General Principles of the European Convention on Human Rights

The European Convention on Human Rights is one of the world's most important and influential human rights documents. It owes its value mainly to the European Court of Human Rights, which applies the Convention rights in individual cases.

This book offers a clear insight into the concepts and principles that are key to understanding the European Convention and the Court's case law. It explains how the Court generally approaches the many cases brought before it and which tools help it to decide on these cases, illustrated by numerous examples taken from the Court's judgments.

Core issues discussed are the types of Convention rights (such as absolute rights); the structure of the Court's Convention rights review; principles and methods of interpretation (such as common ground interpretation and the use of precedent); positive and negative obligations; vertical and horizontal effect; the margin of appreciation doctrine; and requirements for the restriction of Convention rights.

Janneke Gerards is Professor of fundamental rights law at Utrecht University, the Netherlands and Director of the Montaigne Centre for Rule of Law and Administration of Justice. She has published widely in the field of European and national fundamental rights, constitutional law and judicial argumentation, and she teaches in various university and professional training courses on European fundamental rights. Janneke Gerards is also a deputy Judge in the Appeals Court of The Hague, a member of the Human Rights Commission of the Dutch Advisory Council on International Affairs, and a member of the Royal Netherlands Academy of Arts and Sciences.

General Principles of the European Convention on Human Rights

Janneke Gerards

University of Utrecht, the Netherlands

CAMBRIDGE
UNIVERSITY PRESS

CAMBRIDGE
UNIVERSITY PRESS

University Printing House, Cambridge CB2 8BS, United Kingdom

One Liberty Plaza, 20th Floor, New York, NY 10006, USA

477 Williamstown Road, Port Melbourne, VIC 3207, Australia

314–321, 3rd Floor, Plot 3, Splendor Forum, Jasola District Centre, New Delhi – 110025, India

79 Anson Road, #06–04/06, Singapore 079906

Cambridge University Press is part of the University of Cambridge.

It furthers the University's mission by disseminating knowledge in the pursuit of
education, learning, and research at the highest international levels of excellence.

www.cambridge.org
Information on this title: www.cambridge.org/9781108718288
DOI: 10.1017/9781108652926

First published 2019

Printed in the United Kingdom by TJ International Ltd, Padstow Cornwall

A catalogue record for this publication is available from the British Library.

Library of Congress Cataloging-in-Publication Data
Names: Gerards, J. H. (Janneke H.), author.
Title: General principles of the European Convention on Human Rights / Janneke Gerards.
Description: New York : Cambridge University Press, 2019.
Identifiers: LCCN 2018051218 | ISBN 9781108718288 (paperback)
Subjects: LCSH: Convention for the Protection of Human Rights and Fundamental Freedoms
   (1950 November 5) | Human rights–Europe. | Civil rights–Europe. | BISAC: POLITICAL SCIENCE
   / Political Freedom & Security / Human Rights.
Classification: LCC KJC5132 .G475 2019 | DDC 341.4/8094–dc23
LC record available at https://lccn.loc.gov/2018051218

ISBN 978-1-108-71828-8 Paperback

Contents

1 **The Basics of the Convention System**   1
  1.1 Introduction   1
  1.2 Main Principles Underlying the Convention: Effectiveness and
     Subsidiarity   3
  1.3 The Double Role of the European Court of Human Rights   9
  1.4 The Structure of Convention Rights Review   11
  1.5 Typology of Convention Rights from a Perspective of
     Possibilities for Justification   19

2 **The Court's Overall Argumentative Approach – Mediating
  Between the Abstract and the Concrete**   31
  2.1 Introduction   31
  2.2 Object of Review: Legislation and/or Individual Decisions   32
  2.3 Individual Redress or General Convention Interpretation?   36
  2.4 The Role of Precedent in the Court's Case Law   37
  2.5 Case-based Review, Incrementalism and the Search for a
     Reflective Equilibrium   41
  2.6 Legal Effect of the Court's Interpretations; 'Res Interpretata' 44

3 **Principles Governing the Interpretation and Application
  of Convention Rights**   46
  3.1 Introduction   46
  3.2 The ECHR and the Vienna Convention on the Law of Treaties   47
  3.3 Evolutive Interpretation and the Convention as a
     'Living Instrument'   51
  3.4 Meta-teleological Interpretation and the Underlying Values
     of the Convention   59
  3.5 Autonomous Interpretation   67

4 **Methods of Convention Interpretation**   78
  4.1 Introduction   78
  4.2 Textual Interpretation   79
  4.3 Interpretation in light of the *Travaux Préparatoires*   83
  4.4 Internally Harmonising Interpretation   87
  4.5 Common Ground or Consensus Interpretation   93

5 Positive and Negative Obligations   108
  5.1 Introduction   108
  5.2 Definition of Positive Obligations   110
  5.3 Types of Positive Obligations   121
  5.4 The Relation Between Negative and Positive Obligations   132

6 Vertical and Horizontal Effect   136
  6.1 Introduction   136
  6.2 Direct Responsibility of the State for Interferences with
      Convention Rights   138
  6.3 Indirect Horizontal Effect   144

7 The Margin of Appreciation Doctrine   160
  7.1 Introduction   160
  7.2 The Development, Function and Effects of the Margin of
      Appreciation Doctrine   163
  7.3 Applicability of the Margin of Appreciation Doctrine   168
  7.4 Determining the Scope of the Margin of Appreciation   172
  7.5 Continued Relevance of the Margin of Appreciation Doctrine?   196

8 Justification of Restrictions I – Lawfulness   198
  8.1 Introduction   198
  8.2 Autonomous and Substantive Interpretation   199
  8.3 A Basis in Domestic Law   200
  8.4 Accessibility   203
  8.5 Foreseeability   205
  8.6 Absence of Arbitrariness   212
  8.7 Procedural Safeguards   214

9 Justification of Restrictions II – Legitimate Aim   220
  9.1 Exhaustive Lists of Legitimate Aims and Their Importance   220
  9.2 Application and Interpretation of the Legitimate Aim Requirement   221
  9.3 Discrepancy Between Stated and Real Aims   225
  9.4 Plurality of Aims   226
  9.5 Interconnectedness of Legitimate Aim and Proportionality   227

10 Justification of Restrictions III – Necessity, Proportionality and Fair Balance   229
   10.1 Formulas, Tests and Standards   229
   10.2 Necessity, a Pressing Social Need and the Least Restrictive
       Means Test   233
   10.3 The Relevant and Sufficient Test   239
   10.4 Fair Balance, Proportionality and Related Tests   242
   10.5 Procedural Review   258

Index   261

1 The Basics of the Convention System

1.1 Introduction

The European Convention on Human Rights ('Convention' or 'ECHR') was opened for signature in Rome on 4 November 1950 and it entered into force in 1953. It is a unique document which has had tremendous impact on the theory and practice of protecting fundamental rights in Europe. One of the main explanations for this impact is that the drafters of the Convention did not only lay down a well-considered list of human rights, but also designed a system to monitor compliance. Originally, the system was intended as a kind of alarm bell, which could signify the risk that a State would fall into totalitarianism and which could be rung by both States and individuals.[1] The main role in this system is played by the European Court of Human Rights ('Court' or 'ECtHR'), which was established in 1959. This Court was set up 'to ensure the observance of the engagements undertaken by the High Contracting Parties in the Convention and the Protocols thereto' (Article 19 ECHR). Its jurisdiction extends 'to all matters concerning the interpretation and application of the Convention and the Protocols thereto' (Article 32(1) ECHR).

Over the past seven decades, the Convention system has developed considerably. Currently, the Court is generally regarded as one of the world's most influential and effective international institutions.[2] The Court receives about 40,000 to 60,000 applications each year, which indicates the trust which individuals have in the ability of the Court to provide protection and offer redress if Convention rights have been violated. Moreover, many of the judgments of the European Court of Human Rights are eventually complied with, even if it occasionally takes a long time to achieve this.[3] In addition, these judgments appear to have a great impact on

---

[1] On this objective of the Convention, see further e.g. E. Bates, *The Evolution of the European Convention on Human Rights: From its Inception to the Creation of a Permanent Court of Human Rights* (Oxford University Press, 2010).

[2] H. Keller and A. Stone Sweet, 'Introduction: The Reception of the ECHR in National Legal Orders' in H. Keller and A. Stone Sweet (eds.), *A Europe of Rights. The Impact of the ECHR on National Legal Systems* (Oxford University Press, 2008), pp. 3–28 at 3.

[3] Individual judgments are usually executed, if only by paying a certain amount of compensation to the victim; this is not to say, however, that structural or systemic problems causing these individual cases to be brought are actually solved; see further e.g. L.R. Glas, *The Theory, Potential and Practice of*

national law.[4] In the Netherlands, for example, the entire system for legal protection against administrative decisions was overhauled after just one judgment of the Court made clear that the old system offered individuals too little access to court.[5] The Nordic countries have changed their age-old 'closed-shop' systems, which compelled workers to become members of trade unions, after the Court had found that this was contrary to the freedom of association.[6] In Italy, efforts are being made to make court procedures more efficient.[7] Central and Eastern European States try to comply with the Court's judgments when restoring property that has been nationalised under communist regimes and, more generally, to model their legal systems to the standards set in the Convention.[8] In Russia, the Constitutional Court has based numerous decisions on the case law of the ECtHR.[9] Indeed, a 2016 study has shown that at some point, every single State has made at least some fundamental, structural or systemic change in national law and policy in response to a judgment of the Court.[10]

These examples show the great impact of the Convention. However, they equally show the challenges confronting the Court. Each year, the Court is asked to hand

---

Procedural Dialogue in the European Convention on Human Rights System (Antwerp: Intersentia, 2016) at 45–8.

[4] See e.g. L.R. Helfer, 'Redesigning the European Court of Human Rights: Embeddedness as a Deep Structural Principle of the European Human Rights regime', *European Journal of International Law*, 19 (2008), 125–9; P. Popelier, C. Van de Heyning and P. van Nuffel (eds.), *Human Rights Protection in the European Legal Order: The Interaction between the European and the National Courts* (Antwerp: Intersentia, 2011); J.H. Gerards and J.W.A. Fleuren (eds.), *Implementation of the European Convention on Human Rights and of the Judgments of the ECtHR in National Case Law. A comparative analysis* (Antwerp: Intersentia, 2014); I. Motoc and I. Ziemele (eds.), *The Impact of the ECHR on Democratic Change in Central and Eastern Europe* (Cambridge University Press, 2016).

[5] *Benthem v. the Netherlands*, ECtHR 23 October 1985, 8848/80.

[6] In particular *Sørensen and Rasmussen v. Denmark*, ECtHR (GC) 11 January 2006, 52562/99 and 52620/99.

[7] This has been attempted in response to *Bottazzi v. Italy*, ECtHR (GC) 28 July 1999, 34884/97, but without much success; see *Gaglione and Others v. Italy*, ECtHR 21 December 2010, 45867/07; for the efforts made, see www.coe.int/t/dghl/monitoring/execution/Reports/pendingCases_en.asp, last accessed 30 November 2018.

[8] See *Broniowski v. Poland*, ECtHR (GC) 22 June 2004, 31443/96 and the follow-up decision in *Wolkenberg and Others v. Poland*, ECtHR 4 December 2007 (dec.), 50003/99. More generally, for the impact on the national law in these states, see Motoc and Ziemele, *supra* n. 4.

[9] A. Matta and A. Mazmanyan, 'Russia: In Quest for a European Identity' in P. Popelier, S. Lambrecht and K. Lemmens (eds.), *Criticism of the European Court of Human Rights. Shifting the Convention System: Counter-dynamics at the National and EU Level* (Antwerp: Intersentia, 2016), pp. 481–502 at 499 and A.I. Kovler, 'European Convention on Human Rights in Russia: Fifteen Years Later', in Motoc and Ziemele, *supra* n. 4, pp. 351–71 at 356.

[10] See the report by the Legal Affairs and Human Rights Department of the Parliamentary Assembly of the Council of Europe, *Impact of the European Convention on Human Rights in States Parties: Selected Examples* (Strasbourg, 8 January 2016) AS/Jur/Inf (2016) 04. Moreover, such changes are made in response both to judgments against that particular State and to judgments against other States, as is clear from Gerards and Fleuren, *supra* n. 4. See further K.J. Alter, L.R. Helfer and M.R. Madsen, 'How Context Shapes the Authority of International Courts', *Law and Contemporary Problems*, 79 (2016), 1–36 at 10–11 and 16.

down judgments in thousands of cases brought by individuals from all over Europe – the States Parties to the Convention range from Iceland to Azerbaijan and from Monaco to Georgia. Cases relate to such wide-ranging topics as racial violence,[11] the loss of a social security benefit[12] or a prohibition of pre-natal screening of embryos.[13] They may be about important matters such as inhumane prison conditions or torture, but they may also concern relatively minor issues such as administrative fines for speeding or a minor shortcoming in judicial proceedings. They also often concern highly divisive and contested matters such as abortion, the reducibility of lifelong prison sentences, expulsion of terrorism suspects or rights for religious minorities. In all of these cases, the Court must determine which restrictions amount to genuine violations of fundamental rights that cannot be condoned. In doing so, the Court must also take account of its position as an international court that has to judge cases coming from sovereign States, which may have very different constitutional systems and traditions from each other, and which may harbour significantly different values and opinions on contested fundamental rights issues.

The objective of this book is to explain in detail how the Court protects the Convention rights while working within a complex context. This can only be done if the basic principles governing the Court's work are well understood. This first chapter therefore first explains two main principles underlying the Convention system as a whole: the principles of effective protection of fundamental rights, and of subsidiarity (Section 1.2). Thereafter, the double role of the Court within the Convention system is set out: offering individual redress and clarifying Convention rights standards (Section 1.3). To comprehend how the Convention system works, it is further necessary to gain a sound understanding of the structure of the Convention rights. For that reason, Section 1.4 sets out the three main stages of the Court's review, which correspond to the structure of most of the Convention rights. Finally, Section 1.5 provides for a typology of Convention rights according to the possibilities for regulating the exercise of these rights.

1.2 Main Principles Underlying the Convention: Effectiveness and Subsidiarity

1.2.1 Effective Protection of Convention Rights

According to the Convention's Preamble, one of the primary objectives of the Convention is 'the maintenance and further realisation of Human Rights and Fundamental Freedoms'. According to the same Preamble, the one reason to draft

---

[11] E.g. *Fedorchenko and Lozenko v. Ukraine*, ECtHR 20 September 2012, 387/03.
[12] E.g. *Czaja v. Poland*, ECtHR 2 October 2012, 5744/05.
[13] E.g. *Costa and Pavan v. Italy*, ECtHR 28 August 2012, 54270/10.

the Convention was to provide the protection of those rights which were considered the most important within 'like-minded European countries', which have 'a common heritage of political traditions, ideals, freedom and the rule of law'.[14] The Court has referred to this objective of effective protection of fundamental rights as constantly informing its interpretation and application of the Convention. In one of its very first judgments, the *Belgian Linguistics* case of 1968, the Court emphasised that 'the general aim set for themselves by the Contracting Parties through the medium of the European Convention on Human Rights, was to provide effective protection of fundamental human rights'.[15] In 1979, in *Airey*, the Court rephrased the principle of effectiveness in a formula that it still uses today in many of its judgments: 'The Convention is intended to guarantee not rights that are theoretical or illusory but rights that are practical and effective.'[16] In its *Soering* judgment of 1989, the Court connected this principle of effectiveness to the nature and objectives of the Convention and to its own work in interpreting its provisions:

> In interpreting the Convention regard must be had to its special character as a treaty for the collective enforcement of human rights and fundamental freedoms ... Thus, the object and purpose of the Convention as an instrument for the protection of individual human beings require that its provisions be interpreted and applied so as to make its safeguards practical and effective ... In addition, any interpretation of the rights and freedoms guaranteed has to be consistent with the general spirit of the Convention, an instrument designed to maintain and promote the ideals and values of a democratic society.[17]

Thus, the notion of effectiveness provides the Court with important guidance in interpreting the Convention and in assessing the reasonableness and acceptability of interferences with the Convention rights.

The Court has also connected the principle of effectiveness to the obligation in Article 1 of the Convention to 'secure to everyone within their jurisdiction the rights and freedoms defined in the Convention and its Protocols'. In *Osman*, for example, the Court rejected the limited interpretation which the respondent government had suggested of its duty to protect the right to life (Article 2 of the Convention) against interferences by third parties: 'Such a rigid standard must be considered to be incompatible with the requirements of Article 1 of the Convention and the obligations of Contracting States under that Article to secure the practical and effective protection of the rights and freedoms laid down therein, including Article 2.'[18] By means of this connection, the principle of effectiveness also forms an important basis for the development and recognition of so-called 'positive' obligations of the

---

[14] Preamble ECHR.   [15] *Belgian Linguistics Case*, ECtHR 23 July 1968, 1474/62, para. I.B.5.

[16] *Airey v. Ireland*, ECtHR 9 October 1979, 6289/73, para. 24.

[17] *Soering v. the United Kingdom*, ECtHR 7 July 1989, 14038/88, para. 87.

[18] *Osman v. the United Kingdom*, ECtHR 28 October 1998, 23452/94, para. 116.

States to protect Convention rights. In many cases, the Court has accepted that national authorities must act to make sure that individuals can genuinely and effectively enjoy the rights granted to them. To guarantee the right to life, for example, it is not only necessary that State agents refrain from killing citizens without there being a compelling justification for this, but that the State must also take adequate legal and practical measures to avoid a known, real and immediate risk that a person will be harmed.[19] Chapters 5 and 6 further discuss this notion of positive obligations and its connection to the notion of effective protection.

1.2.2 Subsidiarity and Primarity

According to Article 1 of the Convention, the primary responsibility for offering effective protection of the Convention rights lies with the national authorities, who must 'secure the Convention rights to everyone within their jurisdiction'.[20] This can be called the principle of 'primarity'.[21] The Court's task is mainly one of checking whether the national authorities have complied with the obligations they have undertaken under the Convention. Very roughly, this is what is called 'subsidiarity'.[22]

Originally, the notions of primarity and subsidiarity did not have a place in the text of the Convention,[23] but the Court has developed them as principles in its case law. It did so for the first time in the *Belgian Linguistics* case, which was decided in 1968. In its judgment, the Court focused on its own subsidiary role:

[T]he Court cannot disregard those legal and factual features which characterise the life of the society in the State which, as a Contracting Party, has to answer for the measure in dispute. In so doing it cannot assume the rôle of the competent national authorities, for it would thereby lose sight of the subsidiary nature of the international machinery of collective enforcement established by the Convention. The national authorities remain free to choose the measures which they consider appropriate in those matters which are

---

[19] *Osman*, para. 116.

[20] See e.g. F. Tulkens, *How Can We Ensure Greater Involvement of National Courts in the Convention System? Dialogue Between Judges* (European Court of Human Rights, Council of Europe, 2012), pp. 6–10 at 6–7.

[21] J. Christoffersen, *Fair Balance: Proportionality, Subsidiarity and Primarity in the European Convention on Human Rights* (Leiden/Boston: Martinus Nijhoff Publishers, 2009).

[22] Much more has been written on subsidiarity and there are various different theoretical understandings of this notion. See e.g. R. Spano, 'Universality or Diversity of Human Rights? Strasbourg in the Age of Subsidiarity', *Human Rights Law Review*, 14 (2014), 487; A. Mowbray, 'Subsidiarity and the European Convention on Human Rights', *Human Rights Law Review*, 15 (2015), 313; O.M. Arnardóttir, 'The Brighton Aftermath and the Changing Role of the European Court of Human Rights', *Journal of International Dispute Settlement*, 9 (2018), 223–39.

[23] They will be laid down in the Convention's Preamble once Protocol No. 15 enters into force; see CETS No. 213. In Summer 2018, the Protocol was ratified by forty-three of the forty-seven Member States of the Council of Europe.

governed by the Convention. Review by the Court concerns only the conformity of these measures with the requirements of the Convention.[24]

In the later *Handyside* case, the Court addressed subsidiarity in relation to the primary responsibilities of the States Parties in greater depth.[25] This case concerned the 'Little Red Schoolbook', a booklet for teenagers which contained (allegedly rather subversive) information on – among others – matters of sexuality. The British authorities had chosen to prohibit the distribution of the booklet in schools because it would endanger 'good morals'. This evoked the question of whether such a prohibition was compatible with the freedom of expression, protected by Article 10 ECHR.[26] Before answering this question, the Court discussed the division of tasks within the Convention system. First, it explained the rationale for primarity and the consequences of this concept:

> The Convention leaves to each Contracting State, in the first place, the task of securing the rights and liberties it enshrines. The institutions created by it make their own contribution to this task but they become involved only through contentious proceedings and once all domestic remedies have been exhausted ... In particular, it is not possible to find in the domestic law of the various Contracting States a uniform European conception of morals. The view taken by their respective laws of the requirements of morals varies from time to time and from place to place, especially in our era which is characterised by a rapid and far-reaching evolution of opinions on the subject. By reason of their direct and continuous contact with the vital forces of their countries, State authorities are in principle in a better position than the international judge to give an opinion on the exact content of these requirements as well as on the 'necessity' of a 'restriction' or 'penalty' intended to meet them ... [I]t is for the national authorities to make the initial assessment of the reality of the pressing social need implied by the notion of 'necessity' in this context.[27]

Subsequently, the Court defined its own role and, in doing so, gave shape to the notion of 'subsidiarity':

> Nevertheless, [the Convention] does not give the Contracting States an unlimited power of appreciation. The Court, which ... is responsible for ensuring the observance of those States' engagements (Article 19), is empowered to give the final ruling on whether a 'restriction' or 'penalty' is reconcilable with freedom of expression as protected by Article 10. The domestic margin of appreciation thus goes hand in hand with a European supervision. Such supervision concerns both the aim of the measure challenged and its 'necessity'; it covers not only the basic legislation but also the decision applying it, even one given by an independent court.[28]

---

[24] *Belgian Linguistics case*, ECtHR 23 July 1968, 1474/62, para. I.B.10. See also Christoffersen, *supra* n. 21, at 248.
[25] *Handyside v. the United Kingdom*, ECtHR 7 December 1976, 5493/72.   [26] *Ibid.*
[27] *Ibid.*, para. 48.   [28] *Ibid.*, para. 49.

Thus, in the Court's view, the subsidiarity principle means that the States have some leeway to regulate and restrict the exercise of Convention rights in the way they think is best suited to national views and national (legal and constitutional) traditions. Such leeway exists especially in controversial cases where there is no European consensus on how a right can best be regulated, or where the national authorities are clearly better placed than the Court to decide how national sensitivities or national constitutional traditions can be heeded, or where a balance needs to be struck in regulating complex socio-economic matters. This leeway is often expressed in terms of granting a 'margin of appreciation' to the State.[29] However, the quoted considerations also show that such a margin of appreciation, even if it is wide, is far from equal to the possibility of exercising full and unhampered discretion. The Court's task may be subsidiary, but the Court is still competent to supervise national compliance with the Convention. In other words, subsidiarity means that the Court can and will police the borders of the exercise of national discretion. This is significant because, in line with Articles 19 and 32 of the Convention, it is up to the Court to define the minimum level of protection that the States must guarantee in exercising its primary role. This means that there is little subsidiarity involved in the Court's task to provide definitions of core Convention terms and concepts, set and refine relevant standards and criteria for review, and clarify how these can be applied in case of doubt.[30] In fact, the notion of subsidiarity mainly comes into play with regard to the application of such definitions or standards in individual cases. How the Court has given effect to this in practice, and when there may still be an effect on interpretation and standard-setting in general terms, is the subject of discussions in subsequent chapters.

In addition to the effect of subsidiarity on the Court's review in individual cases, the Court has explained that 'subsidiarity' means that the national authorities must have sufficient room to detect and correct mistakes, flaws or omissions in their protection of Convention rights. This explanation constitutes the rationale for its interpretation of several admissibility requirements in the Convention, such as the requirement that all (effective) domestic remedies are exhausted before an applicant can bring a complaint before the Strasbourg Court.[31] In *Demopoulos*, the Court explained how its interpretation of this requirement can be linked to the principle of subsidiarity:

> It is primordial that the machinery of protection established by the Convention is subsidiary to the national systems safeguarding human rights. This Court is concerned with the supervision of the implementation by Contracting States of their obligations under the

---

[29] See in more detail Chapter 7.

[30] This is also recognised by the States Parties, in particular in the High Level Declarations of Interlaken (2010) and Brighton (2013).

[31] Article 35(1) ECHR.

Convention. It cannot, and must not, usurp the role of Contracting States whose responsibility it is to ensure that the fundamental rights and freedoms enshrined therein are respected and protected on a domestic level. The rule of exhaustion of domestic remedies is therefore an indispensable part of the functioning of this system of protection. States are dispensed from answering before an international body for their acts before they have had an opportunity to put matters right through their own legal system and those who wish to invoke the supervisory jurisdiction of the Court as concerns complaints against a State are thus obliged to use first the remedies provided by the national legal system ... The Court cannot emphasise enough that it is not a court of first instance; it does not have the capacity, nor is it appropriate to its function as an international court, to adjudicate on large numbers of cases which require the finding of basic facts or the calculation of monetary compensation – both of which should, as a matter of principle and effective practice, be the domain of domestic jurisdictions.[32]

Consequently, subsidiarity is an important notion in the procedural choices made by the Court, such as in deciding on the admissibility of individual complaints or in giving advice to States as to how they could implement certain judgments. Since this book concentrates on the substantive principles of Convention law, such procedural consequences are not specifically discussed here, but they are mentioned throughout the book where relevant.[33]

Although the principles of subsidiarity and primacy have been developed in the case law of the Court, in recent years, the States Parties have agreed that they are so important that they deserve to be expressly mentioned in the Convention. Following the entry into force of Protocol No. 15 (which was signed in 2013 and has yet to be ratified by a few States),[34] the final paragraph of the Preamble will read as follows: 'Affirming that the High Contracting Parties, in accordance with the principle of subsidiarity, have the primary responsibility to secure the rights and freedoms defined in this Convention and the Protocols thereto, and that in doing so they enjoy a margin of appreciation, subject to the supervisory jurisdiction of the European Court of Human Rights established by this Convention.' This codification of these principles is not intended to make any difference to the way they have been developed in the Court's case law, however, and the Court will retain the competence to interpret these notions as it thinks fit.[35]

---

[32] *Demopoulos and Others v. Turkey*, ECtHR (GC) 1 March 2010 (dec.), 46113/99, para. 69.

[33] In more detail on the procedural effects of the notions of primarity and subsidiarity (as well as of effectiveness), see e.g. Glas, *supra* n. 3.

[34] In November 2018, the Protocol was ratified by forty-five States. It has to be ratified by all forty-seven States in order to enter into force.

[35] Explanatory Memorandum to Protocol No. 15, ETS-no. 213, paras. 7–9 and Opinion of the Court on Draft Protocol No. 15 to the European Convention on Human Rights, 6 February 2013, www.echr.coe.int/Documents/2013_Protocol_15_Court_Opinion_ENG.pdf, last accessed 30 November 2018.

1.3   The Double Role of the European Court of Human Rights

As explained above, the main objective of the Convention system is to protect the fundamental rights guaranteed in the Convention text and Protocols to everyone within the jurisdiction of the States Parties. The States have undertaken to guarantee these rights and they have thereby accepted an obligation to do so in an effective manner. However, due to national oversights, mistakes or even structural problems in upholding rule of law principles, there may be shortcomings in the domestic protection of Convention rights. It is then the Court's task to step in and offer subsidiary protection of the Convention. In offering this subsidiary protection, two major roles or functions for the Court can be distinguished.[36]

Based on Article 19 ECHR, the Court's first and main function is that of supervising the compliance by the States with their obligations under the Convention in concrete cases and of offering individual redress if need be. It is generally accepted that these tasks form the cornerstone of the Convention system.[37] As a completely external, independent and uninvolved institution, the Court is well placed to decide whether a State has failed to comply with its obligations under the Convention in individual cases. It does so by assessing the facts of the case and reviewing the reasonableness of the arguments brought forward by parties. The Court may also offer individual redress if it finds that persons or legal entities have been harmed by violations of their Convention rights by national governments or government agents.[38] Such redress may consist of obliging the State to pay just satisfaction to a victim to compensate for pecuniary or non-pecuniary damage, but the Court may also suggest individual or general measures to be taken to solve systemic problems in Convention protection on a national level.[39]

---

[36] See also F. de Londras, 'Dual Functionality and the Persistent Frailty of the European Court of Human Rights', *European Human Rights Law Review*, 1 (2013), 38–46, and J.H. Gerards and L.R. Glas, 'Access to Justice in the European Convention on Human Rights System', *Netherlands Quarterly of Human Rights*, 35 (2017), 11–30.

[37] See e.g. *Report of the Committee of Minister's Steering Committee for Human Rights (CDDH) on Measures Requiring Amendment of the European Convention on Human Rights* (Strasbourg, February 2012, CDDH(2012)R74 Addendum I). For more elaboration, see Gerards and Glas, *supra* n. 36.

[38] This is often regarded as the most important function of the Court; see e.g. P. Leach, 'On Reform of the European Court of Human Rights', *European Human Rights Law Review*, 6 (2009), 725–35; H. Keller, A. Fischer and D. Kühne, 'Debating the Future of the European Court of Human Rights after the Interlaken Conference: Two Innovative Proposals', *European Journal of International Law*, 21 (2010), 1025–48; *Report of the Committee of Minister's Steering Committee for Human Rights (CDDH) on Measures Requiring Amendment of the European Convention on Human Rights* (Strasbourg, February 2012, CDDH(2012)R74 Addendum I).

[39] For the various possibilities of offering redress and the shifts visible in the Court's case law, see e.g. L.R. Glas, 'Changes in the Procedural Practice of the European Court of Human Rights: Consequences

When exercising this role of supervision and offering individual redress, the Court will assess each admissible individual case on its merits, and it will look into the particular circumstances of the case in evaluating the reasonableness of restrictions. As phrased in its *Sunday Times* judgment, 'the Court has to be satisfied that the interference was necessary having regard to the facts and circumstances prevailing in the specific case before it'.[40] As is further explained in Chapter 2, the central importance of the individual assessment of each case on the merits has led to an often strongly case-based and contextualised case law.

The second main function of the Court is of a more constitutional nature, namely to clarify the minimum level of protection of fundamental rights that should be guaranteed in all Convention States.[41] This function is expressed in the text of the Convention where the Preamble stresses the importance of a system of *collective* enforcement of fundamental rights.[42] Given the fundamental character of the Convention rights, it would be unacceptable if the exercise of those rights were to depend on where the individual happened to live. Someone living in Germany should enjoy the equal right to remain free of torture or discrimination and to express himself freely as someone living in Russia.[43] Only a central institution such as the Court can uniformly establish the meaning of fundamental rights and define a minimum level of fundamental rights protection that must be guaranteed in all the States of the Council of Europe.[44] This means that the Court has an essential role to play in standard-setting, even if States may always provide additional protection (Article 53 ECHR).[45] The Court has explained this in *Soering*, connecting this constitutional function to the principle of effectiveness:

> [T]he object and purpose of the Convention as an instrument for the protection of individual human beings require that its provisions be interpreted and applied so as to make its safeguards practical and effective . . . In addition, any interpretation of the rights and freedoms guaranteed

---

for the Convention System and Lessons to be Drawn', *Human Rights Law Review*, 14 (2014), 671–99, and Gerards and Glas, *supra* n. 36.

[40] *Sunday Times v. the United Kingdom*, ECtHR 26 April 1979, 6538/74, para. 65.

[41] Cf. S. Greer and L. Wildhaber, 'Revisiting the Debate about "Constitutionalising" the European Court of Human Rights', *Human Rights Law Review*, 12 (2012), 655–87; de Londras, *supra* n. 36, at 38.

[42] See also T. Hammarberg, 'The Court of Human Rights versus the "*Court of Public Opinion*"' in *How Can We Ensure Greater Involvement of National Courts in the Convention System?* Dialogue between judges (European Court of Human Rights, Council of Europe 2012), pp. 30–6 at 31; Gerards and Glas, *supra* n. 36.

[43] Cf. D. Galligan and D. Sandler, 'Implementing Human Rights' in S. Halliday and P. Schmidt (eds.), *Human Rights Brought Home. Socio-legal Studies of Human Rights in the National Context* (Oxford: Hart, 2004) at 31.

[44] See further J.H. Gerards, 'Uniformity and the European Court of Human Rights', in K. Lemmens, S. Parmentier and L. Reyntjens (eds.), *Liber Amicorum Paul Lemmens* (in press).

[45] A. Stone Sweet, 'The European Convention on Human Rights and National Constitutional Reordering', *Cardozo Law Review*, 33 (2012), 1859–68, calling this the Court's 'oracular' or 'law-making' function.

has to be consistent with 'the general spirit of the Convention, an instrument designed to maintain and promote the ideals and values of a democratic society'.[46]

This means that the Court cannot limit its work to deciding individual cases on their merits. In accordance with Article 32 of the Convention, its task is 'not only to decide those cases brought before the Court but, more generally, to elucidate, safeguard and develop the rules instituted by the Convention'.[47] European governments generally support the Court's constitutional role. They recently even adopted a new Protocol to the Convention (Protocol No. 16) to create an advisory procedure, which is expressly intended to reinforce the ECtHR's role of providing general interpretations of the ECHR.[48]

Just like the Court's task of offering individual redress, the need to set a minimum level of protection and to provide generally applicable interpretations inform many of the argumentative approaches adopted by the Court.[49] These general principles and doctrines are illuminated in Chapters 3 and 4.

1.4   The Structure of Convention Rights Review

1.4.1   The Three Stages of Convention Rights Review

The Convention and its Protocols contain a wide range of fundamental rights, varying from the right to life (Article 2 ECHR) to the right to property (Article 1 of Protocol No. 1), and from the freedom of expression (Article 10 ECHR) to the freedom to choose one's residence (Article 2 of Protocol No. 4). Given the variety of rights and their differences in nature, it is not surprising that there are also differences in the extent to which the States may regulate their enjoyment. These differences are reflected in the text of the Convention: all provisions of the Convention and the Protocols which protect fundamental rights have their own format. For example, Article 3 of the Convention contains a clean and straightforward prohibition: 'No one shall be subjected to torture or to inhuman or degrading treatment or punishment.'

---

[46] *Soering v. the United Kingdom*, ECtHR 7 July 1989, 14038/88; see also *Rantsev v. Cyprus and Russia*: 'Although the primary purpose of the Convention system is to provide individual relief, its mission is also to determine issues on public-policy grounds in the common interest, thereby raising the general standards of protection of human rights and extending human rights jurisprudence throughout the community of the Convention States' (ECtHR 7 January 2010, 25965/04, para 197).

[47] *Ireland v. the United Kingdom*, ECtHR 18 January 1978, 5310/71, para 154.

[48] Protocol No. 16, ETS-No. 214. For its constitutional purpose, see e.g. *Reflection Paper on the Proposal to Extend the Court's Advisory Jurisdiction* (Strasbourg, March 2012) #3853038, www.echr.coe.int/Documents/2013_Courts_advisory_jurisdiction_ENG.pdf, last accessed 30 November 2018.

[49] See also Gerards and Glas, *supra* n. 36 and J.H. Gerards, 'The European Court of Human Rights', in A. Jákab, A. Dyevre and G. Itzcovich (eds.), *Comparative Constitutional Reasoning* (Cambridge University Press, 2017), pp. 237–76.

Article 12 is equally clear and straightforward, but it is different from Article 3 in that it refers to national law setting the conditions for enjoying the right contained in this provision: 'Men and women of marriageable age have the right to marry and to found a family, according to the national laws governing the exercise of this right.'

Both provisions are also very different from Article 8, which contains two paragraphs:

1. Everyone has the right to respect for his private and family life, his home and his correspondence.
2. There shall be no interference by a public authority with the exercise of this right except such as is in accordance with the law and is necessary in a democratic society in the interests of national security, public safety or the economic well-being of the country, for the prevention of disorder or crime, for the protection of health or morals, or for the protection of the rights and freedoms of others.

Such differences are important for the possibilities for national regulation and restriction of fundamental rights, and the Court's review thereof. There are also notable similarities, however, and indeed, in general, it can be seen that the Court's review of all Convention provision takes place in three cumulative stages, which are closely related to the very concept and structure of fundamental rights.[50] If an allegation is made at the Court that a Convention right has been infringed, the first question that arises is whether one of the Convention provisions is applicable at all. This is *stage 1*, the stage of determination of applicability or of interpretation (Section 1.4.2). Second, the question is whether the facts disclose that this right is interfered with: this is *stage 2*, the stage of determination of an interference (Section 1.4.3). And third, if the Court has found that there is an interference with a Convention right, it must explore where there is a possibility for justification of that interference, and if there is, whether there is such a justification in the case at hand. This is *stage 3*, the stage of justification of restrictions (Section 1.4.4). Whether, how and to what extent such a justification for an interference with a Convention right can be accepted depends on the nature of the Convention provision that is invoked. For that reason, Section 1.5 provides a typology of Convention rights according to the possibilities for justification.

1.4.2 Stage 1 – Determination of Applicability and Interpretation

It can be said that the Court is engaged in determining the applicability of the Convention, if it finds, for example, that the right to enjoy undisturbed sleep at night can be understood as falling under the scope of protection of the right to one's

[50] In more detail, see J.H. Gerards and H.C.K. Senden, 'The Structure of Fundamental Rights and the European Court of Human Rights', *International Journal of Constitutional Law*, 7 (2009), 619–53.

private life mentioned in Article 8 ECHR.[51] To determine whether a set of facts is covered by a specific provision of the Convention, it is thus necessary for the Court to define the various terms and notions contained in the Convention, such as 'torture' (Article 3), 'private life' (Article 8) or 'possessions' (Article 1 of Protocol No. 1). It does so by interpreting them, using a number of principles and techniques that are further discussed in Chapters 3 and 4.

Next to issues of interpretation, the determination of applicability may raise questions of proof. It will be up to an applicant to show that the claimed Convention provision does apply in his case, which means that he will have to adduce sufficient proof to show that he has actually suffered the alleged violation of the Convention. Such issues of evidence will not be dealt with in this book, since they are procedural rather than substantive in nature.[52] Nevertheless, it is important to note that interpretative and evidentiary issues are often intertwined. An example of this, which also can illustrate the Court's general approach to the first stage, can be found in *Sandu*.[53] In this case, the applicants had complained about the fact that in the 1990s, the agricultural land they owned or rented had come under the control of the self-proclaimed Moldovan Transdniestrian Republic (MRT). Originally, the MRT authorities had allowed the applicants to continue using their land for agricultural purposes, but in 2004, they declared that the land was the property of the MRT. The applicants could continue working it, but only on condition that they paid rent to the local MRT authorities. The applicants had refused to sign the rental contracts because they felt they were already the lawful owners or tenants of the land.[54] The MRT authorities then blocked all access to their land, to the effect that the harvest was lost, and some agricultural machines were seized.[55] The applicants lodged a complaint with the Court, alleging a violation of their right to property as protected by Article 1 of Protocol No. 1. The first question the Court had to answer in this case was whether the applicants actually could claim to have 'possessions' under Article 1 of Protocol No. 1. This raised an issue of evidence, since the Russian government, which was held to be responsible for the MRT's decisions and acts, had submitted that the applicants had failed to show that they were owners or tenants of the land in question. The Court answered the question of proof of ownership by investigating the documentary evidence the applicants had submitted, such as certificates of the land registry, deeds of gift and legal succession certificates. Based on this information, it established that all applicants could claim to have rights to

---

[51] Cf. *Powell and Rayner v. the United Kingdom*, ECtHR 21 February 1990, 9310/81; *Hatton and Others v. the United Kingdom*, ECtHR (GC) 8 July 2003, 36022/97.

[52] See in more detail on matters of proof e.g. J. Mačkić, *Proving Discriminatory Violence at the European Court of Human Rights* (Leiden: Brill/Nijhoff, 2018).

[53] *Sandu and Others v. the Republic of Moldova and Russia*, ECtHR 17 July 2018, 21034/05.

[54] *Ibid.*, para. 13.   [55] *Ibid.*

work the land. Subsequently, a question of interpretation arose, since some of the applicants were agricultural companies which did not own, and only rented, the land they worked. Consequently, according to the Russian government, they could not claim 'ownership'. In this regard, the Court held as follows:

> Recalling that the concept of 'possessions' in Article 1 of Protocol No. 1 to the Convention has an autonomous meaning which is not limited to ownership of physical goods, but covers also certain other rights and interests constituting assets ... the Court considers that the right to use land, on the basis of rent contracts, connected to the conduct of a business, conferred on the applicant companies title to a substantive interest protected by Article 1 of Protocol No. 1 to the Convention ... The applicant companies thus had 'possessions' within the meaning of that provision.[56]

The Court thus provided a wide reading of the notion of 'possessions', which encompassed not only actual ownership, but also some related rights, such as the ability to conduct a business based on a rent contract. This exercise of interpretation allowed the Court to establish that the Convention did actually apply. If that would not have been the case and a set of facts would not be seen to be covered by any provision of the Convention, the Court would have needed to declare the case inadmissible and it could not have continued to assess the alleged limitation on its merits.[57]

1.4.3   Stage 2 – Interference with the Exercise of a Convention Right or Freedom

Once it has been established that the facts of a case are covered by one of the provisions of the Convention, the next question to arise is whether the claimed right has been interfered with, and therefore whether the case actually discloses a limitation or a restriction of the exercise of the right. The Court does not always pay separate attention to this question. In many cases, it simply assumes that there is an interference once it has established that a claim comes within the scope of protection of a certain Convention provision.[58] The Court may also accept the applicant's statement that the State's action interfered with the exercise of a right without providing any substantive reasoning,[59] or it may decide not to investigate

---

[56] *Ibid.*, para. 77.

[57] See, for example, *Károly Nagy v. Hungary*, ECtHR (GC) 14 September 2017, 56665/09, paras. 64 et seq. In this case, the Court had to determine the applicability of the right to a fair trial, Article 6 of the Convention. It found that the case did not concern a 'right' in the sense of that provision, which meant that the provision did not apply and the case had to be declared inadmissible *ratione materiae*. See similarly and for more elaboration, *Denisov v. Ukraine*, ECtHR (GC) 25 September 2018, 76639/11, paras. 93–4.

[58] *Mariya Alekhina and Others v. Russia*, ECtHR 17 July 2018, 38004/12.

[59] E.g. *Fränklin-Beentjes and Ceflu-Luz da Floresta v. the Netherlands*, ECtHR 6 May 2014 (dec.), 28167/07, para. 36.

the matter any further because the parties agree that there has been an interference.[60] In yet other cases, the Court may fully merge the phases of determination of scope and of interference,[61] or it may express some hesitations about the existence of an interference, but decide not to deal with the issue because it can conclude that the interference does not amount to a violation of the Convention anyway.[62]

However, there are many cases in which the Court expressly deals with the issue of interference. It did so, for example, in the *Sandu* case discussed above.[63] Having found that the various applicants held 'possessions' in the sense of Article 1 of Protocol No. 1 by renting or owning land, it observed that the MRT authorities had not formally deprived them of their property. However, it held as follows:

> Upon the refusal of the applicants to sign such contracts, the authorities between 2004 and 2006 blocked access to the land they owned or rented ... There has therefore been an interference with the applicants' property rights. While this interference does not amount to a deprivation of property or to a control of the use of property, the Court considers that the applicants' inability to cultivate their land falls to be considered under the ... general principle of the peaceful enjoyment of possessions.[64]

This shows the importance of the stage of determining an interference: it may have an impact on the applicable standards for review. For Article 1 of Protocol No. 1, the Court has held that the right to property can be interfered with in different ways – there may be a deprivation of property, an interference with the peaceful enjoyment of property or a case of control of use of property.[65] The different types of interferences are connected to different standards of review in the third stage of review (review of justification). In case of deprivation of property, for example, specific requirements are set relating to compensation, while in cases such as *Sandu*, which relate to the peaceful enjoyment of possessions, the Court will apply more general standards.

The stage of determining the interference is also important if the Court finds that no such interference has occurred. In that case, without further ado, the Court may find that the Convention has not been violated, or it may conclude that the case is

---

[60] E.g. *Labassee v. France*, ECtHR 26 June 2014, 65941/11, para. 49–50; *Otgon v. Moldova*, ECtHR 25 October 2016, 22743/07, para. 17.

[61] E.g. *Flamenbaum and Others v. France*, ECtHR 13 December 2012, 3675/04 and 23264/04, paras. 187–92; *Denisov v. Ukraine*, ECtHR (GC) 25 September 2018, 76639/11, paras. 110 et seq. Sometimes, there is even a merger of all three phases (e.g. *Austrianu v. Romania*, ECtHR 12 February 2013, 16117/02, paras. 104–7) or of the second and third phase (e.g. *Zagrebačka banka d.d. v. Croatia*, ECtHR 12 December 2013, 39544/05, paras. 259–60 and 265).

[62] E.g. *Golemanova v. Bulgaria*, ECtHR 17 February 2011, no. 11369/04, para. 41; *Church of Jesus Christ of Latter-Day Saints v. the United Kingdom*, ECtHR 4 March 2014, 7552/09, para. 35.

[63] See n. 53 and accompanying text.

[64] *Sandu and Others v. the Republic of Moldova and Russia*, ECtHR 17 July 2018, 21034/05, para. 79.

[65] See *ibid.*, para. 78 with further references to case law.

manifestly ill-founded. *Cha'are Shalom Ve Tsedek* is an example of this.[66] In this case, an orthodox Jewish liturgical association had complained about the French legislation on slaughter of animals, which made it impossible to obtain meat that was slaughtered in accordance with the *Kashrut* rules for ritual slaughter (so-called 'glatt' meat). The Court found that the applicants could rely on the freedom of religion protected by Article 9 ECHR, since ritual slaughter was an essential aspect of practice of the Jewish religion.[67] It then continued to assess whether this right was interfered with by the French legislation on slaughtering animals:

> In the Court's opinion, there would be interference with the freedom to manifest one's religion only if the illegality of performing ritual slaughter made it impossible for ultra-orthodox Jews to eat meat from animals slaughtered in accordance with the religious prescriptions they considered applicable. But that is not the case. It is not contested that the applicant association can easily obtain supplies of 'glatt' meat in Belgium. Furthermore, it is apparent from the written depositions and bailiffs' official reports produced by the interveners that a number of butcher's shops ... make meat certified 'glatt' ... available to Jews. It emerges from the case file as a whole, and from the oral submissions at the hearing, that Jews who belong to the applicant association can thus obtain 'glatt' meat ... Since it has not been established that Jews belonging to the applicant association cannot obtain 'glatt' meat, or that the applicant association could not supply them with it ... the Court considers that the refusal of approval complained of did not constitute an interference with the applicant association's right to the freedom to manifest its religion. That finding absolves the Court from the task of ruling on the compatibility of the restriction challenged by the applicant association with the requirements laid down in the second paragraph of Article 9 of the Convention.[68]

The Court adopted a similar approach in *A., B. and C. v. Ireland* on the Irish prohibition of abortion for reasons of health and well-being.[69] The third applicant in the case had stated that the prohibition led to a life-threatening situation, since she suffered from a disease which was highly dangerous in combination with a pregnancy. In her view, the Irish prohibition of abortion therefore had the result of (potentially) interfering with her right to life (Article 2 ECHR), but the Court did not accept this argument:

> The Court notes that ... there was no legal impediment to the third applicant travelling abroad for an abortion ... The third applicant did not refer to any other impediment to her travelling to England for an abortion and none of her submissions about post-abortion

[66] *Cha'are Shalom Ve Tsedek v. France*, ECtHR (GC) 27 June 2000, 27417/95.   [67] *Ibid.*, para. 73.
[68] *Ibid.*, paras. 80–4. See also, for a different conclusion because no alternatives were available to the applicant, *Vartic v. Romania (no. 2)*, ECtHR 17 December 2013, no 14150/08, paras. 51–2.
[69] *A., B. and C. v. Ireland*, ECtHR (GC) 16 December 2010, 25579/05.

complications concerned a risk to her life. In such circumstances, there is no evidence of any relevant risk to the third applicant's life ... Accordingly, the third applicant's complaint under Article 2 of the Convention must be rejected as manifestly ill-founded pursuant to Article 35 §§ 3 and 4 of the Convention.[70]

As with the applicant association in the case about glatt meat, the third applicant in the Irish case had an alternative: she could travel abroad to undergo an abortion. This might seem to indicate that it is always necessary for applicants to show that the interference with a fundamental right makes it impossible to exercise that right. If that cannot be shown, for example because there are alternative ways to still enjoy the right or the interference was not really serious in nature, the Court might hold that the Convention right is not actually affected and there is no need to require a justification for the limitation of that right.[71] If the Court would always apply this standard, however, many complaints would be dismissed at the stage of determining the interference. After all, more often than not, individual complaints will concern a less optimal enjoyment of a certain right rather than the complete impossibility of exercising it. Indeed, the Court does not often end the test of interference in this way. Mostly, the seriousness of an interference or the availability of alternatives to the applicant is a factor the Court considers in the third stage of its review, that is, when deciding on the justification of the interference. This can be illustrated by the judgment in *Mouvement raëlien suisse*.[72] In that case, which concerned a limitation of the freedom of expression, the Court held that 'there has been no general ban on imparting certain ideas, only a ban on the use of regulated and supervised facilities in public space'.[73] It also found that the applicant association was 'able to continue to disseminate its ideas through its website, and through other means at its disposal such as the distribution of leaflets in the street or in letterboxes.'[74] Contrary to what might be expected based on the judgments quoted here, however, the Court did not find that there was no real interference with the right to freedom of expression in this case. Instead, it continued to assess the reasonableness of the interference. Only in the third stage of its review did it hold that the limitations imposed by the government were not disproportionate because of

---

[70] *Ibid.*, paras. 158–9.

[71] For other examples of where the Court held that there was no interference because the applicant was not sufficiently negatively affected by a restriction, see *Malik v. the United Kingdom*, ECtHR 13 March 2012, 23780/08, paras. 105–10; *Labaca Larrea and Others v. France*, ECtHR 7 February 2017 (dec.), 56710/13, 56727/13 and 57412/13, paras. 45–6; *Klein and Others v. Germany*, ECtHR 6 April 2017, 10138/11, para. 116; *T.G. v. Croatia*, ECtHR 11 July 2017, 39701/14, para. 71.

[72] *Mouvement raëlien suisse v. Switzerland*, ECtHR 13 January 2011, 16354/06. For other examples of this type of case, see *Francesco Sessa v. Italy*, ECtHR 3 April 2012, 28790/08, para. 37.

[73] *Mouvement raëlien suisse*, para. 58.   [74] *Ibid.*, para. 75.

the existence of alternatives for the applicant, and it therefore found that there was no violation.[75]

It can be concluded from this that, although in some cases the Court pays express attention to the phase of interference and it often even devotes a special heading to the test of interference, in other cases it implicitly accepts or assumes the existence of an interference, or it merges the test of interference with the test of applicability or that of justification.[76] In most cases, moreover, the seriousness of the interference plays a role only in the third and final stage of the Court's Convention review, which is that of justification of the interference.

1.4.4   Stage 3 – Justification of Interferences or Reasonableness Review

If the Court has found an interference with a Convention right, in many cases this does not yet mean that there is a violation of the Convention. With a few exceptions, Convention rights may not be exercised unfettered and there usually is some leeway for the State to set reasonable limitations or restrictions. It may be reasonable and even desirable, for instance, to tap the telephones of a group suspected of terrorist acts, or to convict a politician for direct incitement to violence. But, of course, restrictions of Convention rights have to be regarded with special concern and they should not be permitted too easily: the Convention rights are simply too important. For that reason, the Convention contains an intricate system of possibilities and conditions for restrictions, which differentiates between the various human rights protected in the Convention.

This system, first, allows the Court to assess if, at all, it is possible to provide a justification for an interference. This will depend on the nature of the right that is at stake. For example, as is further explained in Section 1.5.1, the prohibition of torture of Article 3 ECHR does not provide for any possibility of justification. As soon as the Court has established on the basis of the facts of the case and its interpretation of the notion of 'torture' that the right to remain free of torture has been interfered with, it will find a violation.[77] For other rights, this is different, and the text of the Convention leaves an explicit or implicit possibility for restriction.[78]

---

[75] *Ibid.*; see similarly *Pentikäinen v. Finland*, ECtHR 4 February 2014, 11882/10, paras. 101, 105, 108 and 114. Also if the interference is not very problematic because of the relatively minor nature thereof, the Court usually takes this into consideration as part of its test of justification rather than as part of the second phase of Convention review; see e.g. *Klein and Others v. Germany*, ECtHR 6 April 2017, 10138/11, paras. 77–83 and 99.

[76] See in particular *Denisov v. Ukraine*, ECtHR (GC) 25 September 2018, 76639/11, paras. 110 et seq., where the Court's Grand Chamber expressly decided to insert the review of whether the interference was sufficiently serious into the test of the applicability of Article 8 ECHR.

[77] Cf. e.g. *Saadi v. Italy*, ECtHR (GC) 28 February 2008, 37201/06, para. 127 and paras. 137–49.

[78] See further Section 1.5.

Second, if there is a possibility for justification of restrictions, the Court will have to assess the relevant arguments advanced by the parties against the requirements and conditions that are relevant to the case at hand. Only if this assessment shows that no sufficient justification has been offered can the Court find that the interference with a Convention right amounts to a violation or breach of the Convention. As mentioned, the possibilities and conditions for restriction thereby are different for the different rights protected in the Convention and the Protocols, but there are many general requirements and principles that apply to almost all Convention rights, such as the requirements of lawfulness, a legitimate aim and of a fair balance between the interest involved in a case. These general requirements and principles are further discussed in Chapters 8, 9 and 10 of this book.

Some special possibilities and conditions for restriction can further be found in Articles 15, 16, 17 and 18 ECHR. These provisions allow, for example, for special restrictions to be made in times of emergency (Article 15 ECHR), or they clarify that specific restrictions permitted under the Convention cannot be applied for any other purpose than those for which they have been prescribed (Article 18 ECHR). Of these provisions, only Article 15 will be (briefly) dealt with below (see Section 1.5.2). The other special restrictions are rather too specific for this book, which mainly relate to the general and substantive principles of ECHR law.

1.5   Typology of Convention Rights from a Perspective of Possibilities for Justification

As was mentioned in Section 1.4.1, the Convention contains a wide variety of fundamental rights formulations. This does not always make it easy to know whether and to what extent their enjoyment can be restricted. For that reason, it is useful to provide a brief typology of Convention rights according to the possibility of restricting their exercise. Roughly, six different categories of Convention rights can be distinguished:

1. 'Absolutely absolute' rights or non-derogable rights.
2. Absolute rights that are not 'notstandsfest'.
3. Non-absolute or derogable rights with express, specific limitation clauses.
4. Non-absolute or derogable rights with express, general limitation clauses.
5. Non-absolute or derogable rights without express limitation clauses, which allow for implied or inherent limitations.
6. Other non-absolute or derogable rights.

These categories of rights will be further explained and illustrated hereafter.

1.5.1   Absolutely Absolute Rights or Non-derogable Rights

The first category comprises 'absolutely absolute' or fully non-derogable rights. This means that, at least according to the Court's case law,[79] no limitations to the exercise can be accepted whatsoever, and these rights cannot even be restricted in times of emergency or war (cf. Article 15 ECHR); they are so-called 'notstandsfest'.

The rights belonging to this category are the prohibition of torture and inhuman or degrading treatment or punishment (Article 3 ECHR), the prohibition of slavery (Article 4(1) ECHR), the prohibition of retroactive application of criminal law (Article 7(1) ECHR) and the freedom of conscience (Article 9(1) ECHR). The non-derogable nature of these provisions sometimes can be derived from the lack of express limitation clauses and from the fact that they are not mentioned as derogable rights in times of war or emergency in Article 15 ECHR. For other rights, their absolutely absolute nature is less obvious from the text of the Convention, as is the case for the freedom of conscience as protected by Article 9 ECHR. Although Article 9(2) ECHR contains an express limitation clause, it refers only to limitations of the freedom to manifest one's religion or beliefs. It must be derived from this that the freedom of conscience cannot be justifiably restricted under the Convention.[80]

The Court has emphasised the importance and the consequences of the absolutely absolute nature of these rights in many of its judgments, in particular in relation to

---

[79] In legal scholarship there is considerable debate about the 'absoluteness' of these rights, in particular in relation to Article 3 ECHR; it has been argued (and contested) that in reality, the prohibition of torture and inhuman and degrading treatment is less absolute than it is made to seem by the ECtHR and indeed, this right should be less absolute in cases where there is a conflict between this right and other (nearly) absolute rights, such as the right to life of Article 2 ECHR (see hereafter, Section 1.5.2). For the debate, see in particular S. Greer, 'Should Police Threats to Torture Suspects Always be Severely Punished? Reflections on the *Gäfgen* Case', *Human Rights Law Review*, 11 (2011), 67–88; N. Mavronicola, 'What is an "Absolute Right"? Deciphering Absoluteness in the Context of Article 3 of the European Convention on Human Rights', *Human Rights Law Review*, 12 (2012), 723–58; S. Smet, 'Conflicts between Absolute Rights: A Reply to Steven Greer', *Human Rights Law Review*, 13 (2013) 469–98; S. Smet, 'The "Absolute" Prohibition of Torture and Inhuman or Degrading Treatment in Article 3 ECHR: Truly a Question of Scope Only?' in: E. Brems and J.H. Gerards (eds.), *Shaping Rights in the ECHR: The Role of the European Court of Human Rights in Determining the Scope of Human Rights* (Cambridge University Press, 2014), pp. 273–93; S. Greer, 'Is the Prohibition Against Torture, Cruel, Inhuman or Degrading Treatment Really "Absolute" in International Human Rights Law?' *Human Rights Law Review*, 15 (2015), 101–37; N. Graffin, '*Gäfgen v Germany*, the Use of Threats and the Punishment of Those who Ill-treat During Police Questioning: A Reply to Steven Greer', *Human Rights Law Review*, 17 (2017), 681–99; N. Mavronicola, 'Is the Prohibition Against Torture and Cruel, Inhuman and Degrading Treatment Absolute in International Human Rights Law? A Reply to Steven Greer', *Human Rights Law Review*, 17 (2017), 479–98; S. Greer, 'Is the Prohibition Against Torture, Cruel, Inhuman and Degrading Treatment Really "Absolute" in International Human Rights Law? A Reply to Graffin and Mavronicola', *Human Rights Law Review*, 18 (2018), 297–307; S. Greer, J.H. Gerards and R. Slowe, *Human Rights in the Council of Europe and the European Union. Achievements, Trends and Challenges* (Cambridge University Press, 2018) 146.

[80] Cf. *Kokkinakis v. Greece*, ECtHR 25 May 1993, 14307/88, para. 33.

the prohibition of torture and inhuman and degrading treatment.[81] According to the Court, the Convention prohibits such treatment even in extreme emergency situations, such as the situation in which (threats of) the use of physical violence seem to be the only way to prevent the death of others (the 'ticking bomb scenario'). In the *Gäfgen* case, the Court explained the absolute and non-derogable nature of the prohibition of torture as follows:

> Article 3 of the Convention enshrines one of the most fundamental values of democratic societies. Unlike most of the substantive clauses of the Convention, Article 3 makes no provision for exceptions and no derogation from it is permissible under Article 15 § 2 even in the event of a public emergency threatening the life of the nation . . . [T]he prohibition on ill-treatment of a person applies irrespective of the conduct of the victim or the motivation of the authorities. Torture, inhuman or degrading treatment cannot be inflicted even in circumstances where the life of an individual is at risk . . . Article 3, which has been framed in unambiguous terms, recognises that every human being has an absolute, inalienable right not to be subjected to torture or to inhuman or degrading treatment under any circumstances, even the most difficult. The philosophical basis underpinning the absolute nature of the right under Article 3 does not allow for any exceptions or justifying factors or balancing of interests, irrespective of the conduct of the person concerned and the nature of the offence at issue.[82]

Nevertheless, the absoluteness of the protection offered by these Convention rights in the Court's case law must be nuanced.[83] In particular, the Court has used the possibilities for the determination of the scope of these rights (stage 1 of Convention review) to allow for some leeway. In *Ireland v. the United Kingdom*, for example, it held that

> ill-treatment must attain a minimum level of severity if it is to fall within the scope of Article 3. The assessment of this minimum is, in the nature of things, relative; it depends on all the circumstances of the case, such as the duration of the treatment, its physical or mental effects and, in some cases, the sex, age and state of health of the victim, etc.[84]

The Court has developed relatively clear and detailed standards to define when this threshold is met. In its judgment in *Paposhvili*, for example, it clarified when it would be contrary to Article 3 to expel a seriously ill person to a third country lacking in access to good-quality health care.[85] The threshold of severity then will

---

[81] E.g. *Saadi v. Italy*, ECtHR (GC) 28 February 2008, 37201/06, para. 127 and paras. 137–49.

[82] *Gäfgen v. Germany*, ECtHR (GC) 1 June 2010, 22978/05, paras. 87 and 107.

[83] There is much scholarly debate on this; see the sources mentioned *supra* n. 79.

[84] *Ireland v. the United Kingdom*, ECtHR 18 January 1978, 5310/71, para. 162. See further on this the debate referred to *supra* n. 79.

[85] *Paposhvili v. Belgium*, ECtHR (GC) 13 December 2018, 41738/10.

only be met if the person facing expulsion is close to death,[86] or in other 'very exceptional cases'. In *Paposhvili*, the Court explained that this notion referred to situations

> involving the removal of a seriously ill person in which substantial grounds have been shown for believing that he or she, although not at imminent risk of dying, would face a real risk, on account of the absence of appropriate treatment in the receiving country or the lack of access to such treatment, of being exposed to a serious, rapid and irreversible decline in his or her state of health resulting in intense suffering or to a significant reduction in life expectancy.[87]

This high threshold clearly limits the number of factual situations in which the absolute provision of Article 3 applies. More importantly, the Court may use the threshold approach to introduce some elements of justification and reasonableness in its review.[88] In the case of *N. v. the United Kingdom*, for example, the Court referred to the following reasons for setting high thresholds for applying Article 3 to cases of expulsion of ill persons:

> inherent in the whole of the Convention is a search for a fair balance between the demands of the general interest of the community and the requirements of the protection of the individual's fundamental rights ... Advances in medical science, together with social and economic differences between countries, entail that the level of treatment available in the Contracting State and the country of origin may vary considerably. While it is necessary, given the fundamental importance of Article 3 in the Convention system, for the Court to retain a degree of flexibility to prevent expulsion in very exceptional cases, Article 3 does not place an obligation on the Contracting State to alleviate such disparities through the provision of free and unlimited health care to all aliens without a right to stay within its jurisdiction. A finding to the contrary would place too great a burden on the Contracting States.[89]

Would this have been a case on a non-absolute Convention provision, such considerations would have formed part of the concrete balancing exercise conducted as part of the test of justification.[90] In practice, thus, the line between absolute and non-absolute rights is less sharply drawn than could be expected. From a conceptual and structural perspective, however, the difference is still important. In cases about

---

[86] *Ibid.*, para. 181; see also *N. v. the United Kingdom*, ECtHR 7 May 2008 (GC), 26565/05 and *D. v. the United Kingdom*, ECtHR 2 May 1997, 30240/96, para. 43.

[87] *Paposhvili*, para. 183.

[88] See also e.g. *S.F. and Others v. Bulgaria*, ECtHR 7 December 2017, 8138/16, para. 92.

[89] *N. v. the United Kingdom*, para. 44. The Court does not always seem to want to take such circumstances into account; with respect to the conditions of detention of asylum seekers, for example, see *J.R. and Others v. Greece*, ECtHR 25 January 2018, 22696/16, para. 137.

[90] See further Chapter 6.

absolute rights, the Court will not expressly or formally enter the third stage of Convention review, and it will not assess the arguments for justification in line with the standards discussed in Chapters 8, 9 and 10. Instead, once the Court has established that an individual has suffered inhuman or degrading treatment or has been tortured, it will immediately find a violation. By contrast, if the treatment does not meet the minimum threshold, it falls outside the scope of protection of the Convention and the complaint will be declared inadmissible.[91] This is different only if the set of facts can be said to be covered by one of the other provisions, such as the right to respect for one's private life as protected by Article 8 ECHR. In that case, the Court may turn to assess the case based on the standards for that particular provision as a kind of fall-back option.[92] This shows that the correct classification of a certain set of facts as being covered by one or the other Convention provision is very important for the applicable standards and, eventually, the outcome of the case.[93]

1.5.2 Absolute Rights That Are not 'Notstandsfest'

The second category comprises Convention rights that are of an absolute nature, but only to the extent that they can never be derogated from in times of peace. In case of an emergency threatening the life of the nation, however, Article 15 ECHR permits certain limitations and restrictions to be made to the exercise of these rights. Examples of rights belonging to this category are the prohibition of forced labour (Article 4(2) and (3)(c) ECHR) and the right to liberty (Article 5 ECHR). Although the latter right can also be restricted in times of peace, special limitations can be accepted in times of emergency. In *Hassan*, for example, the Court mentioned that

> internment in peacetime does not fall within the scheme of deprivation of liberty governed by Article 5 of the Convention without the exercise of the power of derogation under Article 15 . . . It can only be in cases of international armed conflict, where the taking of prisoners of war and the detention of civilians who pose a threat to security are accepted features of international humanitarian law, that Article 5 could be interpreted as permitting the exercise of such broad powers.[94]

If no formal declaration of a state of war or of emergency has been made under Article 15 ECHR, or if the Court finds that there was no real public emergency

---

[91] For an example, see *Budina v. Russia*, ECtHR 18 June 2009 (dec.), 45603/05 ('even though the applicant's situation was difficult . . . the Court is not persuaded that in the circumstances of the present case the high threshold of Article 3 has been met. It follows that this complaint is manifestly ill-founded and must be rejected.').

[92] On this issue of classification and safety nets, see e.g. J.H. Gerards, 'The ECtHR's Response to Fundamental Rights Issues Related to Financial and Economic Difficulties: The Problem of Compartmentalisation', *Netherlands Quarterly of Human Rights*, 33 (2015), 274–92.

[93] *Ibid.*

[94] *Hassan and Others v. the United Kingdom*, ECtHR (GC) 16 September 2014, no. 29750/09, para. 104.

threatening the life of the nation, the additional possibilities for restriction do not exist.[95] Moreover, even if there is an emergency, the States may make use of their right of derogation only 'to the extent strictly required by the exigencies of the situation'.[96] In reviewing the compatibility with this requirement, the Court will give weight to such factors as the nature of the rights affected by the derogation and the circumstances leading to, and the duration of, the emergency situation.[97] Moreover, restrictive measures which are not lawful can never be said to have been strictly required by the exigencies of the situation.[98]

1.5.3   Rights with Express, Specific Limitation Clauses

Several provisions of the Convention and its Protocols contain express limitation clauses that define a number of very specific conditions for a restriction to be permitted. A case in point is the right to life as protected by Article 2 ECHR. The second paragraph of Article 2 provides for three narrowly circumscribed exceptions to this right, namely deprivation of life which is the result of the use of force which is absolutely necessary (a) in defence of any person from unlawful violence; (b) in order to effect a lawful arrest or to prevent the escape of a person lawfully detained; (c) in action lawfully taken for the purpose of quelling a riot or insurrection. These exception clauses, moreover, are very narrowly construed by the Court.[99] The reason for this is that Article 2 'ranks as one of the most fundamental provisions in the Convention, one which, in peace time, admits of no derogation under Article 15. Together with Article 3, it enshrines one of the basic values of the democratic societies making up the Council of Europe'.[100] For these reasons, the right to life of Article 2 sometimes is referred to as an absolutely absolute provision (see category 1), but obviously this is only true insofar as the limited exceptions of Article 2(2) ECHR do not apply.

Equally limited and well-defined limitation clauses can be found in Article 4(3) ECHR (prohibition of forced labour), Article 5 (right to liberty) and Article 6 (right to a fair trial). In relation to Article 6, however, the Court has also recognised a number of inherent limitations (see below, category 5, Section 1.5.5). In addition, in some ECHR provisions, a combination can be found of a general limitation clause (see below, category 4) and a more specified clause. An example is the last sentence of Article 10(1) ECHR, which stipulates that 'this Article shall not prevent States from

[95] *Ibid.* On the Court's competence to review the existence of a public emergency threatening the life of the nation, see e.g. *A. v. the United Kingdom*, ECtHR (GC) 19 February 2009, 3455/05, paras. 175–81 and *Mehmet Hasan Altan v. Turkey*, ECtHR 20 March 2018, 13237/17, paras. 88–94.
[96] Article 15(1) ECHR. See for further elaboration of this standard *Ireland v. the United Kingdom*, ECtHR 18 January 1978, 5310/71, paras. 215 et seq.; *A. v. the United Kingdom*, ECtHR (GC) 19 February 2009, 3455/05, paras. 182 et seq.
[97] E.g. *A. v. the United Kingdom*, ECtHR (GC) 19 February 2009, 3455/05, para. 173.
[98] *Mehmet Hasan Altan v. Turkey*, ECtHR 20 March 2018, no 13237/17, para. 140.
[99] See *McCann and Others v. the United Kingdom*, ECtHR 27 September 1995, 18984/91, paras. 147–50.
[100] *Giuliani and Gaggio v. Italy*, ECtHR (GC) 24 March 2011, 23458/02, para. 174.

requiring the licensing of broadcasting, television or cinema enterprises'. The Court has held that such specific limitation clauses must be construed in conformity with the requirements following from the general limitation clause. In *Demuth*, the Court explained how this works:

> [T]he object and purpose of the third sentence of Article 10 § 1 is to make it clear that States are permitted to regulate by means of a licensing system the way in which broadcasting is organised in their territories, particularly in its technical aspects. The latter are undeniably important, but the grant or refusal of a licence may also be made conditional on other considerations, including such matters as the nature and objectives of a proposed station, its potential audience at national, regional or local level, the rights and needs of a specific audience and the obligations deriving from international legal instruments. This may lead to interferences whose aims will be legitimate under the third sentence of paragraph 1, even though they may not correspond to any of the aims set out in paragraph 2. The compatibility of such interferences with the Convention must nevertheless be assessed in the light of the other requirements of paragraph 2.[101]

In practice, thus, in such cases the various requirements and conditions for restriction are applied cumulatively.[102]

1.5.4   Rights with Express, General Limitation Clauses

The fourth and best-known category comprises those Convention provisions which provide a general definition of the protected right in the first paragraph of the Article and contain a general limitation clause in the second paragraph. Although the general limitation clauses contain a number of standards and conditions to be met, they are defined with less precision and less detail than the specific limitation clauses of, for example, Article 2(2) ECHR. General limitation clauses of this type can be found in Articles 8, 9, 10 and 11 of the Convention (protecting, respectively, the right to private and family life, religion, expression, and assembly and association), Article 1 of Protocol No. 1 (right to property) and Article 2 of Protocol No. 4 (freedom of movement).

Although these limitation clauses are generally similar in their formulation and structure, there are some notable differences which can be explained from the particular character of the various Convention rights and the desirability of providing narrowly drafted and well-specified possibilities for exception. Articles 8 to 11 ECHR disclose relevant differences, for example, as to the aims which may legitimately be pursued. Article 10(2) ECHR mentions maintaining the authority and impartiality of the judiciary as a legitimate aim, while this aim cannot be found in Articles 8, 9 or 11. Likewise, Article 8(2) ECHR allows for restrictions of the right to respect for one's

---

[101]   *Demuth v. Switzerland*, ECtHR 5 November 2002, 38743/97, para. 33.
[102]   See also e.g. *Glas Nadezhda EOOD and Elenkov v. Bulgaria*, ECtHR 11 October 2007, 14134/02, para. 44.

private and family life in the interests of the economic well-being of the country, while this motive is not supposed to play a role in relation to limitations of the freedom of expression, religion and assembly. Furthermore, only Article 10(2) expressly mentions the duties and responsibilities related to the exercise of the right, while only Article 11(2) refers to the imposition of lawful restrictions on the exercise of these rights by members of the armed forces, of the police, or of the administration of the State. In applying the limitation clauses, such differences have to be heeded.

The most common requirements for restriction mentioned in these limitation clauses are that a restriction must be prescribed by law and necessary in a democratic society to pursue a legitimate aim. Because of the importance of these requirements for the possibilities for regulating the Convention rights, these are discussed in depth in Chapters 8, 9 and 10.

1.5.5 Rights without Express Limitation Clauses; Implied or Inherent Limitations

Several Convention provisions do not contain express, specific or general limitation clauses, but according to the Court's case law this does not yet mean they must be considered to protect absolute and non-derogable rights. Indeed, for some rights, the Court has accepted that it is self-evident that these rights cannot be exercised in an absolute manner. An example is the right of access to a court, which follows from Article 6 ECHR. The Court recognised this right as forming an inherent part of the right to a fair trial in the *Golder* case, but it also recognised that there would be implied limitations in the enjoyment of this right: 'The Court considers ... that the right of access to the courts is not absolute. As this is a right which the Convention sets forth ... without, in the narrower sense of the term, defining, there is room, apart from the bounds delimiting the very content of any right, for limitations permitted by implication.'[103] In subsequent case law, the Court has further elaborated on this, and it has defined the applicable standards for assessment of restrictions:

> The right of access to the courts secured by Article 6 § 1 of the Convention is not absolute, but may be subject to limitations; these are permitted by implication since the right of access by its very nature calls for regulation by the State. In this respect, the Contracting States enjoy a certain margin of appreciation, although the final decision as to the observance of the Convention's requirements rests with the Court. It must be satisfied that the limitations applied do not restrict or reduce the access left to the individual in such a way or to such an extent that the very essence of the right is impaired. Furthermore, a limitation will not be compatible with Article 6 § 1 if it does not pursue a legitimate aim

---

[103] *Golder v. the United Kingdom*, ECtHR 21 February 1975, 4451/70, para. 37.

and if there is not a reasonable relationship of proportionality between the means employed and the aim sought to be achieved.[104]

Other examples of rights for which the Court has accepted inherent or implied limitations are the right to education (Article 2 of Protocol No. 1)[105] and the right to free elections (Article 3 of Protocol No. 1).[106] A possibility for restriction is also implied in the prohibition of discrimination of Article 14, even though the French text of the latter provision would seem to forbid every difference in treatment in the exercise of the Convention rights and freedoms. The Court explained this in the *Belgian Linguistics* case as follows:

> 10. In spite of the very general wording of the French version ('sans distinction aucune'), Article 14 does not forbid every difference in treatment in the exercise of the rights and freedoms recognised. This version must be read in the light of the more restrictive text of the English version ('without discrimination'). In addition, and in particular, one would reach absurd results were one to give Article 14 an interpretation as wide as that which the French version seems to imply. One would, in effect, be led to judge as contrary to the Convention every one of the many legal or administrative provisions which do not secure to everyone complete equality of treatment in the enjoyment of the rights and freedoms recognised. The competent national authorities are frequently confronted with situations and problems which, on account of differences inherent therein, call for different legal solutions; moreover, certain legal inequalities tend only to correct factual inequalities. The extensive interpretation mentioned above cannot consequently be accepted.[107]

The Court therefore held that the principle of equality of treatment would only be violated if a difference in treatment has no objective and reasonable justification:

> The existence of such a justification must be assessed in relation to the aim and effects of the measure under consideration, regard being had to the principles which normally prevail in democratic societies. A difference of treatment in the exercise of a right laid down in the Convention must not only pursue a legitimate aim: Article 14 is likewise violated when it is clearly established that there is no reasonable relationship of proportionality between the means employed and the aim sought to be realised.[108]

It can be seen from this that the Court applies many of the standards contained in the express limitation clauses by analogy in cases where such clauses are lacking.

Finally, it is important to note that even if the Court has accepted implied or inherent limitations in relation to specific provisions, this does not mean that *all*

---

[104] *Prince Hans-Adam II of Liechtenstein v. Germany*, ECtHR (GC) 12 July 2001, 42527/98, para. 44.
[105] See already the *Belgian Linguistics* case, ECtHR 23 July 1968, 1474/62, para. I.B.5 and see *Golder v. the United Kingdom*, ECtHR 21 February 1975, 4451/70, para. 38.
[106] *Mathieu-Mohin and Clerfayt v. Belgium*, ECtHR 2 March 1987, 9267/81, para. 52.
[107] *Belgian Linguistics* case, ECtHR 23 July 1968, 1474/62, para. I.B.10.   [108] *Ibid.*

Convention provisions allow for them. This is obviously true for the absolutely absolute rights discussed above (categories 1 and 2), but it also may be so in relation to other rights, such as the right to a fair trial protected by Article 6(1) ECHR. In *Campbell and Fell*, for example, the Court remarked that

> [i]t is true that the Court has recognised that to a certain extent the right of access to the courts secured by Article 6 may be subject to limitations permitted by implication ... However, that recognition resulted from the fact that the right in question was inherent in the first sentence of Article 6 para. 1 but was not defined therein. Again, unlike the first sentence, the second sentence does already contain a detailed list of express exceptions. ... [T]he Court does not consider that that principle [of public pronouncement of a judgment] may be regarded as subject to an implied limitation as suggested by the Government.[109]

However, it cannot be derived from this that all rights specifically protected by Article 6 have an absolute nature. For the right to be defended by a lawyer, which is provided for by Article 6(3)(c) ECHR, the Court held as follows in *Correia de Matos*:

> The minimum rights listed in Article 6 § 3, which exemplify the requirements of a fair trial in respect of typical procedural situations which arise in criminal cases, are not aims in themselves: their intrinsic aim is always to contribute to ensuring the fairness of the criminal proceedings as a whole ... Article 6 § 3 (c) confers on a person charged with a criminal offence the right 'to defend himself in person or through legal assistance of his own choosing'. Notwithstanding the importance of the relationship of confidence between a lawyer and his client, the latter right is not absolute ... [I]t is necessarily subject to certain limitations where free legal aid is concerned and also where it is for the courts to decide whether the interests of justice require that the accused be defended by counsel appointed by them.[110]

Thus, it is clear that the Court will determine for each of the Convention rights individually whether they can reasonably be regarded as subject to implied limitations.

1.5.6   Other Non-absolute or Derogable Rights

Finally, some Convention provisions do provide possibilities for limitation, but they are difficult to place in one of the previous categories. A notorious example is Article 12 ECHR, which stipulates that 'men and women of marriageable age have the right to marry and to found a family, according to the national laws governing the exercise of this right'. Thus, it appears from the text of this provision that the possibilities for limitation of this right have to be found in national law, rather than

---

[109] *Campbell and Fell v. the United Kingdom*, ECtHR 28 June 1984, 7819/77 and 7878/77, para. 90; see also *Fazliyski v. Bulgaria*, ECtHR 16 April 2013, 40908/05, para. 66.

[110] *Correia de Matos v. Portugal*, ECtHR (GC) 4 April 2018, 56402/12, paras. 120–1.

in the Convention. The Court has specified in its case law, however, that this does not leave the conditions for marriage entirely within the remit of the States:

> The exercise of this right gives rise to personal, social and legal consequences. As to both procedure and substance it is subject to the national laws of the Contracting States, but the limitations thereby introduced must not restrict or reduce the right in such a way or to such an extent that the very essence of the right is impaired . . . In consequence, the matter of conditions for marriage in the national laws is not left entirely to Contracting States as being within their margin of appreciation. This would be tantamount to finding that the range of options open to a Contracting State included an effective bar on any exercise of the right to marry.[111]

In *Frasik*, however, the Court explained that the special wording of Article 12 is not without significance:

> In contrast to Article 8 of the Convention, which sets forth the right to respect for private and family life, and with which the right 'to marry and to found a family' has a close affinity, Article 12 does not include any permissible grounds for an interference by the State that can be imposed under paragraph 2 of Article 8 'in accordance with the law' and as being 'necessary in a democratic society', for such purposes as, for instance, 'the protection of health or morals' or 'the protection of the rights and freedoms of others'. Accordingly, in examining a case under Article 12 the Court would not apply the tests of 'necessity' or 'pressing social need' which are used in the context of Article 8 but would have to determine whether, regard being had to the State's margin of appreciation, the impugned interference was arbitrary or disproportionate.[112]

Finally, the Court also explained the meaning of the reference to national laws in *Frasik*:

> The Convention institutions have accepted that limitations on the right to marry laid down in the national laws may comprise formal rules concerning such matters as publicity and the solemnisation of marriage. They may also include substantive provisions based on generally recognised considerations of public interest, in particular concerning capacity, consent, prohibited degrees of affinity or the prevention of bigamy. In the context of immigration laws and for justified reasons, the States may be entitled to prevent marriages of convenience, entered solely for the purpose of securing an immigration advantage. However, the relevant laws – which must also meet the standards of accessibility and clarity required by the Convention – may not otherwise deprive a person or a category of persons of full legal capacity of the right to marry with the partners of their choice.[113]

This last consideration suggests that the Court, regardless of the special way in which Article 12 is drafted, will apply a test of proportionality which is similar to the

---

[111] *Frasik v. Poland*, ECtHR 5 January 2010, 22933/02, para. 88.   [112] *Ibid.*, para. 90.
[113] *Ibid.*, para. 89.

one applied in relation to other Convention rights, as is discussed hereafter in Chapter 6.[114] Nevertheless, it will clearly also ensure that national legislation and national policy choices are respected as much as possible, in line with the principle of subsidiarity, and its review will come down to a mere test of arbitrariness.

---

[114] This is confirmed by the way the Court usually applies a proportionality test in relation to Article 12; see e.g. *O'Donoghue and Others v. the United Kingdom*, ECtHR 14 December 2010, 34848/07, paras. 84 et seq.; *Chernetsky v. Ukraine*, ECtHR 8 December 2016, 44316/07, paras. 28 et seq.; *Babiarz v. Poland*, ECtHR 10 January 2017, 1955/10, paras. 47 et seq.

2 The Court's Overall Argumentative Approach – Mediating Between the Abstract and the Concrete

2.1 Introduction

Pursuant to Article 32(1) ECHR, the Court's jurisdiction extends to all matters concerning the interpretation and application of the Convention and its Protocols. As explained in Chapter 1, one of the Court's main tasks is to provide individual justice and individual redress, but it must also provide general explanations of the Convention and for constitutional standard-setting. Chapter 1 has also shown that, for each individual case, the Court will have to assess whether a Convention provision applies, whether there is an interference and whether such an interference can be held to be justified. Finally, the Court will have to interpret and apply the Convention in a way that protects the various fundamental rights in an effective manner, while respecting the principles of primarity and subsidiarity.

One of the main challenges these tasks set for the Court is that it has to deal with the tension between the individual and the general, or the abstract and the concrete. On the one hand, the Court is asked to decide in individual cases and offer redress if the Convention has been violated in the individual circumstances of the case. This requires concrete interpretations and application of the Convention. On the other hand, the Court must also provide general standards and criteria, which necessarily have to go beyond the individual case and must be rather abstract in nature. Although most of its judgments are structured according to the three stages of review discussed in Section 1.4, the need to mediate between the individual and the general strongly determines its overall argumentative approach. For this reason, this topic is addressed separately in this chapter.

First, Section 2.2 explains what the Court regards as the object of review in cases where an alleged violation of the Convention is caused by legislation: is this the legislation as such (which would invite general and more abstract review), or is it the individual decision applying this legislation (which would invite individualised and more concrete review), or perhaps both? The chapter then turns to discussing how the Court has tried to reconcile its task of offering individual justice and general constitutional interpretations (Section 2.3). Specific attention is paid in this regard to the role of precedent-based reasoning in the Court's case law (Section 2.4) and to case-based review, incrementalism and the development of general principles (Section 2.5). Finally, the legal effect of these general principles is discussed, in contrast to the application thereof to the facts of the individual case (Section 2.6).

2.2 Object of Review: Legislation and/or Individual Decisions

Because of the Court's task of having to offer individual redress if there is a concrete violation of the Convention, it will always need to assess the individual facts and circumstances of the case to see whether they disclose a violation of the Convention. This starting point raises complex questions if an individual complaint finds its basis in legislation, since this is necessarily general in nature. In particular, the question then arises of what exactly will be the object of the Court's review. In theory, three answers can be given to this question, all three of which eventually lead to a finding in the individual case at hand:

1. the Court can review only the individual application of general legislation;
2. it can review the underlying legislation and, if it finds that this violates the Convention, this automatically implies that there is a violation in the individual case; or
3. it can first review the underlying legislation and decide that this is compatible with the Convention, and then continue to review whether the individual application still violated the Convention.

All three answers can be seen in the Court's case law, with the addition of some combinations.

First, in many cases, the Court has held that purely concrete review is the preferable option and no abstract review of the underlying legislation is needed. In *Perinçek*, for example, the applicant complained about his conviction for making a statement in public to the effect that there had not been an Armenian genocide.[1] This conviction was based on a provision of the Swiss Criminal Code, Article 261 *bis* (4), which stated that any person who seeks to justify a genocide or other crimes against humanity shall be punishable by a custodial sentence of up to three years or a fine.[2] The Court held that it would be best if it would apply only a concrete review of the individual application of this provision:

> In the present case, the Court is not required to determine whether the criminalisation of the denial of genocides or other historical facts may in principle be justified. Unlike the constitutional courts of France and Spain, which were entitled to – and indeed duty-bound – to [*sic*] examine the legislative provisions in this respect in the abstract . . . in a

---

[1] *Perinçek v. Switzerland*, ECtHR (GC) 15 October 2015, 27510/08.   [2] *Ibid.*, para. 32.

case which has its origin in an individual application the Court is constrained by the facts of the case ... It can thus only review whether or not the application of Article 261 *bis* § 4 of the Swiss Criminal Code in the case of the applicant was 'necessary in a democratic society' within the meaning of Article 10 § 2 of the Convention.[3]

This approach fits in a long line of case law in which the Convention bodies have found that they are only competent to examine the compatibility of national legislation with the Convention in respect of its application to a specific case, and not the legislation as such.[4]

In addition to the first approach, there are numerous cases in which the Court *does* review the underlying legislation, but it also looks into the individual application in the concrete circumstances of the case. As the Court held in *Sunday Times*[5] in relation to Article 10 ECHR:

> the Court's supervision under Article 10 covers not only the basic legislation but also the decision applying it ... It is not sufficient that the interference involved belongs to that class of the exceptions listed in Article 10 (2) which has been invoked; neither is it sufficient that the interference was imposed because its subject-matter fell within a particular category or was caught by a legal rule formulated in general or absolute terms: the Court has to be satisfied that the interference was necessary having regard to the facts and circumstances prevailing in the specific case before it.[6]

This second approach will usually lead to a two-step review, in which the Court first reviews the legislation in the abstract and then looks into the application to the facts of the case. An example of this can be seen in *Daróczy*, which concerned legislation on registration of surnames.[7] When the applicant married in 1950, her married name was incorrectly registered on her marriage certificate as Tiborné Daróczy. No one had ever noted the mistake and she had used the surname ever since. When she lost her identity card in 2004, however, the error was detected and a new card was issued which correctly indicated her name as Tibor Ipolyné Daróczy. The applicant's request for permission to continue to use the name Tiborné Daróczy was dismissed because of the applicable legislation on the registration of surnames. The Court held that such an argument, *in abstracto*, made sense: 'The Court accepts that due regard has to be given to the accuracy of the official registers and their protection is a core public interest.'[8] The Court further acceded that States should enjoy considerable discretion concerning the regulation of names.[9] However, it also held that there was a need to look into the concrete circumstances of the case:

---

[3] *Ibid.*, para. 226.
[4] See already e.g. *X. v. Austria*, EComHR 10 December 1976, 7045/75, at 88, referring to a Commission decision of 1961.
[5] *Sunday Times v. the United Kingdom (No. 1)*, ECtHR 26 April 1979, 6538/74.   [6] *Ibid.*, para. 65.
[7] *Daróczy v. Hungary*, ECtHR 1 July 2008, 44378/05.   [8] *Ibid.*, para. 29.   [9] *Ibid.*, para. 32.

Imposing a restriction on one's right to bear or change a name without justified and relevant reasons is not compatible with the purpose of Article 8 of the Convention, which is to protect individuals' self-determination and personal development ... Formal reference to a legitimate aim – like, in this case, ensuring the authenticity of the State Registry – in the absence of any actual prejudice to the rights of others cannot justify a restriction of that right. In the present case, the Government did not put forward any convincing argument showing that the genuineness of the system of the State registries or the rights of the applicant's late husband were at real risk. The restriction imposed on the applicant was therefore unacceptably rigid and completely disregarded her interests, in that she has been forced to alter a name which she has used for more than 50 years and which, beyond its relevance in self-identification and self-determination ... also gave her a strong personal link to her husband. Having regard to the above arguments, the considerations relied on by the Government cannot be said to outweigh the interests claimed by the applicant under Article 8 of the Convention in requesting to continue using the name she has borne for more than 50 years. A fair balance has therefore not been struck.

Accordingly, there has been a violation of Article 8 of the Convention.[10]

Of course, in some cases, the abstract review of legislation may already disclose that the legislation violates the Convention. In that case, which is the third option open to the Court, the Court usually does not see a need to look further into the facts of the case, since the very incompatibility of the underlying legislation with the Convention will automatically imply that its individual application is flawed. In some such cases, it has held that it would not even be reasonable to require an individual to complain about a concrete interference. The most famous example of this is the *Dudgeon* case, where the applicant had complained about legislation that criminalised homosexual conduct.[11] Dudgeon had not been subjected to criminal prosecution for homosexual acts, but he stated that he experienced fear, suffering and psychological distress as a result of the very existence of this legislation. The Court agreed with Dudgeon that in this case, the legislation as such should be the object of review, instead of its individual application:

[T]he maintenance in force of the impugned legislation constitutes a continuing interference with the applicant's right to respect for his private life (which includes his sexual life) within the meaning of Article 8 para. 1. In the personal circumstances of the applicant, the very existence of this legislation continuously and directly affects his private life ... either he respects the law and refrains from engaging – even in private with consenting male partners – in prohibited sexual acts to which he is disposed by reason of

---

[10] *Ibid.*, paras. 32–5.   [11] *Dudgeon v. Ireland*, ECtHR 22 October 1981, 7525/76.

his homosexual tendencies, or he commits such acts and thereby becomes liable to criminal prosecution.[12]

Subsequently, the Court assessed the arguments the Irish government had advanced to justify the legislation and it concluded that 'the reasons given by the Government, although relevant, are not sufficient to justify the maintenance in force of the impugned legislation'.[13] It therefore could find a violation of the Convention without looking into any concrete application of the legislation.[14]

Finally, in some cases the Court combines the different approaches. This can be illustrated by the *Bayev* case, which concerned the prohibition of public statements aimed at the promotion of homosexuality among minors (so-called 'homo propaganda') in various regions in Russia.[15] Based on the relevant legislation, the applicants had been fined for, among others, holding banners in front of a school with texts such as 'Homosexuality is normal' or 'I am proud of my homosexuality'. The applicants in the case had not so much complained about these concrete fines, but about the very existence of the legislation on which these individual decisions were based. The Court – probably for that reason – decided to opt for a mixed approach:

> The measures taken against the applicants were based on the legislative provisions specifically adopted to outlaw the promotion of homosexuality and non-traditional sexual relations among minors ... The Court reiterates that, in order to determine the proportionality of a general measure, it must primarily assess the legislative choices underlying it, regard being had to the quality of the parliamentary and judicial review of the necessity of the measure, and the risk of abuse if a general measure were to be relaxed. In doing so it will take into account its implementation in the applicants' concrete cases, which is illustrative of its impact in practice and is thus material to the measure's proportionality.[16]

It justified its deviation from *Perinçek* by holding that 'the Court's assessment in this case will focus on the necessity of the impugned laws as general measures, an approach which is to be distinguished from a call to review domestic law in the abstract'.[17] Eventually, however, the Court's assessment was not very different from the kind of abstract assessment it made in *Dudgeon*, as is witnessed by its conclusion in *Bayev*:

---

[12] *Ibid.*, para. 41.   [13] *Ibid.*, para. 61.
[14] For some specific types of cases, the Court has developed a slightly different and situation-specific approach. See particularly in relation to secret surveillance measures: *Roman Zakharov v. Russia*, ECtHR (GC) 4 December 2015, 47143/06, para. 171 and *Centrum för Rättvisa v. Sweden*, ECtHR 19 June 2018, 35252/08, paras. 92–3.
[15] *Bayev and Others v. Russia*, ECtHR 20 June 2017, 67667/09.   [16] *Ibid.*, para. 63.   [17] *Ibid.*

In the light of the above considerations the Court finds that the legal provisions in question do not serve to advance the legitimate aim of the protection of morals, and that such measures are likely to be counterproductive in achieving the declared legitimate aims of the protection of health and the protection of rights of others. Given the vagueness of the terminology used and the potentially unlimited scope of their application, these provisions are open to abuse in individual cases, as evidenced in the three applications at hand. Above all, by adopting such laws the authorities reinforce stigma and prejudice and encourage homophobia, which is incompatible with the notions of equality, pluralism and tolerance inherent in a democratic society. The foregoing considerations are sufficient to enable the Court to conclude that in adopting the various general measures in question and by implementing them in the applicants' cases the Russian authorities overstepped the margin of appreciation afforded by Article 10 of the Convention. Accordingly, there has been a violation of this provision.[18]

The most important conclusion that can be derived from this is that the Court, in the end, is clearly concerned with the individual applicant and the harm he has suffered as a result of an interference with a Convention right. It matters less if this interference is caused by the legislation as such, by its individual application or by an intricate combination of both.

2.3   Individual Redress or General Convention Interpretation?

Whether the Court assesses the Convention compatibility of an individual interference as such or it also reviews general legislation, it is always acting in its first main function, which is to offer individual redress to victims of fundamental rights violations (see Section 1.3). As explained in Section 1.3, however, the Court's role is a double one, since it also serves to provide general interpretations of the Convention. An important consequence of this is that the Court will not always limit its review to the facts of the case in hand, but it may provide more general explanations and interpretations that also may be relevant to other cases. For example, in *Opuz*, where the Court was asked to assess a case on domestic violence against women, it considered that 'the issue of domestic violence, which can take various forms ranging from physical to psychological violence or verbal abuse, cannot be confined to the circumstances of the present case. It is a general problem which concerns all member States and which does not always surface since it often takes place within personal relationships or closed circuits.'[19] For that reason, the Court did not only review whether the applicant had been a victim of a violation of the Convention because of the domestic violence she had suffered, but it also

---

[18] *Ibid.*, paras. 83–4.   [19] *Opuz v. Turkey*, ECtHR 9 June 2009, 33401/02, para. 132.

provided a number of standards to help determine the obligations of States to protect against such violence and to establish whether domestic violence might amount to gender discrimination.

The Court's task of providing general explanations of the Convention is also reflected in judgments, mostly of the Grand Chamber, where it decides to revisit and reconsider the standards and interpretations it has given in previous case law. An example of this can be seen in the admissibility decision in *Stec*, a case which concerned the question of whether non-contributory social benefits could be regarded as 'possessions' under the right to property as protected by Article 1 Protocol No. 1.[20] Before this case was decided, there was considerable ambiguity about this issue, as the Court expressly recognised:

> The Commission, and the Court in some cases, continued to find that a welfare benefit or pension fell within the scope of Article 1 of Protocol No. 1 only where contributions had been made to the fund that financed it . . . In other cases, however, the Court held that even a welfare benefit in a non-contributory scheme could constitute a possession for the purposes of Article 1 of Protocol No. 1.[21]

Under the heading 'The approach to be applied henceforth', the Court then indicated its resolve to provide a new, unambiguous and general interpretation of Article 1, Protocol No. 1: 'Against this background, it is necessary to examine afresh the question whether a claim to a non-contributory welfare benefit should attract the protection of Article 1 of Protocol No. 1.'[22] The Court decided that the new interpretation should be that both contributory and non-contributory benefits fall within the scope of Article 1 of Protocol No. 1. This clearly was aimed to be an interpretation that would not only matter to the facts of *Stec*, but also for all subsequent cases to be decided on the issue. Thus, the Court's focus clearly was much more on its constitutional and general interpretative role than on its role of offering individual redress and assessing whether there was a concrete violation of the Convention.[23]

2.4　The Role of Precedent in the Court's Case Law

The Convention system is not formally a precedent-based system where precedents are binding unless they are expressly overruled in later judgments. Given the Court's primary role of offering individual redress, each case could therefore be assessed

---

[20] *Stec and Others v. the United Kingdom*, ECtHR (GC) 6 July 2005 (dec.), 65731/01 and 65900/01.
[21] *Ibid.*, para. 46.　　[22] *Ibid.*, para. 47.
[23] Although, eventually, in its judgment on the merits, the Court also addressed the merits of the individual complaint; see *Stec and Others v. the United Kingdom*, ECtHR (GC) 12 April 2006, 65731/01 and 65900/01.

completely on its own merits, without taking account of any previous judgments. Nevertheless, the Court has chosen to develop an approach that comes rather close to a precedent-based system. The Court explained this approach in *Cossey*:

> [T]he Court is not bound by its previous judgments ... However, it usually follows and applies its own precedents, such a course being in the interests of legal certainty and the orderly development of the Convention case-law. Nevertheless, this would not prevent the Court from departing from an earlier decision if it was persuaded that there were cogent reasons for doing so. Such a departure might, for example, be warranted in order to ensure that the interpretation of the Convention reflects societal changes and remains in line with present-day conditions.[24]

Indeed, arguments based on precedent are apparent in virtually all of the Court's judgments, except for the very first ones. Under the heading 'general principles', the Court almost always provides an overview of relevant previous judgments and the main general standards of interpretation or application that can be derived from these. In some cases, the Court does not even give a fresh summary of the general principles, but it simply copies the relevant paragraphs out of a previous judgment,[25] or it only refers to the paragraph numbers of a relevant precedent.[26] The Court then will apply these standards to the individual case, which often means that its substantive argumentation can be limited and it does not need to provide a principled interpretation in each and every case. Sometimes the Court can even import entire holdings of earlier judgments to a new case if the facts and legal situations are sufficiently comparable. The *Sandu* case,[27] for example, which was also discussed in Chapter 1, concerned restrictions on the use of land by landowners which had been imposed by the authorities of the self-proclaimed 'Moldovan Transdniestrian Republic'. One of the issues that arose before the Court is whether the two respondent States, Moldova and Russia, could be held responsible for the alleged violations under Article 1 of the Convention. The Court had already extensively dealt with this issue in several other cases.[28] Although these cases concerned

---

[24] *Cossey v. the United Kingdom*, ECtHR 27 September 1990, 10843/84, para. 35. See also e.g. *Christine Goodwin v. the United Kingdom*, ECtHR (GC) 11 July 2002, 28957/95, para. 74.

[25] E.g. *Rashad Hasanov and Others v. Azerbaijan*, ECtHR 7 June 2018, 48653/13, para. 116; *Cabral v. the Netherlands*, ECtHR 28 August 2018, 37617/10, para. 32.

[26] E.g. *Sandu and Others v. Moldova and Russia*, ECtHR 17 July 2018, 21034/05, para. 33: 'The Court recalls that the general principles concerning the issue of jurisdiction under Article 1 of the Convention in respect of acts and facts occurring in the Transdniestrian region of Moldova were set out in *Ilaşcu and Others* (cited above, §§ 311–19), *Catan and Others* (cited above, §§ 103–7) and, more recently, *Mozer* (cited above, §§ 97–98).'

[27] *Sandu and Others v. Moldova and Russia*, ECtHR 17 July 2018, 21034/05.

[28] In particular *Ilaşcu and Others v. Moldova and Russia*, ECtHR 8 July 2004, 48787/99; *Ivanţoc and Others v. Moldova and Russia*, ECtHR 15 November 2011, 23687/05; *Catan and Others v. Moldova*

very different issues, such as the lawfulness and conditions of detention or access to education, in *Sandu* the Court held as follows:

> The Court sees no grounds on which to distinguish the present case from *Ilaşcu and Others*, *Ivanţoc and Others*, *Catan and Others*, and *Mozer* . . . taking into account the fact that the main events complained of happened in 2004–2006, a period covered by the findings in *Mozer* . . . It follows that the applicants in the present case fell within the jurisdiction of the Russian Federation under Article 1 of the Convention. Consequently, the Court dismisses the Russian Government's objections *ratione personae* and *ratione loci*.[29]

This approach of precedent-based reasoning allows the Court to dispose of many cases in an efficient manner and offer individual redress. Moreover, from a perspective of clarification of standards and the Court's constitutional function, this approach usually does not pose a problem either, at least as long as the precedent referred to actually provides a principled and substantive argumentation explaining the applicable interpretation. In this regard, the case law is sometimes lacking. For example, the *Donaldson* case concerned the prohibition of wearing an 'Easter lily' in commemoration of the Irish republican combatants who died during or were executed after the 1916 Easter Rising.[30] The question arose of whether such a symbol could be regarded as an 'expression' in the sense of Article 10 ECHR. In answering this question, the Court referred to a precedent:

> Having regard to the case of *Vajnai v. Hungary*, no. 33629/06, § 29, 8 July 2008, in which it held that the display of vestimentary symbols, albeit outside prison walls, fell within the ambit of Article 10, the Court agrees that the applicant's decision to wear an Easter lily must be regarded as a way of expressing his political views.[31]

However, in *Vajnai*, the Court did not provide any substantive arguments either. There it merely held that the decision of the applicant to wear a five-pointed red star must be regarded as his way of expressing his political views and, for that reason, the case fell within the ambit of Article 10.[32] Thus, precedent-based reasoning is not always fully satisfactory.[33]

The Court's use of precedent further shows two classic strategies of judicial argumentation: distinguishing and departure from precedent. The strategy of 'distinguishing' means that the Court explains that the factual or legal situation in a previous judgment differs from the case at hand and therefore the case should be decided

---

and Russia, ECtHR (GC) 19 October 2012, 43370/04; *Mozer v. Moldova and Russia*, ECtHR (GC) 23 February 2016, 11138/10.

[29] *Sandu*, paras. 36–7.   [30] *Donaldson v. the United Kingdom*, ECtHR 25 January 2011, 56975/09.
[31] *Ibid.*, para. 20.   [32] *Vajnai v. Hungary*, ECtHR 8 July 2008, 33629/06, para. 47.
[33] See further J.H. Gerards, 'The Prism of Fundamental Rights', *European Constitutional Law Review*, 8 (2012), 173–202.

differently or based on different standards. This strategy allows the Court to judge the new case individually on its merits, or perhaps sidestep less fortunate standards that have been developed in an earlier case or line of case law.[34] An example of this can be seen in *Antwi*, which concerned the intended expulsion of a migrant who had entered Norway with a forged identity and who had then lived in Norway for about six years.[35] In the meantime, he had married a Norwegian national and, together, they had a daughter. In the arguments Antwi presented to the Court, he strongly referred to the Court's judgment in *Nunez*, which was a similar case in which the Court had applied rather lenient standards to the benefit of the applicant.[36] Perhaps because this had evoked some national criticism, or because the Court was not entirely pleased with the way it decided *Nunez*, in *Antwi*, it decided to distinguish the case:

> [T]he Court considers that there are certain fundamental differences between the present case and that of Nunez where it found that the impugned expulsion of an applicant mother would give rise to a violation of Article 8 of the Convention. In reaching this finding, the Court attached decisive weight to the exceptional circumstances pertaining to the applicant's children in that case, which were recapitulated ... in its judgment ([*Nunez*], § 84) ... Unlike what had been the situation of the children of Mrs Nunez, the third applicant [the first applicant's child] had not been made vulnerable by previous disruptions and distress in her care situation (compare *Nunez* ... §§ 79 to 81). Also, the duration of the immigration authorities' processing of the matter was not so long as to give reason to question whether the impugned measure fulfilled the interests of swiftness and efficiency of immigration control that was the intended purpose of such administrative measures (compare *Nunez* ... § 82) ... There being no exceptional circumstances at issue in the present case, the Court is satisfied that sufficient weight was attached to the best interests of the child in ordering the first applicant's expulsion.[37]

With this reasoning, the Court made it clear that application of the lenient approach in *Nunez* would be strictly limited to a narrow set of factual circumstances, rendering that case less relevant as a precedent.

In other cases, but only rarely, the Court explicitly departs from its precedents. Mostly, it will do so because it has turned out that the existing precedents have

---

[34] See e.g. J.H. Gerards, 'The European Court of Human Rights and the National Courts – Giving Shape to the Notion of "Shared Responsibility"' in J.H. Gerards and J.W.A. Fleuren (eds.), *Implementation of the European Convention on Human Rights and of the Judgments of the ECtHR in National Case Law. A Comparative Analysis* (Antwerp: Intersentia, 2014), pp. 13–94, at 60, with further references to examples in the Court's case law on voting rights for prisoners.

[35] *Antwi and Others v. Norway*, ECtHR 14 February 2012, 26940/10.

[36] *Nunez v. Norway*, ECtHR 28 June 2011, 55597/09.

[37] *Antwi*, paras. 100–3. For a similar example, see *Goudswaard-Van der Lans v. the Netherlands*, ECtHR 22 September 2005 (dec.), 75255/01, distinguishing that case from *Kjartan Ásmundsson v. Iceland*, ECtHR 12 October 2004, 60669/00.

created too much uncertainty, or the formulated standards appear to be difficult to apply in practice. A famous example is *Vilho Eskelinen*, which concerned the thorny issue of the applicability of the right of access to a court to disputes of civil servants.[38] In *Pellegrin*, the Court had established an autonomous interpretation with a view to the application of Article 6 in this type of cases.[39] In *Vilho Eskelinen*, however, the Court concluded that the standard it had defined in *Pellegrin* had not proved to be workable and, for that reason, it decided to revise its earlier approach:

> the Court finds that the functional criterion adopted in *Pellegrin* must be further developed. While it is in the interests of legal certainty, foreseeability and equality before the law that the Court should not depart, without good reason, from precedents laid down in previous cases, a failure by the Court to maintain a dynamic and evolutive approach would risk rendering it a bar to reform or improvement.[40]

The Court then chose to develop a new set of standards for determining the applicability of Article 6, which was only minimally similar to that used in *Pellegrin*. In this case, and also in a case such as *Stec* (discussed above), the Court was very open and honest about the need to depart from its earlier approach or to harmonise conflicting or diverging lines of precedent.[41] In most cases, however, the Court does not explicitly depart from the standards and general principles defined in a precedent, but it rather 'further develops'[42] or 'clarifies'[43] them, or it opts for a 'calibrated approach'.[44] Regardless of the terminology, however, these are all clear indications of changes in the Court's general principles that may have an impact on future judgments and decisions.

2.5 Case-based Review, Incrementalism and the Search for a Reflective Equilibrium

The Court's double role of offering individual justice and of providing general explanations may further beg the question of how the two interrelate. Roughly, the Court can be seen to apply two approaches to reconcile its double role. The first approach is for the Court to work from case-based and individualised judgments to

---

[38] *Vilho Eskelinen v. Finland*, ECtHR (GC) 19 April 2007, 63235/00.
[39] *Pellegrin v. France*, ECtHR (GC) 8 December 1999, 28541/95, para. 63.
[40] *Vilho Eskelinen*, para. 56.
[41] For an express example of the latter, see also *Idalov v. Russia*, ECtHR (GC) 22 May 2012, 5826/03, para. 127 and *Denisov v. Ukraine*, ECtHR (GC) 25 September 2018, 76639/11, para. 93.
[42] E.g. *Buzadji v. Moldova*, ECtHR (GC) 5 July 2016, 23755/07, para. 96.
[43] E.g. *Muršić v. Croatia*, ECtHR (GC) 20 October 2016, 7334/13, para. 91.
[44] E.g. *A. and B. v. Norway*, ECtHR (GC) 15 November 2016, 24130/11 and 29758/11, para. 107.

the definition of general principles, which can be called 'incrementalism'.[45] The Court often uses this approach if it has to address a relatively new and potentially sensitive and divisive subject matter. In a series of judgments on assisted suicide and euthanasia, for example, the Court has gradually developed its interpretation of Article 8 from 'not excluding' that a right to assisted suicide could be covered by the right to personal autonomy in 2002, to unreservedly and clearly accepting the applicability of Article 8 to such cases in 2011.[46] In an incremental, yet effective way, this has allowed the Court to cover the sensitive terrain of euthanasia and withdrawal of life-sustaining treatment. In the same vein, the Court seems to have chosen for incrementalism in imposing positive obligations on the States to provide legal recognition of relationships between same-sex couples,[47] as well as in cases on a right to access to information under Article 10 ECHR.[48] In all such cases, the value of incrementalism for the Court is in the possibility to change position if its approach is met with national criticism, while still retaining a relatively high level of protection of Convention rights – if only because certain procedural obligations are imposed on the States and individual redress is offered.

Of course, this incremental and precedent-based approach may have the disadvantage that it offers little clarity about the standards and general interpretation of the Convention. The solution it has found to this is that many of its general interpretations are, in fact, based on the outcomes of its individualised decision-making in previous cases. Once in a while, the Court – mostly in its Grand Chamber formation – sits down to distil the common elements and criteria from its judgments

---

[45] See further J.H. Gerards, 'Margin of Appreciation and Incrementalism in the Case-Law of the European Court of Human Rights', *Human Rights Law Review*, 18 (2018), section 3.B. This section is based on that article.

[46] Compare *Pretty v. the United Kingdom*, ECtHR 29 April 2002, 2346/02, para. 67 and *Haas v. Switzerland*, ECtHR 20 January 2011, 31322/07, para. 51; see also *Koch v. Germany*, ECtHR 19 July 2012, 497/09, para. 52. In a 2013 case, the Court even went one step further, stating that the right to end one's life actually falls within the scope of protection of Article 8 of the Convention (*Gross v. Switzerland*, ECtHR 14 May 2013, 67810/10, para. 60). These cases paved the way for a more principled stand in cases on ending life-sustaining treatment, in particular *Lambert v. France*, ECtHR (GC) 5 June 2015, 46043/14 and (as an application of that judgment) *Gard and Others v. the United Kingdom*, ECtHR 27 June 2017 (dec.), 39793/17.

[47] This is witnessed by the very gradual approach taken in the line of cases ranging from *Schalk and Kopf v. Austria*, ECtHR 24 June 2010, 30141/04 and *X v. Austria*, ECtHR (GC) 19 February 2013, 19010/07 via *Vallianatos and Others v. Greece*, ECtHR (GC) 7 November 2013, 29381/09 and 32684/09 to, more recently (and still very strongly case-based) *Oliari and Others v. Italy*, ECtHR 21 July 2015, 18766/11 and 36030/11 and (less strictly case-based and more principled) *Taddeucci and McCall v. Italy*, ECtHR 30 June 2016, 51362/09 and *Orlandi and Others v. Italy*, ECtHR 14 December 2017, 26431/12. On this development, see also in-depth N.R. Koffeman, *Morally Sensitive Issues and Cross-Border Movement in the EU* (Antwerp: Intersentia, 2015).

[48] See *Magyar Helsinki Bizottság v. Hungary*, ECtHR (GC) 8 November 2016, 18030/11, in which the Court clarified the general principles that slowly emerged from a longer line of (sometimes seemingly inconsistent) judgments, summed up in paras. 127 et seq.

in previous cases and reformulate them in terms of 'general principles derived from the Court's case law'.[49] These principles and criteria then serve as standards or yardsticks to be applied by the Court as well as by national authorities in subsequent cases. Hence, justice is done to the Court's overall task to 'elucidate, safeguard and develop the rules instituted by the Convention'.

The second approach the Court can take to mediate between case-based decision-making and setting general standards is the exact opposite to the strategy of incrementalism. It then starts off a new line of case law by defining a general principle, only later refining it by application in concrete cases. A famous example is the assistance by a lawyer during police interrogations.[50] In *Salduz*, the Court confronted the question head-on of whether such assistance must be offered.[51] It provided detailed reasoning on the importance of such assistance for the rights of the suspect, and it held that such assistance should, in principle, always be offered.[52] The States responded to this judgment in different ways,[53] causing many new cases to be brought. As a result, the Court has had to deal with numerous post-*Salduz* cases in which it was required to clarify, revise and refine the meaning of its first judgment.[54] In deciding on these cases, the Court once again relied on its particularised, case-based approach, taking into account the precise circumstances of every applicant and only gradually lifting the remaining uncertainties regarding the judgment in *Salduz*. Eventually, it appeared from all these concrete applications that the previously established general standards were not sufficiently workable and clear. For that reason, the Court in *Ibrahim* chose to reformulate and refine the general standards, taking due account of the difficulties that had been demonstrated in the individual cases.[55]

Whether the Court adopts the first strategy of incrementalism or the second strategy of case-based refinement of general principles, it is clear that there is a

---

[49] Gerards, *supra* n. 34, at 68.

[50] There are more examples of this approach, although they are relatively rare; see e.g. *Hirst (No. 2) v. the United Kingdom*, ECtHR (GC) 6 October 2005, 74025/01; *Kafkaris v. Cyprus*, ECtHR (GC) 12 February 2008, 21906/04; *Rantsev v. Cyprus and Russia*, ECtHR 7 January 2010, 25965/04. These cases formed the starting point for long lines of judgments specifying and detailing the general principles established in these judgments on, respectively, the right to vote for prisoners, irreducible life sentences and human trafficking.

[51] *Salduz v. Turkey*, ECtHR (GC) 27 November 2008, 36391/02.

[52] *Ibid.*, para. 55: 'as a rule, access to a lawyer should be provided as from the first interrogation of a suspect by the police, unless it is demonstrated in the light of the particular circumstances of each case that there are compelling reasons to restrict this right.'

[53] See the national reports in Gerards and Fleuren, *supra* note 34.

[54] E.g. *Diriöz v. Turkey*, ECtHR 31 May 2012, 38560/04; *Carine Simons v. Belgium*, ECtHR 28 August 2012 (dec.), 71407/10; *Sîrghi v. Romania*, ECtHR 24 May 2016, 19181/09. The Court has even opened a fact sheet on the issue (see www.echr.coe.int/Documents/FS_Police_arrest_ENG.pdf, last accessed 30 November 2018).

[55] *Ibrahim and Others v. the United Kingdom*, ECtHR 13 September 2016, 50541/08, para. 257.

continuous movement from definition of general principles to refinement in individual cases, to redefinition of general principles, to further refinement in individual cases, and so on.[56] The most apt description of the Court's overall argumentative approach therefore might be that of a search for a 'reflective equilibrium'.[57] This characterisation does justice to the Court's practice of 'going back and forth' between principles and concrete circumstances.

2.6   Legal Effect of the Court's Interpretations; 'Res Interpretata'

Finally, it is useful to pay some attention to the legal effect of the interpretations provided by the Court. According to Article 46 ECHR, the Court's judgments are officially only binding on the parties to the case. Thus, strictly speaking, if a violation has been found in a case against the respondent State, the other forty-six States Parties do not have to comply with the judgment or even bother to read it.[58] It has become accepted, however, that this limitation of the binding effect of the Court's judgments is only relevant for the concrete evaluation of an alleged violation and its justification, that is, the so-called operative part of the judgment.[59] By contrast, the Court's interpretations of the notions contained in the Convention are of a general nature and they can be regarded as determining the meaning of the various terms and concepts contained in the Convention.[60] This was expressly recognised by the Parliamentary Assembly of the Council of Europe in 2000:

---

[56] See further J.H. Gerards, 'The European Court of Human Rights' in A. Jákab, A. Dyevre and G. Itzcovich (eds.), *Comparative Constitutional Reasoning* (Cambridge University Press, 2017), pp. 237–76.

[57] *Ibid.* Cf. J. Rawls, *A Theory of Justice* (Cambridge, MA: Belknap, 1971) at 20; the Court's approach then seem to match well with Rawls' own reference to Goodwin's rather circular theory of justification; see N. Goodman, *Fact, Fiction and Forecast*, 4th edn (Cambridge, MA: Belknap, 1983) at 63 and H. Putman's Introduction, at ix.

[58] Cf. E. Klein, 'Should the Binding Effect of the Judgments of the European Court of Human Rights be Extended?' in P. Mahoney, F. Matscher, H. Petzold and L. Wildhaber (eds.), *Protecting Human Rights: The European Perspective* (Cologne: Heymanns, 2000), pp. 705–13 at 706; G. Ress, 'The Effect of Decisions and Judgments of the European Court of Human Rights in the Domestic Legal Order', *Texas International Law Journal* 40 (2005), 359 at 374.

[59] Cf. L. Garlicki, 'Contrôle de constitutionnalité et contrôle de conventionalité. Sur le dialogue des juges', in *La conscience des droits. Mélanges en l'honneur de Jean-Paul Costa* (Paris: Dalloz, 2011), pp. 271–80 at 280 and, in the same volume, A. Drzemczewski, 'Quelques reflexions sur l'autorité de la chose interprétée par la Cour de Strasbourg', pp. 243–8, at 246.

[60] See J. Vélu, 'Considérations sur quelques aspects de la coopération entre la Cour européenne des droits de l'homme et les juridictions nationales' in P. Mahoney et al., *supra* note 58, pp. 1511–1525 at p. 1521. See also M. Marmo, 'The Execution of Judgments of the European Court of Human Rights – A Political Battle', *Maastricht Journal of European and Comparative Law*, 15 (2008), 235–58 at 242–3.

The principle of solidarity implies that the case law of the Court forms part of the Convention, thus extending the legally binding force of the Convention *erga omnes* (to all the other parties). This means that the states parties not only have to execute the judgments of the Court pronounced in cases to which they are party, but also have to take into consideration the possible implications which judgments pronounced in other cases may have for their own legal system and legal practice.[61]

In line with this, the European government leaders have expressly committed themselves to 'taking into account the Court's developing case law, also with a view to considering the conclusions drawn from a judgment finding a violation of the Convention by another State, where the same problem exists within their own legal system'.[62] This legal effect is commonly called the *res interpretata* or 'force of interpretation' of the general principles the Court has accepted in its case law. This also has been expressly embraced and underlined by the Court to mean that '[i]n carrying out this scrutiny, and bearing in mind that the Court provides final authoritative interpretation of the rights and freedoms defined in Section I of the Convention, the Court will consider whether the national authorities have sufficiently taken into account the principles flowing from its judgments on similar issues, even when they concern other States'.[63]

Thus, *de facto*, the Court's well-established interpretations, that is, the general principles it has defined in its judgments, can be considered to be binding on the States. Put differently, the States are obliged to comply with the Convention as it is explained by the Court. Indeed, a different view would be difficult to reconcile with the Convention's objective of maintaining a uniform minimum level of protection throughout Europe. This objective requires at the very least that all States accept that a general interpretation given in one case, which establishes a certain minimum level of protection, is equally pertinent and applicable in all similar cases. All the same, it is important to emphasise that this *res interpretata* is only recognised for the general and well-established interpretations as they are expressed in the 'general principles' section of the Court's judgments. The application of those principles to the concrete facts of the case remains highly particularised and its concrete findings are only binding for the parties to the case, as is understandable from the Court's role of also having to offer individual redress. This approach both confirms and reconciles the two main roles played by the Court.

---

[61] PACE Resolution 1226/2000, *Execution of Judgments of the European Court of Human Rights*, 28 September 2000 (30th Sitting), para. 3.

[62] High Level Conference on the Future of the European Court of Human Rights, Interlaken Declaration, 19 February 2010 – Action plan, para. B.4.c.

[63] *Opuz v. Turkey*, ECtHR 9 June 2009, 33401/02, para. 163.

3 Principles Governing the Interpretation and Application of Convention Rights

3.1 Introduction

In Chapter 1, it was explained that the Court's work is strongly driven by the overall objective of providing an effective protection to the fundamental rights laid down in the Convention. The first principle underlying the system therefore is the *effectiveness principle*. Such effective protection is secured by the organs working within the Convention system – mainly the Court, but also, for example, the Committee of Ministers – together with the States Parties to the Convention. In this respect, the primary responsibility to secure the Convention rights lies with the States, the Court's task being supervisory and subsidiary in nature. This is the *subsidiarity principle*. In addition, in Section 1.3, the double task of the Court was described as having to offer both individual redress and general interpretations of the Convention. As has been discussed in Chapter 2, these principles, objectives and tasks interact in the Court's case law in many ways. In particular, the Court's argumentative approach has been characterised as a continuous search for a balance between the abstract (providing general interpretations) and the concrete (offering individual redress).

These important principles of effectiveness and subsidiarity, and the search for a 'reflective equilibrium' are not alone in guiding the Court in its work of interpreting and applying the Convention. Both in determining the scope of application of the Convention (which requires interpretation of the terms and notions of the various Convention provisions, as explained in Section 1.4.2) and in applying the Convention rights to the concrete case before the Court (which requires an assessment of interference and justification, as explained in Sections 1.4.3 and 1.4.4), the Court also makes use of a number of other general principles and starting points that determine its argumentative approach and the practical meaning and impact of its judgments. It is useful to have an insight into these principles and starting points in order to understand the methods the Court sometimes uses in Convention interpretation (Chapter 4), the positive obligations doctrine (Chapter 5), the vertical and horizontal effect of the Convention (Chapter 6), the development and application of the margin of appreciation doctrine (Chapter 7), and the way the Court assesses justifications for restrictions (Chapters 8, 9 and 10).

This chapter therefore discusses the most important of these principles, connecting them with the two main principles of effectiveness and subsidiarity discussed in Chapter 1. Attention is first paid to the relevance of the rules of interpretation provided by the Vienna Convention on the Law of Treaties and the special nature of the Convention as a 'law-making treaty' (Section 3.2). Subsequently, three principles are discussed that are of primary importance to the interpretation and determination of scope of the Convention after the principles of effectiveness and subsidiarity. These are the notion that the ECHR is a 'living instrument', which has to be interpreted in an evolutive and dynamic manner (Section 3.3), the principle that the Convention should be interpreted in line with the underlying values of the Convention ('meta-teleological interpretation') (Section 3.4) and the principle of autonomous interpretation (Section 3.5).

3.2   The ECHR and the Vienna Convention on the Law of Treaties

As for all treaty bodies, an important starting point for the Court in its interpretation of the Convention is the 1969 Vienna Convention on the Law of Treaties ('Vienna Convention'). In 1975, even before the Vienna Convention had entered into force, the Court recognised the importance of the rules for treaty interpretation contained in this Convention in the *Golder* case:

> The Court is prepared to consider . . . that it should be guided by Articles 31 to 33 of the Vienna Convention of 23 May 1969 on the Law of Treaties . . . [I]ts Articles 31 to 33 enunciate in essence generally accepted principles of international law to which the Court has already referred on occasion. In this respect, for the interpretation of the European Convention account is to be taken of those Articles subject, where appropriate, to 'any relevant rules of the organization' – the Council of Europe – within which it has been adopted (Article 5 of the Vienna Convention).[1]

Article 31(1) of the Vienna Convention stipulates the main principle for interpretation of international treaties: 'A treaty shall be interpreted in good faith in accordance with the ordinary meaning to be given to the terms of the treaty in their context and in the light of its object and purpose.' Article 31(2) then explains the 'context' referred to in this first paragraph. This context is constituted by the text, Preamble and annexes of a treaty, but also, among others, by any agreement made between the parties in connection to the conclusion of a treaty. The third paragraph of Article 31 furthermore explains that, next to this context, account has to be taken of any subsequent agreements between the parties regarding the interpretation or application of a treaty,

---

[1] *Golder v. the United Kingdom*, ECtHR 21 February 1975, 4451/70, para. 29.

any subsequent State practice in the application of the treaty that shows an agreement between the parties regarding its interpretation, and any relevant rules of international law applicable in the relation between the parties. Finally, Article 31(4) explains that the States Parties can give a special meaning to a term contained in a Convention and that this, then, has to be respected.

In addition, Article 32 of the Vienna Convention mentions that other instruments, such as the preparatory works of a treaty and the circumstances of its conclusion, can be used as a supplementary means of interpretation if the meaning of a treaty provision is still ambiguous or obscure after application of the tools provided by Article 31, or if the interpretation based on Article 31 would lead to a result that is manifestly absurd or unreasonable.

Finally, since the Convention and its Protocols are authenticated in two different languages (English and French), Article 33 of the Vienna Convention is also relevant. This provision states, among other things, that the text of both authentic language versions is equally authoritative (Article 33(1)) and that the terms of the treaty are presumed to have the same meaning in each authentic version (Article 33(3)), except when the parties have agreed that, in case of divergence, a particular text shall prevail. If the parties have not agreed on a particular interpretation but the language versions still diverge, Article 33(4) provides that Articles 31 and 32 can be used to solve the divergence. If that does not help, the meaning must be adopted that best reconciles the texts, having regard to the object and purpose of the treaty.

In *Witold Litwa*, the Court explained the meaning of these rules of the Vienna Convention for its interpretation of the ECHR.[2] The Court started by giving its general perspective on the connection between the various principles defined in Article 31:

> [T]he Court reiterates that, in the way it is presented in the general rule of interpretation laid down in Article 31 of the Vienna Convention, the process of discovering and ascertaining the true meaning of the terms of the treaty is a unity, a single combined operation. This general rule, closely integrated, places on the same footing the various elements enumerated in the four paragraphs of that Article ... The sequence in which those elements are listed in Article 31 of the Vienna Convention regulates, however, the order which the process of interpretation of the treaty should follow.[3]

Thus, the Court accepted the Vienna Convention's starting point that a textual interpretation of the Convention is of primary importance to the definition of the terms and notions contained in the Convention. This understanding can be adjusted, however, if it does not fit well within the typical ECHR context.

---

[2] *Witold Litwa v. Poland*, ECtHR 4 April 2000, 26629/95.　　[3] *Ibid.*, paras. 58–9.

The interrelationship between the different tools of interpretation the Vienna Convention offers can also be illustrated by the *Witold Litwa* case. In this case, the Court was asked to explain the notion of 'alcoholics', for which Article 5(1)(e) ECHR provides that they can be legitimately detained. One of the arguments the applicant had made was that this provision could not be applied to persons who were 'merely' intoxicated, since they could not be identified by the notion of 'alcoholics'. Following the order of Article 31(1) of the Vienna Convention, the Court first observed that the word 'alcoholics', in its common usage, indeed denotes persons who are addicted to alcohol. It also noted, however, that in Article 5(1) ECHR, the notion is found in a context that includes a reference to several other categories of persons, such as drug addicts and vagrants. The Court perceived a link between these groups, that they may all be deprived of their liberty either in order to be given medical treatment, or because of considerations dictated by social policy, or on both medical and social grounds.[4] It concluded from this that the main objective of Article 5(1) ECHR is to legitimise detention of persons if they are a danger to public safety or their own safety.[5] According to the Court, this *ratio legis* indicated that the object and purpose of this provision could not be interpreted as only allowing the detention of 'alcoholics' in the limited sense of persons in a clinical state of 'alcoholism'.[6] Instead, persons who are not medically diagnosed as 'alcoholics', but whose behaviour under the influence of alcohol poses a threat to public order or themselves, can also be taken into custody for the protection of the public or their own interests, such as their health or personal safety.[7] Finally, the Court pointed out that this meaning of the term 'alcoholics' was confirmed by the preparatory work of the Convention.[8] Thus, the *Witold Litwa* judgment shows the importance of the principles constituted by Articles 31 and 32 of the Vienna Convention in answering concrete questions of Convention interpretation.

The Court also takes account of Article 33 of the Vienna Convention in its case law. In the *Belgian Linguistics* case, for example, it was asked to reconcile the meaning of the French and English language versions of Article 14 ECHR.[9] The French version mentions that the rights and freedoms protected by the Convention and its Protocols must be secured 'sans aucune distinction', whereas the English language versions says that they must be guaranteed 'without discrimination'. Compared to the English version, the French version thus seems to provide a stricter prohibition of discrimination, encompassing every case of unequal treatment, even if it does not amount to discrimination. The Court held that, in this particular context, the English text version should prevail:

---

[4] *Ibid.*, para. 60.   [5] *Ibid.*   [6] *Ibid.*, para. 61.   [7] *Ibid.*   [8] *Ibid.*, para. 63.
[9] *Belgian Linguistics* case, ECtHR 23 July 1968, 1474/62.

In spite of the very general wording of the French version ('sans distinction aucune'), Article 14 does not forbid every difference in treatment in the exercise of the rights and freedoms recognised. This version must be read in the light of the more restrictive text of the English version ('without discrimination'). In addition, and in particular, one would reach absurd results were one to give Article 14 an interpretation as wide as that which the French version seems to imply. One would, in effect, be led to judge as contrary to the Convention every one of the many legal or administrative provisions which do not secure to everyone complete equality of treatment in the enjoyment of the rights and freedoms recognised. The competent national authorities are frequently confronted with situations and problems which, on account of differences inherent therein, call for different legal solutions; moreover, certain legal inequalities tend only to correct factual inequalities. The extensive interpretation mentioned above cannot consequently be accepted.[10]

The context of the provision and the object and purpose of the Convention thus proved decisive for the Court's interpretation of Article 14 ECHR.

Hence, Articles 31–33 of the Vienna Convention have clear significance for the Court's interpretations.[11] Nevertheless, the Court has put this relevance into perspective. In particular, it has held that the special characteristics of the Convention may justify a different weight to be given to some of the interpretative principles of the Vienna Convention as compared to others. In *Wemhoff*, it explained that, '[g]iven that [the Convention] ... is a law-making treaty, it is also necessary to seek the interpretation that is most appropriate in order to realise the aim and achieve the object of the treaty, not that which would restrict to the greatest possible degree the obligations undertaken by the Parties'.[12] The 'law-making' nature of the Convention sets it apart from other treaties, which may comprise 'mere reciprocal engagements between Contracting States'.[13] In addition, as the Court pointed out in *Soering*, the very nature of the Convention makes that the effectiveness principle, as explained in Chapter 1, is of overriding importance in giving meaning to its provisions:

In interpreting the Convention regard must be had to its special character as a treaty for the collective enforcement of human rights and fundamental freedoms ... Thus, the object and purpose of the Convention as an instrument for the protection of individual human beings require that its provisions be interpreted and applied so as to make its safeguards practical and effective ... In addition, any interpretation of the rights and freedoms guaranteed has

---

[10] *Ibid.*, para. I.B.10.

[11] See for more recent confirmation of the Court's early judgment e.g. *Marguš v. Croatia*, ECtHR (GC) 27 May 2014, 4455/10, para. 129; *Al-Dulimi and Montana Management Inc. v. Switzerland*, ECtHR (GC) 21 June 2016, 5809/08, para. 134.

[12] *Wemhoff v. Germany*, ECtHR 27 June 1968, 2122/64, 'as to the law', para. 8. See more recently also e.g. *Magyar Helsinki Bizottság v. Hungary*, ECtHR (GC) 8 November 2016, 18030/11, para. 138.

[13] E.g. *Ibid.*, para. 122.

to be consistent with the general spirit of the Convention, an instrument designed to maintain and promote the ideals and values of a democratic society.[14]

As such, this is not contrary to the Vienna Convention, which in Article 31 expressly provides for interpretations in the light of the object and purpose of a treaty as well as for interpretations taking the context of the specific treaty instrument into account.[15] It does mean, however, that the Court sometimes pays less attention to the early methods of interpretation mentioned in Article 31 of the Vienna Convention, such as textual interpretation or references to the preparatory works, and emphasises specific Convention methods of interpretation such as 'meta-teleological interpretation' and common ground or consensus interpretation.[16] This impact of the special character of the Convention and its objectives on the Court's methods of interpretation is further explored in Chapter 4.

3.3 Evolutive Interpretation and the Convention as a 'Living Instrument'

3.3.1 Rationale: The Convention as a 'Living Instrument'

The fundamental rights laid down in the Convention are not static, but their content and meaning are subject to continuous development in response to societal and technological developments.[17] The Court has expressly recognised this dynamic nature of the Convention rights in an early formula in *Tyrer*: 'The Court must also recall that the Convention is a living instrument which . . . must be interpreted in the light of present-day conditions.'[18] In later cases, the Court has explained that this means that, in interpreting the Convention, it must take account of 'evolving norms

---

[14] *Soering v. the United Kingdom*, ECtHR 7 July 1989, 14038/88, para. 87. For more recent confirmation of this approach, see e.g. *Perinçek v. Switzerland*, ECtHR (GC) 15 October 2015, 27510/08, paras. 149–51.

[15] In particular, the Preamble of the Convention and the objectives of the Statute of the Council of Europe could be seen to provide this wider context explaining the object and purpose of the Convention; on this, see e.g. F. Matscher, 'Methods of Interpretation of the Convention' in R.St.J. Macdonald, F. Matscher and H. Petzold (eds.), *The European System for the Protection of Human Rights* (Dordrecht/Boston/London: Martinus Nijhoff, 1993), pp. 63–81 at 71.

[16] For a clear example, see *Magyar Helsinki Bizottság v. Hungary*, ECtHR (GC) 8 November 2016, 18030/11, paras. 134–56.

[17] See further e.g. A. Mowbray, 'Between the Will of the Contracting Parties and the Needs of Today: Extending the Scope of Convention Rights and Freedoms Beyond What Could Have Been Foreseen by the Drafters of the ECHR' in E. Brems and J.H. Gerards, *Shaping Rights in the ECHR: The Role of the European Court of Human Rights in Determining the Scope of Human Rights* (Cambridge University Press, 2013), pp. 17–37.

[18] *Tyrer v. the United Kingdom*, ECtHR 25 April 1978, 5856/72, para. 31.

of national and international law in its interpretation of Convention norms'.[19] This basic principle is often summarised as the Court's 'evolutive and dynamic' approach to Convention interpretation.[20] This evolutive interpretation finds its basis in the effectiveness principle explained in Chapter 1. If the Court did not take account of recent developments in society and technology in explaining the meaning of the Convention, it would be difficult for it to provide an effective protection of the Convention rights. The Court clearly stated this in *Christine Goodwin*:

> [S]ince the Convention is first and foremost a system for the protection of human rights, the Court must have regard to the changing conditions within the respondent State and within Contracting States generally and respond, for example, to any evolving convergence as to the standards to be achieved ... It is of crucial importance that the Convention is interpreted and applied in a manner which renders its rights practical and effective, not theoretical and illusory. A failure by the Court to maintain a dynamic and evolutive approach would indeed risk rendering it a bar to reform or improvement.[21]

A clear example of how the principles of evolutive and dynamic interpretation and effective protection of Convention rights interact can be seen in *Rantsev*.[22] This case concerned a situation of human trafficking, which is a notion that is nowhere to be found in the text of the Convention and its Protocols. This evoked the question of whether it is indeed possible to bring cases about human trafficking and related forms of exploitation within the Convention's scope of protection. Basing its interpretation on a typical 'living instrument' and effectiveness-based line of argumentation, the Court provided the following reasoning to bring human trafficking within the scope of application of Article 4 ECHR:

> The absence of an express reference to trafficking in the Convention is unsurprising. The Convention was inspired by the Universal Declaration of Human Rights, proclaimed by the General Assembly of the United Nations in 1948, which itself made no express mention of trafficking. In its Article 4, the Declaration prohibited 'slavery and the slave trade in all their forms'. However, in assessing the scope of Article 4 of the Convention, sight should not be lost of the Convention's special features or of the fact that it is a living instrument which must be interpreted in the light of present-day conditions. The increasingly high standards required in the area of the protection of human rights and fundamental liberties

---

[19] E.g. *Demir and Baykara v. Turkey*, ECtHR (GC) 12 November 2008, 34503/97, para. 68.

[20] See in particular e.g. S.C. Prebensen, 'Evolutive Interpretation of the European Convention on Human Rights' in P. Mahoney (ed.), *Protecting Human Rights: The European Perspective* (Cologne: Heymanns, 2000), pp. 1123–37 and H.C.K. Senden, *Interpretation of Fundamental Rights in a Multilevel Legal System. An Analysis of the European Court of Human Rights and the Court of Justice of the European Union* (Antwerp: Intersentia, 2011) at 169 et seq.

[21] *Christine Goodwin v. the United Kingdom*, ECtHR (GC) 11 July 2002, 28957/95, para. 74.

[22] *Rantsev v. Cyprus and Russia*, ECtHR 7 January 2010, 25965/04.

correspondingly and inevitably require greater firmness in assessing breaches of the fundamental values of democratic societies . . .

The Court notes that trafficking in human beings as a global phenomenon has increased significantly in recent years . . . The conclusion of the Palermo Protocol in 2000 and the Anti-Trafficking Convention in 2005 demonstrate the increasing recognition at international level of the prevalence of trafficking and the need for measures to combat it . . . The Court considers that trafficking in human beings, by its very nature and aim of exploitation, is based on the exercise of powers attaching to the right of ownership . . . There can be no doubt that trafficking threatens the human dignity and fundamental freedoms of its victims and cannot be considered compatible with a democratic society and the values expounded in the Convention. In view of its obligation to interpret the Convention in light of present-day conditions, the Court considers it unnecessary to identify whether the treatment about which the applicant complains constitutes 'slavery', 'servitude' or 'forced and compulsory labour'. Instead, the Court concludes that trafficking itself, within the meaning of Article 3(a) of the Palermo Protocol and Article 4(a) of the Anti-Trafficking Convention, falls within the scope of Article 4 of the Convention.[23]

This statement shows that the Court underpinned its new interpretation by using an intricate combination of the notion of the Convention as a living instrument, the principle of effectiveness and a number of contextual interpretative principles provided by the Vienna Convention, such as the object and purpose of the Convention and international consensus.[24] In particular, the Court's reasoning demonstrates that evolutive interpretation is closely connected to a search for common European standards that can be derived from a growing State practice, the coming into being of new European or international treaties and the case law of the Court. Interpretation of the Convention 'in the light of present-day conditions' or as a 'living instrument' thus often entails 'common ground interpretation' or 'consensus interpretation', as is further detailed in Section 4.5. In addition, the statement shows that the Court attaches great weight to notions of human dignity and democracy as the main values underlying the Convention. This is closely connected to another principle of interpretation that is typical for the Court's approach, which is 'meta-teleological interpretation'. This principle is further explored in Section 3.4.

3.3.2 Temporal Effect of Evolutive Interpretations

Although the principle of evolutive interpretation is well established for the Convention system, it raises a few difficult questions, such as: from what moment in

---

[23] *Ibid.*, paras. 277–82.
[24] The Court has long used this principle in this manner. For an early example, see *Marckx v. Belgium*, ECtHR 13 June 1979, 6833/74, para. 41.

time can the States Parties to the Convention reasonably be expected to take account of a new Convention interpretation? After all, evolutive interpretation can have the effect that an interpretation is given to the Convention that the original drafters of the Convention and the States acceding to the treaty could not easily have foreseen.[25] The general rule applied by the Court is that cases have to be judged based on the standards recognised at the time of the Court's examination.[26] If it would have to judge events in the past according to the jurisprudence prevailing at the time when the events occurred, 'virtually no change in case-law would be possible'.[27] For example, in *Schalk and Kopf*, the Court held that the evolution in European views on same-sex partnerships should lead to the recognition that the emotional and sexual relationship of a same-sex couple could no longer just be seen to constitute 'private life', but that a same-sex couple cohabiting in a stable *de facto* partnership also fell within the notion of 'family life'.[28] In a later case decided in the same year, *P.B. and J.S.*, the Court accepted that it followed from this that it was contrary to the Convention that the national legislation – which predated the *Schalk and Kopf* case – did not provide a possibility for same-sex partners to have health care insurance based on the same footing as cohabiting partners of different sex.[29] The dissenting judges in this case criticised this finding and considered that it was not fair to the States to apply the Court's new interpretation to legislation and decisions predating the *Schalk and Kopf* judgment:

> We find it quite understandable that, at the material time, the Austrian authorities should have denied the first applicant's request on the ground that ... [the applicable legislation] could not be interpreted so as to include homosexual relationships. To be sure, at that time very few European States had enacted legislation on registered partnerships ... and there was also a very small number of States that treated on an equal footing, for social security purposes, two cohabiting persons of the opposite sex and two homosexuals living together ... [A]t the material time there was no European consensus as to whether homosexual couples should be treated on an equal footing with heterosexual couples, even unmarried ones, for various legal purposes in general, and for that of social security in particular. In these conditions we find it difficult to accept that the decisions by the various competent Austrian authorities rejecting the applicants' request, all those decisions having

---

[25] Cf. Mowbray, *supra* n. 17.

[26] Cf. *Lucky Dev v. Sweden*, ECtHR 27 November 2014, 7356/10, para. 50 and see, more implicitly, *Borg v. Malta*, ECtHR 12 January 2016, 37537/13, paras. 59–63.

[27] *Ibid.*   [28] *Schalk and Kopf v. Austria*, ECtHR 24 June 2010, 30141/04.

[29] *P.B. and J.S. v. Austria*, ECtHR 22 July 2010, 18984/02. See similarly, but then in relation to other benefits enjoyed by different-sex couples compared to same-sex couples, *Taddeuci and McCall v. Italy*, ECtHR 30 June 2016, 51362/09.

been issued between 1997 and 2001 ... may be regarded as contrary to Articles 8 and 14 taken together.[30]

In other cases too, dissenting judges have criticised the retroactive effect of the Court's new interpretations, and have invited the Court to give more attention to this.[31] Indeed, in some cases, the Court has acknowledged that it may be problematic for the States to be judged on newly formed standards in a situation predating the formulation of these standards. An early example of this can be found in its judgment in the *Marckx* case.[32] There the Court held that present-day conditions stood in the way of discriminatory treatment of children born out of wedlock, but it expressly limited the consequences of this interpretation:

> Admittedly, it is inevitable that the Court's decision will have effects extending beyond the confines of this particular case ... Nonetheless, it remains true that the Government have an evident interest in knowing the temporal effect of the present judgment. On this question, reliance has to be placed on two general principles of law which were recently recalled by the Court of Justice of the European Communities[33] 'the practical consequences of any judicial decision must be carefully taken into account', but 'it would be impossible to go so far as to diminish the objectivity of the law and compromise its future application on the ground of the possible repercussions which might result, as regards the past, from such a judicial decision' (8 April 1976, Defrenne v. Sabena, Reports 1976, p. 480). The European Court of Human Rights interprets the Convention in the light of present-day conditions but it is not unaware that differences of treatment between 'illegitimate' and 'legitimate' children, for example in the matter of patrimonial rights, were for many years regarded as permissible and normal in a large number of Contracting States ... Evolution towards equality has been slow and reliance on the Convention to accelerate this evolution was apparently contemplated at a rather late stage ... Having regard to all these circumstances, the principle of legal certainty, which is necessarily inherent in the law of the Convention as in Community Law, dispenses the Belgian State from re-opening legal acts or situations that antedate the delivery of the present judgment. Moreover, a similar solution is found in certain Contracting States having a constitutional court: their public law limits the retroactive effect of those decisions of that court that annul legislation.

The Court thus restricted the temporal effect of its new interpretation to cases that would arise after the judgment in *Marckx* had been pronounced. The Court has also opted for this approach in some other cases, mainly in the area of equal treatment of

---

[30] *P.B. and J.S.*, joint partly dissenting opinion of Judges Vajić and Malinverni.
[31] E.g. *Lucky Dev v. Sweden*, ECtHR 27 November 2014, 7356/10, Joint concurring opinion of Judges Villiger, Nussberger and De Gaetano.
[32] *Marckx v. Belgium*, ECtHR 13 June 1979, 6833/74.   [33] Now the European Union.

men and women in the sphere of social security and social benefits.[34] In those cases, the Court held that it is nowadays accepted that most gender-based differences can no longer be sustained, but it also recognised that this understanding has grown gradually and over a long period in time. For that reason, it has held that national legislatures cannot be held accountable for taking a rather long time to remove any remaining differences in treatment between men and women in this area. In addition, even if the Court has accepted that a new interpretation is applicable to legislation or decisions predating the relevant judgment, it may allow the State significant leeway to adduce a justification for the resulting interference with the Convention, and it may not find a violation as a result.[35]

3.3.3   Limits to Evolutive Interpretation

Over time, the principle of evolution has led the Court to gradually widen the scope of protection of the Convention. Over the sixty years of its existence, the Court has read many new rights and obligations into the Convention, ranging from the right to access to information for 'public watchdogs' such as journalists or non-governmental organisations (NGOs)[36] to an obligation to provide legal recognition of same-sex partnerships.[37] Nevertheless, it is generally accepted that evolutive interpretation is not without its limits and it should not result in treaty-making by means of case law.[38] Indeed, the Court is not always ready to adopt an evolutive interpretation if this would imply that new rights would be read into the Convention.[39] An earlier example of such a limitation is the case of *Johnston*, which concerned the question whether the right to marriage, protected by Article 12 ECHR,

---

[34] See e.g. *Stec and Others v. the United Kingdom*, ECtHR (GC) 6 July 2005 (dec.), 65731/01 and 65900/01, paras. 54–66; *Runkee and White v. the United Kingdom*, ECtHR 10 May 2007, 42949/98, para. 24; *Twizell v. the United Kingdom*, ECtHR 20 May 2008, 25379/02, para. 24; *Andrle v. the Czech Republic*, ECtHR 17 February 2011, 6268/08, paras. 49–51. For a similar approach regarding other types of different treatment in social security cases, see e.g. *Stummer v. Austria*, ECtHR (GC) 7 July 2011, 37452/02 and *Manzanas Martin v. Spain*, ECtHR 3 April 2012, 17966/10. For limitation of the retroactive effect of a newly growing consensus in a different context than that of social security measures, see e.g. *Zhelyazkov v. Bulgaria*, ECtHR 9 October 2012, 11332/04, para. 36.

[35] See e.g. *Aldeguer Tomás v. Spain*, ECtHR 14 June 2016, 35214/09, where the Court applied the new reading of Article 8 ECHR as set out in *Schalk and Kopf* (discussed above) (para. 75), but it also held that the difference in treatment between same-sex and different-sex couples in 2005 could not be held to concern similar cases (para. 87) and that 'the Spanish legislature cannot be criticised under the terms of the Convention for not having introduced the 2005 or the 2007 legislation at an earlier date which would have entitled the applicant to obtain the benefit of a survivor's pension' (para. 90).

[36] *Magyar Helsinki Bizottság v. Hungary*, ECtHR (GC) 8 November 2016, 18030/11.

[37] *Orlandi and Others v. Italy*, ECtHR 14 December 2017, 26431/12.   [38] See Prebensen, *supra* n. 20.

[39] This situation is to be distinguished from that in which the Court does not yet note a sufficient evolution to justify a new interpretation (see e.g. *Schalk and Kopf v. Austria*, ECtHR 24 June 2010, 30141/04, paras. 58 and 62; there are developments, however, as is witnessed by e.g. *Orlandi and Others v. Italy*, ECtHR 14 December 2017, 26431/12, para. 205); this type of situation is further discussed in Section 4.5 on consensus or common ground interpretation.

encompasses a right to a divorce.[40] The Court first explained that the principles of the Vienna Convention make it difficult to see how a right to divorce could be read into Article 12 ECHR:

> The Court agrees … that the ordinary meaning of the words 'right to marry' is clear, in the sense that they cover the formation of marital relationships but not their dissolution … Moreover, the foregoing interpretation of Article 12 is consistent with its object and purpose as revealed by the travaux préparatoires … In explaining to the Consultative Assembly why the draft of the future Article 12 did not include the words ['and its dissolution'], Mr. Teitgen, Rapporteur of the Committee on Legal and Administrative Questions, said: 'In mentioning the particular Article of the Universal Declaration, we have used only that part of the paragraph of the Article which affirms the right to marry and to found a family, but not the subsequent provisions of the Article concerning equal rights after marriage, since we only guarantee the right to marry.' … In the Court's view, the travaux préparatoires disclose no intention to include in Article 12 any guarantee of a right to have the ties of marriage dissolved by divorce.[41]

The Court then observed that the applicants had argued that a different reading should be given in light of the significant social developments that had occurred since the Convention was drafted, but it did not agree: 'It is true that the Convention and its Protocols must be interpreted in the light of present-day conditions … However, the Court cannot, by means of an evolutive interpretation, derive from these instruments a right that was not included therein at the outset. This is particularly so here, where the omission was deliberate.'[42] Thus, the Court held that evolutive interpretation cannot go so far as to allow the Court to read rights into the text of the Convention which the drafting States have deliberately chosen to exclude. The Court confirmed this in a decision in the *Quark Fishing* case, in which the applicants had claimed that the system for making declarations to the ECHR, set out in Article 56 ECHR, was outdated:

> Interpretation, albeit a necessary tool to render the protection of Convention rights practical and effective, can only go so far. It cannot unwrite provisions contained in the Convention. If the Contracting States wish to bring the declarations system to an end, this can only be possible through an amendment to the Convention to which those States agree and give evidence of their agreement through signature and ratification.[43]

Nevertheless, the Court is not always as strict as these judgments seem to imply. In *Al-Saadoon and Mufdhi*, for example, it had to answer the question of whether a prohibition of the death penalty can be read into the right to life of Article 2 ECHR.[44]

---

[40] *Johnston and Others v. the United Kingdom*, ECtHR 18 December 1986, 9697/82.
[41] *Ibid.*, para. 52.   [42] *Ibid.*, para. 53.
[43] *Quark Fishing Ltd. v. the United Kingdom*, ECtHR 19 September 2006 (dec.), 15305/06.
[44] *Al-Saadoon and Mufdhi v. the United Kingdom*, ECtHR 2 March 2010, 61498/08.

Importantly, Article 2(1) ECHR expressly excludes the death penalty from the scope of protection of this provision: 'No one shall be deprived of his life intentionally save in the execution of a sentence of a court following his conviction of a crime for which this penalty is provided by law.' Indeed, for that reason, two Protocols have been added to the Convention in order to prohibit the death penalty, one abolishing it in times of peace (Protocol No. 6) and a later one abolishing it in all circumstances (Protocol No. 13). At the time, some States Parties to the Convention deliberately chose not to sign or ratify these Protocols, which meant that for them, the exception of Article 2(1) still applied. Interpreting Article 2(1) as excluding this exception thus would seem to be difficult in light of the interpretative principles applied in *Johnston* and *Quark Fishing.* The Court concluded the following:

> All but two of the member States have now signed Protocol No. 13 and all but three of the States which have signed it have ratified it. These figures, together with consistent State practice in observing the moratorium on capital punishment, are strongly indicative that Article 2 has been amended so as to prohibit the death penalty in all circumstances. Against this background, the Court does not consider that the wording of the second sentence of Article 2 § 1 continues to act as a bar to its interpreting the words 'inhuman or degrading treatment or punishment' in Article 3 as including the death penalty.

Hence, if the consensus between the States is sufficiently strong as to reflect a very clear State practice, the Court may use evolutive interpretation to 'rewrite' the Convention.[45]

3.3.4   Evolutive Interpretation = Progressive Interpretation?

One final issue to be discussed in relation to evolutive interpretation is whether it might sometimes lead to a lesser degree of protection of Convention rights, depending on the direction taken by the evolution of European opinions. After all, it is conceivable that there is a general tendency towards lowering the level of protection of certain rights in certain situations (one might think of the protection of some procedural rights in times of terrorist attacks) or for certain groups (such as terrorist suspects or migrants). However, the effectiveness principle and the Preamble to the Convention do not support such a possibility of 'regressive evolution'.[46] The Preamble states that the aim of the Council of Europe is 'the maintenance and further realisation' of human rights and fundamental freedoms, which suggests a one-way dynamic in the direction of offering more rather than less protection of Convention rights.[47] The Court has confirmed this in its case law, in

---

[45] See also, however, the limitations set by textual interpretation; on this, see Section 4.3.
[46] E.g. Prebensen, *supra* n. 20, at 1137.   [47] *Ibid.*

particular in *Selmouni*.[48] In this case, the Court had to decide whether certain treatment should be qualified as 'torture' or as 'inhuman and degrading treatment':

> [H]aving regard to the fact that the Convention is a living instrument which must be interpreted in the light of present-day conditions … the Court considers that certain acts which were classified in the past as 'inhuman and degrading treatment' as opposed to 'torture' could be classified differently in future. It takes the view that the increasingly high standard being required in the area of the protection of human rights and fundamental liberties correspondingly and inevitably requires greater firmness in assessing breaches of the fundamental values of democratic societies.[49]

It is difficult to say whether it is true that the Court consistently provides for more, rather than less protection of all Convention rights in all situations. Indeed, some of the Court's judges have argued that the Court has sometimes taken a regressive rather than a progressive approach.[50] In addition, the expansion of the scope of one Convention right may be to the detriment of another right in cases where there is a conflict of rights. It is clear, however, that, in principle, it strives for progressive evolution to enable effective realisation of the Convention's aim of 'further realisation' of human rights.

3.4 Meta-teleological Interpretation and the Underlying Values of the Convention

3.4.1 Interpretation in light of the General Values Underlying the Convention

It has been explained above that the Court generally interprets the Convention in a practical and effective manner and in the light of present-day conditions. In doing so, it takes account of the object and purpose of the Convention as a whole, in line with the guidelines for interpretation offered by the Vienna Convention on the Law of Treaties. This is a type of teleological interpretation, that is, interpretation based on the purpose or 'telos' of a certain provision. This teleological interpretation takes place at a rather high level of abstraction: in many cases, the Court does not specifically refer to the purposes of a particular Convention provision, but it refers to the general principles and values underlying the Convention as a whole. In line

---

[48] *Selmouni v. France*, ECtHR (GC) 28 July 1999, 25803/94.

[49] *Ibid.*, para. 101; see similarly *A. v. Croatia*, ECtHR 10 October 2010, 55164/08, para. 67.

[50] See in particular P. Pinto de Albuquerque, 'Plaidoyer for the European Court of Human Rights', *European Human Rights Law Review*, 2018, 119–33 at 123, referring to *Hassan v. the United Kingdom*, ECtHR (GC) 16 September 2014, 29750/09; cf. also the separate opinion of Judge Spano, joined by Judges Nicolaou, Bianku and Kalaydjieva.

with the terminology suggested by Lasser, it can thus be said that the Court engages in 'meta-teleological interpretation'.[51] The Court explained the meaning of this meta-teleological interpretation and its interrelationship with the other general principles of Convention interpretation in its judgment in *Soering*, where it held that: 'In addition, any interpretation of the rights and freedoms guaranteed has to be consistent with "the general spirit of the Convention, an instrument designed to maintain and promote the ideals and values of a democratic society"'.[52] This demonstrates that meta-teleological interpretation, effectiveness and evolutive interpretation are intertwined. In fact, they are different aspects of the same overall desire to do justice to the essential object of the Convention, that is, to effectively protect individual fundamental rights and guarantee a reasonable minimum level of protection of fundamental rights throughout Europe. Generally, it can be said that the Court will more easily accept that a Convention provision applies if a case is more closely connected to the core values protected by the Convention, for example, if a case is more closely related to personal autonomy or human dignity. A case in point is *Denisov*, which concerned the dismissal of a judge from his function as president of a high administrative court in Ukraine. In this case, the Court explained in detail in what circumstances such employment-related issues could come within the scope of protection of Article 8 ECHR, the right to respect for one's private life. The Court first, in general terms, explained that activities of a professional or business nature may come close to the notion of personal autonomy:

> It is ... in the course of their working lives that the majority of people have a significant opportunity to develop relationships with the outside world ... Professional life is ... a zone of interaction between a person and others which, even in a public context, may, under certain circumstances, fall within the scope of 'private life'.[53]

The Court mentioned that this would be the case in particular if 'the impugned measure was based on reasons encroaching upon the individual's freedom of choice in the private sphere',[54] or if it was sufficiently established that there were severe consequences on the individual's 'inner circle', his opportunities to establish and develop relationships with others, or the impact on the individual's reputation.[55] In the latter situations, according to the Court, 'the threshold of severity ... assumes crucial importance', in that Article 8 will only apply if the consequences for the individual's private life are 'very serious' and 'affect his or her private life to a very significant degree'.[56] Accordingly, if the very core of the principle of personal

---

[51] Cf. M. Lasser, *Judicial Deliberations. A Comparative Analysis of Judicial Transparency and Legitimacy* (Oxford University Press, 2004) at 206 et seq. See also Senden, *supra* n. 20, at 204.
[52] *Soering v. the United Kingdom*, ECtHR 7 July 1989, 14038/88, para. 87.
[53] *Denisov v. Ukraine*, ECtHR (GC) 25 September 2018, 76639/11, para. 100.   [54] *Ibid.*, para. 103.
[55] *Ibid.*, para. 107.   [56] *Ibid.*, para. 116.

autonomy is at stake, the Court will hold the Convention to apply, but if the case is further removed from this core, it will declare the case inadmissible because the individual's private life is not really affected. In the *Denisov* case, for example, the Court eventually concluded that the judge's private life was not sufficiently seriously harmed, since he had been able to continue to function as a judge (albeit not as an appeal court president) and the criticism that had been uttered in the proceedings against him 'did not affect the wider ethical aspect of the applicant's personality and character'.[57]

Thus, meta-teleological interpretation can be of great importance to the applicability of the Convention and in stages 1 of 2 of the Court's review. It is therefore useful to understand that the Court has distinguished a variety of general principles and values that can be seen as part of the 'general spirit of the Convention' and, together, make up 'the ideals and values of a democratic society'. These principles and values are human dignity, autonomy, democracy and pluralism, which are discussed consecutively hereafter.

3.4.2   Human Dignity

A general principle or value that often influences the Court's Convention interpretations is that of human dignity. This notion often serves as an important basis for the Court to explain the notion of 'private life' as contained in Article 8 ECHR. This can be seen in the *Pretty* case, where the applicant had argued that assisted suicide could be held to constitute an aspect of her private life.[58] The Court was ready to accept this argument, using meta-teleological reasoning:

> The very essence of the Convention is respect for human dignity and human freedom. Without in any way negating the principle of sanctity of life protected under the Convention, the Court considers that it is under Article 8 that notions of the quality of life take on significance. In an era of growing medical sophistication combined with longer life expectancies, many people are concerned that they should not be forced to linger on in old age or in states of advanced physical or mental decrepitude which conflict with strongly held ideas of self and personal identity ... The applicant in this case is prevented by law from exercising her choice to avoid what she considers will be an undignified and distressing end to her life. The Court is not prepared to exclude that this constitutes an interference with her right to respect for private life as guaranteed under Article 8 § 1 of the Convention.[59]

In this statement, the Court emphasised that 'human dignity and human freedom' constitute 'the very essence' of the Convention, and it used these general principles

---

[57] *Ibid.*, para. 129.   [58] *Pretty v. the United Kingdom*, ECtHR 29 April 2002, 2346/02.
[59] *Ibid.*, paras. 65 and 67.

as an important basis for its interpretation of Article 8.[60] Although the Court did not conclusively hold Article 8 to apply to assisted suicide, it was ready to assess whether there was an unjustifiable restriction of the applicant's right to respect for her private life in the concrete case before it.

Importantly, the Court has never attempted to define the notion of human dignity. Just as in *Pretty*, it standardly confines itself to mentioning the notion as an essential value underlying the Convention, without offering further clarification of its meaning.[61]

3.4.3   Personal Autonomy

Next to the principle of human dignity, the Court distinguishes personal autonomy as a core value of the Convention. As such, this notion can be helpful in interpreting the Convention. An illustration of this can be seen in the case of the *Jehovah's Witnesses of Moscow*.[62] The Russian authorities had decided that the Moscow branch of the Jehovah's Witnesses should be dissolved because the manifestation of their religious convictions could be dangerous to their health. More specifically, the authorities were gravely concerned about the religious prescript that Jehovah's Witnesses are not to receive blood transfusions, for example after an accident. The Jehovah's Witnesses claimed that these grounds for dissolution conflicted with their freedom of religion (Article 9 ECHR) and the right to respect for their private lives (Article 8 ECHR). This raised the question of whether the desire to refuse medical treatment, even if necessary to save one's life, is protected by the Convention. Based on the principle of personal autonomy, the Court answered this question in the positive:

> The very essence of the Convention is respect for human dignity and human freedom and the notions of self-determination and personal autonomy are important principles underlying the interpretation of its guarantees ... The ability to conduct one's life in a manner of one's own choosing includes the opportunity to pursue activities perceived to be of a physically harmful or dangerous nature for the individual concerned. In the sphere of medical assistance, even where the refusal to accept a particular treatment might lead to a fatal outcome, the imposition of medical treatment without the consent of a mentally

---

[60] This approach can also be seen in many other cases, ranging from cases on recognition of gender transformations to cases on lifelong sentences or living conditions for asylum seekers. For some more recent examples, see *M.S.S. v. Belgium and Greece*, ECtHR (GC) 21 January 2011, 30696/09, paras. 220–1; *Vinter and Others v. the United Kingdom*, ECtHR (GC) 9 July 2013, 66069/09, para. 113; *Y.Y. v. Turkey*, ECtHR 10 March 2015, 14793/08, para. 58; *Bouyid v. Belgium*, ECtHR (GC) 29 September 2015, 23380/09, paras. 89–90; *Enver Şahin v. Turkey*, ECtHR 30 January 2018, 23065/12, para. 70.

[61] In some cases, the Court provides an indication of its meaning, but it is never really precise; see e.g. *Vinter and Others v. the United Kingdom*, ECtHR (GC) 9 July 2013, 66069/09, para. 113; *McDonald v. the United Kingdom*, ECtHR 20 May 2014, 4241/12, para. 47.

[62] *Jehovah's Witnesses of Moscow and Others v. Russia*, ECtHR 10 June 2010, 302/02.

competent adult patient would interfere with his or her right to physical integrity and impinge on the rights protected under Article 8 of the Convention ...

The freedom to accept or refuse specific medical treatment, or to select an alternative form of treatment, is vital to the principles of self-determination and personal autonomy. A competent adult patient is free to decide, for instance, whether or not to undergo surgery or treatment or, by the same token, to have a blood transfusion. However, for this freedom to be meaningful, patients must have the right to make choices that accord with their own views and values, regardless of how irrational, unwise or imprudent such choices may appear to others ... It was emphasised[63] that free choice and self-determination were themselves fundamental constituents of life and that, absent any indication of the need to protect third parties – for example, mandatory vaccination during an epidemic, the State must abstain from interfering with the individual freedom of choice in the sphere of health care, for such interference can only lessen and not enhance the value of life.[64]

Based on the principle of personal autonomy, often combined with the notion of human dignity, the Court has also held that end-of-life situations may come within the scope of protection of Article 8 ECHR,[65] just like abortion issues[66] or cases about forced sterilisation.[67] Many cases in which the Court invokes personal autonomy thus concern the physical integrity of individuals. The notion is not limited to those situations, however, but it should be given an extensive meaning:

Under this principle protection is given to the personal sphere of each individual, including the right to establish details of their identity as individual human beings ... The Court has held that gender identification, name and sexual orientation and sexual life were details pertaining to an individual's identity falling within the personal sphere protected by Article 8 ... In a more recent judgment, in the case of *S. and Marper v. the United Kingdom* ([GC], nos. 30562/04 and 30566/04, § 66, 4 December 2008), the Court further held that ethnic identity was also a detail pertaining to the individual's identity falling within the ambit of Article 8.[68]

This wide definition implies that cases of clear negative ethnic stereotyping may also come within the scope of protection of Article 8 of the Convention, as the Court held in *R.B. v. Hungary*:

The notion of personal autonomy ... can ... embrace multiple aspects of a person's physical and social identity. The Court has accepted in the past that an individual's ethnic

---

[63] In previous judgments.   [64] *Ibid.*, paras. 135–6.

[65] *Lambert and Others v. France*, ECtHR (GC) 5 June 2015, 46043/14, para. 142.

[66] See e.g. *Tysiąc v. Poland*, ECtHR 20 March 2007, 5410/03, para. 107; *A., B. and C. v. Ireland*, ECtHR (GC) 16 December 2010, 25579/05, para. 216.

[67] See e.g. *V.C. v. Slovakia*, ECtHR 8 November 2011, 18968/07, para. 115.

[68] *Ciubotaru v. Moldova*, ECtHR 27 April 2010, 27138/04, para. 49.

identity must be regarded as another such element . . . In particular, any negative stereotyping of a group, when it reaches a certain level, is capable of impacting on the group's sense of identity and the feelings of self-worth and self-confidence of members of the group. It is in this sense that it can be seen as affecting the private life of members of the group.[69]

This makes clear that personal autonomy does not necessarily only refer to *individual* autonomy and freedom of choice, but it may also relate to one's identification with a particular group. In addition, the Court has held that other individual choices, such as the choice of one's place of residence, may equally come within the sphere of one's personal autonomy,[70] just like informational self-determination (which may be affected by collecting, processing and dissemination of personal data).[71] The case discussed in the introduction to this section, *Denisov*, further illustrates that employment-related restrictions can also relate to personal autonomy as long as they are sufficiently closely related to an individual's private life.[72]

3.4.4 Democracy

Democracy is a third core notion informing the Court's Convention interpretation. In its judgment in *United Communist Party of Turkey*, the Court discussed the importance and meaning of this notion for the Convention system as a whole:

> Democracy is without doubt a fundamental feature of the European public order . . . That is apparent, firstly, from the Preamble to the Convention, which establishes a very clear connection between the Convention and democracy by stating that the maintenance and further realisation of human rights and fundamental freedoms are best ensured on the one hand by an effective political democracy and on the other by a common understanding and observance of human rights . . . The Preamble goes on to affirm that European countries have a common heritage of political tradition, ideals, freedom and the rule of law. The Court has observed that in that common heritage are to be found the underlying values of the Convention . . . it has pointed out several times that the Convention was designed to maintain and promote the ideals and values of a democratic society . . . Democracy thus appears to be the only political model contemplated by the Convention and, accordingly, the only one compatible with it.[73]

Thus defined, the notion of democracy offers the Court guidance in its concrete interpretations of the Convention, especially of those rights that have a clear

---

[69] *R.B. v. Hungary*, ECtHR 12 April 2016, 64602/12, para. 78.
[70] See e.g. *Alkaya v. Turkey*, ECtHR 9 October 2012, 42811/06, para. 30.
[71] See e.g. *Satakunnan Markkinapörssi Oy and Satamedia Oy v. Finland*, ECtHR (GC) 27 June 2017, 931/13, para. 136; *Benedik v. Slovenia*, ECtHR 24 April 2018, 62357/14, para. 102.
[72] *Denisov v. Ukraine*, ECtHR (GC) 25 September 2018, 76639/11.
[73] *United Communist Party of Turkey v. Turkey*, ECtHR 30 January 1998, 19392/92, para. 45.

relation to democracy, such as the freedom of expression, assembly and association, and the right to vote.[74] To protect the essential values of democracy, these rights are usually given a wide interpretation and a strong protection.

At the same time, the Court may also use the notion of democracy to define certain limits to the scope of fundamental rights or the freedom to enjoy them. This can be seen in the summary the Court gave in *Fáber* of its case law on the freedom of expression (Article 10) and assembly (Article 11):

> The guarantees of Article 11 of the Convention apply to all assemblies except those where the organisers and participants have violent intentions or otherwise deny the foundations of a 'democratic society' ... Any measures interfering with freedom of assembly and expression other than in cases of incitement to violence or rejection of democratic principles – however shocking and unacceptable certain views or words used may appear to the authorities – do a disservice to democracy and often even endanger it.[75]

Thus, if the Convention rights are used to undermine democratic values, the limits of Convention protection are reached and individuals cannot successfully invoke these rights.[76] It can also be derived from the Court's consideration, however, that a complex dilemma may arise if a State decides to limit the freedom of expression or assembly (core elements of a well-functioning democracy), because the expressions or actions are inherently undemocratic or serve to undermine the central democratic values.[77] In its case law the Court has strived to steer a careful course between the two, always taking democracy to be the main Convention value that needs to be respected in the best way possible.[78]

---

[74] For an example in which the Court used democracy as a yardstick to assess the fairness of limitations of the right to vote, see e.g. *Anchugov and Gladkov v. Russia*, ECtHR 4 July 2013, 11157/04 and 15162/05, para. 97. For the use of the notion in relation to freedom of expression, see e.g. *Karácsony and Others v. Hungary*, ECtHR (GC) 17 May 2016, 42461/13 and 44357/13, para. 141.

[75] *Fáber v. Hungary*, ECtHR 24 July 2012, 40721/08, para. 37.

[76] See e.g. *Kasymakhunov and Saybatalov v. Russia*, ECtHR 14 March 2013, 26261/05 and 26377/06, paras. 102 et seq.; *Roj TV A/S v. Denmark*, ECtHR 17 April 2018 (dec.), 24683/14, paras. 46–7.

[77] On this dilemma, see further P. de Morree, *Rights and Wrongs Under the ECHR. The Prohibition of Abuse of Rights in Article 17 of the European Convention on Human Rights* (Antwerp: Intersentia, 2016).

[78] It has found, for example, that far-reaching measures such as dissolution of a political party or an association is allowed only in extraordinary situations, where there is a concrete, tangible and immediate risk that the party's actions will undermine democratic values; see e.g. *Refah Partisi (The Welfare Party) and Others v. Turkey*, ECtHR (GC) 13 February 2003, 41340/98, paras. 109 et seq.; *Herri Batasuna and Batasuna v. Spain*, ECtHR 30 June 2009, 25803/04 and 25817/04, paras. 74–83; *Kasymakhunov and Saybatalov v. Russia*, ECtHR 14 March 2013, 26261/05 and 26377/06, paras. 102 et seq.; *Zehra Foundation and Others v. Turkey*, ECtHR 10 July 2018, 51595/07, paras. 61 et seq.

3.4.5   Pluralism

Finally, the Court has recognised the notion of pluralism as an important guiding principle for the interpretation and application of the Convention. Pluralism is a multi-faceted term with its meaning reliant on the context. In relation to the freedom of religion (Article 9 ECHR), for example, the Court has explained its importance as follows:

> As enshrined in Article 9, freedom of thought, conscience and religion is one of the foundations of a 'democratic society' within the meaning of the Convention. It is, in its religious dimension, one of the most vital elements that go to make up the identity of believers and their conception of life, but it is also a precious asset for atheists, agnostics, sceptics and the unconcerned. The pluralism indissociable from a democratic society, which has been dearly won over the centuries, depends on it.[79]

In connection to the freedom of association and assembly, the Court has provided another definition of pluralism:

> While in the context of Article 11 the Court has often referred to the essential role played by political parties in ensuring pluralism and democracy, associations formed for other purposes, including those protecting cultural or spiritual heritage, pursuing various socio-economic aims, proclaiming or teaching religion, seeking an ethnic identity or asserting a minority consciousness, are also important to the proper functioning of democracy. For pluralism is also built on the genuine recognition of, and respect for, diversity and the dynamics of cultural traditions, ethnic and cultural identities, religious beliefs, artistic, literary and socio-economic ideas and concepts. The harmonious interaction of persons and groups with varied identities is essential for achieving social cohesion. It is only natural that, where a civil society functions in a healthy manner, the participation of citizens in the democratic process is to a large extent achieved through belonging to associations in which they may integrate with each other and pursue common objectives collectively.[80]

In relation to freedom of expression, the Court has held, inter alia, that pluralism means that diverse political programmes can be proposed and debated, and there must be effective access for different actors to the audio-visual market (media pluralism).[81] And in non-discrimination cases, the Court has defined pluralism as a check on democracy: 'Although individual interests must on occasion be subordinated to those of a group, democracy does not simply mean that the views of a majority must always prevail: a balance must be achieved which ensures the

---

[79] *Kokkinakis v. Greece*, ECtHR 25 May 1993, 14307/88, para. 31.
[80] *Gorzelik v. Poland*, ECtHR (GC) 17 February 2004, 44158/98, para. 92.
[81] E.g. *Centro Europa 7 S.r.l. and Di Stefano v. Italy*, ECtHR (GC) 7 June 2012, 38433/09, paras. 129–30.

fair treatment of people from minorities and avoids any abuse of a dominant position.'[82]

The exact meaning and importance of the notion of pluralism and how it affects the Court's interpretation thus depends on the applicable Convention right. Just like the notion of democracy, the notion of pluralism can also serve to delimit the enjoyment of Convention rights, for example if the activities of an individual or association are aimed at undermining the values of pluralism.[83]

3.5   Autonomous Interpretation

3.5.1   Rationale: Effective Protection of Convention Rights

The Convention contains many notions and concepts that are also used in national constitutions and legislation, such as 'privacy', 'property', 'court' or 'marriage'. The precise legal meaning of such terms can differ for each individual legal system.[84] For example, what constitutes 'property' in the United Kingdom can be different from what constitutes property in Greece, and while disciplinary proceedings may be conducted before a court in one Convention State, they might not form part of the regular judicial system in another.[85] When interpreting or defining central Convention notions, the Court must therefore choose between respecting the national meaning of such a notion and adopting a definition of its own.

The Court has emphasised that a European, autonomous definition should usually prevail.[86] This is understandable from the perspective that the Convention should guarantee an equal level of protection in all States Parties.[87] Indeed, the Court has expressly stated that the integrity of the objectives of the Convention would be endangered if the Court were to take the national level of protection, or the national definition of certain notions, as a point of departure for its own case law. In particular, this would pose the risk that States try to evade the Court's supervision by narrowly defining the terms and notions that determine the Convention's applicability.[88] In turn, this might have a negative impact on the effective protection of fundamental rights.

---

[82] *İzzettin Doğan and Others v. Turkey*, ECtHR (GC) 26 April 2016, 62649/10, para. 109. See also *Mytilinaios and Kostakis v. Greece*, ECtHR 3 December 2015, 29389/11, para. 56.

[83] E.g. *Zehra Foundation and Others v. Turkey*, ECtHR 10 July 2018, 51595/07, paras. 61 et seq.

[84] Cf. R. Bernhardt, 'Thoughts on the Interpretation of Human Rights Treaties' in R.St.J. Macdonald et al. (eds.), *The European System for the Protection of Human Rights* (Dordrecht: Martinus Nijhoff, 1993), pp. 65–71 at 67.

[85] *Ibid.*

[86] See also Senden, *supra* n. 20, at 298; G. Letsas, 'The Truth in Autonomous Concepts: How to Interpret the ECHR', *European Journal of International Law*, 15 (2004), 279–305 at 282–3.

[87] Matscher, *supra* n. 15, at 73; Senden, *supra* n. 20, at 178 and, for more elaboration, 294–5.

[88] See e.g. *G.I.E.M. S.R.L. and Others v. Italy*, ECtHR (GC) 28 June 2018, 1828/06, para. 216.

The Court explained this rationale in its judgment in *Chassagnou*.[89] The applicants were landholders in France and, as such, they were obliged to be a member of a hunting association (an 'ACCA'). In the applicants' view, this obligatory membership violated the negative aspect of the freedom of association (Article 11 ECHR), that is, the freedom *not* to be a member of an association. The French government, however, argued that ACCAs were semi-public bodies which, for that reason, could not be regarded as associations in the sense of Article 11 ECHR. The Court then stressed the necessity of giving an autonomous reading to the notion of 'association':

> If Contracting States were able, at their discretion, by classifying an association as 'public' or 'para-administrative', to remove it from the scope of Article 11, that would give them such latitude that it might lead to results incompatible with the object and purpose of the Convention, which is to protect rights that are not theoretical or illusory but practical and effective ... Freedom of thought and opinion and freedom of expression, guaranteed by Articles 9 and 10 of the Convention respectively, would thus be of very limited scope if they were not accompanied by a guarantee of being able to share one's beliefs or ideas in community with others, particularly through associations of individuals having the same beliefs, ideas or interests. The term 'association' therefore possesses an autonomous meaning; the classification in national law has only relative value and constitutes no more than a starting-point.[90]

The Court then continued to investigate whether, in its own view, the ACCAs had sufficient characteristics to be regarded as associations for the purposes of Article 11. In this respect, it based its judgment on a number of autonomous standards it had defined earlier in the case of *Le Compte, Van Leuven and De Meyere*, and which related to the question of whether the association would be so strongly integrated into the structures of the States as to make them lose the typically 'private' nature of the type of associations Article 11 ECHR aims to cover.[91] Eventually, it held that Article 11 indeed applied to ACCAs and it found that the obligatory membership was incompatible with that provision.

3.5.2   Limitations

Although autonomous interpretation is the rule under the Convention, the Court has accepted for a few situations that a non-autonomous reading should be given of the Convention.

---

[89] *Chassagnou and Others v. France*, ECtHR (GC) 29 April 1999, 25088/94.
[90] *Chassagnou*, para. 100. See also already *Engel and Others v. the Netherlands*, ECtHR 8 June 1976, 5100/71, para. 81.
[91] *Le Compte, Van Leuven and De Meyere v. Belgium*, ECtHR 23 June 1981, 6878/75 and 7238/75.

First, the Court has pointed out that autonomous interpretation is a kind of one-way street. It only applies if there is a reason to fear that States will use their own national definitions in order to escape accountability under the Convention system, but not if the application of their own definitions would provide more protection of the Convention (as Article 53 ECHR allows). The Court explained this in *Engel*, a case that concerned a set of disciplinary sanctions imposed on conscript soldiers serving in different non-commissioned ranks in the Netherlands armed forces.[92] One of the questions that arose in this respect was whether the right to a fair trial, protected by Article 6 ECHR, would apply to such disciplinary sanctions. In answering this question, the Court also paid attention to when it should provide an autonomous interpretation of the notion of 'criminal charge', and when there would be no need to do so:

> The Convention without any doubt allows the States, in the performance of their function as guardians of the public interest, to maintain or establish a distinction between criminal law and disciplinary law, and to draw the dividing line, but only subject to certain conditions. The Convention leaves the States free to designate as a criminal offence an act or omission not constituting the normal exercise of one of the rights that it protects ... Such a choice, which has the effect of rendering applicable Articles 6 and 7, in principle escapes supervision by the Court ... The converse choice, for its part, is subject to stricter rules. If the Contracting States were able at their discretion to classify an offence as disciplinary instead of criminal, or to prosecute the author of a 'mixed' offence on the disciplinary rather than on the criminal plane, the operation of the fundamental clauses of Articles 6 and 7 would be subordinated to their sovereign will. A latitude extending thus far might lead to results incompatible with the purpose and object of the Convention. The Court therefore has jurisdiction, under Article 6 ... to satisfy itself that the disciplinary does not improperly encroach upon the criminal. In short, the 'autonomy' of the concept of 'criminal' operates, as it were, one way only.[93]

Thus, if the effective protection of the right to a fair trial would be at risk because States deliberately tried to evade this protection by willingly moving parts of criminal law (which would be covered by Article 6) to disciplinary law (which would not be covered), the Court should avoid this by applying an autonomous interpretation. By contrast, the Court can easily leave it to the national authorities' primary responsibility to determine whether they will criminalise and impose sanctions for certain acts at all. After all, as soon as they do so, the Convention will apply, since there will then be a 'criminal charge'.

Second, the Court will not give an autonomous interpretation of notions for which the Convention itself expressly refers to the national laws of the States

---

[92] *Engel and Others v. the Netherlands*, ECtHR 8 June 1976, 5100/71.   [93] *Ibid.*, para. 81.

Parties. An example of this is Article 12 ECHR, which protects the right to marry and found a family for men and women of marriageable age, 'according to the national laws governing the exercise of this right'. The meaning of this reference to national law has been of particular importance in cases on same-sex marriage. In several cases, most notably *Schalk and Kopf*, applicants have argued that Article 12 should be interpreted so as not to exclude the marriage between two men or two women.[94] Relying on the principle of evolutive interpretation, the Court found that indeed, there was considerable development in European opinions on the topic. Moreover, in the more recent EU Charter of Fundamental Rights, the reference to 'men and women' was deliberately dropped from the right to marriage.[95] However, the particular phrasing of Article 12 stood in the way of accepting a new and autonomous definition of the right to marry:

> Regard being had to Article 9 of the Charter, therefore, the Court would no longer consider that the right to marry enshrined in Article 12 must in all circumstances be limited to marriage between two persons of the opposite sex. Consequently, it cannot be said that Article 12 is inapplicable to the applicants' complaint. However, as matters stand, the question whether or not to allow same-sex marriage is left to regulation by the national law of the Contracting State.[96]

Although it seems clear that the Court might change its interpretation in the future when there is an even stronger European consensus regarding same-sex marriages, if there is a national definition of a marriage as one between 'a man and a woman', currently this definition will prevail.

At the same time, it is important to note that the Court has held that this kind of reference to national law does not fully remove a topic from the Court's supervision. Even if national law does not provide for a certain right, the Court's task of offering effective protection of fundamental rights might be given priority. In *Parry*, the Court explained this as follows:

> The exercise of the right to marry gives rise to social, personal and legal consequences and Article 12 expressly provides for regulation of marriage by national law ... The matter of conditions for marriage in national law cannot, however, be left entirely to Contracting States as being within their margin of appreciation. This would be tantamount to finding that the range of options open to a Contracting State included an effective bar on any exercise of the right to marry. The margin of appreciation cannot extend so far. Any limitations introduced must not restrict or reduce the right in such a way or to such an extent that the very essence of the right is impaired.[97]

---

[94] *Schalk and Kopf v. Austria*, ECtHR 24 June 2010, 30141/04, para. 55.   [95] *Ibid.*, paras. 58–60.
[96] *Ibid.*, para. 64.   [97] *Parry v. the United Kingdom*, ECtHR 28 November 2006 (dec.), 42971/05.

Thus, according to the Court's case law, the reference to 'national laws' in Article 12 only concerns the stage of interpretation (stage 1 as defined in Chapter 1.4), but not the stages of determining an interference and assessing the justification of restrictions (stages 2 and 3 as defined in Chapter 1.4).

Finally, in a very limited number of cases, the Court has decided against an autonomous interpretation because of the degree of controversy on the correct definition of a fundamental right between and within the States. A famous example is the definition of the right to life of Article 2 ECHR, which raises the question of when 'life' can be held to begin. If the Court autonomously answered this question by accepting that life starts at conception, or soon afterwards, the text of Article 2 ECHR would imply that unborn life should be protected to an almost absolute degree.[98] Accordingly, in this reading, it would be incompatible with the Convention if a State legally permitted abortion, regardless of the grounds and circumstances the State would advance in justification. By contrast, if the Court accepted that life begins at birth, all abortion legislation would fall outside the scope of protection of Article 2 and no protection would be offered of the right to life of unborn children. Providing a uniform, autonomous interpretation of Article 2 thus presents the Court with a difficult and controversial choice. In 2004, in the *Vo* case, the Court deliberately decided to avoid having to make this choice by refusing to offer an autonomous interpretation:

> [T]he issue of when the right to life begins comes within the margin of appreciation which the Court generally considers that States should enjoy in this sphere, notwithstanding an evolutive interpretation of the Convention, a 'living instrument which must be interpreted in the light of present-day conditions' ... The reasons for that conclusion are, firstly, that the issue of such protection has not been resolved within the majority of the Contracting States themselves ... and, secondly, that there is no European consensus on the scientific and legal definition of the beginning of life ... At best, it may be regarded as common ground between States that the embryo/foetus belongs to the human race. ... Having regard to the foregoing, the Court is convinced that it is neither desirable, nor even possible as matters stand, to answer in the abstract the question whether the unborn child is a person for the purposes of Article 2 of the Convention ('personne' in the French text).[99]

The consequence of the Court's approach in *Vo* is that all issues relating to the right to life of unborn children remain fully within the discretion of the States, which is the opposite of an autonomous approach. The effect of this is illustrated by the Chamber judgment in *Evans*, which, inter alia, concerned the question of whether

---

[98] Article 2 only provides for very limited exceptions; see Section 1.5.2.

[99] *Vo v. France*, ECtHR (GC) 8 July 2004, 53924/00, paras. 82–4.

embryos that have not been used for IVF treatment can be destroyed without violating the right to life of Article 2 ECHR:

> The Court recalls ... that in *Vo v. France* ... it held that, in the absence of any European consensus on the scientific and legal definition of the beginning of life, the issue of when the right to life begins comes within the margin of appreciation which the Court generally considers that States should enjoy in this sphere. Under English law, as was made clear by the domestic courts in the present applicant's case ... an embryo does not have independent rights or interests and cannot claim – or have claimed on its behalf – a right to life under Article 2. There has not, accordingly, been a violation of that provision in the present case.[100]

A certain degree of protection of such aspects of the right to life accordingly can only be provided under national law.[101]

A similar non-autonomous approach can be seen in the case *Kimlya*, which concerned the question of whether the Church of Scientology could be regarded as a religious community and, consequently, whether it could enjoy the protection of the freedom of religion offered by Article 9 ECHR.[102] The Court held that the answer to this question should be primarily given by the national authorities:

> The Court observes that the question whether or not Scientology may be described as a 'religion' is a matter of controversy among the member States. It is clearly not the Court's task to decide *in abstracto* whether or not a body of beliefs and related practices may be considered a 'religion' within the meaning of Article 9 of the Convention. In the absence of any European consensus on the religious nature of Scientology teachings, and being sensitive to the subsidiary nature of its role, the Court considers that it must rely on the position of the domestic authorities in the matter and determine the applicability of Article 9 of the Convention accordingly ... Having regard to the position of the Russian authorities, which have consistently expressed the view that Scientology groups are religious in nature, the Court finds that Article 9 of the Convention is applicable in the case before it.[103]

Consequently, if the applicant happens to live in a State where the Scientology Church is recognised as a religious entity, his complaint about alleged interferences with the freedom of religion will be admissible. This is different if the State does not recognise the Scientology Church and considers it a sect or a non-religious entity.

---

[100] *Evans v. the United Kingdom*, ECtHR 7 March 2006, 6339/05, paras. 46–7. The case was referred to the Grand Chamber, which delivered its judgment on 10 April 2007, but the issue of applicability of Article 2 to the embryos was not raised there.

[101] Thus far, the Court has not been willing to revisit its approach; see e.g. *Parrillo v. Italy*, ECtHR (GC) 27 August 2015, 46470/11, para. 215.

[102] *Kimlya and Others v. Russia*, ECtHR 1 October 2009, 76836/01 and 31782/03.

[103] *Ibid.*, paras. 79 and 81.

Thus, the Court did not provide an interpretation of its own in this case, again with the rationale of a lack of national consensus on the exact meaning of the notion of 'religion'.

The lack of European consensus and the need to respect the principle of subsidiarity may also inspire a non-autonomous approach in cases on less morally sensitive issues than the definition of 'life' or 'religion'. A case in point is *Vilho Eskelinen*, which concerned the applicability of the right to a fair trial of Article 6 ECHR to disputes in which civil servants are involved.[104] The main question of interpretation in such cases is whether these disputes really concern 'civil rights and obligations', which is the term-of-art used in Article 6 ECHR, or whether they are, in fact, about typically public law issues which should be left to the remit of the States Parties. In its answer to this question in *Vilho Eskelinen*, the Court chose to rely on a criterion based on national law:

> [I]t is primarily for the Contracting States, in particular the competent national legislature, not the Court, to identify expressly those areas of public service involving the exercise of the discretionary powers intrinsic to State sovereignty where the interests of the individual must give way. The Court exerts its supervisory role subject to the principle of subsidiarity ... If a domestic system bars access to a court, the Court will verify that the dispute is indeed such as to justify the application of the exception to the guarantees of Article 6. If it does not, then there is no issue and Article 6 § 1 will apply.
>
> [I]n order for the respondent State to be able to rely before the Court on the applicant's status as a civil servant in excluding the protection embodied in Article 6, two conditions must be fulfilled. Firstly, the State in its national law must have expressly excluded access to a court for the post or category of staff in question. Secondly, the exclusion must be justified on objective grounds in the State's interest. The mere fact that the applicant is in a sector or department which participates in the exercise of power conferred by public law is not in itself decisive ... It is also for the State to show that the subject matter of the dispute in issue is related to the exercise of State power or that it has called into question the special bond. Thus, there can in principle be no justification for the exclusion from the guarantees of Article 6 of ordinary labour disputes, such as those relating to salaries, allowances or similar entitlements, on the basis of the special nature of relationship between the particular civil servant and the State in question. There will, in effect, be a presumption that Article 6 applies. It will be for the respondent Government to demonstrate, firstly, that a civil-servant applicant does not have a right of access to a court under national law and, secondly, that the exclusion of the rights under Article 6 for the civil servant is justified.[105]

The applicability of the right of access to a court is therefore determined by the national exclusion of certain categories of cases brought by civil servants. This

---

[104] *Vilho Eskelinen v. Finland*, ECtHR (GC) 19 April 2007, 63235/00.   [105] *Ibid.*, paras. 61–2.

means that this judgment does not disclose a fully autonomous definition of 'civil rights and obligations'. Nevertheless, the approach taken in this case is different from *Vo* and *Kimlya* in that the Court also expressly held that it will always assess the reasonableness of national exclusions of certain categories of civil servants' cases. Thus, it is fair to say that *Vilho Eskelinen* is a case where the Court applies a kind of 'semi-autonomous' interpretation.[106]

3.5.3 Dependency, or the 'In for a penny, in for a pound' Approach

It was mentioned above that the principle of autonomous interpretation is a kind of 'one-way street'. The Court will provide an interpretation of its own only if there is a risk that States avoid applicability of the Convention by providing a narrow reading of the terms and notions determining the scope of its provisions. By contrast, as the Court made clear in *Engel*, there is no objection against providing more protection than the minimum strictly required by the Convention. This is confirmed by Article 53 ECHR, which provides that '[n]othing in this Convention shall be construed as limiting or derogating from any of the human rights and fundamental freedoms which may be ensured under the laws of any High Contracting Party or under any other agreement to which it is a party'. For this additional protection, which is voluntarily offered by the States, the Court will not provide an autonomous inter-pretation. Indeed, one might even expect that the Convention does not apply to such rights and benefits, but their regulation is fully left to the States' discretion. Even so, the Court has construed a certain degree of Convention applicability in this regard by developing an approach that can best be described as the 'in for a penny, in for a pound' principle or the 'dependency' principle.[107] The Court had already used this approach in its judgment in the *Belgian Linguistics* case for the prohibition of discrimination as contained in Article 14 ECHR:[108]

[P]ersons subject to the jurisdiction of a Contracting State cannot draw from Article 2 of the Protocol the right to obtain from the public authorities the creation of a particular kind of educational establishment; nevertheless, a State which had set up such an establishment could not, in laying down entrance requirements, take discriminatory measures within the meaning of Article 14. To recall a further example . . . Article 6 of the Convention does not

---

[106] For similar examples of such a 'semi-autonomous' approach, see *Roche v. the United Kingdom*, ECtHR (GC) 19 October 2005, 32555/96, para. 120 and *Boulois v. Luxembourg*, ECtHR (GC) 3 April 2012, 37575/04, para. 91.
[107] On these notions, see further J.H. Gerards, 'The European Court of Human Rights and the National Courts – Giving Shape to the Notion of "Shared Responsibility"' in J.H. Gerards and J.W.A. Fleuren (eds.), *Implementation of the European Convention on Human Rights and of the judgments of the ECtHR in National Case Law. A Comparative Analysis* (Antwerp: Intersentia, 2014), pp. 13–94 at 49–50.
[108] *Belgian Linguistics* case, ECtHR 23 July 1968, 1474/62.

compel States to institute a system of appeal courts. A State which does set up such courts consequently goes beyond its obligations under Article 6. However it would violate that Article, read in conjunction with Article 14, were it to debar certain persons from these remedies without a legitimate reason while making them available to others in respect of the same type of actions.[109]

Some degree of Convention protection may therefore apply to nationally recognised fundamental rights that are not as such contained in the Convention. In *Micallef*, a Chamber of the Court provided a further rationale for this approach.[110] The case concerned the applicability of the right to a fair trial to cases which do not strictly concern 'civil rights and obligations', but the Court decided to apply Article 6 anyway:

> The Court reiterates that through its system of collective enforcement of the rights it establishes, the Convention reinforces, in accordance with the principle of subsidiarity, the protection afforded at national level … but never limits it (Article 53 of the Convention). The Court does not countenance the view that human rights protection in any particular area should be weaker in Strasbourg than it is in domestic tribunals. That being so, the Court notes that the concept of 'civil right' under Article 6 § 1 cannot be construed as limiting an enforceable right in domestic law within the meaning of Article 53 of the Convention … Moreover, Article 6 reflects the fundamental principle of the rule of law which underpins the whole Convention system and is expressly referred to in the Preamble to the Convention … In a democratic society within the meaning of the Convention, the right to a fair administration of justice holds such a prominent place that a restrictive interpretation of Article 6 § 1 would not correspond to the aim and the purpose of that provision … and this restriction must be very compellingly established. In sum, Article 6 is applicable in the instant case and the application falls within the jurisdiction of the Court ratione materiae.

An example may serve to illustrate the effect of this dependency principle. The case *E.B. v. France* concerned a conflict over the desire of a single, lesbian woman to adopt a child.[111] In a long line of cases, the Court had given an autonomous reading to the notion of respect for family life, protected by Article 8 of the Convention, to the effect that this notion covers only established family life.[112] The creation of a family, either through adoption or otherwise, therefore does not come within the scope of the Convention and the Court normally cannot judge interferences with the desire to found a family on the merits. French legislation, however, did recognise a

---

[109] *Ibid.*, para. I.B.9.
[110] *Micallef v. Malta*, ECtHR 15 January 2008, 17056/06. The case was referred to the Grand Chamber, which delivered its judgment on 15 October 2009, based on different grounds.
[111] *E.B. v. France*, ECtHR (GC) 22 January 2008, 43546/02.
[112] See *Marckx v. Belgium*, ECtHR 13 June 1979, 6833/74, para. 31.

right to adoption and even a right to adoption for singles. In its judgment in *E.B.*, the Court held that *because* this right was recognised in French law, it should be guaranteed in conformity with the Convention:

> The Court, noting that the applicant based her application on Article 14 of the Convention, taken in conjunction with Article 8, reiterates at the outset that the provisions of Article 8 do not guarantee either the right to found a family or the right to adopt ... The right to respect for 'family life' does not safeguard the mere desire to found a family; it presupposes the existence of a family ... With regard to Article 14, which was relied on in the present case, the Court reiterates that it only complements the other substantive provisions of the Convention and the Protocols thereto. It has no independent existence since it has effect solely in relation to 'the enjoyment of the rights and freedoms' safeguarded by those provisions ... The application of Article 14 does not necessarily presuppose the violation of one of the substantive rights protected by the Convention. It is necessary but it is also sufficient for the facts of the case to fall 'within the ambit' of one or more of the Articles of the Convention ... The prohibition of discrimination enshrined in Article 14 thus extends beyond the enjoyment of the rights and freedoms which the Convention and the Protocols thereto require each State to guarantee. It applies also to those additional rights, falling within the general scope of any Convention Article, for which the State has voluntarily decided to provide ... The present case does not concern adoption by a couple or by the same-sex partner of a biological parent, but solely adoption by a single person. Whilst Article 8 of the Convention is silent as to this question, the Court notes that French legislation expressly grants single persons the right to apply for authorisation to adopt and establishes a procedure to that end. Accordingly, the Court considers that the facts of this case undoubtedly fall within the ambit of Article 8 of the Convention. Consequently, the State, which has gone beyond its obligations under Article 8 in creating such a right – a possibility open to it under Article 53 of the Convention – cannot, in the application of that right, take discriminatory measures within the meaning of Article 14 ... Accordingly, Article 14 of the Convention, taken in conjunction with Article 8, is applicable in the present case.[113]

Put differently: once the State is 'in for the penny' of voluntarily recognising a certain Convention-related right, it must be 'in for the pound' of Convention applicability: it must protect the right without discrimination and it must accept that the Court is competent to assess its application.[114]

---

[113] *E.B. v. France*, ECtHR (GC) 22 January 2008, 43546/02, paras. 43–7. The Court has often applied this approach in relation to social security and social benefits, as well as some migration cases; see *Carson v. the United Kingdom*, ECtHR (GC) 16 March 2010, 42184/04, para. 63, and *P.B. and J.S. v. Austria*, ECtHR 22 July 2010, 18984/02, para. 33; *Pajić v. Croatia*, ECtHR 23 February 2016, 68453/13, para. 80; *Aielli and Others v. Italy*, ECtHR 10 July 2018 (dec.), 27166/18 and 27167/18, para. 22.

[114] See also *Pajić v. Croatia*, ECtHR 23 February 2016, 68453/13, para. 80.

Although the Court most commonly applies this dependency approach in relation to the right to non-discrimination, it has also done so for the right to a fair trial and access to a court. As is clear from the cited considerations of the Chamber in *Micallef*, the Court finds it important that individuals do not only have a right to a fair trial in cases where the Court autonomously holds Article 6 to be applicable.[115] These examples show that the 'in for a penny, in for a pound' approach does not reflect an autonomous interpretation of the Convention, but instead is national-law dependent. This may result in national differences in the scope and level of protection of Convention rights, especially where some States have created and recognised many more rights than others. On the other hand, this fits well with the principles of primarity and subsidiarity. By signing and ratifying the Convention, the States have agreed to respect the fundamental rights contained therein for all of their acts, including the prohibition of discrimination and the right to a fair trial.[116] The 'in for a penny, in for a pound' approach builds on this by simply requiring the States to accept the consequences of regulating a matter that affects specific Convention rights.[117] Simultaneously, it allows the Court to supervise the compliance with the prohibition of discrimination and procedural rights, thus enabling it to offer effective protection.

---

[115] See e.g. *Andrejeva v. Latvia*, ECtHR (GC) 18 February 2009, 55707/00, para. 97. To a certain degree, this applies also to Article 5 ECHR (on deprivation of liberty); see in particular *Suso Musa v. Malta*, ECtHR 23 July 2013, 42337/12, para. 97.

[116] The Court confirmed in *G.R. v. the Netherlands* that the right to an effective remedy of Article 13 'guarantees the availability at national level of a remedy to enforce the substance of the Convention rights and freedoms in whatever form they may happen to be secured in the domestic legal order' (ECtHR 10 January 2012, 22251/07, para. 44).

[117] In a rather similar vein, the Court has sometimes held that States that have set certain standards for fundamental rights protection can be required under the Convention to respect their own standards, even if they may not be standards that the Convention itself has set – see e.g. *Orchowski v. Poland*, ECtHR 22 October 2009, 17885/04, para. 123 and *M.S.S.* v. *Belgium and Greece*, ECtHR (GC) 21 January 2011, 30696/09, para. 250.

4 Methods of Convention Interpretation

4.1 Introduction

In many, if not most cases, the Court nowadays relies on precedents in interpreting the Convention. It usually first categorises the case before it, for example as one relating to domestic violence or about press freedom, then sets out the general principles relating to that category of cases that it has established in its previous judgments (as explained in Sections 2.4 and 2.5), and then applies those principles to the facts of the case. Although this application may require some slight adaptation or further refinement of the general principles and standards, in many cases it does not demand much, if any, new interpretative work. Indeed, after nearly sixty years of development and having delivered more than 20,000 judgments,[1] genuinely 'new' cases might rarely be expected to be presented to the Court. Yet, they still occur, which is a logical result of societal, legal and technological developments. Over the past years, for example, cases have been brought on issues such as the ownership of embryos in relation to IVF treatment,[2] the responsibility for defamatory posts on internet fora,[3] data protection and privacy of the use of social media in the workplace,[4] surrogate parenthood,[5] 'push-back' operations in the Mediterranean,[6] expulsion of seriously ill migrants,[7] the execution of decisions by the UN Sanction Committee,[8] sexual abuse of children in Catholic schools,[9] prohibitions of wearing a full-face veil,[10]

---

[1] See *ECHR Overview 1959–2017* (Strasbourg, ECtHR, 2018), at www.echr.coe.int/Documents/ Overview_19592017_ENG.pdf, last accessed 30 November 2018.

[2] *Parrillo v. Italy*, ECtHR (GC) 27 August 2015, 46470/11.

[3] *Delfi AS v. Estonia*, ECtHR (GC) 16 June 2015, 64569/09.

[4] *Satakunnan Markkinapörssi Oy and Satamedia Oy v. Finland*, ECtHR (GC) 27 June 2017, 931/13; *Bărbulescu v. Romania*, ECtHR (GC) 5 September 2017, 61496/08.

[5] *Paradiso and Campanelli v. Italy*, ECtHR (GC) 24 January 2017, 25358/12.

[6] *Hirsi Jamaa and Others v. Italy*, ECtHR (GC) 23 February 2012, 27765/09.

[7] *Paposhvili v. Belgium*, ECtHR (GC) 13 December 2016, 41738/10.

[8] *Nada v. Switzerland*, ECtHR (GC) 12 September 2012, 10593/08; *Al-Dulimi and Montana Management Ltd. v. Switzerland*, ECtHR (GC) 21 June 2016, 5809/08.

[9] *O'Keeffe v. Ireland*, ECtHR (GC) 28 January 2014, 35810/09.

[10] *S.A.S. v. France*, ECtHR (GC) 1 July 2014, 43835/11.

recognition of rights for transsexual and same-sex partners,[11] end-of-life situations,[12] or access to government information.[13]

In some of these cases, reasoning based on precedents may help support the Court's argumentation, but many cases present the Court with new and complex questions of interpretation. To answer these, the Court relies on a number of specific principles and methods of interpretation. The main principles and objectives guiding the Court in its interpretative work and its overall argumentative approach have been explained in Chapters 1, 2 and 3. These principles, however, are still relatively abstract in nature.[14] They are useful in providing a sense of direction to the Court, but often they do not suffice to answer a concrete question of interpretation. For that reason, the Court often also relies on the methods of interpretation as described in the provisions of the Vienna Convention on the Law of Treaties, such as textual interpretation, interpretation in light of the *travaux préparatoires* and internally harmonising interpretation.[15] Hereafter, the Court's use of these three methods is explained (Sections 4.2, 4.3 and 4.4). In addition to these methods, the Court has opted for a particular refinement of one of the Vienna Convention's methods, which is interpretation in harmony with international law and State practice.[16] This refinement, which has the shape of common ground or consensus interpretation, is discussed in Section 4.5.

4.2 Textual Interpretation

Article 31 of the Vienna Convention on the Law of Treaties stipulates that treaty provisions should be interpreted in light of the 'ordinary meaning' of the terms of the treaty.[17] Since the Court has embraced the Vienna Convention as guiding its interpretations, it is not surprising that in many of its judgments, it relies on textual arguments to underpin its interpretation of the Convention. It has proved difficult to determine a term's 'ordinary meaning', however. For that reason, whenever the Court relies on textual interpretation, it prefers to adapt the meaning of a notion to make it fit in the particular legal and Convention context in which it is used. This is

---

[11] *Hämäläinen v. Finland*, ECtHR (GC) 16 July 2014, 37359/09.
[12] *Gross v. Switzerland*, ECtHR (GC) 30 September 2014, 67810/10; *Lambert v. France*, ECtHR 5 June 2015, 46043/14.
[13] *Magyar Helsinki Bizottság v. Hungary*, ECtHR (GC) 8 November 2016.
[14] On the difference between principles and methods of Convention interpretation, see further H.C.K. Senden, *Interpretation of Fundamental Rights in a Multilevel Legal System. An Analysis of the European Court of Human Rights and the Court of Justice of the European Union* (Antwerp: Intersentia, 2011), 44–6.
[15] On the Vienna Convention on the Law of Treaties, see further Section 3.2.
[16] See further Section 4.2.   [17] See further Section 4.2.

clear, for example, from the *Witold Litwa* case, which was discussed in Section 3.2, and which concerned the interpretation of the term 'alcoholic' in relation to the question of whether a drunken person could lawfully be detained under Article 5(1)(e) ECHR.[18] The Court started its reasoning by referring to the ordinary meaning of the term 'alcoholics': 'The Court observes that the word "alcoholics", in its common usage, denotes persons who are addicted to alcohol.'[19] The 'ordinary meaning' of the term did not, however, provide a satisfactory answer to the question if non-addicted, intoxicated persons could also be detained for a while. For that reason, the Court looked into the context offered by the provision in which the term was used and it concluded that the overall purpose of Article 5(1) was to allow States to take persons into custody who pose a threat to public order or to themselves.[20] For that reason, the Court decided that the term 'alcoholic' refers to persons who are in a state of intoxication and who may pose a danger to themselves and others, regardless of whether or not they are addicted to alcohol.[21]

Thus, the meaning of a text is usually established in a rather legal and context-dependent fashion.[22] To give another example: in the *Banković* case, the question was raised if the notion 'within its jurisdiction' in Article 1 ECHR could be read as implying a certain extraterritorial effect.[23] The Court explained that the meaning of this term had to be determined in the appropriate legal context, in this case that of international law:

> As to the 'ordinary meaning' of the relevant term in Article 1 of the Convention, the Court is satisfied that, from the standpoint of public international law, the jurisdictional competence of a State is primarily territorial. While international law does not exclude a State's exercise of jurisdiction extra-territorially, the suggested bases of such jurisdiction (including nationality, flag, diplomatic and consular relations, effect, protection, passive personality and universality) are, as a general rule, defined and limited by the sovereign territorial rights of the other relevant States … Accordingly, for example, a State's competence to exercise jurisdiction over its own nationals abroad is subordinate to that State's and other States' territorial competence … In addition, a State may not actually exercise jurisdiction on the territory of another without the latter's consent, invitation or

---

[18] *Witold Litwa v. Poland*, ECtHR 5 April 2000, 26629/95.   [19] *Ibid.*, para. 60.

[20] *Ibid.*, para. 61; see in more detail Section 3.2. For a similar approach, see *Johnston and Others v. Ireland*, ECtHR 18 December 1986, 9697/82, para. 52.

[21] *Ibid.*

[22] See also e.g. *The National Union of Rail, Maritime and Transport Workers v. the United Kingdom*, ECtHR 8 April 2014, 31045/10, para. 76; *Cyprus v. Turkey*, ECtHR (GC) 12 May 2014 (Just satisfaction), paras. 39–42 (where the Court used textual interpretation merely as a confirmation of interpretation based on other methods).

[23] *Banković and Others v. Belgium, the Czech Republic, Denmark, France, Germany, Greece, Hungary, Iceland, Italy, Luxembourg, the Netherlands, Norway, Poland, Portugal, Spain, Turkey and the United Kingdom*, ECtHR (GC) 12 December 2001 (dec.), 52207/99.

acquiescence, unless the former is an occupying State in which case it can be found to exercise jurisdiction in that territory, at least in certain respects . . . The Court is of the view, therefore, that Article 1 of the Convention must be considered to reflect this ordinary and essentially territorial notion of jurisdiction, other bases of jurisdiction being exceptional and requiring special justification in the particular circumstances of each case.[24]

Reliance on supplementary means of interpretation may also be necessary if it turns out that a purely grammatical interpretation would still allow for different readings of a Convention term. This can be illustrated by the Court's judgment in *Wemhoff*, where it had to interpret the notion that everyone who is arrested or detained is 'entitled to trial within a reasonable time or release pending trial' (Article 5(3) ECHR).[25] The Court held that a textual interpretation would not help it provide a proper reading of this notion and it therefore relied on other means:

> The Court considers that it is of the greatest importance that the scope of this provision should be clearly established. As the word 'reasonable' applies to the time within which a person is entitled to trial, a purely grammatical interpretation would leave the judicial authorities with a choice between two obligations, that of conducting the proceedings until judgment within a reasonable time or that of releasing the accused pending trial, if necessary against certain guarantees. The Court is quite certain that such an interpretation would not conform to the intention of the High Contracting Parties. It is inconceivable that they should have intended to permit their judicial authorities, at the price of release of the accused, to protract proceedings beyond a reasonable time. This would, moreover, be flatly contrary to the provision in Article 6 (1) cited above. To understand the precise scope of the provision in question, it must be set in its context.[26]

In the end, the Court relied on established international law precedents and the object and purpose of the Convention to establish that protection against unduly long detention should continue up to the delivery of judgment.[27] In other cases, the Court has referred to its own precedents as constituting a relevant context to determine the textual meaning of a Convention term. In *Harkins*, for example, the Court was asked to clarify when a complaint is essentially the same as one previously decided by the Court and is therefore inadmissible based on Article 35 (2)(b) ECHR.[28] This article also provides that inadmissibility follows only if the application 'contains no relevant new information'. Interpreting this clause, the Court referred to the meaning of this notion as it was explained in previous decisions:

---

[24] *Ibid.*, paras. 59–60.   [25] *Wemhoff v. Germany*, ECtHR 27 June 1968, 2122/64.
[26] *Ibid.*, paras. 4–5 (As to the law).   [27] *Ibid.*, para. 8 (As to the law).
[28] *Harkins v. the United Kingdom*, ECtHR (GC) 15 June 2017, 71537/14.

To date, the Court has not provided precise guidance on the meaning of 'relevant new information'. However, while the English text of Article 35 § 2 (b) uses the term 'relevant new information', the French text speaks of 'faits nouveaux', a difference which can only be reconciled if the ordinary meaning of 'relevant new information' is understood to be relevant new factual information ... Such an interpretation would be consistent with the Court's approach in deciding whether an application should be rejected under the first limb of Article 35 § 2 (b). While in *X. v. the Federal Republic of Germany* (dec.), no. 4256/69, 14 December 1970 the [former] Commission accepted that in a case concerning a 'continuing situation' a change in the legal classification of a complaint brought about by the coming into force of Protocol No. 4 in the respondent State would constitute 'relevant new information', in subsequent case law the Convention organs have tended to focus on the existence of new facts (see, for example, *Vojnovic* (dec.), §§ 28-30; *Anthony Aquilina*, §§ 34–37; and *X. v. Slovenia* (dec.), §§ 40–42 ...) and rejected attempts to support past complaints with new legal argument (see, for example, *I.J.L. v. the United Kingdom* (dec.) and *Kafkaris* (dec.), § 68...).[29]

Examples of purely textual interpretation in the light of the 'ordinary meaning' of the Convention terms are therefore few and far between; in most cases, support is found in the object and purpose of the Convention, in precedent or in other supplementary means of interpretation.[30] In fact, purely textual interpretation occurs mainly as a check on the use of other principles and methods of interpretation. This particular use of the method can be seen in the *Pretty* case, where the Court was presented with the question of whether the right to life, protected by Article 2 ECHR, can also be seen to comprise a right to die in the context of assisted suicide.[31] The Court answered this question in the negative, based on a textual interpretation of the notion of 'life':

The consistent emphasis in all the cases before the Court has been the obligation of the State to protect life. The Court is not persuaded that 'the right to life' guaranteed in Article 2 can be interpreted as involving a negative aspect ... Article 2 of the Convention is phrased in different terms. It is unconcerned with issues to do with the quality of living or what a person chooses to do with his or her life. To the extent that these aspects are recognised as so fundamental to the human condition that they require protection from State interference, they may be reflected in the rights guaranteed by other Articles of the Convention, or in other international human rights instruments. Article 2 cannot, without a distortion of language, be interpreted as conferring the diametrically opposite right, namely

---

[29] *Harkins*, para. 50. For a similar approach, see *Moohan and Gillon v. the United Kingdom*, ECtHR 13 June 2017 (dec.), 22962/15 and 23345/15, para. 40.

[30] For a rare example, see *Buishvili v. the Czech Republic*, ECtHR 25 October 2012, 30241/11, para. 39.

[31] *Pretty v. the United Kingdom*, ECtHR 29 April 2002, 2346/02.

a right to die; nor can it create a right to self-determination in the sense of conferring on an individual the entitlement to choose death rather than life.[32]

Thus, even if the principles of evolutive and meta-teleological interpretation might point in the direction of an extensive interpretation of Article 2, the Court accepted that there is a limitation to the application of such principles in the actual wording of the Convention. Similarly, in *Ferrazzini*, the Court held that the term 'civil' in 'civil rights and obligations' of Article 6 cannot simply be interpreted away:

> The principle according to which the autonomous concepts contained in the Convention must be interpreted in the light of present-day conditions in democratic societies does not give the Court power to interpret Article 6 § 1 as though the adjective 'civil' (with the restriction that that adjective necessarily places on the category of 'rights and obligations' to which that Article applies) were not present in the text.[33]

Finally, the function of textual interpretation to limit the scope of protection of the Convention was also expressly mentioned in *Cumhuriyet Halk Partisi*:

> [T]he Court once again emphasises that the text of Article 3 of Protocol No. 1 clearly suggests that its ambit is limited to elections – held at reasonable intervals – determining the choice of the legislature, and its wording is a strong indication of the limits of an expansive, purposive interpretation of its applicability. In other words, the object and purpose of the provision have to be ascertained by reference to the wording used in the provision ... In the light of the above considerations and its settled case law on the applicability of Article 3 of Protocol No. 1, the Court thus concludes that the wording of that provision – taking into account its ordinary meaning in context as well as its object and purpose – precludes the possibility of the Court's adopting an expansive interpretation of the provision which would include referendums.[34]

Thus, textual interpretation may form an important check on the – otherwise potentially unlimited – expansion of the scope of protection of the Convention provisions in light of the principle of evolutive interpretation.[35]

4.3 Interpretation in light of the *Travaux Préparatoires*

According to Article 32 of the Vienna Convention on the Law of Treaties, the *travaux préparatoires* or preparatory works of a treaty may be used as a supplementary means in treaty interpretation. The Court's use of the *travaux préparatoires* is in

---

[32] *Ibid.*, para. 39.   [33] *Ferrazzini v. Italy*, ECtHR (GC) 12 July 2001, 44759/98, para. 30.
[34] *Cumhuriyet Halk Partisi v. Turkey*, ECtHR 21 November 2017, 48818/17, paras. 37–8.
[35] Other limits to evolutive interpretation have been discussed in Section 3.3.3.

line with this: although it may refer to the *travaux* in some cases, their content is not decisive and the Court will always also rely on other methods to support its eventual interpretation. This is not only in conformity with the text of Article 32 of the Vienna Convention, but it is also understandable because of the specific nature of the Convention as a 'law-making' human rights treaty, which has to be interpreted in line with the principle of effectiveness and which must be given an evolutive interpretation.[36] In addition, only ten States were involved in drafting the original text of the Convention, whereas thirty-seven Convention States have acceded at a later date. It could be argued that it is not fully appropriate to consider these thirty-seven States to be bound to the objectives and views of the original drafters as they are expressed in the *travaux*. And finally, over time, the *travaux* will have lost some of their relevance because societal views on what fundamental rights have significantly changed and the many technological developments have led to a variety of new fundamental rights issues which the drafters could not even imagine.[37] These various arguments for nuancing the importance of this tool for the Convention context have been confirmed by the Court in its *Loizidou* judgment:

> That the Convention is a living instrument which must be interpreted in the light of present-day conditions is firmly rooted in the Court's case-law ... Such an approach, in the Court's view, is not confined to the substantive provisions of the Convention, but also applies to those provisions ... which govern the operation of the Convention's enforcement machinery. It follows that these provisions cannot be interpreted solely in accordance with the intentions of their authors as expressed more than forty years ago. Accordingly, even if it had been established, which is not the case, that restrictions, other than those *ratione temporis*, were considered permissible ... at a time when a minority of the present Contracting Parties adopted the Convention, such evidence could not be decisive.[38]

In addition, the Court has emphasised in *Naït-Liman* that even the Vienna Convention on the Law of Treaties itself does not give great importance to the *travaux*: 'With regard to the *travaux préparatoires*, the Court notes ... that, in accordance with Article 32 of the Vienna Convention, these are only a 'supplementary means' of interpretation of treaties. It is thus necessary to take them into account on a subsidiary basis and with a certain restraint when interpreting the terms of a treaty'.[39]

---

[36] See further Sections 1.2.1 and 3.2.

[37] See A. Mowbray, 'Between the Will of the Contracting Parties and the Needs of Today: Extending the Scope of Convention Rights and Freedoms Beyond What Could Have Been Foreseen by the Drafters of the ECHR' in E. Brems and J.H. Gerards (eds.), *Shaping Rights in the ECHR: The Role of the European Court of Human Rights in Determining the Scope of Human Rights* (Cambridge University Press, 2013), 17–36.

[38] *Loizidou v. Turkey*, ECtHR 23 March 1995 (Preliminary objections), 15318/89, para. 71.

[39] *Naït-Liman v. Switzerland*, ECtHR (GC) 15 March 2018, 51357/07, para. 192.

Other reasons for the Court to play down the relevance of the *travaux* have been that their contents are not particularly clear or conclusive, and their contents are outdated, as the *Hirsi Jamaa* case can illustrate.[40] The question in the case was whether the prohibition of collective expulsion of aliens (Article 4 of Protocol No. 4) may have a certain extraterritorial effect in that it may also relate to the removal of aliens carried out in the context of interceptions on the high seas, so-called 'push-back' operations. In this respect, the Court noted a few difficulties relating to the use of the *travaux* in helping it answer this question. First, '[t]he *travaux préparatoires* are not explicit as regards the scope of application and ambit of Article 4 of Protocol No. 4'.[41] Second, to the extent that the *travaux* would provide a more or less clear answer, the Court questioned the continued relevance of the Explanatory Report:

> A long time has passed since Protocol No. 4 was drafted. Since that time, migratory flows in Europe have continued to intensify, with increasing use being made of the sea, although the interception of migrants on the high seas and their removal to countries of transit or origin are now a means of migratory control in so far as they constitute tools for States to combat irregular immigration. The economic crisis and recent social and political changes have had a particular impact on certain regions of Africa and the Middle East, throwing up new challenges for European States in terms of immigration control.[42]

In the end, the Court therefore opted for an interpretation in line with the principles of effectiveness and evolutive interpretation. Taking account of 'present-day conditions' and the objectives of the Protocol and the Convention in general, it held that Article 4 of Protocol No. 4 should also be considered to apply to push-back operations conducted outside the territory of the respondent State.[43]

Finally, the Court has sometimes referred to the actual text of the *travaux* to emphasise their limited meaning for the Court's interpretations. For example, the Explanatory Report to Protocol No. 7 states that it 'does not constitute an instrument providing an authoritative interpretation of the text of the Protocol, although it might be of such a nature as to facilitate the understanding of the provisions contained therein'.[44] For that reason, the Court held in *Allen* that it could have little bearing on the Court's interpretation of the Protocol: 'the Explanatory Report itself provides that, although intended to facilitate the understanding of the provisions contained in the Protocol, it does not constitute an authoritative interpretation of the text ... Its references to the need to demonstrate innocence must now be

---

[40] *Hirsi Jamaa and Others v. Italy*, ECtHR (GC) 23 February 2012, 27765/09.

[41] *Ibid.*, para. 174. This is a problem the Court has noted more often; see also e.g. *Magyar Helskinki Bizottság v. Hungary*, ECtHR (GC) 8 November 2016, 18030/11, para. 135; *Naït-Liman v. Switzerland*, ECtHR (GC) 15 March 2018, 51357/07, para. 192.

[42] *Hirsi Jamaa*, para. 176.   [43] *Ibid.*, para. 180.

[44] *Explanatory Report to the Protocol No. 7 to the Convention for the Protection of Human Rights and Fundamental Freedoms* (Strasbourg, 22 November 1984, ETS No. 117), para. II.

considered to have been overtaken by the Court's intervening case-law on Article 6 § 2.'[45] Here, the Court's tendency towards reliance on precedent clearly overrode the relevance of the Explanatory Memorandum.

Despite these nuances, the Court may refer to the *travaux* if it is asked to provide a new interpretation of the Convention.[46] In *Banković*, it thereby explained the weight it can generally give to this instrument:

> [T]he extracts from the *travaux préparatoires* detailed above constitute a clear indication of the intended meaning of Article 1 of the Convention which cannot be ignored. The Court would emphasise that it is not interpreting Article 1 'solely' in accordance with the *travaux préparatoires* or finding those *travaux* 'decisive'; rather this preparatory material constitutes clear confirmatory evidence of the ordinary meaning of Article 1 of the Convention as already identified by the Court (Article 32 of the Vienna Convention 1969).[47]

Moreover, the *travaux* may be useful where a case does not concern the text of the Convention or one of the older Protocols, but of one of the Protocols that have been added more recently. The *travaux* then will be up to date and might accurately reflect a European consensus on the meaning and objectives of the Protocol. To illustrate, in *Korolev*, the Court had to interpret the admissibility requirement that an applicant must have suffered a 'significant disadvantage' as a result of the alleged violation of the Convention.[48] This requirement had been added to the Convention by Protocol No. 14, which entered into force in 2010. In interpreting the new requirement, the Court referred to the aim of the provision as expressed in the explanatory memorandum to the Protocol:

> In view of the circumstances of the present case the Court finds it appropriate to examine at the outset whether the applicant's complaints comply with this new admissibility requirement. In doing so, the Court will bear in mind that the purpose of the new admissibility criterion is, in the long run, to enable more rapid disposal of unmeritorious cases and thus to allow it to concentrate on the Court's central mission of providing legal protection of human rights at the European level (see Explanatory Report to Protocol No. 14, CETS No. 194 ('Explanatory Report'), §§ 39 and 77–79). The High Contracting Parties clearly wished that the Court devote more time to cases which warrant consideration on the merits, whether seen from the perspective of the legal interest of the

---

[45] *Allen v. the United Kingdom*, ECtHR (GC) 12 July 2013, 25424/09, para. 133.
[46] See e.g. *Sergey Zolotukhin v. Russia*, ECtHR (GC) 10 February 2009, 14939/03, para. 107; *Dorado Baúlde v. Spain*, ECtHR 1 September 2015 (dec.), 23486/12, para. 14; *Magyar Helskinki Bizottság v. Hungary*, ECtHR (GC) 8 November 2016, 18030/11, paras. 134–7.
[47] *Banković and Others v. Belgium, the Czech Republic, Denmark, France, Germany, Greece, Hungary, Iceland, Italy, Luxembourg, the Netherlands, Norway, Poland, Portugal, Spain, Turkey and the United Kingdom*, ECtHR (GC) 12 December 2001 (dec.), 52207/99.
[48] *Korolev v. Russia*, ECtHR 1 July 2010 (dec.), 25551/05.

individual applicant or considered from the broader perspective of the law of the Convention and the European public order to which it contributes (see Explanatory Report, § 77).

Making many further references to the Explanatory Report, the Court then continued to establish a few objective criteria for the application of the new rule. Likewise, the Court has extensively referred to the Explanatory Report for the prohibition of discrimination of Protocol No. 12.[49] Although the *travaux* are thus of little relevance to the Convention as such, their value may be significant for the interpretation of more recent Protocols.

4.4   Internally Harmonising Interpretation

An important starting point for the Court's interpretation of the Convention is that the meaning of the various provisions must be internally consistent or harmonious:

> Since the Convention is first and foremost a system for the protection of human rights, the Court must interpret and apply it in a manner which renders its rights practical and effective, not theoretical and illusory. The Convention must also be read as a whole, and interpreted in such a way as to promote internal consistency and harmony between its various provisions.[50]

The admissibility decision in the *Stec* case can serve as an illustration of this method of internally harmonising interpretation.[51] The case concerned the interpretation of the notion of 'possessions' as contained in Article 1 of Protocol No. 1. In some of its previous judgments, the Court had explained that a welfare benefit or pension fell within the scope of Article 1 of Protocol No. 1 only if contributions had been made to the fund that financed it.[52] After having decided that it was now time for a new interpretation, the Court mentioned that, in providing such an interpretation, it would have to secure the internal consistency of the Convention:

> The Convention must also be read as a whole, and interpreted in such a way as to promote internal consistency and harmony between its various provisions . . . It is noteworthy in this respect that, in its case-law on the applicability of Article 6 § 1, the Court originally held

---

[49] See e.g. *Sejdić and Finci v. Bosnia and Herzegovina*, ECtHR (GC) 22 December 2009, 27996/06 and 34836/06, para. 55 and *Savez crkava 'Riječ života' and Others v. Croatia*, ECtHR 9 October 2010, 7798/08, para. 104.

[50] *Demir and Baykara v. Turkey*, ECtHR (GC) 12 November 2008, 34503/97, para. 66. See also e.g. *Leander v. Sweden*, ECtHR 26 March 1987, 9248/81, para. 78.

[51] *Stec and Others v. the United Kingdom*, ECtHR (GC) 6 July 2005 (dec.), 65731/01 and 65900/01.

[52] *Ibid.*, para. 46.

that claims regarding only welfare benefits which formed part of contributory schemes were, because of the similarity to private insurance schemes, sufficiently personal and economic to constitute the subject matter of disputes for 'the determination of civil rights' ... [but in subsequent cases] Article 6 § 1 was held also to apply to a dispute over entitlement to a non-contributory welfare benefit, the Court emphasising that the applicant had an assertable right, of an individual and economic nature, to social benefits. It thus abandoned the comparison with private insurance schemes and the requirement for a form of 'contract' between the individual and the State. In *Schuler-Zgraggen v. Switzerland* (judgment of 24 June 1993, Series A no. 263, p. 17, § 46), the Court held that '... the development in the law ... and the principle of equality of treatment warrant taking the view that today the general rule is that Article 6 § 1 does apply in the field of social insurance, including even welfare assistance'. It is in the interests of the coherence of the Convention as a whole that the autonomous concept of 'possessions' in Article 1 of Protocol No. 1 should be interpreted in a way which is consistent with the concept of pecuniary rights under Article 6 § 1 of the Convention. It is moreover important to adopt an interpretation of Article 1 of Protocol No. 1 which avoids inequalities of treatment based on distinctions which, nowadays, appear illogical or unsustainable.[53]

Other judgments of the Court also express the desire to safeguard the overall consistency and harmony of the Convention.[54] The importance of this is particularly evident in cases where different Convention provisions could be held to apply at the same time, such as the freedom of expression (Article 10) and the freedom of assembly (Article 11) in a case where someone holds a banner during a demonstration, or the freedom of religion (Article 9) and the freedom of expression (Article 10) in a case about the prohibition of wearing a headscarf. In such cases, the Court uses a variation of the principle of internally harmonising interpretation by interpreting and applying the one applicable provision in light of the standards developed for the other. An example can be found in *Jehovah's Witnesses of Moscow*, in which the Court had to decide on the dissolution of the Moscow branch of the Jehovah's Witnesses.[55] Finding that the freedom of religion and association had been affected by this dissolution, it held that

[s]ince religious communities traditionally exist in the form of organised structures, Article 9 must be interpreted in the light of Article 11 of the Convention, which safeguards

---

[53] *Ibid.*, paras. 48–9.
[54] See also, for example, the case law on the interrelationship between the rights to a fair trial and the *ne bis in idem* principle (see e.g. *Zolotukhin v. Russia*, ECtHR (GC) 10 February 2009, 14939/03, para. 52 and *A. and B. v. Norway*, ECtHR (GC) 15 November 2016, 24130/11 and 29758/11, para. 107), or the *Perinçek* case, in which the Court provided an internally harmonising interpretation of the notion of 'law' as contained in both Articles 7 and 10(2) ECHR: *Perinçek v. Switzerland*, ECtHR (GC) 15 October 2015, 27510/08, para. 134.
[55] *Jehovah's Witnesses of Moscow and Others v. Russia*, ECtHR 10 June 2010, 302/02.

associative life against unjustified State interference. Seen in that perspective, the right of believers to freedom of religion, which includes the right to manifest one's religion in community with others, encompasses the expectation that believers will be allowed to associate freely, without arbitrary State intervention. Indeed, the autonomous existence of religious communities is indispensable for pluralism in a democratic society and is thus an issue at the very heart of the protection which Article 9 affords. The State's duty of neutrality and impartiality, as defined in the Court's case-law, is incompatible with any power on the State's part to assess the legitimacy of religious beliefs.[56]

The Court thus decided to approach Article 9 as a *specialis* of Article 11. It also often does so in cases on demonstrations, where it regards the freedom of assembly as a *specialis* of the more general freedom of expression. It then primarily applies the standards developed in relation to the freedom of demonstration, but it provides for internal harmony by expressly taking the specific values protected by the freedom of expression into account. As the Court explained in *Lashmankin*:

> At the outset, the Court notes that in relation to the same facts the applicants rely on two separate Convention provisions: Article 10 and Article 11 of the Convention ... In the Court's opinion, in the circumstances of the present case, Article 10 is to be regarded as a *lex generalis* in relation to Article 11, a *lex specialis* ... The thrust of the applicants' complaints is that the authorities imposed various restrictions on holding of peaceful assemblies thereby preventing them from expressing their views together with other demonstrators. The Court therefore finds that the applicants' complaint should be examined under Article 11 ... That being said, the Court notes that the issues of freedom of expression and freedom of peaceful assembly are closely linked in the present case. Indeed, the protection of personal opinions, secured by Article 10 of the Convention, is one of the objectives of freedom of peaceful assembly as enshrined in Article 11 of the Convention ... In the sphere of political debate the guarantees of Articles 10 and 11 are often complementary, so Article 11, where appropriate, must be considered in the light of the Court's case-law on freedom of expression. The Court reiterates that the link between Article 10 and Article 11 is particularly relevant where the authorities have interfered with the right to freedom of peaceful assembly in reaction to the views held or statements made by participants in a demonstration or members of an association ... The Court will therefore examine the present case under Article 11, interpreted where appropriate in the light of Article 10.[57]

A third function of internally harmonising interpretation can be seen in cases disclosing textual differences between similar notions used in different Convention

---

[56] *Ibid.*, para. 99. See similarly, but then regarding the overlap between Articles 9 and 10: *Ibragim Ibragimov v. Russia*, ECtHR 28 August 2018, 1413/08 and 28621/11, para. 78.

[57] *Lashmankin and Others v. Russia*, ECtHR 7 February 2017, 57818/09, paras. 363–4.

provisions, or between the definition of such notions in the English and French text versions of the Convention. The Court then aims to provide a harmonious interpretation, making use of the tools provided by Article 33 of the Vienna Convention on the Law of Treaties on interpreting diverging authentic text versions. Such a harmonising approach can be seen in the extensive reasoning the Court provided in the *Perinçek* case, which concerned a restriction of the freedom of expression which was allegedly necessary to 'prevent disorder' in the sense of Article 10(2) ECHR:

> When setting forth the various legitimate aims that may justify interferences with the rights enshrined in the Convention and its Protocols, the various Articles in the English text of the Convention and its Protocols use different formulations. Article 10 § 2 of the Convention, as well as Articles 8 § 2 and 11 § 2, contain the term 'prevention of disorder', whereas Article 6 § 1 of the Convention and Article 1 § 2 of Protocol No. 7 speak of the 'interests of public order', Article 9 § 2 of the Convention uses the formula 'protection of public order', and Article 2 § 3 of Protocol No. 4 refers to the 'maintenance of *ordre public*'. While ... when using the same term the Convention and its Protocols must in principle be taken to refer to the same concept, differences in the terms used must normally be presumed to denote a variation in meaning. Seen in this context, the latter formulas appear to bear a wider meaning, based on the extensive notion of public order (*ordre public*) used in continental countries ... – where it is often taken to refer to the body of political, economic and moral principles essential to the maintenance of the social structure, and in some jurisdictions even encompasses human dignity – whereas the former appears to convey a narrower significance, understood in essence in cases of this type as riots or other forms of public disturbance. On the other hand, the French text of Article 10 § 2 of the Convention, as well as those of Articles 8 § 2 and 11 § 2, speak of '*la défense de l'ordre*', which might be perceived as having a wider meaning than the term 'prevention of disorder' in the English text. Yet here also, there is a difference in the formulation, for the French text of Article 6 § 1 of the Convention, as well as those of Article 2 § 3 of Protocol No. 4 and Article 1 § 2 of Protocol No. 7, refer to '*ordre public*' ...
>
> By Article 33 § 1 of the 1969 Vienna Convention on the Law of Treaties, treaties are to be interpreted 'in good faith in accordance with the ordinary meaning to be given to the terms of the treaty in their context and in the light of its object and purpose'. By Article 33 § 3 of that Convention, which deals with the interpretation of treaties which, like the Convention, are authenticated in two or more languages, the terms of a treaty are 'presumed to have the same meaning in each authentic text'. Article 33 § 4 of that Convention says that when a comparison of the authentic texts discloses a difference of meaning that the application of the other rules of interpretation does not remove, the meaning that must be adopted is the one that 'best reconciles the texts, having regard to the object and purpose of the treaty'. These latter rules must be read as elements of the general rule of interpretation laid down in Article 31 § 1 of that Convention ...

The Court has already had occasion to say that these rules ... require it to interpret the relevant texts in a way that reconciles them as far as possible and is most appropriate to realise the object and purpose of the Convention ... Bearing in mind that the context in which the terms at issue were used is a treaty for the effective protection of individual human rights ... that clauses, such as Article 10 § 2, that permit interference with Convention rights must be interpreted restrictively ... and that, more generally, exceptions to a general rule cannot be given a broad interpretation ... the Court finds that, since the words used in the English text appear to be only capable of a narrower meaning, the expressions 'the prevention of disorder' and '*la défense de l'ordre*' in the English and French texts of Article 10 § 2 can best be reconciled by being read as having the less extensive meaning.[58]

This reasoning also shows the interplay between the different methods of interpretation, which, in this case, had the effect of justifying a narrow reading of the restriction clause of Article 10(2) ECHR.

Finally, the method of internally harmonising interpretation is sometimes used to delimit the scope of the Convention. An example of this can be seen in the *Pretty* case, which was discussed in Section 4.2 in relation to textual interpretation.[59] One of the questions raised in that case was whether a prohibition of assisted suicide would be incompatible with the prohibition of inhuman and degrading treatment (Article 3 ECHR), as in some cases, the prohibition would mean that severe and intense physical and mental suffering could not be ended. In this connection, the Court reasoned that Article 3 cannot be given this interpretation for reasons of internal consistency:

While the Court must take a dynamic and flexible approach to the interpretation of the Convention, which is a living instrument, any interpretation must also accord with the fundamental objectives of the Convention and its coherence as a system of human rights protection. Article 3 must be construed in harmony with Article 2, which hitherto has been associated with it as reflecting basic values respected by democratic societies. As found above,[60] Article 2 of the Convention is first and foremost a prohibition on the use of lethal force or other conduct which might lead to the death of a human being and does not confer any right on an individual to require a State to permit or facilitate his or her death ... [T]he positive obligation on the part of the State which is relied on in the present case would not involve the removal or mitigation of harm by, for instance, preventing any ill-treatment by public bodies or private individuals or providing improved conditions or care. It would require that the State sanction actions intended to terminate life, an obligation that cannot be derived from Article 3 of the Convention.[61]

---

[58] *Perinçek v. Switzerland*, ECtHR (GC) 15 October 2015, 27510/08, paras. 146–51.
[59] *Pretty v. the United Kingdom*, ECtHR 29 April 2002, 2346/02.   [60] See Section 5.2.
[61] *Ibid.*, paras. 54–5.

However, other methods and principles of interpretation at times may be more important. For example, in *Bayatyan*, a Chamber of the Court had held that Article 9 ECHR could not be interpreted as containing a right for conscientious objectors to refuse military service.[62] The reason it gave for this was that this provision had to be interpreted in harmony with the provision in Article 4(3)(b) ECHR, which stipulates that the prohibition of forced labour does not include military service or an alternative form of service for conscientious objectors.[63] The Chamber thus gave much value to the argument of internal harmony of the Convention, as well as to an interpretation the former European Commission of Human Rights had provided. This finding was revised by the Grand Chamber in the same case, however, which emphasised the limitations of an internally harmonising approach:

> The Court . . . is not convinced that [the Chamber's] interpretation of Article 4 § 3 (b) reflects the true purpose and meaning of this provision. It notes that Article 4 § 3 (b) excludes from the scope of 'forced or compulsory labour' prohibited by Article 4 § 2 'any service of a military character or, in case of conscientious objectors in countries where they are recognised, service exacted instead of compulsory military service'. The Court further notes in this respect the *travaux préparatoires* on Article 4 . . . In the Court's opinion, the *travaux préparatoires* confirm that the sole purpose of sub-paragraph (b) of Article 4 § 3 is to provide a further elucidation of the notion 'forced or compulsory labour'. In itself it neither recognises nor excludes a right to conscientious objection and should therefore not have a delimiting effect on the rights guaranteed by Article 9. At the same time, the Court is mindful of the fact that the restrictive interpretation of Article 9 applied by the Commission was a reflection of the ideas prevailing at the material time. It considers, however, that many years have elapsed since the Commission first set out its reasoning . . . In the meantime there have been important developments both in the domestic legal systems of Council of Europe member States and internationally. The Court reiterates in this connection that the Convention is a living instrument which must be interpreted in the light of present-day conditions and of the ideas prevailing in democratic States today . . . Furthermore, in defining the meaning of terms and notions in the text of the Convention, the Court can and must take into account elements of international law other than the Convention and the interpretation of such elements by competent organs. The consensus emerging from specialised international instruments may constitute a relevant consideration for the Court when it interprets the provisions of the Convention in specific cases . . . In the light of the foregoing and in line with the 'living instrument' approach, the Court therefore takes the view that it is not possible to confirm the case-law established by the Commission, and that Article 9 should no longer be read in conjunction with Article 4 § 3 (b). Consequently, the applicant's complaint is to be assessed solely under Article 9.[64]

---

[62] *Bayatyan v. Armenia*, ECtHR 27 October 2009, 23459/03.   [63] *Ibid.* (Chamber judgment), para. 63.
[64] *Bayatyan v. Armenia*, ECtHR (GC) 7 July 2011, 23459/03, paras. 100–9.

The Grand Chamber then decided to base its new interpretation on a rather more precedent-orientated reading of Article 9, referring to standards for applicability of the freedom of religion it had defined in its previous case law and taking a strongly case-dependent approach. In the end, it held that objections to military service may fall within the ambit of Article 9, although this would depend on the circumstances of the case.[65] This judgment thus shows the interplay between the different methods of interpretation used by the Court. Even if a particular method of interpretation seems to point in a certain direction – in this case, internally harmonising interpretation should lead to non-applicability of Article 9 – other methods may provide a counter-indication. In making choices in such cases, the Court allows itself to be guided by the general principles discussed in Chapters 1 and 3. The notion of the Convention as a living instrument in *Bayatyan* clearly pointed to accepting a wider scope for Article 9. Using concrete methods of interpretation supporting that reading, this was the conclusion the Court eventually reached.

The judgment in *Bayatyan* also shows the pertinency of another method of interpretation, which is the amount of European consensus and the convergence of State practice. This shows that there should not only be internal harmony in interpreting the Convention, but the Convention must also be read in harmony with foreign and international developments. This is done through application of the 'common ground method', as is discussed in the next section.

4.5   Common Ground or Consensus Interpretation

4.5.1   Rationale

An important method of interpretation for the Court is common ground or consensus interpretation.[66] This implies that the Court can accept a novel interpretation of the Convention if there is a sufficiently clear European consensus on the classification of a certain aspect of a right as part of a Convention right.[67] The use of this method is supported by the Vienna Convention on the Law of Treaties, which stipulates in Article 31(3) that in interpreting a treaty, account has to be taken of any subsequent agreements between the parties regarding the interpretation or

---

[65] *Ibid.*, para. 110.
[66] On this method, see *in extenso* (and with many references) Senden, *supra* n. 14.
[67] This section therefore does not specifically deal with the function of the consensus argument in determining the scope of the margin of appreciation that should be left to the States, which will be discussed in Section 7.4.2. Consensus interpretation as discussed in this chapter mainly relates to stage 1 of the Court's review (see Section 1.4.2), which concerns the determination of applicability of the Convention. However, now that the Court does not always strictly distinguish between the stages and sometimes defines relevant standards of application in stage 3 (justification review, see Section 1.4.4), examples are sometimes given that relate to the Court's review of restrictions.

application of a treaty, any subsequent State practice in the application of the treaty that shows an agreement between the parties regarding its interpretation, and any relevant rules of international law applicable in the relation between the parties.[68] In addition, the common ground method is closely related to the principles of effective and evolutive interpretation.[69] As the Court emphasised in *Christine Goodwin*, developments in national and international law may provide a good basis to arrive at an interpretation of the Convention that is in line with 'present-day conditions' and that provides for real and effective protection of the fundamental rights contained in that instrument:

> [S]ince the Convention is first and foremost a system for the protection of human rights, the Court must have regard to the changing conditions within the respondent State and within Contracting States generally and respond, for example, to any evolving convergence as to the standards to be achieved … It is of crucial importance that the Convention is interpreted and applied in a manner which renders its rights practical and effective, not theoretical and illusory. A failure by the Court to maintain a dynamic and evolutive approach would indeed risk rendering it a bar to reform or improvement.[70]

Consensus interpretation may also enable the Court to arrive at autonomous interpretations that can be relatively easily implemented in national law, since definitions may be chosen that lie close to what is already known and accepted at the national level.[71] Conversely, as was also discussed in relation to autonomous interpretation in Section 3.5, consensus interpretation occasionally may be used to refuse to give a new interpretation if there is insufficient support for it in the laws of the States.[72] By using the method in this manner the Court can leave room for national diversity with regard to sensitive fundamental rights issues and respect the principle of subsidiarity.

4.5.2   Sources of Common Ground Interpretation

The Court can draw from a variety of sources to establish a European common ground regarding the definition of the Convention rights. In particular, the Court often has regard to national law, international and European law (including soft law, and decisions and resolutions of treaty bodies or international organisations)

---

[68] See further Section 3.2.   [69] See further Section 3.3.

[70] *Christine Goodwin v. the United Kingdom*, ECtHR (GC) 11 July 2002, 28957/95, para. 74.

[71] It is important to note, however, that this advantage will be a relative one – whether a definition will really fit in well with national law will depend on the level and the nature of the consensus and on the extent to which the meaning of a notion in the law of a specific State already resembles the ECHR definition. See also M. Cartabia, 'Europe and Rights: Taking Dialogue Seriously', *European Constitutional Law Review*, 5 (2009), 5–31 at 18.

[72] See most famously *Vo v. France*, ECtHR (GC) 8 April 2004, 53924/00, para. 82 (discussed in more detail in Section 3.5.2).

and, more specifically, European Union law. These various sources and their use are discussed hereafter.

a   National Law

Comparing national constitutional texts, legislation and judgments allows the Court to detect an emerging common ground on a specific fundamental rights issue or, by contrast, a lack of European consensus. A famous example of this approach is a sequence of judgments on the legal recognition of gender transformations. In its first judgment on the issue in *Rees*, the Court held that no obligation could be derived from the Convention for the States to formally recognise an individual's new gender (for example, by changing a birth certificate or passport), given the lack of convergence of national law:

> Several States have, through legislation or by means of legal interpretation or by administrative practice, given transsexuals the option of changing their personal status to fit their newly-gained identity. They have, however, made this option subject to conditions of varying strictness and retained a number of express reservations (for example, as to previously incurred obligations). In other States, such an option does not – or does not yet – exist. It would therefore be true to say that there is at present little common ground between the Contracting States in this area and that, generally speaking, the law appears to be in a transitional stage.[73]

After this judgment, which was handed down in 1986, a number of other applications were lodged regarding similar topics. In 1990, the Court decided on the *Cossey* case,[74] in 1992 it dealt with *B. v. France*,[75] and in 1998, it judged on the *Sheffield and Horsham* case.[76] In each case, the Court used a fresh comparative review of State practice, and in each case, it found that more States had accepted some form of legal recognition of gender transformations. Nevertheless, in each case, the Court also concluded that the national laws still did not disclose a sufficient degree of common ground to justify a new Convention interpretation. Eventually, however, in the 2002 *Christine Goodwin* case, the Court ruled differently, and, significantly, it thereby nuanced the importance of full convergence:

> Already at the time of the Sheffield and Horsham case, there was an emerging consensus within Contracting States in the Council of Europe on providing legal recognition following gender re-assignment ... The latest survey submitted by Liberty[77] in the present case shows a continuing international trend towards legal recognition ... In Australia and New

---

[73] *Rees v. the United Kingdom*, ECtHR 17 October 1986, 9532/81, para. 37.
[74] *Cossey v. the United Kingdom*, ECtHR 27 September 1990, 10843/84.
[75] *B. v. France*, ECtHR 25 March 1992, 13343/87.
[76] *Sheffield and Horsham v. the United Kingdom*, ECtHR (GC) 30 July 1998, 22985/93 and 23390/94.
[77] An NGO which intervened in the case.

Zealand, it appears that the courts are moving away from the biological birth view of sex ... and taking the view that sex, in the context of a transsexual wishing to marry, should depend on a multitude of factors to be assessed at the time of the marriage.

The Court observes that in the case of Rees in 1986 it had noted that little common ground existed between States, some of which did permit change of gender and some of which did not and that generally speaking the law seemed to be in a state of transition ... While this would appear to remain the case, the lack of such a common approach among forty-three Contracting States with widely diverse legal systems and traditions is hardly surprising ... The Court accordingly attaches less importance to the lack of evidence of a common European approach to the resolution of the legal and practical problems posed, than to the clear and uncontested evidence of a continuing international trend in favour not only of increased social acceptance of transsexuals but of legal recognition of the new sexual identity of post-operative transsexuals.[78]

This judgment in *Christine Goodwin* shows, first, that it is not always necessary that national law discloses a full consensus between the States Parties on a certain topic, but it may be sufficient if there is 'clear and uncontested evidence of a continuing international trend'.[79] Second, it makes clear that comparative reviews of national law do not necessarily have to be made by the Court itself. Although the Court has a Research and Library Division which can draw up such reports in important cases,[80] the Court may also rely on reports supplied by one of the parties to the case,[81] intervening third parties (such as the NGO Liberty in *Christine Goodwin*)[82] or European international organisations or committees.[83] The Court increasingly also relies on the information acquired through the Supreme Courts Network, which was established in 2015 with the objective of facilitating exchanges of information between the ECtHR and the national courts.[84] Part of this is that the Court can direct formal requests for information to the national supreme courts, which it can then use in drawing up its comparative reports.[85] Third, the judgment

---

[78] *Christine Goodwin v. the United Kingdom*, ECtHR (GC) 11 July 2002, 28957/95, paras. 84–5.

[79] See further on this also hereafter, section 4.5.3.

[80] See e.g. *Labassee v. France*, ECtHR 26 June 2014, 65941/11, paras. 31–3.

[81] See e.g. *Gough v. the United Kingdom*, ECtHR 28 October 2014, 49327/11, paras. 123–6 and 172.

[82] See also e.g. *Oliari and Others v. Italy*, ECtHR 21 July 2015, 18766/11 and 36030/11, paras. 135 et seq.

[83] See e.g. *Strzelecki v. Poland*, ECtHR 10 April 2012, 26648/03, para. 52.

[84] See the *Cooperation Charter of the Supreme Courts Network* (Strasbourg, 2015), www.echr.coe.int/ Documents/SCN_Charter_ENG.pdf and the *Operational Rules of the Supreme Courts Network* (Strasbourg, 13 April 2018), www.echr.coe.int/Documents/SCN_Operational_Rules_ENG.pdf, last accessed 30 November 2018.

[85] See e.g. the overview of requested reports in *Supreme Courts Network Annual Report 2017 – Consolidating the Position of the SCN in the Convention Landscape* (Strasbourg, January 2018), www.echr.coe.int/Documents/SCN_Annual_Report_2017_ENG.pdf, last accessed 30 November 2018.

demonstrates that the Court may not only look into the laws of the States Parties to the Convention, but occasionally also of non-European States, such as Australia and New Zealand.[86] In most cases, however, the Court merely regards such foreign legal developments as a confirmation (or denial) of an overall trend towards recognition of certain rights and as a source of inspiration.[87]

b International and European Instruments and Soft Law

Next to comparative reviews of national law, the Court has found an important source for its common ground reasoning in the existence of international or European treaties, soft law or views and decisions of treaty bodies. Such instruments can be indicative of consensus if they have been negotiated, signed and ratified by a significant number of Convention States. Moreover, the Vienna Convention on the Law of Treaties expressly states that a treaty, such as the Convention, must be interpreted in light of any relevant rules of international law applicable in the relation between the parties.[88] Another advantage of using international sources is that they are often highly specialised. In particular, international treaty bodies or specific international organisations or committees may have an expertise which the Court is lacking.[89] For the Court, this may constitute an important reason for taking international instruments into account. This is witnessed, for example, by its reasoning in the *Opuz* case on domestic violence against women:

> The Court notes at the outset that when it considers the object and purpose of the Convention provisions, it also takes into account the international-law background to the legal question before it. Being made up of a set of rules and principles that are accepted by the vast majority of States, the common international or domestic law standards of European States reflect a reality that the Court cannot disregard when it is called upon to clarify the scope of a Convention provision that more conventional means of interpretation have not enabled it to establish with a sufficient degree of certainty ... In this connection, when considering the definition and scope of discrimination against women, in addition to

---

[86] For other examples, see *Pretty v. the United Kingdom*, ECtHR 29 April 2002, 2346/02, para. 66; *Appleby v. the United Kingdom*, ECtHR 6 May 2003, 44306/98, para. 46; *Oliari and Others v. Italy*, ECtHR 21 July 2015, 18766/11 and 36030/11, para. 177.

[87] See e.g. *Oliari and Others v. Italy*, ECtHR 21 July 2015, 18766/11 and 36030/11, para. 177: 'The same rapid development can be identified globally, with particular reference to countries in the Americas and Australasia ... The information available thus goes to show the continuing international movement towards legal recognition, to which the Court cannot but attach some importance'. By contrast, for confirmation of a lack of consensus, see *Naït-Liman v. Switzerland*, ECtHR (GC) 15 March 2018, 51357/07, para. 200.

[88] Article 31(3)(c) of the Vienna Convention; see also Section 3.2 and see specifically *Mamatkulov and Askarov v. Turkey*, ECtHR (GC) 4 February 2005, 46827/99 and 46951/99, para. 111.

[89] See e.g. *National Federation of Sportspersons' Associations and Unions (FNASS) and Others v. France*, ECtHR 18 January 2018, 48151/11 and 77769/13, para. 181.

the more general meaning of discrimination as determined in its case-law ... the Court has to have regard to the provisions of more specialised legal instruments and the decisions of international legal bodies on the question of violence against women.[90]

Referring to the UN Convention on the Elimination of All Forms of Discrimination Against Women (CEDAW) and the findings of the CEDAW Committee, a resolution of the UN Commission on Human Rights, the Belém do Pará Convention on violence against women, and the rulings of the Inter-American Commission on Human Rights,[91] the Court concluded that '[i]t transpires from the above-mentioned rules and decisions that the State's failure to protect women against domestic violence breaches their right to equal protection of the law'.[92] This conclusion then formed the basis for the Court's own interpretation of the prohibition of discrimination in cases of domestic violence.

However, some governments have pointed out that not all sources of international law can be considered to be equally authoritative. In a 2014 case on trade union freedom, for example, the United Kingdom argued that the Court should not accord too much weight to the views on a specific element of trade union freedom of the European Committee on Social Rights (ECSR) and the International Labour Organisation's Committee (ILO Committee).[93] The Court disagreed with this position. Regarding the ECSR, in particular, it held that 'the interpretative value of the ECSR appears to be generally accepted by States and by the Committee of Ministers. It is certainly accepted by the Court, which has repeatedly had regard to the ECSR's interpretation of the Charter and its assessment of State compliance with its various provisions.'[94] The Court further reasoned that even if the views of the ECSR and the ILO Committee could not be considered decisive,[95] together with the national comparative material, they could be used to show that the United Kingdom 'finds itself at the most restrictive end of a spectrum of national regulatory approaches on this point and is out of line with a discernible international trend calling for a less restrictive approach'.[96]

Thus, even if certain international materials are 'merely' soft law or non-binding instruments, the Court will rely on them if it considers them sufficiently indicative of a consensus. Importantly, however, such materials will not be decisive for the Court's findings, but it will always combine them with other sources and arguments. Indeed, the Court has expressly refused to take any document of international institutions as 'binding', even if it concerns authoritative standards set by highly

---

[90] *Opuz v. Turkey*, ECtHR 9 June 2009, 33401/02, paras. 184–5.   [91] *Opuz*, paras. 186–90.
[92] *Ibid.*, para. 191.
[93] *National Union of Rail, Maritime and Transport Workers v. the United Kingdom*, ECtHR 8 April 2014, 31045/10.
[94] *National Union of Rail, Maritime and Transport Workers*, para. 94.   [95] *Ibid.*, para. 98.
[96] *Ibid.*

specialised bodies. The Court explained this in its judgment in *Muršić*, which concerned the standards to be applied in cases about prison conditions.[97] In such cases, the Court often refers to the work of the European Committee for the Prevention of Torture (CPT), but it pointed out that, even so, it would still need to set its own standards:

> With regard to the standards developed by other international institutions such as the CPT, the Court would note that it has declined to treat them as constituting a decisive argument for its assessment under Article 3 ... The central reason for the Court's reluctance to take the CPT's available space standards as a decisive argument for its finding under Article 3 relates to its duty to take into account all relevant circumstances of a particular case before it when making an assessment under Article 3, whereas other international institutions such as the CPT develop general standards in this area aiming at future prevention ... Moreover, as the CPT has recognised, the Court performs a conceptually different role to the one assigned to the CPT, whose responsibility does not entail pronouncing on whether a certain situation amounts to inhuman or degrading treatment or punishment within the meaning of Article 3 ... The thrust of CPT activity is pre-emptive action aimed at prevention, which, by its very nature, aims at a degree of protection that is greater than that upheld by the Court when deciding cases concerning conditions of detention ... In contrast to the CPT's preventive function, the Court is responsible for the judicial application in individual cases of an absolute prohibition against torture and inhuman or degrading treatment under Article 3 ... Nevertheless, the Court would emphasise that it remains attentive to the standards developed by the CPT.[98]

Reliance on international instruments as confirmation of consensus may also be controversial if the relevant instrument has not been signed or ratified by a majority of the Convention States, or if it has been signed by many States but not by the respondent State.[99] The Court dealt with the first situation in the *Marckx* case, which concerned various issues concerning the legal position of children born out of wedlock.[100] Under Belgian law, the maternal affiliation of an illegitimate child could not be established by its birth alone or by the entry of the mother's name on the birth certificate, but only by following a specific procedure. In ruling on the compatibility of this with the prohibition of discrimination (Article 14) and the right to respect for one's family life (Article 8), the Court took account of international law:

---

[97] *Muršić v. Croatia*, ECtHR (GC) 20 October 2016, 7334/13.   [98] *Ibid.*, paras. 111–13.

[99] See also e.g. P. Pinto de Albuquerque, 'Plaidoyer for the European Court of Human Rights', *European Human Rights Law Review*, 2018, 119–33 at 123.

[100] *Marckx v. Belgium*, ECtHR 13 June 1979, 6833/74, para. 28.

It is true that, at the time when the Convention of 4 November 1950 was drafted,[101] it was regarded as permissible and normal in many European countries to draw a distinction in this area between the 'illegitimate' and the 'legitimate' family. However, the Court recalls that this Convention must be interpreted in the light of present-day conditions ... In the instant case, the Court cannot but be struck by the fact that the domestic law of the great majority of the member States of the Council of Europe has evolved and is continuing to evolve, in company with the relevant international instruments, towards full juridical recognition of the maxim 'mater semper certa est'. Admittedly, of the ten States that drew up the Brussels Convention, only eight have signed and only four have ratified it to date. The European Convention of 15 October 1975 on the Legal Status of Children born out of Wedlock has at present been signed by only ten and ratified by only four members of the Council of Europe. Furthermore, Article 14 (1) of the latter Convention permits any State to make, at the most, three reservations, one of which could theoretically concern precisely the manner of establishing the maternal affiliation of a child born out of wedlock ... However, this state of affairs cannot be relied on in opposition to the evolution noted above. Both the relevant Conventions are in force and there is no reason to attribute the currently small number of Contracting States to a refusal to admit equality between 'illegitimate' and 'legitimate' children on the point under consideration. In fact, the existence of these two treaties denotes that there is a clear measure of common ground in this area amongst modern societies.[102]

Consequently, even if a treaty has not been ratified by a majority of States Parties to the Convention, the Court may regard its very existence as indicative of consensus.[103] In the same vein, the Court usually does not consider it problematic that a particular treaty has not been signed or ratified by the respondent State. This is clear from the *Demir and Baykara* case, which concerned the question of whether the trade union freedom, protected by Article 11 ECHR, also extended to civil servants.[104] The respondent State, Turkey, had always resisted that interpretation and it had deliberately refused to sign and ratify a number of relevant international treaties. The Court did not consider this of any importance in relation to its interpretation of Article 11:

The Court, in defining the meaning of terms and notions in the text of the Convention, can and must take into account elements of international law other than the Convention, the interpretation of such elements by competent organs, and the practice of European States reflecting their common values. The consensus emerging from specialised international

---

[101] The ECHR.   [102] *Ibid.*, para. 41.
[103] See also e.g. *Biao v. Denmark*, ECtHR (GC) 24 May 2016, 38590/10; although the European Convention on Nationality is signed by only twenty of the forty-seven Council of Europe States, the Court found that it 'suggests a certain trend towards a European standard' (para. 132).
[104] *Demir and Baykara v. Turkey*, ECtHR (GC) 12 November 2008, 34503/97.

instruments and from the practice of Contracting States may constitute a relevant consideration for the Court when it interprets the provisions of the Convention in specific cases. In this context, it is not necessary for the respondent State to have ratified the entire collection of instruments that are applicable in respect of the precise subject matter of the case concerned. It will be sufficient for the Court that the relevant international instruments denote a continuous evolution in the norms and principles applied in international law or in the domestic law of the majority of member States of the Council of Europe and show, in a precise area, that there is common ground in modern societies.[105]

Nevertheless, there are some exceptions to the general irrelevance of the number of signatory and ratifying States and non-ratification by the respondent State. A case in point is *Chapman*, in which the Court referred to the Council of Europe's Framework Convention for the Protection of National Minorities.[106] At the time, the Framework Convention had been signed by thirty-seven of the then forty-one Member States of the Council of Europe and it was ratified by twenty-eight.[107] In addition, the need to protect certain minorities, in particular Roma (to which the case pertained) was confirmed by other international instruments.[108] Nevertheless, the Court did not regard this as sufficient proof of a European consensus:

> [T]he Court is not persuaded that the consensus is sufficiently concrete for it to derive any guidance as to the conduct or standards which Contracting States consider desirable in any particular situation. The framework convention, for example, sets out general principles and goals but the signatory States were unable to agree on means of implementation. This reinforces the Court's view that the complexity and sensitivity of the issues involved in policies balancing the interests of the general population, in particular with regard to environmental protection, and the interests of a minority with possibly conflicting requirements renders the Court's role a strictly supervisory one.[109]

Similar considerations can also be seen in more recent judgments. In *X. and Others v. Austria*, on the right to adoption for same-sex partners, the Court first dismissed an argument based on a comparison of national legislation, finding that no conclusions could be drawn from them as to the existence of a possible consensus.[110] It then turned to the consensus argument based on international law: 'In the Court's view, the same holds true for the 2008 Convention on the Adoption of Children. Firstly, it notes that this Convention has not been ratified by Austria. Secondly, given the low number of ratifications so far, it may be open to doubt

---

[105] *Ibid.*, paras. 85–6.
[106] *Chapman v. the United Kingdom*, ECtHR (GC) 18 January 2001, 27238/95.   [107] *Ibid.*, para. 56.
[108] *Ibid.*, para. 93.   [109] *Ibid.*, para. 94.
[110] *X. and Others v. Austria*, ECtHR (GC) 19 February 2013, 19010/07, para. 149.

whether the Convention reflects common ground among European States at present.'[111]

It is difficult to explain these differences between the Court's judgments, but it can be noted that the Court's reasoning in *X. and Others* was critically received by seven dissenting judges.[112] This seems to confirm that the issue of the weight to be given to consensus arguments based on international law is a matter of some controversy within the Court.

c   European Union Law

Finally, European Union law may be a special source for common ground interpretation by the Court. Of course, the EU could be regarded as just another international organisation, and the Court will refer to its instruments in a similar way as it refers to other international law, soft law and decisions by international organisations. Nevertheless, there is good reason for the Court to take express account of EU law, as there is an increasing number of fields where there is a possibility for overlap between the ECHR and EU law, such as in immigration and asylum law, or in relation to data protection. A lack of cooperation between the two systems might then result in inconsistent case law or even to conflicting obligations for the States.[113] There are various means to avoid such inconsistencies, such as informal discussions between the ECtHR and the Court of Justice of the EU, but a solution can also be found in harmonious interpretation or interpretation of ECHR provisions in the light of EU law.[114]

However, one of the difficulties in taking account of EU law in common ground reasoning is that, of the forty-seven States Parties to the Convention, only twenty-eight are bound by EU law (and only twenty-seven after the UK's withdrawal from membership of the EU). The Court has emphasised, therefore, that it cannot directly

---

[111] *Ibid.*, para. 150. Cf. also *A and B v. Norway*, ECtHR (GC) 15 November 2016, 24130/11 and 29758/11, para. 117, where it took account of the limited number of ratifications of Protocol No. 7 to the Convention.

[112] *X. and Others*, Joint partly dissenting opinion of Judges Casadevall, Ziemele, Kovler, Jočienė, Šikuta, De Gaetano and Sicilianos, paras. 12–23.

[113] See e.g. S. Morano-Foadi and S. Andreadikis, 'The Convergence of the European Legal System in the Treatment of Third Country Nationals in Europe: The ECJ and ECtHR Jurisprudence', *European Journal of International Law*, 22 (2011), 1071–88.

[114] See e.g. G. Harpaz, 'The European Court of Justice and its Relations with the European Court of Human Rights: The Quest for Enhanced Reliance, Coherence and Legitimacy', *Common Market Law Review*, 46 (2009), 105–41; C. Van de Heyning and R. Lawson, 'The EU as a Party to the European Convention of Human Rights. EU law and the European Court of Justice Case Law as Inspiration and Challenge to the European Court of Human Rights Jurisprudence' in P. Popelier et al. (eds.), *Human Rights Protection in the European Legal Order: The Interaction between the European and the National Courts* (Antwerp: Intersentia, 2011), pp. 35–64.

import the level of protection offered by EU law.[115] Moreover, even if the relatively recent EU Charter of Fundamental Rights (adopted in 2000) could be an important source, as it reflects the developments in views and opinions in the EU Member States on fundamental rights, it may not be decisive for the Court's reasoning.[116] This is witnessed by the *Schalk and Kopf* case, in which the Court held that there were no sufficient grounds to interpret the right to marry of Article 12 ECHR in line with the new formulation of that right in the EU Charter:

> Turning to the comparison between Article 12 of the Convention and Article 9 of the Charter, the Court [notes] that the latter has deliberately dropped the reference to 'men and women' ... The Commentary of the Charter, which became legally binding in December 2009, confirms that Article 9 is meant to be broader in scope than the corresponding Articles in other human rights instruments ... At the same time, the reference to domestic law reflects the diversity of national regulations, which range from allowing same-sex marriage to explicitly forbidding it. By referring to national law, Article 9 of the Charter leaves the decision whether or not to allow same-sex marriage to the States ... Regard being had to Article 9 of the Charter, therefore, the Court would no longer consider that the right to marry enshrined in Article 12 must in all circumstances be limited to marriage between two persons of the opposite sex. Consequently, it cannot be said that Article 12 is inapplicable to the applicants' complaint. However, as matters stand, the question whether or not to allow same-sex marriage is left to regulation by the national law of the Contracting State ... In that connection, the Court observes that marriage has deep-rooted social and cultural connotations which may differ largely from one society to another. The Court reiterates that it must not rush to substitute its own judgment in place of that of the national authorities, who are best placed to assess and respond to the needs of society.[117]

The Court thus regarded Article 9 of the EU Charter as a relevant instrument in interpreting the Convention, but it did not give any decisive value to this in light of the existing national diversity. The fact that only twenty-eight of the Convention States were engaged in changing the text may have played a role in this respect. To justify a new interpretation of the Convention, the Court will commonly await a

---

[115] See e.g. *NA. v. the United Kingdom*, ECtHR 17 July 2008, 25904/07, para. 107; *Hristozov and Others v. Bulgaria*, ECtHR 13 November 2012, 47039/11 and 358/12, para. 105.

[116] It is therefore relatively often referred to; see e.g. *Bayatyan v. Armenia*, ECtHR (GC) 7 July 2011, 23459/03, para. 106; *Correia de Matos v. Portugal*, ECtHR (GC) 4 April 2018, 56402/12, para. 137. The Court may also refer to other EU materials, however, such as directives, case law of the Court of Justice of the EU or recommendations by the European Parliament. See, for example, *D.H. and Others v. the Czech Republic*, ECtHR (GC) 13 November 2007, 57325/00, paras. 186–9, where the Court clearly chose to incorporate the well-established EU approach to determining indirect discrimination. See also e.g. *J.K. and Others v. Sweden*, ECtHR (GC) 23 August 2016, 59166/12, para. 96.

[117] *Schalk and Kopf v. Austria*, ECtHR 24 June 2010, 30141/04, paras. 60–2.

stronger degree of convergence to be shown by a comparison of national law or by other international law materials.[118] Indeed, where it mentions the EU Charter as a sign of convergence, such a reference is usually embedded in a wider review of national and international instruments which are also indicative of an emerging consensus.[119]

4.5.3   When Is There a Sufficient Common Ground?

One last question that may arise in relation to the common ground method is how exactly the Court can determine that there is sufficient consensus to justify a new interpretation. The previous sections have already demonstrated that in most cases, national laws or international instruments do not disclose a full European consensus.[120] Sometimes, as in *Rees*, this may lead the Court to decide that there is not enough agreement to justify a new interpretation.[121] Likewise, if the comparative data reveals a 'spectrum of national positions' or 'fluctuating developments' in the legal systems,[122] the Court may not be inclined to provide a far-reaching and novel application of the Convention.[123] In other cases, however, even if there is not a full consensus, the Court may still find that there is sufficient common ground if there is a clear tendency towards convergence. Generally, '[t]he Court ... attaches less importance to the lack of evidence of a common European approach to the resolution of the legal and practical problems posed, than to the clear and uncontested evidence of a continuing international trend'.[124]

In other judgments, the Court has mentioned that the yardstick should be whether 'there is as yet any emerging consensus that could assist the Court in its examination'[125] or whether there was at least a 'clear general tendency' towards convergence.[126] Nevertheless, the case law is not fully consistent on this topic. In particular, there is disagreement on a more methodological point. An important

---

[118] It has already found a stronger consensus to exist in *Oliari and Others v. Italy*, ECtHR 21 July 2015, 18766/11 and 36030/11, para. 178.
[119] See e.g. *Bayatyan v. Armenia*, ECtHR (GC) 7 July 2011, 23459/03, paras. 103–8, where the Court also discussed developments in national law, the interpretation given by the UN Human Rights Committee to the ICCPR, and positions taken by the Council of Europe's Committee of Ministers and Parliamentary Assembly.
[120] For a rare example where the Court found that there is a 'uniform approach today by the national legislatures on the subject' (equal treatment of children born out of wedlock), see *Fabris v. France*, ECtHR (GC) 7 February 2013, 16574/08, para. 58.
[121] For some other examples, see *Labassee v. France*, ECtHR 26 June 2014, 65941/11, para. 57; *Hämäläinen v. Finland*, ECtHR (GC) 16 July 2014, 37359/09, paras. 73–4; *Orlandi and Others v. Italy*, ECtHR 14 December 2017, 26431/12, para. 205.
[122] E.g. *Perinçek v. Switzerland*, ECtHR (GC) 15 October 2015, 27510/08, paras. 255–6.
[123] *Ibid.*, para. 257.
[124] *Christine Goodwin v. the United Kingdom*, ECtHR (GC) 11 July 2002, 28957/95, para. 85.
[125] *Appleby and Others v. the United Kingdom*, ECtHR 6 May 2003, 44306/98, para. 46.
[126] E.g. *I.B. v. Greece*, ECtHR 3 October 2013, 552/10, para. 83.

issue in making legal comparisons relates to the level of abstractness that is selected for the comparison. In some cases, the Court seems to require a common ground on a rather concrete level, such as regarding the specific modalities of regulation. This can be illustrated by the Court's judgment in *Hristozov*, a case in which the applicants had claimed a right to access to experimental medical treatment for terminally ill patients:

> As regards the consensus within the Contracting States, the Court observes that, according to the comparative-law information available to it, a number of those States have made provision in their laws for exceptions, in particular in the case of terminally ill patients, to the rule that only authorised medicinal products may be used for medical treatment. They have, however, made this option subject to conditions of varying strictness … On that basis, and on the basis of the manner in which the issue is regulated in the law of the European Union … the Court concludes that there is now a clear trend in the Contracting States towards allowing, under certain exceptional conditions, the use of unauthorised medicinal products. However, that emerging consensus is not based on settled principles in the law of the Contracting States. Nor does it appear to extend to the precise manner in which that use should be regulated.[127]

For that reason, the Court did not want to base any far-reaching conclusions on the consensus argument.[128] By contrast, in other cases, the Court does not so much refer to the lack of convergence on specific issues of regulation, but bases its judgment on a consensus on a more abstract level. In *Lambert*, for example, a case on an end-of-life-situation, the Court noted that:

> no consensus exists among the Council of Europe member States in favour of permitting the withdrawal of artificial life-sustaining treatment, although the majority of States appear to allow it. While the detailed arrangements governing the withdrawal of treatment vary from one country to another, there is nevertheless consensus as to the paramount importance of the patient's wishes in the decision-making process, however those wishes are expressed.[129]

This shows that there is uncertainty regarding the level of abstraction the Court will use to establish a consensus. Indeed, also within the Court, findings such as

---

[127] *Hristozov and Others v. Bulgaria*, ECtHR 13 November 2012, 47039/11 and 358/12, para. 123. See also e.g. *Parrillo v. Italy*, ECtHR (GC) 27 August 2015, 46470/11, paras. 177–8; *Dubská and Krejzová v. the Czech Republic*, ECtHR (GC) 15 November 2016, 28859/11 and 28473/12, para. 183.

[128] Although in this kind of case, the Court also sometimes mentions that a certain matter 'may need to be kept under review in so far as attitudes in European democratic society evolve'; see e.g. *Shindler v. the United Kingdom*, ECtHR 7 May 2013, 19840/09, paras. 110–15; *Jones and Others v. the United Kingdom*, ECtHR 14 January 2014, 34356/06 and 40528/06, para. 215.

[129] *Lambert and Others v. France*, ECtHR (GC) 5 June 2015, 46043/14, para. 147. See also e.g. *Biao v. Denmark*, ECtHR (GC) 24 May 2016, 38590/10, para. 133.

those in the cited examples are often controversial, with dissenting judges assessing the available data based on different levels of abstraction.[130]

Another issue of contention is a temporal issue. Sometimes it may take many years before a case is judged by the Court, and in the meantime many developments may occur in the States or on the international level. This may raise the question of whether a case should be judged based on the level of consensus that existed at the time the alleged interference occurred, or whether the Court should take an 'ex nunc' approach. This question arose in *Zhelyazkov*, concerning the issue of whether the work which the applicant was asked to do in detention could be regarded as falling under the exception to the prohibition of forced labour contained in Article 4(3)(a) ECHR.[131] This provision states that work in prison cannot be regarded as forced labour if it is conducted 'in the ordinary course of detention'. The applicant argued that the non-remuneration of his work made it fall outside that definition and thereby outside the exception. The Court observed that in previous case law, this argument had been rejected, and it then noted that

> there have been subsequent developments in attitudes to that issue, reflected in particular in the 1987 and 2006 European Prison Rules, which call for the equitable remuneration of the work of prisoners – with the 2006 Rules adding 'in all instances' ... Those Rules, and the modification in their wording, reflect an evolving trend. However, the Court does not consider that as matters stood at the time when the applicant was ordered to carry out the work at issue in the present case – approximately two years before the adoption of the 2006 Rules – it could be maintained that there existed an unconditional obligation under Article 4 of the Convention to remunerate the work of all detainees in all circumstances.[132]

The newly grown consensus, as witnessed by a change in the Prison Rules, therefore could not be applied retroactively to the benefit of the applicant. As was shown in Section 3.3.2, however, the Court sometimes also bases new interpretations on the consensus as it existed at the time of the judgment, and it has even applied such new interpretations retroactively. This demonstrates that the Court's approach on the temporal issue is not fully consistent.

---

[130] See e.g. *Dubská and Krejzová v. the Czech Republic*, ECtHR (GC) 15 November 2016, 28859/11 and 28473/12. Whereas the majority had found in this case that there was considerable divergence regarding the exact regulation of home births in the European states, the dissenting judges assessed these data differently, concluding that '[w]hen nearly 50% of the member States provide for and regulate home births (twenty out of the forty-three member States surveyed) and home births are unregulated or under-regulated in twenty-three member States, but no legislation prohibits the assistance of midwives at home births in any of these forty-three States, then there is a consensus in favour of not prohibiting home births among the member States' (Joint dissenting opinion of Judges Sajó, Karakaş, Nicolaou, Laffranque and Keller, para. 28).
[131] *Zhelyazkov v. Poland*, ECtHR 9 October 2012, 11332/04.   [132] *Ibid.*, para. 36.

One last contested issue is whether a majority view can be imposed on a State that strongly objects to a certain interpretation. It was shown in Section 4.5.2 that the Court usually passes by the deliberate non-ratification by States of international treaties. However, in rare cases, the Court may hold differently. A famous case is *F. v. Switzerland*, which concerned a three-year prohibition on remarriage after a divorce in Switzerland. The Court held that Switzerland did not need to comply with the European consensus:

> The Court notes that a waiting period no longer exists under the laws of other Contracting States . . . In this connection, it recalls its case-law according to which the Convention must be interpreted in the light of present-day conditions . . . However, the fact that, at the end of a gradual evolution, a country finds itself in an isolated position as regards one aspect of its legislation does not necessarily imply that that aspect offends the Convention, particularly in a field – matrimony – which is so closely bound up with the cultural and historical traditions of each society and its deep-rooted ideas about the family unit.[133]

It seems that the reasoning provided in this case no longer holds, given the many subsequent judgments in which the Court has adopted new interpretations based on the existence of a strong European consensus, even if not all States agree.[134] Nevertheless, to the extent that a special position of a particular State shows that there is continuous controversy or if it is otherwise clear that the case relates to a highly sensitive moral or social issue, the Court tends to solve this by leaving a wide margin of appreciation in relation to some aspects of the review of restrictions with these rights (stage 3 of its review, see Chapter 1.4.). This specific response by the Court is further discussed in Chapter 7 of this book.

---

[133] *F. v. Switzerland*, ECtHR 18 December 1987, 11329/85, para. 33.

[134] Examples are the acceptance of a prohibition of the death penalty (*Al-Saadoon and Mufdhi*, ECtHR 3 March 2010, 61498/08, para. 120, confirmed for Russia (one of the States which have not so far ratified the death penalty Protocols) in *A.L. (X.W.) v. Russia*, ECtHR 29 October 2015, 44095/14, para. 64); a right to recognition of conscientious objections against military service (*Bayatyan v. Armenia*, ECtHR (GC) 7 July 2011, 23459/03, paras. 103–4); or a prohibition on the restriction of residence rights on HIV-positive non-nationals (see e.g. *Kiyutin v. Russia*, ECtHR 10 March 2011, 2700/10, para. 65; *Novruk and Others v. Russia*, ECtHR 15 March 2016, 31039/11, para. 101).

5 Positive and Negative Obligations

5.1 Introduction

The fundamental rights laid down in the Convention can generally be classified as 'first generation' political rights and liberties.[1] 'Securing' these rights, as the States Parties are bound to do under Article 1 of the Convention, implies that they must abstain from interfering with the free exercise of such rights. For example, the States should not interfere with one's private life by arbitrarily searching one's home, they should not prohibit or censure press publications, and they should not subject suspects to torture. These obligations for the States to abstain from undue interference with the Convention rights and freedoms are called 'negative obligations'.

At the same time, to provide effective protection of the Convention rights, it may not be enough for the States to comply strictly with these negative obligations. For example, the right to a fair trial can only be enjoyed effectively if the State at least establishes and maintains a court system, which would require positive action rather than doing nothing. Indeed, the Court has accepted from a very early stage that purely negative obligations are not the only obligations following from the Convention.[2] The Court has expressed this most clearly in the *Marckx* case, which concerned the right to family life protected by Article 8:

> By proclaiming in paragraph 1 the right to respect for family life, Article 8 signifies firstly that the State cannot interfere with the exercise of that right otherwise than in accordance with the strict conditions set out in paragraph 2 ... [T]he object of the Article is essentially that of protecting the individual against arbitrary interference by the public authorities ... Nevertheless it does not merely compel the State to abstain from such interference: in addition to this primarily negative undertaking, there may be positive obligations inherent

---

[1] Cf. e.g. Ch. Tomuschat, *Human Rights. Between Idealism and Realism*, 3rd edn (Oxford University Press, 2014), pp. 137–8; A.E.M. Leijten, *Core Rights and the Protection of Socio-Economic Interests by the European Court of Human Rights*, PhD thesis, Leiden University (2015), p. 23 et seq.

[2] This was implicitly stated in the *Belgian Linguistics* case, 'relating to certain aspects of the laws on the use of languages in education in Belgium', ECtHR 23 July 1968, 1474/62 paras. I.B.3 and 4. See further on this e.g. M. Beijer, *The Limits of Fundamental Rights Protection by the EU. The Scope for the Development of Positive Obligations* (Antwerp: Intersentia, 2017), 38 et seq.

in an effective 'respect' for family life. This means, amongst other things, that when the State determines in its domestic legal system the regime applicable to certain family ties such as those between an unmarried mother and her child, it must act in a manner calculated to allow those concerned to lead a normal family life.[3]

However, even if the Court made it very clear in this judgment that positive obligations exist, it did not explain the legal basis for their recognition, nor did it set out how and to what degree such positive obligations can be defined and imposed on the States. In subsequent judgments, these questions have been answered by referring to the text of Article 1 of the Convention and a reference to the principle of effectiveness. For example, in *Kontrová*, the Court mentioned that '[i]n assessing the scope of such positive obligations . . . the obligation of Contracting States under Article 1 of the Convention to secure the practical and effective protection of the rights and freedoms laid down therein should be taken into account'.[4]

The Court gave a similar explanation, couched in different terms, in *Plattform 'Ärtzte für das Leben'*, a famous case on the freedom of assembly:

> Genuine, effective freedom of peaceful assembly cannot . . . be reduced to a mere duty on the part of the State not to interfere: a purely negative conception would not be compatible with the object and purpose of Article 11. Like Article 8, Article 11 sometimes requires positive measures to be taken, even in the sphere of relations between individuals, if need be.[5]

As a basis for recognising positive obligations, the Court thus referred to the special nature of the Convention and its overall objectives.[6] It is difficult to find a more principled or detailed argumentation underpinning the positive obligations doctrine in the Court's judgments. Indeed, in *Plattform 'Ärtzte für das Leben'*, the Court mentioned that it 'does not have to develop a general theory of the positive obligations which may flow from the Convention'.[7]

Regardless of such a lack of a 'general theory', it is obvious that the doctrine of positive obligations has great importance for the Convention. The Court's case-based recognition of a wide variety of positive obligations has significantly contributed to the overall strength and scope of the protection offered by the Convention, the incorporation of social and economic rights into the civil and political rights of the Convention, and the recognition of (indirect) effect of the Convention in

---

[3] *Marckx v. Belgium*, ECtHR 13 June 1979, 6833/74, para. 31. See also the equally famous case of *Airey v. the United Kingdom*, ECtHR 9 October 1979, 6289/73, para. 33.

[4] *Kontrová v. Slovakia*, ECtHR 31 May 2007, 7510/04, para. 51.

[5] *Plattform 'Ärtzte für das Leben' v. Austria*, ECtHR 21 June 1988, 10126/82, para. 32.

[6] On these objectives, see further Section 1.2. For a further discussion of the rationales for recognising positive obligations, see e.g. Beijer, *supra* n. 2, at 46 et seq.; V. Stoyanova, *Human Trafficking and Slavery Reconsidered. Conceptual Limits and States' Positive Obligations in European Law* (Cambridge University Press, 2017), 320–1.

[7] *Plattform 'Ärtzte für das Leben' v. Austria*, ECtHR 21 June 1988, 10126/82, para. 31.

relations between individuals and private legal entities or other individuals ('horizontal effect'). To explain the overall meaning and impact of the doctrine, the current chapter focuses on the ways in which the Court generally defines positive obligations and reviews the States' compliance with these obligations (Section 5.2); the different types of positive obligations (Section 5.3); and the relation between positive and negative obligations (Section 5.4). The incorporation of social and economic rights is briefly addressed in relation to the definition of substantive procedural obligations. The indirect horizontal effect of the doctrine of positive obligations is not dealt with in this chapter, but will be discussed separately in Chapter 6.

5.2   Definition of Positive Obligations

The various provisions of the Convention have been formulated with an eye to interferences with the traditionally negative obligations the Convention imposes on the States. In cases concerning such obligations, the structure of the Court's reasoning is usually in line with the three-stage approach discussed in Section 1.4. After having established that the complaint concerns a Convention right (stage 1) and there has been an interference with the exercise or enjoyment of this right (stage 2), it can assess whether the restriction can be justified by applying the relevant conditions and standards contained in express or implied limitation clauses (stage 3).[8] In cases concerning positive obligations, the Court finds less easy guidance in the text and structure of the Convention provisions, and its argumentation may slightly deviate from the scheme established in Section 1.4. Indeed, the Court has developed some special tools to help it define which positive obligations can reasonably be imposed on the States. First, in some cases (mainly in relation to Articles 8–11 ECHR), the Court applies a 'fair balance' test, as is discussed in Section 5.2.1. Second, when a case concerns the need to prevent violations of individuals' physical or mental integrity (mainly Articles 2 and 3 ECHR), the Court may rely on a 'reasonable knowledge and means' test, which is discussed in Section 5.2.2. Third, in yet other cases, such as cases where the Court imposes positive obligations to investigate alleged violations of the Convention, the Court infers these from the general principle of effectiveness (Section 5.2.3). And finally, in many judgments, the Court does not provide a fresh definition of positive obligations at all, but relies on its previous judgments and directly applies the general principles following from these (Section 5.2.4).

---

[8] See further also J.H. Gerards, 'The European Court of Human Rights' in A. Jákab, A. Dyevre and G. Itzcovich (eds.), *Comparative Constitutional Reasoning* (Cambridge University Press, 2017), pp. 237–76 at 249 and 259.

5.2.1   The 'Fair Balance' Test

The name of the 'fair balance' test is derived from a formulation the Court uses in many of its positive obligations cases: 'In determining whether or not a positive obligation exists, regard must be had to the fair balance that has to be struck between the general interest of the community and the interests of the individual, the search for which balance is inherent in the whole of the Convention.'[9] The fair balance test implies that the Court first identifies the various individual and general interests at play in a certain case and, subsequently, assesses which positive action would be needed to strike a fair balance between them. To do so, the Court places the individual interest that would be served by a certain action by the government in one scale of the balance. This is usually the Convention right the applicant has claimed should be effectively protected. In the other scale, the Court places the government interests that would be served by not having to protect the Convention right in a particular manner or to a particular degree. It will then see if it is possible to define a certain type of State action that manages to strike a fair balance between maximum protection of the individual interests concerned and maximum protection of those served by the State. This particular State action is then defined as the positive obligation existing in the concrete case before the Court.

A good example of this fair balance test can be seen in the *Hatton* case, which related to noise disturbance for people living in the vicinity of Heathrow Airport.[10] The applicants claimed that the right to respect for their private lives (protected by Article 8 ECHR) was infringed by the sleep disturbance caused by the many aircraft taking off and landing at night. The question the Court had to answer was whether the national authorities had complied with their positive obligations to effectively protect the private lives of the applicants by regulating the night flights as they had done in the applicable '1993 Scheme', or whether more or different State action had been needed. To understand how the Court determined the fair balance and the State's obligations in this case, it is worth citing the Court's judgment at length:

> The Court has no doubt that the implementation of the 1993 Scheme was susceptible of adversely affecting the quality of the applicants' private life and the scope for their enjoying the amenities of their respective homes, and thus their rights protected by Article 8 of the Convention ...
>
> In order to justify the night flight scheme in the form in which it has operated since 1993, the Government refer not only to the economic interests of the operators of airlines and other enterprises as well as their clients, but also, and above all, to the economic interests of the country as a whole. In their submission these considerations make it necessary to impinge, at least to a certain extent, on the Article 8 rights of the persons affected by the

---

[9] E.g. *Rees v. the United Kingdom*, ECtHR 17 October 1986, 9532/81, para. 37.
[10] *Hatton and Others v. the United Kingdom*, ECtHR (GC) 8 July 2003, 36022/97.

scheme ... It is ... legitimate for the State to have taken the above economic interests into consideration in the shaping of its policy.

Whether in the implementation of that regime the right balance has been struck in substance between the Article 8 rights affected by the regime and other conflicting community interests depends on the relative weight given to each of them ...

As to the economic interests which conflict with the desirability of limiting or halting night flights in pursuance of the above aims, the Court considers it reasonable to assume that those flights contribute at least to a certain extent to the general economy ... A further relevant factor in assessing whether the right balance has been struck is the availability of measures to mitigate the effects of aircraft noise generally, including night noise ... The Court considers it reasonable, in determining the impact of a general policy on individuals in a particular area, to take into account the individuals' ability to leave the area. Where a limited number of people in an area (2 to 3% of the affected population, according to the 1992 sleep study) are particularly affected by a general measure, the fact that they can, if they choose, move elsewhere without financial loss must be significant to the overall reasonableness of the general measure.

On the procedural aspect of the case, the Court notes that a governmental decision-making process concerning complex issues of environmental and economic policy such as in the present case must necessarily involve appropriate investigations and studies in order to allow them to strike a fair balance between the various conflicting interests at stake ... In this respect it is relevant that the authorities have consistently monitored the situation ... The 1993 Scheme had ... been preceded by a series of investigations and studies carried out over a long period of time. The particular new measures introduced by that scheme were announced to the public by way of a Consultation Paper which referred to the results of a study carried out for the Department of Transport, and which included a study of aircraft noise and sleep disturbance ... The applicants and persons in a similar situation ... had access to the Consultation Paper, and it would have been open to them to make any representations they felt appropriate. Had any representations not been taken into account, they could have challenged subsequent decisions, or the scheme itself, in the courts ...

In these circumstances the Court does not find that, in substance, the authorities overstepped their margin of appreciation by failing to strike a fair balance between the right of the individuals affected by those regulations to respect for their private life and home and the conflicting interests of others and of the community as a whole, nor does it find that there have been fundamental procedural flaws in the preparation of the 1993 regulations on limitations for night flights.

There has accordingly been no violation of Article 8 of the Convention.[11]

The fair balance test as applied by the Court in this case comes down to a general test of reasonableness. The Court assessed whether the national authorities had

---

[11] *Ibid.*, paras. 118–30.

sufficiently carefully identified and weighed the conflicting interests concerned and whether they had done so through a fair and open procedure. In *Hatton* it concluded that this had been the case, and it therefore found that the State had sufficiently complied with its positive obligation to effectively protect the individual interests concerned.

The Court will hold differently if it finds that the national authorities did not offer adequate protection of the individual interest and they did not have a good reason for this. An example of this can be seen in *Moreno Gómez*.[12] This case also concerned sleep disturbance, but this time, it was caused by the noise of bars and discotheques:

> The Court notes that the applicant lives in an area that is indisputably subject to night-time disturbances; this clearly unsettles the applicant as she goes about her daily life, particularly at weekends … In view of the volume of the noise – at night and beyond the permitted levels – and the fact that it continued over a number of years, the Court finds that there has been a breach of the rights protected by Article 8.
>
> Although the Valencia City Council has used its powers in this sphere to adopt measures (such as the bylaw concerning noise and vibrations) which should in principle have been adequate to secure respect for the guaranteed rights, it tolerated, and thus contributed to, the repeated flouting of the rules which it itself had established during the period concerned. Regulations to protect guaranteed rights serve little purpose if they are not duly enforced and the Court must reiterate that the Convention is intended to protect effective rights, not illusory ones. The facts show that the applicant suffered a serious infringement of her right to respect for her home as a result of the authorities' failure to take action to deal with the night-time disturbances.
>
> In these circumstances, the Court finds that the respondent State has failed to discharge its positive obligation to guarantee the applicant's right to respect for her home and her private life, in breach of Article 8 of the Convention. There has consequently been a violation of that provision.[13]

Unlike in *Hatton*, the national authorities had not provided any good reasons to justify the unremitting noise disturbance. In particular, they had not explained their lack of enforcement of the noise regulations that were in place. Accordingly, the Court found that they had not managed to strike a fair balance between the need to protect the applicant's Convention rights and to serve the general interest.

Hence, it can be seen that the fair balance test amalgamates the three stages of Convention review that have been distinguished in Section 1.4.[14] Applying a test of

---

[12] *Moreno Gómez*, ECtHR 16 November 2004, 4143/02.   [13] *Ibid.*, paras. 58–63.

[14] See further e.g. J.H. Gerards and H.C.K. Senden, 'The Structure of Fundamental Rights and the European Court of Human Rights', *International Journal of Constitutional Law*, 7 (2009), 619–53 at 634 et seq.; L. Lavrysen, *Human Rights in a Positive State. Rethinking the Relationship Between*

reasonableness or justification (which is applied in stage 3 of the Court's review in negative obligations cases), the Court determines what positive obligations the State would have had to protect a Convention right (stage 1 of the Court's review in negative obligations cases) as well as examining whether the State has complied with them (stage 2 of the Court's review in negative obligations cases).[15] Even if the test is structured differently and it does not carefully follow the three steps explained in Section 1.4, however, it is clear that all three elements still play a role in the Court's reasoning. This is true in particular for the requirements for justification of restrictions, which are discussed in Chapters 8, 9 and 10. The Court has recognised this in many of its judgments, including the *Moreno Gómez* judgment discussed above:[16]

> Whether the case is analysed in terms of a positive duty on the State to take reasonable and appropriate measures to secure the applicants' rights under paragraph 1 of Article 8 or in terms of an interference by a public authority to be justified in accordance with paragraph 2, the applicable principles are broadly similar. In both contexts regard must be had to the fair balance that has to be struck between the competing interests of the individual and of the community as a whole. Furthermore, even in relation to the positive obligations flowing from the first paragraph of Article 8, in striking the required balance the aims mentioned in the second paragraph may be of a certain relevance.[17]

Thus, the Court's review in positive obligations cases where the fair balance test is applied is generally based on similar standards as its review in cases about negative interferences. The main difference is that the Court's review in negative obligations cases is usually more clearly structured, as it is more expressly based on the three-stage approach.[18] In some positive obligations cases, however, the Court's approach is even more similar to that taken in relation to negative interferences.[19] In those cases the Court first establishes whether a reasonable interpretation of the Convention would require certain positive State action. If it has thus established the existence of prima facie positive obligation for the

---

Positive and Negative Obligations under the European Convention on Human Rights (Antwerp: Intersentia, 2016), 221 et seq.

[15] On the stages of review, see Section 1.4.

[16] *Moreno Gómez v. Spain*, ECtHR 16 November 2004, 4143/02.

[17] *Ibid.*, para. 55. See, in different words, also e.g. *Rees v. the United Kingdom*, ECtHR 17 October 1986, 9532/81, para. 37.

[18] See also Gerards and Senden, *supra* n. 14 at 637 et seq.

[19] See also L. Lavrysen, 'The Scope of Rights and the Scope of Obligations. Positive Obligations' in E. Brems and J.H. Gerards, *Shaping Rights in the ECHR: The Role of the European Court of Human Rights in Determining the Scope of Human Rights* (Cambridge University Press, 2014), pp. 162–82.

State, it examines whether there were objective and solid arguments for not fully complying with that obligation. An example of this approach can be found in *Dubetska*, where the applicants had complained about the nuisance and health problems caused by a coal mine close to their homes.[20] In this case, the Court first established that the combination of the intensity and duration of the nuisance and its physical and mental effects on the applicants' health and quality of life shows a strong enough link between the pollutant emissions and the State to raise an issue of the State's responsibility under Article 8 of the Convention.[21]

It thus recognised a certain prima facie obligation of the State to protect the applicants against the interferences with their enjoyment of their homes and private lives. Subsequently, the Court held that it should investigate whether the State had done enough to meet this prima facie positive obligation: 'It remains to be determined whether the State, in securing the applicants' rights, has struck a fair balance between the competing interests of the applicants and the community as a whole, as required by paragraph 2 of Article 8.'[22] In this regard, the Court paid attention to the various individual and general interests concerned and the procedural steps the national authorities had taken to balance these interests.[23] In the end, it found a violation of Article 8:

> The Court appreciates that tackling environmental concerns associated with the operation of two major industrial polluters, which had apparently been malfunctioning from the start and piling up waste for over fifty years, was a complex task which required time and considerable resources, the more so in the context of these facilities' low profitability and nationwide economic difficulties, to which the Government have referred. At the same time, the Court notes that these industrial facilities were located in a rural area and the applicants belonged to a very small group of people (apparently not more than two dozen families) who lived nearby and were most seriously affected by pollution. In these circumstances the Government has failed to adduce sufficient explanation for their failure to either resettle the applicants or find some other kind of effective solution for their individual burden for more than twelve years.[24]

Hence, the Court rather carefully distinguished between, on the one hand, the determination of the scope of application of a Convention right and the obligations following from the recognition of such a right (stages 1 and 2) and, on the other hand, the question to what extent the compliance with such obligations can be

---

[20] *Dubetska and Others v. Ukraine*, ECtHR 10 February 2011, 30499/03. See also e.g. *Fadeyeva v. Russia*, ECtHR 9 June 2005, 55723/00; *Brânduşe v. Romania*, ECtHR 7 April 2009, 6586/03.
[21] *Dubetska*, para. 123.   [22] *Ibid.*, para. 124.   [23] *Ibid.*, paras. 146–54.   [24] *Ibid.*, para. 155.

expected of the State (stage 3). It should be noted, however, that the application of this 'three-stage test' in positive obligations cases is relatively rare.[25]

5.2.2   The 'Reasonable Knowledge and Means' Test

The second method the Court uses to establish positive obligations can be termed the 'reasonable knowledge and means' test.[26] The Court has developed this test in relation to cases on the use of (lethal) violence or ill-treatment by third parties, but it is also applied in other cases concerning Articles 2 or 3 of the Convention.[27] In all such cases, the question may arise as to what extent the State should act to protect the lives and physical integrity of those within its jurisdiction. The Court explained the general standards it would use to answer to this question in *Osman*.[28] The applicants in this case had argued that the police had not taken sufficient action to protect the lives of the second applicant and his father, who had been seriously threatened by another individual. The Court first emphasised that in relation to this type of cases, the State may incur positive obligations to provide effective protection:

> The Court notes that the first sentence of Article 2 § 1 enjoins the State not only to refrain from the intentional and unlawful taking of life, but also to take appropriate steps to safeguard the lives of those within its jurisdiction ... It is common ground that the State's obligation in this respect extends beyond its primary duty to secure the right to life by putting in place effective criminal-law provisions to deter the commission of offences against the person backed up by law-enforcement machinery for the prevention, suppression and sanctioning of breaches of such provisions. It is thus accepted by those appearing before the Court that Article 2 of the Convention may also imply in certain well-defined circumstances a positive obligation on the authorities to take preventive operational measures to protect an individual whose life is at risk from the criminal acts of another individual. The scope of this obligation is a matter of dispute between the parties.[29]

Turning to the scope of the State's obligation to take preventive measures in order to safeguard an individual's life, the Court held that

> [f]or the Court, and bearing in mind the difficulties involved in policing modern societies, the unpredictability of human conduct and the operational choices which must be made in

---

[25] Moreover, in some of these cases on environmental pollution, the Court decides to apply a negative obligations test rather than a positive obligations one; see e.g. *Dzemyuk v. Ukraine*, ECtHR 4 September 2014, 42488/02, para. 90.

[26] On this test, see also e.g. Lavrysen, *supra* n. 14, at 131 et seq.; D. Xenos, *The Positive Obligations of the State under the European Convention of Human Rights* (Abingdon: Routledge, 2012), 74 et seq.

[27] See e.g. *X and Y v. the Netherlands*, ECtHR 26 March 1985, 8978/80; *O'Keeffe v. Ireland*, ECtHR (GC) 28 January 2014, 35810/09, para. 144.

[28] *Osman v. the United Kingdom*, ECtHR 28 October 1998, 23452/94.   [29] *Ibid.*, para. 115.

terms of priorities and resources, such an obligation must be interpreted in a way which does not impose an impossible or disproportionate burden on the authorities. Accordingly, not every claimed risk to life can entail for the authorities a Convention requirement to take operational measures to prevent that risk from materialising. Another relevant consideration is the need to ensure that the police exercise their powers to control and prevent crime in a manner which fully respects the due process and other guarantees which legitimately place restraints on the scope of their action to investigate crime and bring offenders to justice, including the guarantees contained in Articles 5 and 8 of the Convention.

   In the opinion of the Court where there is an allegation that the authorities have violated their positive obligation to protect the right to life in the context of their above-mentioned duty to prevent and suppress offences against the person ... it must be established to its satisfaction that the authorities knew or ought to have known at the time of the existence of a real and immediate risk to the life of an identified individual or individuals from the criminal acts of a third party and that they failed to take measures within the scope of their powers which, judged reasonably, might have been expected to avoid that risk. The Court does not accept the Government's view that the failure to perceive the risk to life in the circumstances known at the time or to take preventive measures to avoid that risk must be tantamount to gross negligence or wilful disregard of the duty to protect life ... Such a rigid standard must be considered to be incompatible with the requirements of Article 1 of the Convention and the obligations of Contracting States under that Article to secure the practical and effective protection of the rights and freedoms laid down therein, including Article 2 ... For the Court, and having regard to the nature of the right protected by Article 2, a right fundamental in the scheme of the Convention, it is sufficient for an applicant to show that the authorities did not do all that could be reasonably expected of them to avoid a real and immediate risk to life of which they have or ought to have knowledge. This is a question which can only be answered in the light of all the circumstances of any particular case.[30]

Accordingly, a preventive positive obligation arises if the authorities knew or ought to have known of a real and immediate risk to the life of an identified individual or individuals from the criminal acts of a third party. This is the 'reasonable knowledge' part of the test. Subsequently, it must be shown that the authorities failed to take measures within the scope of their powers which, judged reasonably, might have been expected to avoid that risk. This is the 'reasonable means' part of the test.

   Over time, the Court has further refined this test. As for the reasonable knowledge part, for example, it has clarified issues of burden of proof and evidence, and it has pointed out that there is not always a need of a concrete risk for an identifiable

---

[30] *Ibid.*, paras. 116–17.

person to pose a threat to another person's life, as it held in *Osman*, but there may be more general obligations to afford protection against harm to individual's health and lives.[31] The Court has further applied the test to new contexts, such as extraordinary rendition,[32] the risks of dangerous substances or activities such as asbestos or deep diving,[33] and sexual abuse of children in schools.[34] In these instances, the assessment is necessarily strongly case-dependent.

The application of the reasonable means part of the test equally depends on the circumstances of the case.[35] Many specific and detailed explanations of what exactly can be expected of the State can be seen in relation to specific fields of application, such as domestic violence,[36] human trafficking[37] and sexual exploitation,[38] or decisions to allow (potentially dangerous) prisoners and mentally ill persons to go on prison leave or enjoy other forms of liberty.[39] For example, the Court has defined some specific requirements in relation to dangerous industrial activities in *Öneryildiz*.[40] In that case, the Court clarified that in determining the State's responsibility for taking preventive measures it should take account of factors such as 'the harmfulness of the phenomena inherent in the activity in question, the contingency of the risk to which the applicant was exposed by reason of any life-endangering circumstances, the status of those involved in bringing about such circumstances, and whether the acts or omissions attributable to them were deliberate'.[41]

Consequently, in these cases, the Court applies contingent tests to establish whether the State has met its positive obligations under the Convention, which take careful account of both the need for effective protection of Convention rights and what can be reasonably expected from the State in the exercise of its powers. It might be stated that the result is very similar to the fair balance test, but the test is couched in different wording.

---

[31] See e.g. *Bljakaj v. Poland*, ECtHR 18 September 2014, 74448/12, para. 108.

[32] See e.g. *El-Masri v. the Former Yugoslav Republic of Macedonia*, ECtHR (GC) 13 December 2012, 39630/09, para. 215.

[33] E.g. *Vilnes and Others v. Norway*, ECtHR 5 December 2013, 52806/09, para. 222; *Brincat and Others v. Malta*, ECtHR 24 July 2014, 60908/11, paras. 103 et seq.

[34] *O'Keeffe v. Ireland*, ECtHR (GC) 28 January 2014, 35810/09, paras. 149 et seq.

[35] See e.g. *Marro and Others v. Italy*, ECtHR 8 April 2014 (dec.), 29100/07.

[36] E.g. *Opuz v. Turkey*, ECtHR 9 June 2009, 33401/02, para. 130 et seq.; *A. v. Croatia*, ECtHR 14 October 2010, 55164/08, paras. 57 et seq.; *T.M. and C.M. v. Moldova*, ECtHR 28 January 2014, 26608/11, paras. 36 et seq.

[37] See e.g. *Rantsev v. Cyprus and Russia*, ECtHR 7 January 2010, 25965/04, paras. 286 and 289.

[38] See e.g. *S.M. v. Croatia*, ECtHR 19 July 2018, 60561/14, paras. 55 et seq.

[39] E.g. *Mastromatteo v. Italy*, ECtHR 24 October 2002, 37703/97; *Choreftakis and Choriftaki v. Greece*, ECtHR 17 January 2012, 46846/08; *Fernandes de Oliveira v. Portugal*, ECtHR 28 March 2017, 78103/14.

[40] *Öneryildiz v. Turkey*, ECtHR (GC) 30 November 2004, 48939/99, para. 71.   [41] *Ibid.*, para. 73.

5.2.3   Effectiveness-based Definition of Positive Obligations

The fair balance test and the reasonable knowledge and means test are fairly detailed ways for the Court to define positive obligations and to see whether they have been respected in a concrete case. In many other cases, however, the Court mainly relies on the general principles of interpretation, such as effectiveness and evolutive interpretation, to underpin the acceptance of a new positive obligation.[42] An early example can be found in *X and Y v. the Netherlands*.[43] Y had mental disabilities, and lived in a private home for children with similar disabilities where she was sexually assaulted and raped by the son-in-law of the director. Y's father, X, had asked the police to institute criminal proceedings, but this proved impossible under national law because Y had not lodged the complaint herself. It did not make a difference to this, according to the domestic legislation, that Y was not able to do so herself because of her mental disability. Moreover, because Y was over sixteen years old, her father could not lodge the complaint on her behalf. According to the applicants, the impossibility of having criminal proceedings instituted violated Y's privacy rights under Article 8 ECHR. The Court agreed:

> The Court recalls that although the object of Article 8 is essentially that of protecting the individual against arbitrary interference by the public authorities, it does not merely compel the State to abstain from such interference: in addition to this primarily negative undertaking, there may be positive obligations inherent in an effective respect for private or family life … These obligations may involve the adoption of measures designed to secure respect for private life even in the sphere of the relations of individuals between themselves … The Court finds that the protection afforded by the civil law in the case of wrongdoing of the kind inflicted on Miss Y is insufficient. This is a case where fundamental values and essential aspects of private life are at stake. Effective deterrence is indispensable in this area and it can be achieved only by criminal-law provisions; indeed, it is by such provisions that the matter is normally regulated. Moreover … this is in fact an area in which the Netherlands has generally opted for a system of protection based on the criminal law. The only gap … is as regards persons in the situation of Miss Y; in such cases, this system meets a procedural obstacle which the Netherlands legislature had apparently not foreseen … Thus, [none of the provisions] of the Criminal Code provided Miss Y with practical and effective protection. It must therefore be concluded, taking account of the nature of the wrongdoing in question, that she was the victim of a violation of Article 8 of the Convention.[44]

Hence, the Court accepted a positive obligation for the State to provide effective deterrence to help protect the fundamental value of physical and mental integrity against interferences by third parties. This obligation was given the shape of

---

[42] See also Lavrysen, *supra* n. 14, at 146 et seq.
[43] *X and Y v. the Netherlands*, ECtHR 26 March 1985, 8978/80.   [44] *Ibid.*, paras. 23–30.

requirement to fill any gaps in the Criminal Code that would make it impossible to prosecute perpetrators of rape and sexual assault. Importantly, the Court did not use a fair balance test or a reasonable knowledge and means test to define this obligation, but it referred to what would be needed in order to provide effective protection of the 'fundamental values and essential aspects' of private life. Many other positive obligations find their basis in similar reasoning. This is witnessed in particular by the Court's reasoning in *McCann* to underpin the obligation for the States to conduct an effective investigation into an allegation that individuals had been killed under the responsibility of the respondent State:

> The Court confines itself to noting . . . that a general legal prohibition of arbitrary killing by the agents of the State would be ineffective, in practice, if there existed no procedure for reviewing the lawfulness of the use of lethal force by State authorities. The obligation to protect the right to life under this provision, read in conjunction with the State's general duty under Article 1 of the Convention to 'secure to everyone within their jurisdiction the rights and freedoms defined in [the] Convention', requires by implication that there should be some form of effective official investigation when individuals have been killed as a result of the use of force by, *inter alios*, agents of the State.[45]

In this case, too, the positive obligation for the State and its scope were based on the Court's own interpretation of what would be required to guarantee an effective protection of the Convention, rather than a fair balance test or a reasonable knowledge and means test.

5.2.4   Precedent-based Definition of Positive Obligations

Finally, in many cases the Court does not apply any of the three methods discussed above. There is no need for it to do so if it has already established the existence of a certain positive obligation in earlier case law. In line with its overall argumentative approach described in Chapter 2, the Court may choose to define such positive obligations as part of the general principles relevant to the interpretation and application of the Convention in specific types of situation. For example, in relation to Articles 2 and 3 ECHR, as was discussed in Section 5.2.3, the Court accepted in *McCann* that the State has a positive obligation to investigate cases where individuals have been killed.[46] This general obligation has been further refined and detailed in many subsequent judgments, and they were brought together as part of the 'General Principles' section in *Nachova*:

> The obligation to protect the right to life under Article 2 of the Convention, read in conjunction with the State's general duty under Article 1 of the Convention to 'secure to

---

[45] *McCann and Others v. the United Kingdom*, ECtHR 27 September 1995, 18984/91, para. 161.
[46] *Ibid.*

everyone within [its] jurisdiction the rights and freedoms defined in [the] Convention', requires by implication that there should be some form of effective official investigation when individuals have been killed as a result of the use of force ... The essential purpose of such an investigation is to secure the effective implementation of the domestic laws safeguarding the right to life and, in those cases involving State agents or bodies, to ensure their accountability for deaths occurring under their responsibility ...

The authorities must act of their own motion once the matter has come to their attention. They cannot leave it to the initiative of the next-of-kin either to lodge a formal complaint or to request particular lines of inquiry or investigative procedures ... For an investigation into alleged unlawful killing by State agents to be effective, the persons responsible for and carrying out the investigation must be independent and impartial, in law and in practice ... The investigation must also be effective in the sense that it is capable of leading to a determination of whether the force used was or was not justified in the circumstances and to the identification and punishment of those responsible ... The authorities must have taken the reasonable steps available to them to secure the evidence concerning the incident, including, inter alia, eye-witness testimony and forensic evidence. The investigation's conclusions must be based on thorough, objective and impartial analysis of all relevant elements and must apply a standard comparable to the 'no more than absolutely necessary' standard required by Article 2 § 2 of the Convention. Any deficiency in the investigation which undermines its capability of establishing the circumstances of the case or the person responsible is liable to fall foul of the required measure of effectiveness.[47]

Once such general principles have been established, which has happened for the great majority of cases, the Court does not need to apply any fair balance or reasonable knowledge and means test, nor does it have to refer to the principle of effectiveness to justify a new positive obligation. The Court can simply reiterate the accepted positive obligations as general principles and apply the resulting standards to the facts of the case, if needed with some further refinement or redefinition.[48] The use of the three other tests and bases for defining positive obligations is thus reserved for setting standards regarding yet unexplored issues.

5.3   Types of Positive Obligations

Using the methods discussed above, the Court has accepted a wide variety of positive obligations in its case law. The Court itself distinguishes between two main types of positive obligations: substantive positive obligations and procedural

---

[47] *Nachova and Others v. Bulgaria*, ECtHR (GC) 6 July 2005, 43577/98 and 43579/98, paras. 110–13.
[48] For two recent examples out of many, see *Fernandes de Oliveira v. Portugal*, ECtHR 28 March 2017, 78103/14, paras. 65–81 and *Sarishvili-Bolkvadze v. Georgia*, ECtHR 19 July 2018, 58240/08, paras. 67–98.

positive obligations.[49] These two main types of obligations are discussed hereafter (Sections 5.3.1 and 5.3.2), whereby Section 5.3.1 also pays attention to a particular effect of the Court's recognition of such obligations, which is the recognition of social and economic rights as part of the Convention. In Section 5.3.3, some other possible typologies of positive obligations are discussed.

5.3.1 Substantive Positive Obligations and the Relation Between Civil/Political and Socio-economic Rights

Substantive positive obligations are notoriously difficult to define other than as obligations that are not predominantly procedural in nature. They are very diverse, since their content and scope will depend on the circumstances of the case and the nature of the individual and general interests at stake. The Court has recognised such divergent obligations as those to provide active police protection to protestors threatened by a hostile audience,[50] offer facilities to detainees to conceive a child,[51] protect playing children from harm by unexploded mines,[52] carefully plan and control any law enforcement operations in which violence is likely to be used,[53] protect pluralism of the media and free access to information,[54] provide alternatives to military duty for conscientious objectors[55] or provide minimum subsistence in situations of extreme deprivation.[56] Substantive positive obligations may moreover range from the obligation to introduce legislation[57] and the obligation for national

---

[49] See also Lavrysen, *supra* n. 14, at 47; Beijer, *supra* n. 2, at 55.

[50] *Plattform 'Ärzte für das Leben' v. Austria*, ECtHR 21 June 1988, 10126/82; *Christian Democratic People's Party v. Moldova (No. 2)*, ECtHR 2 February 2010, 25196/04, para. 25; *Fáber v. Hungary*, ECtHR 24 July 2012, 40721/08; *Promo Lex and Others v. Moldova*, ECtHR 24 February 2015, 30587/13; *Karaahmed v. Bulgaria*, ECtHR 24 February 2015, 30587/13.

[51] *Dickson v. the United Kingdom*, ECtHR (GC) 4 December 2007, 44362/04, although the Court was very nuanced in defining the scope of this obligation.

[52] *Oruk v. Turkey*, ECtHR 4 February 2014, 33647/04; *Sarihan v. Turkey*, ECtHR 6 December 2016, 55907/08.

[53] E.g. *Isayeva and Others v. Russia*, ECtHR 24 February 2005, 57950/00, paras. 180 et seq.; *Giuliani and Gaggio v. Italy*, ECtHR (GC) 24 March 2011, 23458/02, paras. 254 et seq.; *Tagayeva and Others v. Russia*, ECtHR 13 April 2017, 26562/07, paras. 481 et seq.

[54] *Manole and Others v. Moldova*, ECtHR 17 September 2009, 13936/02, paras. 100 and 107; *Frasila and Ciocirlan v. Romania*, ECtHR 10 May 2012, 25329/03; *Centro Europa 7 S.r.l. and Di Stefano v. Italy*, ECtHR 7 June 2012, 38433/09; *Aydogan and Dara Radyo Televizyon Yayıncılık Anonim Şirketi v. Turkey*, ECtHR 13 February 2018, 12261/06.

[55] *Savda v. Turkey*, ECtHR 12 June 2012, 42730/05.

[56] *M.S.S. v. Belgium and Greece*, ECtHR (GC) 21 January 2011, 30696/09, para. 253.

[57] E.g. *X and Y v. the Netherlands*, ECtHR 26 March 1985, 8970/80, para. 27; *Bărbulescu v. Romania*, ECtHR (GC) 5 September 2017, 61496/08, para. 115.

courts to interpret the Convention in a certain way[58] to the requirement of con-ducting a certain (different) policy[59].[60]

The wide variety of substantive positive obligations and their strong contingency makes it difficult to provide any further classification or general discussion.[61] All the same, it is possible to point out one important effect of the recognition of substantive positive obligations, which is a certain blurring of the distinction between political and civil rights (which traditionally require that the government abstains from interferences) and social and economic rights (which mainly ask for positive State action).[62] The Court has consciously accepted this 'socialising' conse-quence of the positive obligations doctrine in its judgment in the *Airey* case.[63] This case concerned the question of whether the State would be obliged to provide subsidised legal aid if that would be necessary to enable an individual to have effective access to court. The respondent State had objected to the recognition of any obligations in this field, also in view of the mainly economic nature of the resulting 'right to subsidised legal aid'. The Court found that the civil/political or socio-economic nature of an obligation could not have any significant bearing for its recognition under the Convention:

> The Government's principal argument rests on what they see as the consequence of the Commission's opinion, namely that, in all cases concerning the determination of a 'civil right', the State would have to provide free legal aid ... [I]n their submission, the Convention should not be interpreted so as to achieve social and economic developments in a Contracting State; such developments can only be progressive.
>
> The Court is aware that the further realisation of social and economic rights is largely dependent on the situation – notably financial – reigning in the State in question. On the other hand, the Convention must be interpreted in the light of present-day conditions ... and it is designed to safeguard the individual in a real and practical way as regards those areas with which it deals ... Whilst the Convention sets forth what are essentially civil and political rights, many of them have implications of a social or economic nature. The Court therefore considers, like the Commission, that the mere fact that an interpretation of the Convention may extend into the sphere of social and economic rights should not be a

---

[58] E.g. *Pla and Puncernau v. Andorra*, ECtHR 13 July 2004, 69498/01; *Khurshid Mustafa and Tarzibachi v. Sweden*, ECtHR 16 December 2008, 23883/06.

[59] Cf. *Hatton and Others v. the United Kingdom*, ECtHR (GC) 8 July 2003, 6022/97.

[60] Sometimes, however, obligations to regulate are classified as procedural rather than substantive obligations; the distinction between the two is not clear-cut. See e.g. Lavrysen, *supra* n. 14, at 53.

[61] The Court itself has expressly recognised this; see e.g. *Hämäläinen v. Finland*, ECtHR (GC) 16 July 2014, 37359/09, para. 66: '[H]aving regard to the diversity of the practices followed and the situations obtaining in the Contracting States, the notion's requirements will vary considerably from case to case.'

[62] See also Section 5.1.   [63] *Airey v. Ireland*, ECtHR 9 October 1979, 6289/73.

decisive factor against such an interpretation; there is no water-tight division separating that sphere from the field covered by the Convention.[64]

In *Airey*, this led the Court to accept that the State must provide legal assistance for impecunious applicants. Similarly, in other cases, the Court has accepted obligations to prevent or remedy concrete cases of severe pollution and environmental damage[65] or to provide minimum subsistence[66].[67] Nevertheless, although some substantive obligations may be far-reaching and their recognition has resulted in the inclusion of many socio-economic rights in the Convention, the Court's approach is often cautious and it certainly has accepted some limitations.[68] In *Sentges*, for example, the Court stressed that in previous judgments, it had held

> that Article 8 may impose such positive obligations on a State where there is a direct
> and immediate link between the measures sought by an applicant and the latter's private
> life ... However, Article 8 does not apply to situations concerning interpersonal relations of
> such broad and indeterminate scope that there can be no conceivable link between the
> measures the State is urged to take and an individual's private life ... Article 8 cannot be
> considered applicable each time an individual's everyday life is disrupted, but only in the
> exceptional cases where the State's failure to adopt measures interferes with that
> individual's right to personal development and his or her right to establish and maintain
> relations with other human beings and the outside world. It is incumbent on the
> individual concerned to demonstrate the existence of a special link between the situation
> complained of and the particular needs of his or her private life.[69]

This meant that no positive obligation could be imposed on the respondent State to provide the applicant with a robotic arm, which he arguably needed to lead an autonomous life in dignity.[70] In the same vein, the Court has held that the Convention does not imply a general right to free medical care, nor does it imply any

---

[64] *Ibid.*, para. 26. See also e.g. *Sidabras and Džiautas v. Lithuania*, ECtHR 27 July 2004, 55480/00 and 59330/00, para. 47; *Stec v. the United Kingdom*, ECtHR (GC) 6 July 2005 (dec.), 65731/01 and 65900/01; *Demir and Baykara v. Turkey*, ECtHR (GC) 12 November 2008, 34503/97, para. 84.

[65] E.g. *Mileva and Others v. Bulgaria*, ECtHR 25 November 2010, 43449/02 and 21475/04, paras. 98–102.

[66] *M.S.S. v. Belgium and Greece*, ECtHR (GC) 21 January 2011, 30696/09, paras. 253 et seq.

[67] See for other examples A.E.M. Leijten, 'Defining the Scope of Economic and Social Guarantees in the Case Law of the ECtHR' in E. Brems and J.H. Gerards (eds.), *Shaping Rights in the ECHR: The Role of the European Court of Human Rights in Determining the Scope of Human Rights* (Cambridge University Press, 2014), pp. 109–36.

[68] Cf. also Xenos, *supra* n. 26, at 84; Lavrysen, *supra* n. 14, at 137 (referring to the 'proximity' test); Beijer, *supra* n. 2, at 67.

[69] *Sentges v. the Netherlands*, ECtHR 8 July 2003 (dec.), 27677/02.

[70] See similarly e.g. also *Botta v. Italy*, ECtHR 24 February 1998, 21439/93; *Marzari v. Italy*, ECtHR 4 May 1999 (dec.), 36448/97; *Pentiacova and Others v. Moldova*, ECtHR 4 January 2005 (dec.), 14462/03; *Mółka v. Poland*, ECtHR 11 April 2006 (dec.), 56550/00; *Farcaş v. Romania*, ECtHR 14 September 2010 (dec.), 32596/04.

positive obligations to general preventive health care.[71] Similarly, it has never imposed general positive obligations to provide a certain level of social security or social benefits. The only situation in which such obligations could arise has been defined in *Budina* as that 'where an applicant, in circumstances wholly dependent on State support, found herself faced with official indifference when in a situation of serious deprivation or want incompatible with human dignity'.[72] Moreover, even though the applicant in *Budina* clearly found herself in a destitute situation, this was not enough for the Court to conclude that there was a positive obligation for the State to provide her with additional means of subsistence:

> Turning to the facts of the present application, the Court notes that the applicant's income within the period in question was not high in absolute terms. However, the applicant has failed to substantiate her allegation that the lack of funds translated itself into concrete suffering. On the contrary, in her observations the applicant explained that in 2008 her pension was enough for flat maintenance, food, and hygiene items, but was not enough for clothes, non-food goods, sanitary and cultural services, health and sanatorium treatment. Of these latter items, it appears that the applicant was in fact eligible for free medical treatment ... Indeed there is no indication in the materials before the Court that the level of pension and social benefits available to the applicant have been insufficient to protect her from damage to her physical or mental health or from a situation of degradation incompatible with human dignity ... Therefore even though the applicant's situation was difficult, especially from 2004 to 2007, the Court is not persuaded that in the circumstances of the present case the high threshold of Article 3 has been met.[73]

Also in relation to protection of the environment, the Court has qualified in *Ivan Atanasov* that positive obligations cannot arise 'every time environmental deterioration occurs: no right to nature preservation is included as such among the rights and freedoms guaranteed by the Convention or its Protocols'.[74] The Court further emphasised in this case that a State's obligations under Article 8 come into play only if there is a direct and immediate link between the impugned situation and the applicant's home or private or family life, and if a minimum level of severity has been attained.[75]

Accordingly, even if the positive obligations doctrine has blurred the dividing line between socio-economic rights and civil and political rights, it is evident that the

---

[71] *Pentiacova and Others v. Moldova*, ECtHR 4 January 2005 (dec.), 14462/03; *Shelley v. the United Kingdom*, ECtHR 4 January 2008 (dec.), 23800/06. See also *Hristozov and Others v. Bulgaria*, ECtHR 13 November 2012, 47039/11 and 358/12.

[72] *Budina v. Russia*, ECtHR 18 June 2009 (dec.), 45603/05.

[73] *Ibid.* So far, the existence of such an extreme situation of deprivation has only been recognised in *M.S.S. v. Belgium and Greece*, ECtHR (GC) 21 January 2011, 30696/09, paras. 253 et seq. and *Nencheva and Others v. Bulgaria*, ECtHR 18 June 2013, 48609/06.

[74] E.g. *Ivan Atanasov v. Bulgaria*, ECtHR 2 December 2010, 12853/03, para. 66.   [75] *Ibid.*, para. 75.

Court will not lightly accept the existence of positive obligations in a purely socio-economic rights context.[76]

5.3.2 Procedural Positive Obligations

Originally, procedural positive obligations have been defined mainly in the case law related to the right to life of Article 2 ECHR and the prohibition of torture and inhuman and degrading treatment of Article 3 ECHR.[77] If someone has died or suffered from inhuman treatment and it is likely that the State can be held responsible for this, the State is required to guarantee some form of effective official investigation.[78] Obligations accepted in this regard include that the investigation must be conducted *ex officio*, which means that the State cannot wait until an official request or complaint is lodged but has to act of its own accord; the investigation must be completely independent; it must be adequate in the sense that it must be capable of leading to the identification and punishment of those responsible; reasonable steps must be available to the authorities to secure the evidence concerning the incident; and the next-of-kin must be able to participate effectively.[79] Moreover, an effective remedy must be provided to the victim or his family to obtain redress[80] and, in some cases, criminal prosecution of those responsible is necessary.[81] In *Šilih*, the Court even held that the procedural obligations of Article 2 can be seen as an independent and autonomous set of obligations arising from the Convention: 'Although it is triggered by the acts concerning the substantive aspects

---

[76] In addition, the Court in these cases often leaves a wide margin of appreciation to the States, which means they have much leeway to determine how and to what degree they can meet positive obligations. On this, see further Section 7.4.3 and cf. A.E.M. Leijten, 'From *Stec* to *Valkov*: Possessions and Margins in the Social Security Case Law of the European Court of Human Rights', *Human Rights Law Review*, 13 (2013), 309–49.

[77] For further classification and more detail, see e.g. Lavrysen, *supra* n. 14, at 57 et seq.

[78] See e.g. *McCann v. the United Kingdom*, ECtHR (GC) 27 September 1995, 18984/91, para. 161; see further e.g. A.R. Mowbray, 'Duties of Investigation under the European Convention on Human Rights', 51 *International and Comparative Law Quarterly* 437 (2002) and E. Brems, 'Procedural Protection: An Examination of Procedural Safeguards Read into Substantive Convention Rights' in E. Brems and J.H. Gerards (eds.), *Shaping Rights in the ECHR: The Role of the European Court of Human Rights in Determining the Scope of Human Rights* (Cambridge University Press, 2014), pp. 137–61.

[79] E.g. *Anguelova v. Bulgaria*, ECtHR 13 June 2002, 38361/97, para. 138–9; *Nachova v. Bulgaria*, ECtHR (GC) 6 July 2005, 43577/98 and 43579/98, para. 111; *Ramsahai v. the Netherlands*, ECtHR (GC) 15 May 2007, 52391/99, paras. 326 et seq.; *Nachova v. Bulgaria*, ECtHR (GC) 6 July 2005, 43577/98 and 43579/98, para. 113.

[80] E.g. *Calvelli and Ciglio v. Italy*, ECtHR (GC) 17 February 2002, 32967/96, para. 51.

[81] E.g. *Öneryildiz v. Turkey*, ECtHR (GC) 30 November 2004, 48939/99, para. 93 and *Budayeva and Others v. Russia*, ECtHR 20 March 2008, 15339/02, para. 142. This is usually different for cases where a death is not caused intentionally, for example because it is the result of medical negligence or medical errors; see e.g. *Gray v. Germany*, ECtHR 22 May 2014, 49278/09, para. 81.

of Article 2 it can give rise to a finding of a separate and independent "interference" … In this sense it can be considered to be a detachable obligation arising out of Article 2 capable of binding the State.'[82] Consequently, even if the Court does not have sufficient information to allow it to conclude that the State has respected its substantive obligations under the Convention (such as the obligation to prevent someone from harm), it can still find a violation of the Convention if it turns out that the State has not done enough to investigate a suspicious case of death or ill-treatment.[83] The requirements the Court sets for the quality of national procedures thereby are very similar to the fair trial rights protected by Article 6 ECHR. As the Court has held in *Tunç*, however, the safeguards provided are not necessarily to be assessed in the same manner.[84] In particular, the Court emphasised that the procedural positive obligations of Article 2 call for a concrete examination of the independence of the investigation in its entirety, rather than an abstract assessment:[85]

> In this regard, the Court considers it appropriate to specify that compliance with the procedural requirement of Article 2 is assessed on the basis of several essential parameters: the adequacy of the investigative measures, the promptness of the investigation, the involvement of the deceased person's family and the independence of the investigation. These elements are inter-related and each of them, taken separately, does not amount to an end in itself … They are criteria which, taken jointly, enable the degree of effectiveness of the investigation to be assessed. It is in relation to this purpose of an effective investigation that any issues … must be assessed.[86]

The Court's review of the compliance with the procedural positive obligations of investigation will thus be an overall assessment, where slight shortcomings regarding one particular obligation can be compensated for and remedied in other stages of the domestic proceedings.

In addition to the many procedural obligations *ex post*, the Court has recognised several procedural positive obligations of an *ex ante* nature.[87] In the particular context of dangerous activities, the Court has placed special emphasis on regulations geared to the particular features of the activity in question. According to its judgment in *Kolyadenko*, such regulations

---

[82] *Šilih v. Slovenia*, ECtHR (GC) 9 April 2009, 71463/01, para. 159.

[83] See e.g. *Mehdiyev v. Azerbaijan*, ECtHR 18 June 2015, 59075/09.

[84] *Mustafa Tunç and Fecire Tunç v. Turkey*, ECtHR (GC) 14 April 2014, 24014/05, para. 220.

[85] *Ibid.*, para. 222.

[86] *Ibid.*, para. 225. See similarly, in comparison to the procedural requirements of Articles 5 and 6 ECHR, in *I.R. and G.T. v. the United Kingdom*, ECtHR 28 January 2014 (dec.), 14876/12 and 63339/12, para. 61.

[87] Cf. e.g. *Öneryildiz v. Turkey*, ECtHR (GC) 30 November 2004, 48939/99, para. 90; *Budayeva and Others v. Russia*, ECtHR 20 March 2008, 15339/02, paras. 147 et seq.

must govern the licensing, setting up, operation, security and supervision of the activity and must make it compulsory for all those concerned to take practical measures to ensure the effective protection of citizens whose lives might be endangered by the inherent risks. Among these preventive measures particular emphasis should be placed on the public's right to information, as established in the case law of the Convention institutions. The relevant regulations must also provide for appropriate procedures, taking into account the technical aspects of the activity in question, for identifying shortcomings in the processes concerned and any errors committed by those responsible at different levels.[88]

Similarly, in the context of prevention of harm done by third parties, such as ill-treatment, murder, rape or child abuse, the Court has pointed out that 'effective measures of deterrence against grave acts … can only be achieved by the existence of effective criminal-law provisions backed up by law enforcement machinery'.[89] The precise form of such regulations and procedures will depend on the particular nature of the risk for a Convention violation.[90] In relation to child sexual abuse, for example, the Court has held that existence of useful detection and reporting mechanisms are fundamental to the effective implementation of the relevant criminal laws.[91] Other examples are cases where an interference with a Convention right is possibly related to racist or otherwise discriminatory motives. In such cases, the Court has identified a particular duty for the States to take all reasonable procedural steps to unmask such a motive and to establish whether or not hatred or prejudice may have played a role in the events,[92] and they should provide penalty-enhancing provisions or separate criminalisation of discriminatory violence.[93]

Such *ex ante* and *ex post* procedural positive obligations have also been accepted in relation to other Convention provisions.[94] For example, the Court has accepted obligations of a procedural nature under Article 8 ECHR in connection to, inter alia, custody and access rights,[95] damage to one's reputation[96] and access to one's personal data;[97] under Article 9 in relation to employment discrimination based

---

[88] *Kolyadenko and Others v. Russia*, ECtHR 28 February 2012, 17423/05, paras. 158–9.

[89] E.g. *X and Y v. the Netherlands*, ECtHR 26 March 1985, 8978/80, para. 27; *O'Keeffe v. Ireland*, ECtHR (GC) 28 January 2014, 35810/09, para. 148.

[90] See e.g. in relation to domestic violence, *Opuz v. Turkey*, ECtHR 9 June 2009, 33401/02; in relation to human trafficking, *Rantsev v. Cyprus and Turkey*, ECtHR 7 January 2010, 25965/04; in relation to violations of integrity, *Söderman v. Sweden*, ECtHR (GC) 12 November 2013, 5786/08.

[91] E.g. *Juppala v. Sweden*, ECtHR 2 December 2008, 18620/03, para. 42.

[92] *Nachova and Others v. Bulgaria*, ECtHR (GC) 6 July 2005, 43577/98 and 43579/98, para. 160; see also e.g. *Identoba and Others v. Georgia*, ECtHR 12 May 2015, 73235/12, para. 67.

[93] E.g. *Yotova v. Bulgaria*, ECtHR 23 October 2012, 43606/04, paras. 109–10.

[94] For an overview, see e.g. Brems, *supra* n. 78.

[95] E.g. *Venema v. the Netherlands*, ECtHR 17 December 2002, 35731/97, paras. 91 et seq.

[96] E.g. *Özpinar v. Turkey*, ECtHR 19 October 2010, 20999/04, paras. 77–9; *Mitkus v. Latvia*, ECtHR 2 October 2012, 7259/03.

[97] E.g. *Joanna Szulc v. Poland*, ECtHR 13 November 2012, 43932/08.

on political conviction or religion,[98] or protection against religious violence;[99] under Article 10 in relation to defamation cases;[100] under Article 14 in relation to various forms of discriminatory treatment and discriminatory violence;[101] under Article 1 of Protocol No. 1 in relation to deprivation of property;[102] and under Article 3 of Protocol No. 1 as regards limitations of the right to vote.[103]

In addition to this, the Court has accepted a number of procedural obligations in cases where a State has voluntarily decided to provide a higher level of protection to Convention rights than is strictly required by the Court's case law.[104] The Court considered in *A., B. and C. v. Ireland*, for instance, that there was no obligation under the Convention to provide a right to abortion, and the States enjoy a wide discretion in defining the circumstances in which an abortion will be permitted.[105] Nevertheless, once that decision is taken, the Court requires that 'the legal framework devised for this purpose should be shaped in a coherent manner which allows the different legitimate interests involved to be taken into account adequately and in accordance with the obligations deriving from the Convention'.[106] In particular, such a regime should provide an accessible and effective procedure by which a pregnant woman could establish whether she qualified for a lawful abortion.[107] Accordingly, as soon as a right is voluntarily provided to individuals which is somehow connected to a Convention right, the obligation arises to guarantee the effective exercise of such rights through the creation of a suitable legal framework surrounded by adequate procedural safeguards.

5.3.3   Other Typologies of Positive Obligations

Next to the distinction between procedural and substantive positive obligations, some other classifications of positive obligations have been presented in scholarly literature.[108] For example, Lavrysen has distinguished between *vertical positive obligations*, which directly govern the relation between an individual and the State,

---

[98] E.g. *Redfearn v. the United Kingdom*, ECtHR 6 November 2012, 47335/06; *Eweida and Others v. the United Kingdom*, ECtHR 15 January 2013, 48420/10.

[99] E.g. *Begheluri and Others v. Georgia*, ECtHR 7 October 2014, 28490/02, para. 165.

[100] E.g. *Lombardi Vallauri v. Italy*, ECtHR 20 October 2009, 39128/05, paras. 52-5; *Etxeberria and Others v. Spain*, ECtHR 30 June 2009, 35579/03.

[101] E.g. *Horváth and Kiss v. Hungary*, ECtHR 29 January 2013, 11146/11.

[102] E.g. *Zagrebačka banka d.d. v. Croatia*, ECtHR 12 December 2013, 39544/05.

[103] E.g. *Grosaru v. Romania*, ECtHR 2 March 2010, 78039/01, para. 47.

[104] This is the 'dependency' or 'in for a penny, in for a pound' approach, which was discussed in Section 3.5.3.

[105] *A., B. and C. v. Ireland*, ECtHR (GC) 16 December 2010, 25579/05, para. 249.

[106] *Ibid.*, para. 249.   [107] *Ibid.*, para. 267.

[108] See e.g. C. Dröge, *Positive Verpflichtungen der Staaten in der Europäischen Menschenrechtskonvention* [Positive Obligations of the States in the European Convention on Human Rights] (Berlin: Springer, 2003); Xenos, *supra* n. 26; Lavrysen, *supra* n. 14, at 45 et seq.; Beijer, *supra* n. 2, at 55 et seq.

and *horizontal positive obligations*, which concern the action the State should take to secure the Convention rights in the 'horizontal' relationship between private parties.[109] Vertical obligations are thereby closely related to negative obligations, because they are often directly linked to the State's obligation to refrain from interfering with the exercise of fundamental rights. One may think here, for example, of the positive obligation to provide humane detention conditions,[110] which is closely connected to the prohibition of inhuman or degrading treatment,[111] or the obligation to recognise the legal status of persons who have undergone gender transformation,[112] which is closely connected to the right to respect for one's private and family life.[113] By contrast, the cases of *Osman* or *X and Y v. the Netherlands*, discussed in Section 5.2, concerned obligations for the States to protect the right to life and the integrity of the person, not against the State, but against interferences by third parties.[114] This distinction between horizontal and vertical positive obligations is further explored in Chapter 6, which is concerned with the horizontal and vertical effect of the Convention more generally.

A second typology has been proposed by Van Kempen.[115] He has distinguished between categories of *dependent, supporting, intrinsic* and *autonomous positive obligations*. These categories can be placed on a sliding scale, ranging from obligations which are very closely related to the traditional type of negative obligations following from the Convention, to obligations which do have a more independent or autonomous nature, and which are further removed from the original negative obligations inherent in the Convention. Dependent positive obligations in this typology are those obligations which come into being because a State has not complied with its negative obligations to respect fundamental rights. For example, if the State decides to detain an individual, it impinges on his right to liberty protected by Article 5 of the Convention, which is a 'negative' interference. Certain positive obligations can be accepted to directly follow from such deprivation of liberty, such as the obligation to detain persons in conditions respecting their human dignity and create facilities necessary to guarantee their human rights.[116] Examples are obligations to ensure medical care,[117] the possibility for a prisoner to

---

[109] See in particular Lavrysen, *supra* n. 14, at 78 et seq.

[110] See e.g. *Kudła v. Poland*, ECtHR (GC) 26 October 2000, 30210/96, para. 94; *Muršić v. Croatia*, ECtHR (GC) 20 October 2016, 7334/13, para. 99.

[111] Lavrysen, *supra* n. 14, at 79.

[112] E.g. *Christine Goodwin v. the United Kingdom*, ECtHR (GC) 11 July 2002, 28957/95, para. 93.

[113] Lavrysen, *supra* n. 14, at 103.   [114] For more examples, see Lavrysen, *supra* n. 14, at 82 et seq.

[115] P.H. van Kempen, *Repressie Door Mensenrechten* [Repression by Human Rights], inaugural lecture, Radboud University Nijmegen 2008, 16–18.

[116] *Kudła v. Poland*, ECtHR (GC) 26 October 2000, 30210/96, para. 94; *Muršić v. Croatia*, ECtHR (GC) 20 October 2016, 7334/13, para. 99.

[117] E.g. *Logvinenko v. Ukraine*, ECtHR 14 October 2010, 13448/07, paras. 66 et seq.

have contact with family members[118] or the facilities needed for a detainee to meet a solicitor.[119] Similarly, if the State interferes with its negative obligation to respect individuals' private lives by assembling and storing information about their health, this may incur a dependent positive obligation to guarantee the confidentiality of and access to such information.[120] The second category of obligations – supporting positive obligations – directly contributes to the State's respect for negative obligations, but they are less clearly connected to them than are dependent positive obligations. The State can be obliged, for example, to ensure that police officers and military personnel are trained well in order to prevent unnecessary or disproportionate interferences with the right to life.

Third, Van Kempen has distinguished intrinsic positive obligations in relation to, for example, the right to education. Since such a right would be meaningless if no educational facilities exist, certain positive obligations may be recognised to provide a minimal educational framework, as the Court has already recognised in the *Belgian Linguistics* case.[121] Similarly, it could be stated that the right to free elections can only be effectively exercised if some kind of electoral system is in place, which inherently or intrinsically implies a positive obligation to ensure that such a system is created.

Finally, autonomous positive obligations are positive obligations which are still somehow connected to negative obligations and which can help to ensure the effective enjoyment thereof, yet can be defined entirely autonomously or independently from such negative obligations. Examples may be the requirement for the States to conduct a policy to minimise the damage resulting from natural disasters,[122] or the obligation to actively combat human trafficking.[123] Such positive obligations hardly correspond to negative obligations of the States. After all, States cannot easily be held accountable for the damage done by natural disasters, while in the case of human trafficking, usually it is not the State but third parties who cause the interference with fundamental rights. Nevertheless, it is clear that such positive obligations are connected to the effective exercise and enjoyment of the rights and freedoms protected in the Convention.

According to Van Kempen, there is a difference between these types of obligations as regards the degree to which it is self-evident that they are recognised to effectively secure the Convention rights. For autonomous positive obligations, stronger support is needed (for instance, by reference to the general principles of

---

[118] E.g. *Petrov v. Bulgaria*, ECtHR 22 May 2008, 15197/02, 51.
[119] E.g. *Gagiu v. Romania*, ECtHR 24 February 2009, 63258/00.
[120] E.g. *I. v. Finland*, ECtHR 17 July 2008, 20511/03.
[121] See the *Belgian Linguistics* case, ECtHR 23 July 1968, 1474/62.
[122] E.g. *Budayeva and Others v. Russia*, ECtHR 20 March 2008, 15339/02.
[123] E.g. *Rantsev v. Cyprus and Russia*, ECtHR 7 January 2010, 25965/04.

the Convention) than for dependent positive obligations. The Court itself does not in this way distinguish between the obligations, however, which means that this typology is mainly useful for analytical purposes.

5.4   The Relation Between Negative and Positive Obligations

There are significant differences between negative and positive obligations. Whereas negative obligations logically and directly follow from the text of the Convention, positive obligations are only implied therein.[124] Generally, moreover, positive obligations refer to State action, whereas negative obligations require States to abstain from interfering.[125] The Court further relies on different methods to define positive obligations, such as its fair balance test, the reasonable knowledge and means test, or the effectiveness-based test. Furthermore, and in particular, there is an important difference between positive and negative obligations as regards absolute rights. As was explained in Section 1.5, interferences with such rights, such as the prohibition of torture, can never be justified. However, positive obligations relating to such rights seem to be less absolutely defined, and they seem to allow more room for restriction. An example can be seen in relation to Article 2 ECHR. This is not an absolute provision in the sense that no exceptions are permitted whatsoever.[126] The second paragraph of Article 2 allows for very strictly circumscribed exceptions, such as the use of lethal violence in absolutely necessary self-defence. However, the Court has accepted that the provision is otherwise absolute: if none of the exceptions of the second paragraph applies, there is no possibility of justification of State acts which lead to someone's death.[127] This might cause some difficulties in practice, however, since it seems that the second paragraph does not cover all conceivable and reasonable situations of exception. If a case arises in which the Court finds that some lenience is in place, it therefore seems that it makes an effort to frame the case in terms of positive obligations rather than negative obligations, with the consequence that some balancing of interests is possible and – indirectly – an exception can be carved out.

An example of this approach can be found in the *Watts* case.[128] Mrs Watts lived in a care home for elderly people which was about to be renovated. For that reason, all residents were to be moved to alternative housing. The family was concerned about the consequences for Mrs Watts, who had limited life expectancy and for whom it clearly would be best to remain in her current home. The claim before the Court was that the risk inherent in the transfer to a new residential care home

---

[124] Beijer, *supra* n. 2, at 42–4.   [125] Beijer, *supra* n. 2, at 44.   [126] See also Section 1.5.3.
[127] *Ibid.*   [128] *Watts v. the United Kingdom*, ECtHR 4 May 2010 (dec.), 53586/09.

constituted a violation of her right to life. Although it might have been possible to frame this complaint as a direct interference with the right to life, which occasionally is also held to apply in life-threatening situations,[129] the Court decided to examine it on the basis of the State's positive obligations.[130] Having made a detailed assessment of all the circumstances of the case, and having conducted an overall reasonableness review, it concluded that Article 2 was not violated by the transfer: '[H]aving regard to the operational choices which must be made by local authorities in their provision of residential care to the elderly and the careful planning and the steps which have been undertaken to minimise any risk to the applicant's life, the Court considers that the authorities have met their positive obligations under Article 2.'[131] Evidently, this was a type of conclusion the Court could not have reached if it had chosen to treat this case as one about negative obligations.

The Court also struggled with the absolute nature of Article 2, and has found positive obligations to be the answer in some end-of-life cases. As the Court held in *Pretty*, Article 2 cannot be seen to encompass a right to die. In *Lambert*, however, the partner of Vincent Lambert, supported by a medical team, considered it to be in line with Lambert's wishes and interests that the life-sustaining treatment given to him would be ended.[132] This case raised a difficult debate on whether such a decision would entail actively putting an end to Vincent Lambert's life (which would conflict with the State's negative obligations) or whether not continuing to provide him with nutrition and hydration in fact constituted an inaction that should be examined from the perspective of positive obligations. The Court opted for the latter approach:

> The Court notes that both the applicants and the Government make a distinction between the intentional taking of life and 'therapeutic abstention' ... and stresses the importance of that distinction. In the context of the French legislation, which prohibits the intentional taking of life and permits life-sustaining treatment to be withdrawn or withheld only in certain specific circumstances, the Court considers that the present case does not involve the State's negative obligations under Article 2, and will examine the applicants' complaints solely from the standpoint of the State's positive obligations.[133]

This approach allowed the Court to embark on a detailed assessment to see whether there were sufficient procedural guarantees surrounding the decision of withdrawal of the life-sustaining treatment, whether Lambert's wishes and those of persons close to him were respected, and, overall, whether a fair decision was taken in the

---

[129] See e.g. *Colak and Tsakiridis v. Germany*, ECtHR 5 March 2009, 77144/01 and 35493/05, para. 29.
[130] *Watts*, para. 85.   [131] *Ibid.*, para. 92.
[132] *Lambert and Others v. France*, ECtHR (GC) 5 June 2015, 46043/14.   [133] *Ibid.*, para. 124.

case.[134] The Court thereby adopted a type of reasonableness review that it could not have applied had it qualified this case as one concerning negative obligations.

These two cases illustrate that the distinction between the two types of obligations continues to be important. Yet, even so, they also illustrate that the line between the two types of obligation is a very fine one.[135] Indeed, the Court has expressly recognised this, as it did, for example, in these terms in *Keegan*: 'the boundaries between the State's positive and negative obligations under this provision do not lend themselves to precise definition.'[136]

In some cases, positive and negative obligations may even completely coincide. An example can be seen in *Demir and Baykara*, where the question arose of whether the Turkish refusal to recognise the legal personality of a trade union established by civil servants could be seen as an interference with its negative obligations under Article 11 ECHR, or whether it had to be regarded as a non-compliance with the positive obligation to legally recognise this type of trade union.[137] The Court indicated that it would not only be difficult, but also of little relevance to try to strictly distinguish between these obligations in this type of case:

> [The Court] considers that the present case can be analysed either as an interference with Article 11 or as a failure by the State to comply with its positive obligation to secure the applicants' rights under this provision. In the particular circumstances of the present case, the Court considers that both approaches are possible given the mixture of action and inaction on the part of the authorities with which it is confronted. Accordingly, it will proceed on the basis that this part of the case should be analysed from the standpoint of whether there was an interference with the applicants' rights but it will also have regard to the State's positive obligations in so doing.

In *Ališić*, the Court even expressly held that there was no need for it to differentiate between the two types of obligations:

> In the present case, the applicants complained of their inability to withdraw their savings from their accounts with the banks in question. Their deposits had become unavailable owing to such factors as the lack of funds in the relevant banks, the imposition by law of a freezing of the accounts and the failure by national authorities to take measures with a view to enabling deposit holders in the applicants' situation to dispose of their savings. This state of affairs may well be examined in terms of an interference with the effective exercise of the right protected by Article 1 of Protocol No. 1 or in terms of a failure to secure the exercise of that right . . . Having regard to the particular circumstances of the present case, the Court considers it unnecessary to categorise its examination of the case strictly as being

---

[134] *Ibid.*, paras. 143 et seq.   [135] See also Beijer, *supra* n. 2, at 91.
[136] *Keegan v. the United Kingdom*, ECtHR 26 May 1994, 16969/90, para. 49.
[137] *Demir and Baykara v. Turkey*, ECtHR (GC) 12 November 2008, 34503/97.

under the head of positive or negative obligations of the respondent States. The Court will determine whether the conduct of the respondent States – regardless of whether that conduct may be characterised as an interference or as a failure to act, or a combination of both – was justifiable in view of the principles of lawfulness, legitimate aim and 'fair balance'.[138]

Indeed, in many cases, State inaction can be qualified just as easily as a (continuing) interference with a fundamental right and as non-compliance with a positive obligation.[139] Consequently, even if the positive obligations doctrine has been of great importance for the development of the Convention and it has had great impact on the Convention's scope and the nature of the rights and obligations recognised, nowadays there is much pertinence to the Court's own finding that there are no clear boundaries between the two types of obligations and that the applicable principles are roughly similar.[140] It often seems an issue of grown conventions that in some cases, a positive obligations approach is used, whereas other cases are categorised as negative obligations cases. Indeed, often the issue is what would be the most relevant line of precedent rather than whether, judging the facts, the case can best be qualified as one about either positive or negative obligations.[141]

---

[138] *Ališić and Others v. Bosnia and Herzegovina, Croatia, Serbia, Slovenia and the former Yugoslav Republic of Macedonia*, ECtHR (GC) 16 July 2014, 60642/08, para. 102; see similarly e.g. *Lukats v. Romania*, ECtHR 5 April 2016, 24199/07, para. 49. In other cases, the Court may not very clearly distinguish between the two different types of obligations either, for example by first quoting the relevant general principles for positive obligations and ruling that they will apply to the case, and then finding that the case concerns an interference with a Convention right (which implies that the perspective is one of negative obligations); see e.g. *A.-M.V. v. Finland*, ECtHR 23 March 2017, 53251/13, paras. 70–7. This approach is not altogether common, however; in many judgments, the Court still expressly decides whether it will treat the case as one about negative or about positive obligations; see, for example, *Hämäläinen v. Finland*, ECtHR (GC) 16 July 2014, 37359/09, paras. 63–4.

[139] Compare, for example, the approach taken in *Steel and Morris v. the United Kingdom*, ECtHR 15 February 2005, 68416/01 with *Airey v. Ireland*, ECtHR 9 October 1979, 6289/73, and see the difference in approach of the majority and the dissenting judge Martens in *Cossey v. the United Kingdom*, ECtHR 27 September 1990, 10843/84.

[140] In some literature, it therefore has been submitted that it would be better to remove the strict distinction and apply a different approach instead; see in particular Gerards and Senden, *supra* n. 14; Lavrysen, *supra* n. 14, at 305 et seq.

[141] See e.g. *McDonald v. the United Kingdom*, ECtHR 20 May 2014, 4241/12, para. 48, where, under the heading 'Positive obligation or interference with a right?' the Court was mainly looking for the 'appropriate comparator' case in its own body of case law.

6 Vertical and Horizontal Effect

6.1 Introduction

The Convention was originally designed to protect individuals, groups of individuals, NGOs and private legal entities from interferences with their fundamental rights by the States. The States wield sovereign power and they may affect individuals' lives in many different ways: by means of legislation and administrative decisions, by judgments in individual cases, by police or military intervention, and so on. After the two world wars had proved that States can misuse this power in terrible ways, and thereby deeply harm individuals' dignity, autonomy and freedom, one of the main objectives of the Convention was to restrain States' exercise of power by creating a collective framework of enforcement, and supranational supervision by an independent court. This explains why so many negative obligations have been laid down in the Convention and why restrictions of rights are only allowed if they meet certain conditions.

The Convention is thus mainly intended to govern so-called 'vertical' relations, that is, relations in which the national governments wield power over individuals and private legal entities. In this highly imbalanced relationship, where powers are used top-down, the Convention rights protect the individual against intrusive and arbitrary legislation and decisions. It has long been thought that a similar power imbalance does not exist between individuals *inter se* or between individuals and private legal entities. In these so-called 'horizontal' relations, the parties were considered more or less equal and they were deemed free to determine their own relationships. To the extent that regulation was needed, horizontal relations were governed by private law, such as the law of obligations and of negligence, and partly by criminal law, such as by legislation on ill-treatment or burglary. To the extent that individual interests were affected that could be regarded as fundamental rights, such as privacy interests or property rights, these were considered to be sufficiently covered by these provisions of private and criminal law. In light of the presumed power balance between private parties, there did not seem to be any further need for protection of fundamental rights.

Over time, however, it has become increasingly clear that power imbalances also exist in private law relationships. The relationship between an employer and an employee is an obvious example, especially if the employer is a large company employing hundreds or thousands of workers. Large companies also may wield significant power in other spheres, for example by collecting and processing personal data of clients or by creating and using algorithms to select what information internet users receive. Over time, it has come to be acknowledged that individuals, groups, organisations and companies may pose just as great a risk to the effective enjoyment of fundamental rights as public bodies and government agents. Terrorist attacks, murder, assault and domestic violence have come to be regarded as violating fundamental rights, such as the right to life and the right to respect for one's bodily and mental integrity. It has also come to be recognised that associations and political parties may violate the prohibition of discrimination if they exclude certain groups or persons as members or if they incite to hatred, and news media are understood to interfere with reputation and privacy rights if they publish ugly articles on the rich and famous. Indeed, nowadays, many horizontal issues are framed in terms of fundamental rights.

The Convention itself has not kept pace with these developments and changing perspectives. Its text has never been amended to reflect the increasing need for protection of fundamental rights against acts and omissions of private parties. It is still not possible to lodge individual applications at the Court to complain about an interference with one's Convention rights caused by an employer, a neighbour, a company, a religious organisation, an editor or any other individual or private entity.[1] Article 34 only allows individual applications to be lodged against one of the High Contracting Parties. In addition, even if there are some exceptions to this rule, the Court has not held that private entities or individuals have obligations under the Convention to protect and respect other persons' fundamental rights.[2]

Nevertheless, over time, the Court has found various ways to extend the protection offered by the Convention rights to horizontal relations. This chapter therefore focuses on the scope of protection of the Convention in vertical and horizontal relations. First, in Section 6.2, the direct Convention responsibilities of the States are

---

[1] See e.g. *Reynbakh v. Russia*, ECtHR 20 September 2005, 23405/03, para. 18; *Bogomolova v. Russia*, ECtHR 20 June 2017, 13812/09, para. 38.

[2] Exceptions can mainly be seen in the domain of freedom of expression, where Article 10(2) ECHR expressly states that journalists might have certain 'duties and responsibilities' in exercising this freedom. These duties and responsibilities might be particularly important, for example, for news websites that also run a web forum on which defamatory, discriminatory or insulting comments are posted. Even then, however, the Court will not directly hold the journalist or owner of a website responsible, but it will review whether the domestic authorities, in dealing with such an issue, have sufficiently respected and fairly balanced the various conflicting Convention rights. For an example, see *Delfi AS v. Estonia*, ECtHR (GC) 16 June 2015, 64569/09, paras. 134 et seq.

explained. The point at which an organisation or institution can be regarded as a 'public authority' to be held directly accountable for respecting the Convention is discussed (Section 6.2.1) and, in addition, it is explained that public authorities are always obliged to act in accordance with the Convention, even if they behave as private parties (Section 6.2.2). Subsequently, Section 6.3 sets out how the Convention may have an impact on horizontal relationships. In this respect, attention is paid to the positive obligations of the State to provide effective regulation and enforcement in such horizontal relationships (Section 6.3.1), as well as to the obligations for national courts to take the Convention rights into account when deciding on private law matters (Section 6.3.2).

6.2   Direct Responsibility of the State for Interferences with Convention Rights

6.2.1   Definition of 'The State' – Public Authorities

Because of the importance of the effective protection of Convention rights, and in light of the primary responsibility of the States to provide such protection, the Court has always provided a wide definition of 'the State'. In particular, the Court has made sure that States cannot escape their responsibilities by delegating parts of their power to private legal entities or associations.[3] The Court has done so by giving an autonomous reading to the notions of a 'public authority' and a 'governmental organisation'. Even if an entity is not regarded as a public body according to national law, it still may qualify as such under the Convention and, accordingly, the State may be held accountable for its acts and omissions.

This strategy of autonomous interpretation can be illustrated by the *Wós* case.[4] The applicant in this case, a Polish citizen, had been subjected to forced labour in Germany during World War II. In the 1990s, several treaties were negotiated between Poland and Germany about the settlement of any claims arising out of the war period. A Polish-German Reconciliation Foundation was established to deal with any such claims for compensation. The applicant's claim was dismissed, however, because of the conditions which the Reconciliation Foundation had set for the acceptance of claims. The applicant complained before the Court about the decision to refuse to grant him compensation. As a preliminary issue, the Court decided to determine whether Poland's responsibility under the Convention was engaged in respect of the Reconciliation Foundation. In this respect, the Court noted

---

[3] Logically, this also means that the State cannot escape its obligations under the Convention by delegating certain powers to decentralised or federal authorities; see e.g. *Demirbaş and Others v. Turkey*, ECtHR 9 November 2010 (dec.), 1093/08.

[4] *Wós v. Poland*, ECtHR 1 March 2005 (dec.), 22860/02.

that, according to the interpretation adopted by the domestic courts, the Foundation was not part of the public administration.[5] It then decided to adopt an autonomous interpretation in order to prevent the situation that Poland could not be held responsible for the policy in relation to the compensation payments:

> The Court considers that the fact that a State chooses a form of delegation in which some of its powers are exercised by another body cannot be decisive for the question of State responsibility *ratione personae*. In the Court's view, the exercise of State powers which affects Convention rights and freedoms raises an issue of State responsibility regardless of the form in which these powers happen to be exercised, be it for instance by a body whose activities are regulated by private law. The Convention does not exclude the transfer of competences under an international agreement to a body operating under private law provided that Convention rights continue to be secured … The responsibility of the respondent State thus continues even after such a transfer. The Court observes that the respondent State has decided to delegate its obligations arising out of international agreements to a body operating under private law. In the Court's view, such an arrangement cannot relieve the Polish State of the responsibilities it would have incurred had it chosen to discharge these obligations itself, as it could well have done … It should be recalled in this respect that the Convention is intended to guarantee rights that are not theoretical or illusory, but rights that are practical and effective. In conclusion, having regard to all the above considerations, the Court considers that the specific circumstances of the present case give rise to the conclusion that the actions of the Polish-German Reconciliation Foundation in respect of both compensation schemes are capable of engaging the responsibility of the State.[6]

The Court's strategy of autonomous interpretation may evoke the question of how it decides that a private legal entity really is a 'governmental organisation' or a 'public authority'. In many cases, this question is easily answered, because it is simply not disputed that a body (such as a hospital or a university) is a public authority; in those cases, the Court will proceed on that basis.[7] For cases of controversy, the Court originally only offered some rather vague standards,[8]

---

[5] *Ibid.*, para. 69.

[6] *Ibid.*, paras. 71–4. See also e.g. *Costello-Roberts v. the United Kingdom*, ECtHR 25 March 1993, 13134/87, para. 27; *Storck v. Germany*, ECtHR 16 May 2005, para. 102; *Frăsilă and Ciocîrlan v. Romania*, ECtHR 10 May 2012, 25329/03, para. 66.

[7] E.g. *Glass v. the United Kingdom*, ECtHR 9 March 2004, 61827/00, para. 71; *Marić v. Croatia*, ECtHR 12 June 2014, 50132/12, para. 61; *Rubins v. Latvia*, ECtHR 13 January 2015, 79040/12, para. 43.

[8] See e.g. *Mihăilescu v. Romania*, ECtHR 26 August 2003 (dec.), 47748/99; *Mykhaylenky and Others v. Ukraine*, ECtHR 30 November 2004, 35091/02, paras. 43–6; *Novoseletskiy v. Ukraine*, ECtHR 22 February 2005, 47148/99, paras. 80–2; *Reynbakh v. Russia*, ECtHR 20 September 2005, 23405/03, para. 18; *Yershova v. Russia*, ECtHR 8 April 2010, 1387/04, paras. 55–63; *Saliyev v. Russia*, ECtHR 21 October 2010, 35016/03, paras. 64–70.

but in recent years, the Court has further specified these criteria. Of particular relevance in this respect is the *Kotov* case.[9] Kotov had deposited his savings with the commercial bank Yurak, but when he requested the closure of his account, the bank informed him that it was unable to repay his capital plus interest as its funds were insufficient. The bank was declared insolvent, but under the relevant legislation, Kotov belonged to the first class of creditors, whose claims were to be satisfied before others. However, the liquidator decided to create a special group of privileged creditors within the first class, including disabled persons, war veterans and persons in need, who were to receive full satisfaction before the other creditors in the first class. In the end, almost all of the funds were used for repayment of these privileged creditors and Kotov was left with less than 1 per cent of the amount owed to him by the bank. At the Court, Kotov complained about his inability to obtain the payment of the amount due to him because of the unlawful distribution of assets by the liquidator. The Russian government argued, however, that the liquidator was a private person according to Russian law and did not act as a State agent. The Court therefore had to determine whether there was direct State responsibility for the liquidator's acts, or, put differently, if the liquidator could be regarded as a public authority in the Court's autonomous definition. In this respect, the Court took into account how strongly the State and the public interest were involved in relation to five aspects: (a) appointment;[10] (b) supervision and accountability;[11] (c) objectives;[12] (d) powers;[13] and (e) functions.[14] Summarising the outcomes of the factual and legal assessment of these five aspects, the Court concluded that

> [i]t would appear that the liquidator, at the relevant time, enjoyed a considerable amount of operational and institutional independence, as State authorities did not have the power to give instructions to him and therefore could not directly interfere with the liquidation process as such. The State's involvement in the liquidation procedure resulted only from its role in establishing the legislative framework for such procedures, in defining the functions and the powers of the creditors' body and of the liquidator, and in overseeing observance of the rules. It follows that the liquidator did not act as a State agent. Consequently, the respondent State cannot be held directly responsible for his wrongful acts in the present case. The fact that a court was entitled to review the lawfulness of the liquidator's actions does not alter this analysis.[15]

In *Ališić*, the Court further clarified the applicable key criteria, holding that account must be taken of 'the company's legal status (under public or private law); the nature of its activity (a public function or an ordinary commercial business); the context of its operation (such as a monopoly or heavily regulated

---

[9] *Kotov v. Russia*, ECtHR (GC) 3 April 2012, 54522/00.   [10] *Ibid.*, paras. 100–1.
[11] *Ibid.*, paras. 102–3.   [12] *Ibid.*, para. 104.   [13] *Ibid.*, para. 105.   [14] *Ibid.*, para. 106.
[15] *Ibid.*, para. 107.

business); its institutional independence (the extent of State ownership); and its operational independence (the extent of State supervision and control)'.[16] It also explained that the overall conclusion to be based on these criteria should be that a legal entity can only be absolved from direct responsibility under the Convention if it in fact enjoyed 'sufficient institutional and operational independence from the State'.[17] The various criteria therefore should be applied in combination, without one criterion being more important or conclusive than the others.

Even if the Court holds, as it eventually did in *Kotov*, that there is no direct State responsibility for the acts of a private entity, this is not necessarily the end of the matter. As is further explained in Section 6.3, the State may still incur a positive obligation to make sure that the Convention rights are effectively protected against the acts of the responsible private legal entity, such as the liquidator in *Kotov*.[18] The *Danilenkov* case may serve to illustrate this.[19] The case concerned an issue of alleged trade union busting by the Kaliningrad Seaport Company. The Russian government had advanced a number of arguments to show that this company could not be regarded as a public authority and therefore, it could not be held responsible for its acts before the Court. The Court, however, reasoned as follows:

> The Court notes that the parties disagree as to whether the circumstances of the present case involved direct intervention by the State, given the status of the Kaliningrad seaport company. It considers that it is not necessary to rule on this issue, since the responsibility of the Russian Federation would, in any case, be engaged if the matters complained of resulted from a failure on its part to secure to the applicants under domestic law the rights set forth in Article 11 of the Convention.[20]

This consideration also shows that the Court's construction of indirect State responsibility is often more important than its answer to the question of whether a legal entity is primarily public or private in nature,[21] which explains why there is no detailed case law on the definition of a public authority.[22] This indirect State responsibility is further discussed in Section 6.3.

---

[16] *Ališić and Others v. Bosnia and Herzegovina, Croatia, Serbia, Slovenia and the former Yugoslav Republic of Macedonia*, ECtHR (GC) 16 July 2014, 60642/08, para. 114.
[17] *Ibid.*, para. 115.   [18] *Kotov*, para. 108.
[19] *Danilenkov and Others v. Russia*, ECtHR 30 July 2009, 67336/01.   [20] *Ibid.*, para. 120.
[21] See also e.g. *Palomo Sánchez v. Spain*, ECtHR (GC) 12 September 2011, 28955/06, para. 60.
[22] Importantly, there is a significant body of case law on a related matter, which is whether individuals can claim the negative right to freedom of association in relation to associations with a primarily public nature. This issue is not addressed specifically here, since this chapter is mainly concerned with States' responsibility for the effective protection of Convention rights and not with the personal scope of application of the various Convention rights as such. Some important cases in this respect are *Le Compte, Van Leuven and De Meyere v. Belgium*, ECtHR 23 June 1981, 6878/75 and 7238/75, paras. 64–5; *Chassagnou v. France*, ECtHR (GC) 29 April 1999, 67336/01, paras. 100–2; *Herrmann v. Germany*, ECtHR (GC) 20 January 2011, 9300/07, paras. 76–9; *Mytilinaios and Kostakis v. Greece*,

6.2.2   Private Law Acts by Public Authorities

The responsibility of the States to respect the Convention does not only pertain to typical public law acts, such as adopting legislation and administrative decisions, rendering judgments in civil law cases, prosecuting suspects under criminal law, law enforcement by the police, etc. Also if the State acts in a private law capacity, for instance as an employer or in offering services, it has to respect the various Convention rights. The Court emphasised this in *Schmidt and Dahlström*, a case on trade union freedom: 'The Convention nowhere makes an express distinction between the functions of a Contracting State as holder of public power and its responsibilities as employer. In this respect, Article 11 is no exception ... Article 11 is accordingly binding upon the "State as employer", whether the latter's relations with its employees are governed by public or private law.'[23] Accordingly, there is no need for the Court to assess whether certain activities (such as employment, supplying information and offering postal services, education or health care) have a typically public law nature or whether they are governed by private law. It will suffice to establish that it is the State that has acted, in accordance with the criteria discussed in Section 6.2.1.[24]

Likewise, once it has been established that an interference can be imputed to a public authority or a State agent, it is not necessary for the Court to find out in which capacity that authority or agent acted. In *Peev*, for example, the applicant was employed by the Prosecutor's Office in Bulgaria. After he had published a letter in a newspaper making allegations against the Chief Prosecutor, he was refused access to his office.[25] When he later returned, it appeared that his desk had been searched and sealed, and that a number of documents had disappeared. At the Court,

---

ECtHR 3 December 2015, 29389/11, paras. 36–45. There is also a body of case law on another related issue, which is that public authorities cannot themselves lodge a complaint at the Court, since they do not belong to one of the categories of applicants competent to do so under Article 34 ECHR. Because this is a procedural rather than a substantive matter, this issue is not specifically addressed in this chapter either. For some examples, see *Radio France and Others v. France*, ECtHR 23 September 2003 (dec.), 53984/00, para. 26; *Österreichischer Rundfunk v. Austria*, ECtHR 7 December 2006, 35841/02, paras. 46–53; *Islamic Republic of Iran Shipping Lines v. Turkey*, ECtHR 13 December 2007, 40998/98, paras. 78–82; *Východoslovenská vodárenská spoločnost a.s. v. Slovakia*, ECtHR 2 July 2013 (dec.), paras. 32–8; *Ärztekammer für Wien and Dorner v. Austria*, ECtHR 16 February 2016, 8895/10, paras. 35–45; *Bursa Barosu Başkanlığı and Others v. Turkey*, ECtHR 19 June 2018, 25680/05, para. 112.

[23] *Schmidt and Dahlström v. Sweden*, ECtHR 6 February 1976, 5589/72, para. 33. See more recently e.g. *Nenkova-Lalova v. Bulgaria*, ECtHR 11 December 2012, 35745/05, para. 50; *Matúz v. Hungary*, ECtHR 21 October 2014, 73571/10, para. 26; *Ebrahimian v. France*, ECtHR 26 November 2015, 64846/11, para. 47.

[24] See e.g. on employment decisions by public universities, *Rubins v. Latvia*, ECtHR 13 January 2015, 79040/12, para. 44, and on disclosure of confidential health information by a doctor in a public hospital, *Mockutė v. Lithuania*, ECtHR 26 February 2018, 66490/09, paras. 98–9.

[25] *Peev v. Bulgaria*, ECtHR 26 July 2007, 64209/01.

he complained that the search had violated his privacy rights, but the government maintained that it could not be held responsible for the search because it had not been conducted by the public prosecutor in the exercise of his functions but by the Prosecutor's Office as an employer. The Court disagreed with the government:

> On this point, the Court notes that . . . the applicant's office was sealed off by the prosecutor S.D., who was evidently acting under the pretext of his authority and with the acquiescence of the police officer on duty, and who told the officer that the applicant had been dismissed . . . The national courts found that the person who had carried out the search, be it the same prosecutor S.D. or another person, had access to the Courts of Justice building, admittance to which was restricted, and was apparently connected to the Chief Prosecutor . . . The material obtained during the search was later brought before the Chief Prosecutor and was used by him to terminate the applicant's employment . . . In these circumstances, there is no reason to assume that the search was an act carried out by persons in their private capacity. It is immaterial whether the persons who carried out the search acted as public prosecutors or as representatives of the applicant's employer, the Prosecutor's Office, because in any event they were acting as agents of the State. In this connection, the Court reiterates that the responsibility of a State under the Convention may arise for the acts of all its organs, agents and servants. Acts accomplished by persons in an official capacity are imputed to the State in any case. In particular, the obligations of a Contracting Party under the Convention can be violated by any person exercising an official function vested in him . . . The Court thus concludes that the search amounted to an interference by a public authority with the applicant's right to respect for his private life.[26]

In whatever capacity the State acted in searching and sealing the applicant's desk, it was clear that the State had been at work and it therefore could be held responsible for its acts before the Court.[27]

It is still important, however, to determine whether the behaviour that is complained about really can be attributed to the State, especially if it concerns an act by an individual person. For example, in *V.K. v. Russia*, a boy complained that he had been ill-treated by the teachers of a public nursery school.[28] As punishment, the teachers had forced him to stand in the entrance hall, barefoot and wearing only his underpants, they had taped his mouth shut with tape, and they had hit him on the back with their fists.[29] The Court held that in such a case, it must determine whether the teachers acted as private persons or as State agents, which meant that it had to investigate if the impugned acts were sufficiently clearly connected to the performance of their professional duties.[30] In this regard, the Court mentioned that it should assess the issue of State responsibility along the following lines:

---

[26] *Ibid.*, para. 41.

[27] See similarly e.g. *Hovhannisyan v. Armenia*, ECtHR 19 July 2018, 18419/13, para. 55.

[28] *V.K. v. Russia*, ECtHR 7 March 2017, 68059/13.   [29] *Ibid.*, para. 16.   [30] *Ibid.*, para. 173.

A Contracting State will be responsible under the Convention for violations of human rights caused by acts of its agents carried out in the performance of their duties. The Court has held that where the behaviour of a State agent is unlawful, the question of whether the impugned acts can be imputed to the State requires an assessment of the totality of the circumstances and consideration of the nature and circumstances of the conduct in question ... The Court reiterates that whether a person is an agent of the State for the purposes of the Convention is defined on the basis of a multitude of factors, none of which is determinative on its own. The key criteria used to determine whether the State is responsible for the acts of a person, whether formally a public official or not, are as follows: manner of appointment, supervision and accountability, objectives, powers and functions of the person in question.[31]

For the circumstances of the case, the Court established that nursery schools in Russia are usually public or municipal institutions, they receive State or municipal funding, and they offer the basic public service of educating children. While performing their functions, the teachers therefore were to be regarded as State agents. The Court further established that the ill-treatment happened during school hours and the impugned acts were connected to their role as teachers. The State therefore bore direct responsibility for the violation of Article 3 ECHR.[32] Conversely, if the acts of an individual are far removed from the performance of a State agent's duties, they cannot be imputed to the State and the State cannot be held responsible for them under the Convention.[33] In those cases, however, indirect State responsibility can often be construed by arguing that the State should have done more to protect an individual from harm, as will be explained in the next section.[34]

6.3   Indirect Horizontal Effect

In the cases discussed in Section 6.2, the direct responsibility of the State was engaged for acts and omissions of its agents and authorities. Even though they may be governed by private law, they are usually considered as 'vertical' ('top-down') relationships because of the involvement of the State. In many cases, however, the interference with a Convention right is not caused by a public authority or a State agent, but it is effected by the acts of private entities or

---

[31] *Ibid.*, paras. 174–5.

[32] *Ibid.*, paras. 180–4. See also e.g. *Sašo Gorgiev v. the former Yugoslav Republic of Macedonia*, ECtHR 19 April 2012, 49382/06, paras. 46 et seq.

[33] See e.g. *Reilly v. Ireland*, ECtHR 23 September 2014, 51083/09, paras. 53–6.

[34] See Section 6.3.1. For an example in which this approach was chosen and in which, for that reason, it did not matter if the harm had been inflicted by State agents or by private individuals, see *Hovhannisyan v. Armenia*, ECtHR 19 July 2018, 18419/13, para. 55.

individuals. As was mentioned in the introduction to this chapter, the Convention does not apply to such 'horizontal' relations. Nevertheless, the Court has developed two strategies that have created a strong degree of indirect protection of Convention rights in this type of relationships. The first strategy is to impose positive obligations on the State to ensure an effective protection of the Convention in relations between individuals or private entities, as is discussed in Section 6.3.1. The second strategy is to hold national courts (as organs of the State) accountable for applying the Convention provisions and the standards developed in the Court's case law in horizontal cases, as is explained in Section 6.3.2.

6.3.1 Positive Obligations to Protect Convention Rights in Horizontal Relations

The first way for the Court to realise a certain degree of horizontal effect is by imposing a positive obligation on the States to ensure effective protection of Convention rights in the relation between private parties. The *Bărbulescu* case offers an example of this.[35] Bărbulescu was employed as a sales engineer by a private company. At his employer's request, for the purpose of responding to customers' enquiries, he had created a Yahoo Messenger account. At one point, his manager decided to dismiss him, since the monitoring and recording of his Yahoo Messenger account showed that he had been using it for personal purposes against the internal rules. Bărbulescu complained about his employer's breach of the secrecy of his correspondence. This case was clearly about a relationship between an employer and an employee that was covered by civil law. Indeed, the Court expressly held that the monitoring of Bărbulescu's communications and the inspection of their content could not be regarded as an interference with his right by a State authority.[36] It also emphasised, however, that in a case such as this one, the State still had to ensure that employees are protected from unforeseeable and arbitrary interferences with their rights by their employer:

> The Court's task in the present case is ... to clarify the nature and scope of the positive obligations that the respondent State was required to comply with in protecting the applicant's right to respect for his private life and correspondence in the context of his employment ... The Court observes that it has held that in certain circumstances, the State's positive obligations under Article 8 of the Convention are not adequately fulfilled unless it secures respect for private life in the relations between individuals by setting up a legislative framework taking into consideration the various interests to be protected in a particular context ... The domestic authorities should ensure that the introduction by an employer of measures to monitor correspondence and other communications, irrespective

---

[35] *Bărbulescu v. Romania*, ECtHR (GC) 5 September 2017, 61496/08.   [36] *Ibid.*, para. 109.

of the extent and duration of such measures, is accompanied by adequate and sufficient safeguards against abuse.[37]

The Court then listed six factors which domestic authorities should address in this type of case, such as an adequate notification of the possibility of the employer's monitoring of correspondence, the extent of the monitoring by the employer, the consequences of the monitoring, and the safeguards offered against arbitrary use.[38] In Bărbulescu's case, the Court assessed whether the domestic authorities had taken due account of these criteria, and it noted several shortcomings:

> [I]t appears that the domestic courts failed to determine, in particular, whether the applicant had received prior notice from his employer of the possibility that his communications on Yahoo Messenger might be monitored; nor did they have regard either to the fact that he had not been informed of the nature or the extent of the monitoring, or to the degree of intrusion into his private life and correspondence. In addition, they failed to determine, firstly, the specific reasons justifying the introduction of the monitoring measures; secondly, whether the employer could have used measures entailing less intrusion into the applicant's private life and correspondence; and thirdly, whether the communications might have been accessed without his knowledge.[39]

Consequently, the Court found that the domestic authorities had not afforded sufficient protection to Bărbulescu's right to respect for his private life and correspondence, which amounted to a violation of Article 8 ECHR.[40] This example clearly illustrates the working of the Court's construction of indirect horizontal effect: it is not the employer who is held responsible for the violation of the Convention, but the State, which is obliged to ensure that, in the concrete case, the employee's rights were respected. Directly, therefore, the State is held responsible, but indirectly, a judgment such as Bărbulescu has great significance for the underlying horizontal relationship, as well as for national private and employment law more generally.

In many cases of this type, the Court does not indicate very clearly which State authority on the national level should be responsible for ensuring that the various criteria are taken into account. This may be the domestic courts, but criteria such as those mentioned in Bărbulescu could also be inserted into statutory legislation. Indeed, the Court often takes the position that it is the State that should guarantee respect for the Convention, and it is up to the State to decide how it wants to meet this obligation.[41] Nevertheless, in some cases, the Court is rather more precise, for

---

[37] *Ibid.*, paras. 114–15 and 120.   [38] *Ibid.*, paras. 121–2.   [39] *Ibid.*, para. 140.
[40] *Ibid.*, para. 141.
[41] Cf. J.H. Gerards, 'The European Court of Human Rights and the National Courts – Giving Shape to the Notion of "Shared Responsibility"' in J.H. Gerards and J.W.A. Fleuren (eds.), *Implementation of the European Convention on Human Rights and of the Judgments of the ECtHR in National Case Law. A Comparative Analysis* (Antwerp: Intersentia, 2014), pp. 13–94 at 25.

instance by indicating that horizontal protection of fundamental rights should be effected by means of (a) criminal law or other types of legislation, (b) effective law enforcement, (c) operational measures or (d) effective legal remedies. These four options are briefly discussed hereafter.

a   Criminal Law Legislation in Horizontal Relationships

Although the Convention protects people's lives, their physical and mental integrity, and their freedom against unjustified interference by the States, these rights are often violated by other human beings. Murder, acts of terrorism, abduction, sexual assault, violence, ill-treatment, child abuse, desecration of graves, discrimination – all such acts clearly infringe the rights protected by the Convention. On the national level, the protection of fundamental rights against such acts is usually guaranteed by criminal law, which is meant to have a preventive and deterrent effect as well as offering redress to the victim. Sometimes, however, the relevant legislation may contain gaps to the effect that aims cannot be realised. In those cases, it is possible to claim before the Court that the State has not complied with its positive obligations to provide effective criminal law provisions. This can be illustrated by the case of *M.C. v. Bulgaria*.[42] In Bulgaria, rape cases were prosecuted only if it was clear that the victim had actively resisted. The applicant, however, had been scared and embarrassed, and she had not had the strength to resist or scream. For that reason, the national authorities found that the allegation of rape had not sufficiently been proved. For the Court, this showed that the State had been lacking in its compliance with the Convention:

> Positive obligations on the State are inherent in the right to effective respect for private life under Article 8; these obligations may involve the adoption of measures even in the sphere of the relations of individuals between themselves. While the choice of the means to secure compliance with Article 8 in the sphere of protection against acts of individuals is in principle within the State's margin of appreciation, effective deterrence against grave acts such as rape, where fundamental values and essential aspects of private life are at stake, requires efficient criminal-law provisions. Children and other vulnerable individuals, in particular, are entitled to effective protection ... On that basis, the Court considers that States have a positive obligation inherent in Articles 3 and 8 of the Convention to enact criminal-law provisions effectively punishing rape and to apply them in practice through effective investigation and prosecution ... [T]he Court is persuaded that any rigid approach to the prosecution of sexual offences, such as requiring proof of physical resistance in all circumstances, risks leaving certain types of rape unpunished and thus jeopardising the effective protection of the individual's sexual autonomy. In accordance with contemporary standards and trends in that area, the member States' positive obligations under

---

[42]   *M.C. v. Bulgaria*, ECtHR 4 December 2003, 39272/98.

Articles 3 and 8 of the Convention must be seen as requiring the penalisation and effective prosecution of any non-consensual sexual act, including in the absence of physical resistance by the victim.[43]

Indeed, the Court had already held in *X and Y v. the Netherlands* that civil law remedies would not suffice in such cases:

> [T]he Court finds that the protection afforded by the civil law in the case of wrongdoing of the kind [sexual assault and rape] inflicted on Miss Y [a girl with mental disabilities] is insufficient. This is a case where fundamental values and essential aspects of private life are at stake. Effective deterrence is indispensable in this area and it can be achieved only by criminal-law provisions; indeed, it is by such provisions that the matter is normally regulated.[44]

The Court has accepted similar obligations to provide an effective system of criminal law provisions in relation to other serious offences against individuals' lives, freedom and integrity, such as domestic violence,[45] human trafficking and exploitation,[46] child abuse,[47] and violence or degrading treatment motivated by ethnic or religious hatred or homophobia.[48] However, in *Söderman*, it held that criminal law measures are not always necessary and in less serious cases, civil law remedies can suffice:

> More generally ... in respect of less serious acts between individuals, which may violate psychological integrity, the obligation of the State under Article 8 to maintain and apply in practice an adequate legal framework affording protection does not always require that an efficient criminal-law provision covering the specific act be in place. The legal framework could also consist of civil-law remedies capable of affording sufficient protection ... The Court notes, for example, that in some previous cases concerning the protection of a person's picture against abuse by others, the remedies available in the member States have been of a civil-law nature, possibly combined with procedural remedies such as the granting of an injunction.[49]

---

[43] *Ibid.*, paras. 150, 153 and 166.

[44] *X and Y v. the Netherlands*, ECtHR 26 March 1985, 8978/80, para. 27.

[45] E.g. *Opuz v. Turkey*, ECtHR 9 June 2009, 33401/02, paras. 138 et seq.

[46] E.g. *Siliadin v. France*, ECtHR 26 July 2005, 73316/01, para. 89; *Rantsev v. Cyprus and Russia*, ECtHR 7 January 2010, 25965/04, paras. 284–5; *L.E. v. Greece*, ECtHR 21 January 2016, 71545/12, paras. 64 et seq.

[47] See e.g. *O'Keeffe v. Ireland*, ECtHR (GC) 28 January 2014, 35810/09, para. 148.

[48] See e.g. *97 Members of the Gldani Congregation of Jehovah's Witnesses and 4 Others v. Georgia*, ECtHR 3 May 2007, 71156/01, paras. 133–4; *Begheluri and Others v. Georgia*, ECtHR 7 October 2014, 28490/02, paras. 97–8; *Karaahmed v. Bulgaria*, ECtHR 24 February 2015, 30587/13, paras. 93 et seq.

[49] *Söderman*, ECtHR (GC) 12 November 2013, 5786/08, para. 85.

In relation to cases of unintentional harm, such as medical negligence cases or cases where injuries resulted from an accident, the Court has also accepted that States could meet their obligations by introducing civil law or disciplinary remedies, and there is no specific need for criminal law provisions.[50]

b   Other Legislative Measures

In many areas of life, it thus may not be necessary to rely on criminal law to prevent, deter or punish individuals from violating fundamental rights. Nevertheless, the Court has found that legislation still might be the most appropriate way to regulate a private law relationship and effectuate the protection offered by the Convention. The *Redfearn* case illustrates that the States may have a positive obligation to provide such legislation.[51] Redfearn was a bus driver for a local bus company. When he was elected as a local councillor for the British National Party (which, at the time, was only open to white nationals and resisted any form of integration of non-European persons), the company dismissed him because it feared that Redfearn's 'continued employment would give rise to considerable anxiety among passengers and their carers'.[52] At the time, there was no legislation in place that allowed Redfearn – who was still in his first year of employment – to effectively challenge his dismissal. Before the Court, he complained that the lack of protection against dismissal had infringed his freedom of association, as protected by Article 11 ECHR. The Court agreed:

> Although the essential object of Article 11 is to protect the individual against arbitrary interference by public authorities with the exercise of the rights protected, the national authorities may in certain circumstances be obliged to intervene in the relationships between private individuals by taking reasonable and appropriate measures to secure the effective enjoyment of the right to freedom of association ... Therefore, although the matters about which the applicant complained did not involve direct intervention or interference by the State, the United Kingdom's responsibility will be engaged if these matters resulted from a failure on its part to secure to the applicant under domestic law his right to freedom of association. In other words there is also a positive obligation on the authorities to provide protection against dismissal by private employers where the dismissal is motivated solely by the fact that an employee belongs to a particular political party (or at least to provide the means whereby there can be an independent evaluation of the

---

[50] See hereafter, Section 6.3.1(b) and (d). For an example of an accident for which the State held responsibility but which occurred outside the sphere of medical negligence, see *Gorgiev v. the Former Yugoslavian Republic of Macedonia*, ECtHR 19 April 2012, 26984/05, para. 63. If the case goes beyond a mere accident, an error of judgment or medical negligence however, recourse to criminal law may still be necessary (see e.g. *Sinim v. Turkey*, ECtHR 6 June 2017, 9441/10, paras. 62 et seq.; *Lopes de Sousa Fernandes v. Portugal*, ECtHR (GC) 19 December 2017, para. 215).
[51] *Redfearn v. the United Kingdom*, ECtHR 6 November 2012, 47335/06.   [52] *Ibid.*, para. 11.

proportionality of such a dismissal in the light of all the circumstances of a given case) . . . Consequently, the Court considers that it was incumbent on the respondent State to take reasonable and appropriate measures to protect employees, including those with less than one year's service, from dismissal on grounds of political opinion or affiliation, either through the creation of a further exception to the one-year qualifying period or through a free-standing claim for unlawful discrimination on grounds of political opinion or affiliation. As the United Kingdom legislation is deficient in this respect, the Court concludes that the facts of the present case give rise to a violation of Article 11 of the Convention.[53]

Such obligations to take measures have also been accepted in other spheres of life. In relation to health care institutions, for example, the Court has made clear that the State should have in place regulations compelling both public and private hospitals to adopt appropriate measures for the protection of their patients' lives and physical integrity.[54] Mostly, however, the exact modalities of regulation remain within the discretion of the States, and minor deficiencies in the legislative framework may sometimes be excused if the case shows that, as a whole, sufficient protection is given to the relevant Convention rights.[55]

c Enforcement and Operational Acts and Measures

Simply providing a sound legislative framework to govern horizontal relations does not suffice to offer effective protection to the Convention. In addition to this, the State must ensure that this framework is effectuated in practice. As the Court held in general terms in *Lopes de Sousa Fernandes*, '[i]t must . . . be emphasised that the States' obligation to regulate must be understood in a broader sense which includes the duty to ensure the effective functioning of that regulatory framework. The regulatory duties thus encompass necessary measures to ensure implementation, including supervision and enforcement.'[56]

An illustration of the requirement of effective enforcement can be seen in the *Moreno Gómez* case, which was discussed in Chapter 5.[57] The case concerned the sleep disturbance caused by the noise of bars, cafés and discotheques in a residential neighbourhood in Valencia. In this case, the Court held that the lack of protection of Moreno Gómez's private life and respect to her home was due to the underperformance of the local authorities in enforcing the noise regulations:

---

[53] *Ibid.*, paras. 42–3 and 57.
[54] See e.g. *Trocellier v. France*, ECtHR 5 October 2006 (dec.), 75725/01; *Csoma v. Romania*, ECtHR 15 January 2013, 8759/05, paras. 41–2; *Lambert and Others v. France*, ECtHR 5 June 2015, 46043/14, paras. 140 and 151; *Lopes de Sousa Fernandes v. Portugal*, ECtHR (GC) 19 December 2017, 56080/13, paras. 166 and 186.
[55] *Ibid.*, para. 188.   [56] *Ibid.*, para. 189.
[57] *Moreno Gómez v. Spain*, ECtHR 16 November 2004, 4143/02.

The present case does not concern interference by public authorities with the right to respect for the home, but their failure to take action to put a stop to third-party breaches of the right relied on by the applicant ... Although the Valencia City Council has used its powers in this sphere to adopt measures (such as the bylaw concerning noise and vibrations) which should in principle have been adequate to secure respect for the guaranteed rights, it tolerated, and thus contributed to, the repeated flouting of the rules which it itself had established ... Regulations to protect guaranteed rights serve little purpose if they are not duly enforced and the Court must reiterate that the Convention is intended to protect effective rights, not illusory ones. The facts show that the applicant suffered a serious infringement of her right to respect for her home as a result of the authorities' failure to take action to deal with the night-time disturbances. In these circumstances, the Court finds that the respondent State has failed to discharge its positive obligation to guarantee the applicant's right to respect for her home and her private life, in breach of Article 8 of the Convention.[58]

In addition to this general obligation to enforce existing legislation, the Court has accepted a wide range of obligations to provide substantive, preventive and operational measures and actions to ensure effective protection of fundamental rights in horizontal relationships. In Chapter 5, some of these were already mentioned, such as the obligation for the police to take action if there is an immediate risk of harm to the life and limb of a concrete individual.[59] The Court has imposed similar obligations in many other contexts, varying from the obligation to take measures to facilitate the reunion of children and a parent after child abduction[60] or the obligation to act if an allegedly illegal group deliberately tries to prevent the publication and distribution of a newspaper,[61] to the obligation to ensure that persons taking part in a demonstration or in acts of worship are not harassed by a 'hostile audience',[62] and the obligation to guarantee that hospitals and doctors

---

[58] *Ibid.*, paras. 57 and 61–2. In other contexts, see e.g. *Rantsev v. Cyprus and Russia*, ECtHR 7 January 2010, 25965/04, para. 285; *Frăsilă and Ciocîrlan v. Romania*, ECtHR 10 May 2012, 25329/03, para. 71; *Cevrioğlu v. Turkey*, ECtHR 4 October 2016, 69546/12, paras. 61 et seq.

[59] See *Osman v. the United Kingdom*, ECtHR 28 October 1998, 23452/94, paras. 115–16; see more recently also e.g. *Rantsev v. Cyprus and Russia*, ECtHR 7 January 2010, 25965/04, para. 286. For an extensive overview of relevant case law in this field, see also e.g. *Cavit Tınarlıoğlu v. Turkey*, ECtHR 2 February 2016, 3648/04, paras. 63 et seq.

[60] See e.g. *Hokkanen v. Finland*, ECtHR 23 September 1994, 19823/92, para. 58; *Ignaccolo-Zenide v. Romania*, ECtHR 25 January 2000, 31679/96, para. 94; *Mamousseau and Washington v. France*, ECtHR 6 December 2007, 39388/05, para. 83; *Neulinger and Shuruk v. Switzerland*, ECtHR (GC) 6 July 2010, 41615/07, paras. 139–40; *Z. v. Latvia*, ECtHR (GC) 26 November 2013, 27853/09, paras. 101 et seq.; *Sévère v. Austria*, ECtHR 21 September 2017, 53661/15, paras. 103 et seq.

[61] *Özgür Gündem v. Turkey*, ECtHR 16 March 2000, 23144/93, para. 44.

[62] See e.g. *Plattform 'Ärtzte für das Leben' v. Austria*, ECtHR 21 June 1988, para. 32; *Promo Lex and Others v. Moldova*, ECtHR 24 February 2015, 42757/09, para. 22; *Karaahmed v. Bulgaria*, ECtHR 24 February 2015, 30587/13, paras. 91 et seq.

inform their patients about the potential risks of medical treatment.[63] This variety shows that the scope and nature of these obligations is dependent on the type of situation and the circumstances of the case.[64]

d Obligation to Provide an Effective Remedy and a Fair Balance

The example of *Bărbulescu* given above already showed that the Court often requires that there is not only legislation and enforcement but also access to a judicial remedy for the individual to complain about the acts of a private party, such as an employer.[65] In *Sovtransavto Holding*, the Court formulated this requirement in even more general terms:

> The Court reiterates that by virtue of Article 1 of the Convention each Contracting Party 'shall secure to everyone within [its] jurisdiction the rights and freedoms defined in . . . [the] Convention'. The obligation to secure the effective exercise of the rights defined in that instrument may result in positive obligations for the State . . . As regards the right guaranteed by Article 1 of Protocol No. 1, those positive obligations may entail certain measures necessary to protect the right of property . . . even in cases involving litigation between individuals or companies. This means, in particular, that the States are under an obligation to afford judicial procedures that offer the necessary procedural guarantees and therefore enable the domestic courts and tribunals to adjudicate effectively and fairly any disputes between private persons.[66]

This shows that the mere existence of a remedy is not enough to meet the State's positive obligations under the Convention. The domestic courts really must be competent to review the legality of the contested decision, identify and take into account all the interests of the parties involved, strike a fair balance and provide reasons for their judgments. The Court found a violation of the Convention in this respect in *Schüth*, which concerned the dismissal of an organist working at a Catholic parish church because of his extramarital relationship:

> The Court would first note that, by putting in place both a system of employment tribunals and a constitutional court having jurisdiction to review their decisions, Germany has in theory complied with its positive obligations towards citizens in the area of labour law, an area in which disputes generally affect the rights of the persons concerned under Article 8 of the Convention. In the present case the applicant was thus able to bring his case before

---

[63] E.g. *Trocellier v. France*, ECtHR 5 October 2006 (dec.), 75725/01; *Csoma v. Romania*, ECtHR 15 January 2013, 8759/05, para. 42.

[64] See further Sections 5.2 and 5.3.1.

[65] *Bărbulescu v. Romania*, ECtHR (GC) 5 September 2017, 61496/08, para. 122.

[66] *Sovtransavto Holding v. Ukraine*, ECtHR 25 July 2002, 48553/99, para. 96. See also e.g. *Vulakh and Others v. Russia*, ECtHR 10 January 2012, 33468/03, para. 45; *Matrakas and Others v. Poland and Greece*, ECtHR 7 November 2013, 47268/06, para. 146.

an employment tribunal, which had to determine whether the dismissal was lawful under ordinary domestic labour law, while having regard to ecclesiastical labour law, and to balance the competing interests of the applicant and the employing Church ... [However, the Court] is ... of the view that the employment tribunals did not sufficiently explain the reasons why, according to the findings of the Employment Appeal Tribunal, the interests of the Church far outweighed those of the applicant, and that they failed to weigh the rights of the applicant against those of the employing Church in a manner compatible with the Convention ... Consequently, having regard to the particular circumstances of the case, the Court finds that the German authorities did not provide the applicant with the necessary protection and that there has, accordingly, been a violation of Article 8 of the Convention.[67]

To be effective, moreover, remedies should be able to lead to sufficient redress for the victim of an interference. The Court has emphasised this, for example, in the context of breaches of individuals' right to life occurring in hospitals or other health care facilities:

> In the specific sphere of medical negligence the obligation may ... be satisfied if the legal system affords victims a remedy in the civil courts, either alone or in conjunction with a remedy in the criminal courts, enabling any liability of the doctors concerned to be established and any appropriate civil redress, such as an order for damages and for the publication of the decision, to be obtained. Disciplinary measures may also be envisaged.[68]

Hence, merely providing theoretical possibilities to bring civil court actions or disciplinary proceedings is not enough. Such a system must be seen to operate effectively, within a reasonable time and allowing the courts to adequately assess the liability of the one allegedly responsible for a violation.[69] In addition, there must be the possibility of obtaining a fair amount of compensation if it turns out that a fundamental right has been infringed, even if this does not necessarily have to be pecuniary compensation.[70]

---

[67] *Schüth v. Germany*, ECtHR 23 September 2010, 1620/03, paras. 59 and 74–5. See also e.g. *Eweida and Others v. the United Kingdom*, ECtHR 15 January 2013, 48420/10, para. 94; *I.B. v. Greece*, ECtHR 3 October 2013, 552/10, paras. 8790. Cf. also *Vulakh and Others v. Russia*, ECtHR 10 January 2012, 33468/03, para. 45. By contrast, if the overall approach taken by the national courts makes clear that they have struck a fair balance between the interests concerned, the Court will generally hold that the State has respected its positive obligations; see e.g. *Obst v. Germany*, ECtHR 23 September 2010, 425/03, para. 45; *Köpke v. Germany*, ECtHR 5 October 2010 (dec.), 420/07; *Eweida and Others v. the United Kingdom*, ECtHR 15 January 2013, 48420/10, para. 109.

[68] *Calvelli and Ciglio v. Italy*, ECtHR (GC) 17 January 2002, 32967/96, para. 51.

[69] *Ibid.*, para. 53. See also e.g. *Csoma v. Romania*, ECtHR 15 January 2013, 8759/05, para. 68; *Vasileva v. Bulgaria*, ECtHR 17 March 2016, 23796/10, para. 64.

[70] See e.g. *G.R. and R.B. v. Moldova*, ECtHR 18 December 2012, paras. 32–5; *Kahn v. Germany*, ECtHR 17 March 2016, 16313/10, para. 65; *Egill Einarsson v. Iceland (No. 2)*, ECtHR 17 July 2018, 31221/15, para. 36.

e   Limits to Positive Obligations in Horizontal Relationships

The examples discussed in this section make clear that there is a considerable, albeit indirect, horizontal effect of the Convention. The Court has imposed many obligations on the States to draft legislation, take preventive or enforcement measures, and provide remedies, which have the result that private parties are increasingly obliged to respect the Convention rights. Nevertheless, the Court sometimes accepts limits to these obligations. Usually it does so by means of its application of the fair balance test that has been described in Section 5.2.1. An example of this can be found in a case where the private owner of the 'Galleries', a large shopping mall in the city centre of a British town, had prohibited the distribution of leaflets and collection of signatures for a petition against a local infrastructural project.[71] The local authorities had not taken action against this prohibition, but the Court did not find that this amounted to a violation of the Convention:

> The issue to be determined is whether the respondent State has failed in any positive obligation to protect the exercise of the applicants' Article 10 rights from interference by others – in this case, the owner of the Galleries … In the present case, the restriction on the applicants' ability to communicate their views was limited to the entrance areas and passageways of the Galleries. It did not prevent them from obtaining individual permission from businesses within the Galleries (the manager of a hypermarket granted permission for a stand within his store on one occasion) or from distributing their leaflets on the public access paths into the area. It also remained open to them to campaign in the old town centre and to employ alternative means, such as calling door-to-door or seeking exposure in the local press, radio and television … The Court does not consider, however, that the applicants can claim that they were, as a result of the refusal of the private company, Postel, effectively prevented from communicating their views to their fellow citizens … Balancing the rights in issue and having regard to the nature and scope of the restriction in this case, the Court does not find that the respondent State failed in any positive obligation to protect the applicants' freedom of expression.[72]

Similarly, in *Remuszko*, the Court nuanced the State's positive obligations when a publishing company had refused a request to publish a paid advertisement for a book in a newspaper.[73] The Court held that the freedom of expression did not require the domestic courts to order a newspaper to publish an advertisement:

> The Court notes at the outset that the application concerns the outcome of a dispute between two private parties … The Court is of the view that in such a situation the right

---

[71] *Appleby and Others v. the United Kingdom*, ECtHR 6 May 2003, 44306/98.
[72] *Ibid.*, paras. 41 and 47.   [73] *Remuszko v. Poland*, ECtHR 16 July 2013, 1562/10.

invoked by the applicant has to be interpreted and applied with due consideration for the rights of the press protected under Article 10 of the Convention. The Court has already held that privately owned newspapers must be free to exercise editorial discretion in deciding whether to publish articles, comments and letters submitted by private individuals or even by their own staff reporters and journalists. The State's obligation to ensure the individual's freedom of expression does not give private citizens or organisations an unfettered right of access to the media in order to put forward opinions ... In the Court's view these principles apply also to the publication of advertisements. An effective exercise of the freedom of the press presupposes the right of the newspapers to establish and apply their own policies in respect of the content of advertisements. It also necessitates that the press enjoys freedom to determine its commercial policy in this respect and to choose those with whom it deals ... The Court is ... satisfied that the courts carefully weighed the applicant's interests against the legitimate rights of the publishers, such as their own freedom of expression and economic freedom ... The Court agrees with the analysis of the case carried out by the domestic courts. It finds that their conclusion that, in a pluralistic media market press, publishers should not be obliged to carry advertisements proposed by private parties is compatible with the freedom of expression standards under the Convention.[74]

The fair balance test may thus delimit the scope of the positive obligations in cases between private parties. If there is not a very far-reaching interference and the very essence of a right is not affected, there is still significant leeway for the States to decide for themselves if and how they need to intervene.

6.3.2 Responsibility of the National Courts to Apply the Convention

In Section 6.3.1, various positive obligations have been discussed which have been imposed on the States to protect the Convention rights in horizontal relations. Another route to effectuating indirect horizontal effect of the Convention is through the national courts. As organs of the State, the domestic courts have a direct and primary responsibility under Article 1 ECHR to secure the Convention rights in their interpretation and application of national law.[75] In general terms, the Court held in *Paulić* that 'no legal provision of domestic law should be interpreted and applied in a manner incompatible with [the respondent State's] obligations under the Convention'.[76]

It follows from the Court's case law that the national courts also incur this obligation in the sphere of private law, such as in the interpretation of contracts. In *Pla and Puncernau*, for example, the Andorran courts had interpreted a testamentary provision (which had been drafted about fifty years before) in accordance

---

[74] *Ibid.*, paras. 76, 79 and 86.   [75] See also Gerards, *supra* n. 41, at 21 et seq.
[76] *Paulić v. Croatia*, ECtHR 22 October 2009, 3572/06, para. 42.

with the (supposed) intent of the testatrix.[77] The Court found the courts' interpretation unacceptable since it conflicted with the non-discrimination principle laid down in the Convention. It also held that in relation to contracts, the domestic courts have to strive for an interpretation that is in accordance with the Convention:

> The Court reiterates that the Convention, which is a dynamic text and entails positive obligations for States, is a living instrument, to be interpreted in the light of present-day conditions ... Thus, even supposing that the testamentary disposition in question did require an interpretation by the domestic courts, that interpretation could not be made exclusively in the light of the social conditions existing when the will was made or at the time of the testatrix's death, namely in 1939 and 1949 ... Where such a long period has elapsed, during which profound social, economic and legal changes have occurred, the courts cannot ignore these new realities ... [A]ny interpretation, if interpretation there must be, should endeavour to ascertain the testator's intention and render the will effective, while bearing in mind that 'the testator cannot be presumed to have meant what he did not say' and without overlooking the importance of interpreting the testamentary disposition in the manner that most closely corresponds to domestic law and to the Convention as interpreted in the Court's case-law.[78]

The Court held similarly in *Khurshid Mustafa and Tarzibachi* on a provision in a tenancy agreement that prohibited tenants from erecting outdoor aerials and other objects on the house.[79] The applicants had violated this provision by mounting a satellite dish in order to receive television programmes in Arabic and Farsi. After a warning, the landlord gave the applicants notice of termination and successfully initiated judicial proceedings to seek execution of this notice. At the Court, the applicants complained that the enforcement of the tenancy agreement had breached their freedom of information as protected by Article 10 ECHR. Recalling its findings in *Pla and Puncernau*, the Court held that the Swedish courts had been obliged to ensure that their interpretation of the tenancy agreement in the light of Swedish legislation was compatible with the Convention:

> Admittedly, the Court is not in theory required to settle disputes of a purely private nature. That being said, in exercising the European supervision incumbent on it, it cannot remain passive where a national court's interpretation of a legal act, be it a testamentary disposition, a private contract, a public document, a statutory provision or an administrative practice appears unreasonable, arbitrary, discriminatory or, more broadly, inconsistent with the principles underlying the Convention ... In the present case the Court

---

[77] *Pla and Puncernau v. Andorra*, ECtHR 13 July 2004, 69498/01.
[78] *Ibid.*, para. 62. See also E. Bjorge, 'National Supreme Courts and the Development of ECHR Rights', *International Journal of Constitutional Law*, 9 (2011), 5–31, giving more examples of cases from which it appears that national courts must apply the principle of evolutive interpretation.
[79] *Khurshid Mustafa and Tarzibachi v. Sweden*, ECtHR 16 December 2008, 23883/06.

notes that the Court of Appeal ... applied and interpreted not only the tenancy agreement concluded between the applicants and the landlord but also Chapter 12 of the Land Code. Further, it ruled on the applicants' right to freedom of information laid down in the Swedish Constitution and the Convention. Domestic law, as interpreted in the last resort by the Court of Appeal, therefore made lawful the treatment of which the applicants complained ... In effect, the applicants' eviction was the result of the court's ruling. The Court finds that the responsibility of the respondent State within the meaning of Article 1 of the Convention for any resultant breach of Article 10 may be engaged on this basis.[80]

Assessing the interests of the applicants and those of the landlord, the Court concluded that the Swedish Court of Appeal had not attached sufficient weight to the applicants' interest in receiving the television broadcast and the lack of safety threats posed by the satellite dish. The Court therefore found a violation in this private law case.

Finally, the positive obligations to provide an effective judicial remedy, discussed in Section 6.3.1 under (d), also have their bearing on the national courts. In particular, the Court's case law implies that they have to carefully establish the interests of the private parties involved in a conflict and provide a fair balance. This can be illustrated by the first *Von Hannover* case, which concerned the publication of photographs of the private life of Caroline von Hannover, the Princess of Monaco.[81] Caroline von Hannover thought this to be an interference with her private life and she tried to have the publication prohibited by the national courts. She did not succeed, however, because the national courts held that famous persons should show a greater tolerance of this kind of intrusion. The case was clearly horizontal in nature: the privacy interests of the Princess clashed with the freedom of expression of the newspapers and magazines and the right of the public to receive such information. The Princess, however, reframed the case as a vertical one by stating before the Court that the German court decisions had infringed her right to respect for her private and family life protected by Article 8 of the Convention.[82] Without paying attention to the underlying, horizontal nature of the conflict, the Court examined whether the national courts had interpreted the applicable legislation in a way compatible with the Convention:

The Court finds it hard to agree with the domestic courts' interpretation of section 23(1) of the Copyright (Arts Domain) Act, which consists in describing a person as such as a figure of contemporary society 'par excellence'. Since that definition affords the person very limited protection of their private life or the right to control the use of their image, it could conceivably be appropriate for politicians exercising official functions. However, it cannot be justified for a 'private' individual, such as the applicant, in whom the interest of the

---

[80] *Ibid.*, paras. 33–4.   [81] *Von Hannover v. Germany*, ECtHR 24 June 2004, 59320/00.
[82] *Ibid.*, para. 43.

general public and the press is based solely on her membership of a reigning family, whereas she herself does not exercise any official functions. In any event the Court considers that, in these conditions, the Act has to be interpreted narrowly to ensure that the State complies with its positive obligation under the Convention to protect private life and the right to control the use of one's image ... [I]n the Court's opinion the criteria established by the domestic courts were not sufficient to ensure the effective protection of the applicant's private life and she should, in the circumstances of the case, have had a 'legitimate expectation' of protection of her private life.[83]

This approach is characteristic of much of the Court's extensive case law on conflicts between the freedom of expression and the rights to reputation and respect for one's private life. It does not seem to make any difference for the Court's review whether the original, national case was governed by private law or by criminal law (where the prosecution means that the State's responsibility for the limitation of the freedom of expression is directly engaged). In most cases, the Court mainly examines whether the national courts have given too much or too little weight to specific interests and whether they have sufficiently taken the Court's own standards into account.[84] For example, in a second case brought by the Princess of Monaco,[85] the Court defined a number of criteria the national courts should take into account, such as the extent to which a publication contributed to a debate of general interest, the fame of the person concerned, the content and consequences of the publication, and the circumstances in which photos were taken.[86] In a third case on the Von Hannover family, this time relating to a press publication featuring the Prince of Monaco, the Court found it 'appropriate to make the preliminary observation that its role in this case consists primarily in verifying whether the domestic courts whose decisions are contested by the applicants struck a fair balance between the rights at stake and ruled in accordance with the criteria established by it for that purpose'.[87] Indeed, the Court has generally accepted that it can only substitute its own view for that of the domestic courts if they have failed to undertake a balancing exercise in conforming with the standards defined by the Court.[88] In most cases, the Court therefore merely investigates whether the national courts have taken these

---

[83] *Ibid.*, paras. 72 and 78.   [84] See also the examples mentioned above, Section 6.3.1(e).

[85] *Von Hannover (No. 2) v. Germany*, ECtHR (GC) 7 February 2012, 40660/08 and 60641/08.

[86] *Ibid.*, paras. 108–26.

[87] *Couderc and Hachette Filipacchi Associés v. France*, ECtHR (GC) 10 November 2015, 40454/07, para. 95. See also e.g. *Rubins v. Latvia*, ECtHR 13 January 2015, 79040/12, para. 77.

[88] See e.g. *MGN Limited v. the United Kingdom*, ECtHR 11 January 2011, 39401/04, paras. 150 and 155; *Palomo Sánchez and Others v. Spain*, ECtHR (GC) 12 September 2011, 28955/06, para. 57; *Von Hannover (No. 2) v. Germany*, ECtHR (GC) 7 February 2012, 40660/08 and 60641/08, para. 107; *Satakunnan Markkinapörssi Oy and Satamedia Oy v. Finland*, ECtHR (GC) 27 June 2017, 931/13, para. 198.

standards into account and whether they had done so in a serious and adequate manner.[89] Nevertheless, indirectly, the Court's standards thereby have a strong influence on the way in which horizontal cases are decided in the national courts, as well as on the obligations that private parties (such as publishers, employers or insurance companies) bear in respecting fundamental rights.[90]

---

[89] For an example, see *Sihler-Jauch and Jauch v. Germany*, ECtHR 24 May 2016 (dec.), 68273/10 and 34194/11, paras. 32–40.

[90] For some examples of judgments which might lead – indirectly – to specific obligations for private entities to respect and protect fundamental rights, see *Delfi AS v. Estonia*, ECtHR (GC) 16 June 2015, 64569/09; *Vukota-Bojić v. Switzerland*, ECtHR 18 October 2016, 61838/10; *Bărbulescu v. Romania*, ECtHR (GC) 5 September 2017, 61496/08; *Satakunnan Markkinapörssi Oy and Satamedia Oy v. Finland*, ECtHR (GC) 27 June 2017, 931/13.

7 The Margin of Appreciation Doctrine

7.1 Introduction

In Chapter 1, it was explained that it is an important task for the Court to define a minimum level of protection of Convention rights. Only then can it be guaranteed that the Convention rights are secured to everyone on an equal footing, regardless of whether they are living in Russia, Luxembourg, Andorra, or in any of the forty-four other States Parties. To provide such an equal level of protection, and to make sure the rights are protected effectively, it has been shown in Chapters 2–6 that the Court uses a wide range of instruments, varying from autonomous, meta-teleological and evolutive interpretation to the definition of positive obligations and of general standards and principles.

In using these instruments, the Court cannot simply choose a maximalist approach, striving for the highest thinkable level of protection of fundamental rights in all forty-seven Convention States.[1] The first reason for this is institutional in nature and has to do with the Court's position in the Convention system.[2] In this respect, the second core principle of the Convention system can be recalled, which is the principle of subsidiarity.[3] This principle expresses that the States bear the primary responsibility for the protection of the Convention rights, whereas the Court exercises a subsidiary role of supervision. This subsidiary role comes down to checking whether the States have lived up to their responsibilities and have effectively secured the Convention to those falling within their jurisdiction. As long as the States respect the limits set by the Convention and the case law of the Court, however, they retain their discretion to decide which measures, restrictions or exceptions are necessary and reasonable.

---

[1] This introduction is partly based on earlier writing, in particular J.H. Gerards, 'Uniformity and the European Court of Human Rights' in K. Lemmens, S. Parmentier and L. Reyntjens (eds.), *Liber Amicorum Paul Lemmens* (in press).

[2] See e.g. O.M. Arnardóttir, 'Rethinking the Two Margins of Appreciation', *European Constitutional Law Review*, 12 (2016), 27–53 at 40.

[3] See Section 1.2.2.

The second reason why a maximalist approach would be difficult to realise is connected to the inherent indeterminacy of the Convention. Regardless of the powerful rhetoric of the universality of human rights, there is relatively little consensus on the exact meaning of fundamental rights.[4] Such consensus may exist where the core of the Convention rights is concerned, and on a relatively high level of abstraction. (Almost) everyone will agree, for example, that the prohibition of torture means that the police may not use iron bars to hurt a suspect so as to make him confess a crime he has not committed, or that the right to family life means that a child may not be removed from its parents without good reason.[5] Matters become rather more complicated where the periphery of fundamental rights is concerned, or, in some cases, on a more concrete level of abstraction. For example, there can be considerable controversy over the question of whether the right to remain free from degrading treatment implies that undocumented aliens, too, have a right to food and shelter.[6] Similarly, there may be little consensus on the question of whether the right to family life encompasses a right to have more than two registered parents, for example where a child is raised by a male same-sex couple and was born to a female friend.[7] The text of the Convention offers few clues on solving such issues.[8] The formulation of the Convention rights is open and fairly indeterminate. For example, the Convention may clearly say that protection should be offered against inhuman and degrading treatment, but it does not explain what this means; or it may stipulate that family life should be respected, but it does not describe what, then, constitutes a 'family'. Even if the Court has a wide range of interpretative tools available, as has been shown in Chapters 2, 3 and 4, they may not always indicate a straightforward and unambiguous solution to such difficult issues of interpretation. It has been shown in Sections 4.2 and 4.3 that textual interpretation and interpretation based on the *travaux préparatoires* often do not provide a conclusive answer

---

[4] See further e.g. R.D. Sloane, 'Outrelativizing Relativism: A Liberal Defense of the Universality of International Human Rights', *Vanderbilt Journal of Transnational Law*, 34 (2001), 527–96 and E. Brems, *Human Rights: Universality and Diversity* (Leiden/Boston: Martinus Nijhoff Publishers, 2001). More specifically for the ECHR context, see S. Greer, 'Universalism and Relativism in the Protection of Human Rights in Europe: Politics, Law and Culture' in P. Agha (ed.), *Human Rights between Law and Politics: The Margin of Appreciation Doctrine in Post-National Contexts* (London: Bloomsbury/Hart, 2017), pp. 17–26.

[5] Cf. B. Baade, 'The ECtHR's Role as a Guardian of Discourse: Safeguarding a Decision-Making Process Based on Well-established Standards, Practical Rationality, and Facts', *Leiden Journal of International Law*, 31 (2018), 335–61 at 339.

[6] See e.g. *Hunde v. the Netherlands*, ECtHR 5 July 2016 (dec.), 17931/16.

[7] See more generally on these issues: N.R. Koffeman, *Morally Sensitive Issues and Cross-Border Movement in the EU. The Cases of Reproductive Matters and Legal Recognition of Same-sex Relationships* (Cambridge: Intersentia, 2015).

[8] For elaboration, see e.g. H.C.K. Senden, *Interpretation of Fundamental Rights in a Multilevel Legal System. An Analysis of the European Court of Human Rights and the Court of Justice of the European Union* (Antwerp: Intersentia, 2011); also Baade, *supra* n. 5, at 341.

to difficult questions, precisely because of the indeterminacy of the provisions and the continuous developments in the European societies and technologies. Consensus sometimes may be a shaky basis for the determination of a uniform definition of fundamental rights, as with evolutive and meta-teleological interpretation.[9] This makes it very difficult to find an appropriate and uncontested basis for a uniform definition of Convention rights. In some cases it therefore may be more appropriate – and easier – for the Court to avoid a uniform, maximalist application of the Convention than to accept one.

The third main reason why the Court is hesitant to take a maximalist approach is more practical or epistemic in nature.[10] Many fundamental rights issues require difficult factual or legal assessments. It will usually be easier for the national authorities to see which measures and remedies fit best into the system than it is for the Court, and whether an issue should be regulated by means of constitutional amendments, statutory legislation, bylaws or policy instruments, or individual decision-making by public bodies or courts. Similarly, as has been shown in Chapter 5, regulation of fundamental rights often demands that operational or policy choices be made, and to facilitate such choices, a detailed identification and assessment of facts, risks, alternatives and potential consequences is required. National authorities are involved in making such choices and assessments on a daily basis and they have the necessary expertise to do so. National legislators and policy-makers are generally well equipped to assess the economic, social or technical consequences of certain decisions, as well as estimate the constitutional, moral and ethical values related to some contested issues. Similarly, national courts are close to the parties and experts involved and they may hear, for example, all the parties in a case about their views on a particular arrangement. By contrast, the Court stands at a relative distance from this, and has much less capacity to gauge the epistemic validity of certain national decisions than the national authorities. Indeed, the principles of primarity and subsidiarity find an important basis in this epistemic argument of capacity, and they result in a logical division of labour. By contrast, a far-reaching, maximalist protection of all Convention rights by the Court would be hard to reconcile with these principles.

The three reasons mentioned above disclose an inherent tension in the Convention system, which was already alluded to in Chapter 1. On the one hand, the Court has to provide effective protection of fundamental rights and ensure that everyone can equally enjoy these rights, yet on the other hand, it has to allow sufficient freedom to the States and respect their special abilities and powers to make choices

---

[9] See, respectively, Sections 4.5, 3.3.3 and 3.4.

[10] See further e.g. J. Fahner, *Intensity of Review in International Courts and Tribunals: A Comparative Analysis of Deference,* PhD thesis, University of Luxembourg/University of Amsterdam (2018), section 4.2.

and decisions, also in light of the inherent indeterminacy of the Convention. It is against this backdrop and for this reason that the Court has developed its famous yet complex margin of appreciation doctrine, on which this chapter is focused.[11] First, some insight is given into the development of this doctrine in the Court's case law, and its main rationale and functions as described by the Court (Section 7.2). Section 7.3 explains the types of cases where the doctrine is applied, and in Section 7.4 the various factors determining the scope of the margin and their interaction are discussed. Finally, in Section 7.5 some attention is paid to the difference between doctrine and reality in the Court's case law.

7.2   The Development, Function and Effects of the Margin of Appreciation Doctrine

The Court started its development of the margin of appreciation doctrine in the *Belgian Linguistics* case.[12] There the Court referred to some of the reasons discussed in Section 7.1 as determining the Court's overall approach in assessing national interferences with Convention rights:

> In attempting to find out in a given case, whether or not there has been an arbitrary distinction, the Court cannot disregard those legal and factual features which characterise the life of the society in the State which, as a Contracting Party, has to answer for the measure in dispute. In so doing it cannot assume the rôle of the competent national authorities, for it would thereby lose sight of the subsidiary nature of the international machinery of collective enforcement established by the Convention. The national authorities remain free to choose the measures which they consider appropriate in those matters which are governed by the Convention. Review by the Court concerns only the conformity of these measures with the requirements of the Convention.[13]

The Court elaborated on this in the *Handyside* case, which is generally regarded as the judgment in which the Court introduced the margin of appreciation doctrine.[14] The case concerned a little book with information for teenagers which was to be

---

[11] The chapter will thereby mainly rely on the doctrine's function in helping the Court decide on the deference it will pay to the national authorities. Many different conceptualisations of the doctrine are possible, however. For other analyses of the doctrine, see e.g. G. Letsas, 'Two Concepts of the Margin of Appreciation', *Oxford Journal of Legal Studies*, 26 (2006), 705–32; Arnardóttir, *supra* n. 2 (with further references).

[12] *Belgian Linguistics Case*, ECtHR 23 July 1968, 1474/62, para. I.B.10. Before this case, the former European Commission of Human Rights had already used a variation of the doctrine in its report in *Lawless v. Ireland*, EComHR 19 December 1959, 332/57, at 85.

[13] *Belgian Linguistics Case*, para. 1.B.10.

[14] *Handyside v. the United Kingdom*, ECtHR 7 December 1976, 5493/72.

distributed at schools, but which was found by the national courts to contain obscenities. The distribution of the book was therefore prohibited with the aim of protecting public morals, and all copies were seized. The Court had to answer the question of whether the prohibition and seizure could be considered to be reasonable in the light of the freedom of expression, protected by Article 10 ECHR. In doing so, under the second paragraph of Article 10, it had to assess whether the prohibition was 'prescribed by law', pursued a 'legitimate aim' (in this case the protection of morals) and was 'necessary in a democratic society'. Before the Court embarked on this assessment, it first defined its own position and overall approach:

> The Court points out that the machinery of protection established by the Convention is subsidiary to the national systems safeguarding human rights ... The Convention leaves to each Contracting State, in the first place, the task of securing the rights and liberties it enshrines. The institutions created by it make their own contribution to this task but they become involved only through contentious proceedings and once all domestic remedies have been exhausted ...
>
> These observations apply, notably, to Article 10 para. 2. In particular, it is not possible to find in the domestic law of the various Contracting States a uniform European conception of morals. The view taken by their respective laws of the requirements of morals varies from time to time and from place to place, especially in our era which is characterised by a rapid and far-reaching evolution of opinions on the subject. By reason of their direct and continuous contact with the vital forces of their countries, State authorities are in principle in a better position than the international judge to give an opinion on the exact content of these requirements as well as on the 'necessity' of a 'restriction' or 'penalty' intended to meet them ... [I]t is for the national authorities to make the initial assessment of the reality of the pressing social need implied by the notion of 'necessity' in this context.
>
> Consequently, Article 10 para. 2 leaves to the Contracting States a margin of appreciation. This margin is given both to the domestic legislator ('prescribed by law') and to the bodies, judicial amongst others, that are called upon to interpret and apply the laws in force.
>
> Nevertheless, Article 10 para. 2 does not give the Contracting States an unlimited power of appreciation. The Court, which ... is responsible for ensuring the observance of those States' engagements (Article 19), is empowered to give the final ruling on whether a 'restriction' or 'penalty' is reconcilable with freedom of expression as protected by Article 10. The domestic margin of appreciation thus goes hand in hand with a European supervision. Such supervision concerns both the aim of the measure challenged and its 'necessity'; it covers not only the basic legislation but also the decision applying it, even one given by an independent court ... It follows from this that it is in no way the Court's task to take the place of the competent national courts but rather to review under Article 10 the decisions they delivered in the exercise of their power of appreciation. However, the Court's supervision would generally prove illusory if it did no more than examine these

decisions in isolation; it must view them in the light of the case as a whole, including the publication in question and the arguments and evidence adduced by the applicant in the domestic legal system and then at the international level. The Court must decide, on the basis of the different data available to it, whether the reasons given by the national authorities to justify the actual measures of 'interference' they take are relevant and sufficient under Article 10 para. 2.[15]

These considerations show that it is not only the specifically supranational, subsidiary role of the Court that explains the choice for a 'margin of appreciation doctrine' (the institutional reason mentioned in Section 7.1), but also the so-called 'better placed argument' (the epistemic reason mentioned in Section 7.1). The Court expressly mentioned that the States are in principle in a better position than it is itself to assess the necessity of certain restrictive measures to achieve a certain aim. Notably, however, this epistemic reason for allowing the State a certain margin of appreciation may not be as strong in each individual case. In some cases, the Court may be just as well equipped as national authorities to give its opinion, for example where the interpretation of the terms and notions of the Convention is concerned or where a necessity test does not require a particularly close assessment of national facts and circumstances. This already indicates that there may be a certain need for variation in the amount of discretion that is left to the States. After all, if States were granted the same wide margin of appreciation in all cases, the supervision of the Court would always be restrained. This would result in a rather empty concept of fundamental rights and a relatively low overall level of protection. The strength of the margin of appreciation doctrine is, therefore, in its flexibility and variability.[16] Indeed, the main function of the margin of appreciation doctrine is to allow the Court to vary the intensity of its review of the States' compliance with the negative and positive obligations following from the Convention.

As is further explained in Section 7.3, the Court generally distinguishes between a 'narrow margin', a 'certain margin' and a 'wide margin'. These formulas cannot be regarded as indicating specific tests or levels that result in a certain apportionment of the burden of proof or in an exact set of standards of review.[17] Nevertheless, there is a difference in consequence between a wide margin and a narrow one. If a wide

---

[15] *Ibid.*, paras. 48–50.

[16] Cf. R.St.J. Macdonald, 'The Margin of Appreciation' in R.St.J. Macdonald et al. (eds.), *The European System for the Protection of Human Rights* (Dordrecht: Martinus Nijhoff, 1993), pp. 83–124 at 123; Y. Arai-Takahashi, *The Margin of Appreciation Doctrine and the Principle of Proportionality in the Jurisprudence of the ECHR* (Antwerp: Intersentia, 2002) 236; A. Ostrovsky, 'What's So Funny About Peace, Love, and Understanding? How the Margin of Appreciation Doctrine Preserves Core Human Rights within Cultural Diversity and Legitimises International Human Rights Tribunals', *Hanse Law Review*, (2005) 47, 58.

[17] For elaboration, see J. Christoffersen, *Fair Balance: Proportionality, Subsidiarity and Primarity in the European Convention on Human Rights* (Leiden/Boston: Martinus Nijhoff Publishers, 2009) 265

margin is allowed to the national authorities, the Court will examine the choices made by the national authorities rather superficially to see whether the result is not (clearly) unreasonable or disproportionate. The judgment in *James* is an example of such deferential or restrained review, and concerned the regulation of property under Article 1 of Protocol No. 1.[18] In this case, the Court left a margin of appreciation to the respondent State, in accordance with the *Handyside* case. It then explained what this would mean for its assessment of the legislative measures under review:

> It is, so the applicants argued, only if there was no other less drastic remedy for the perceived injustice that the extreme remedy of expropriation could satisfy the requirements of Article 1. This amounts to reading a test of strict necessity into the Article, an interpretation which the Court does not find warranted. The availability of alternative solutions does not in itself render the . . . legislation unjustified; it constitutes one factor, along with others, relevant for determining whether the means chosen could be regarded as reasonable and suited to achieving the legitimate aim being pursued, having regard to the need to strike a 'fair balance'. Provided the legislature remained within these bounds, it is not for the Court to say whether the legislation represented the best solution for dealing with the problem or whether the legislative discretion should have been exercised in another way.[19]

Furthermore, if the margin of appreciation is wide, the burden of proof to show that a restriction is unjustified is often placed with the applicants. An example of this can be found in the Court's decision in *Greenpeace*, where the applicant had complained that the German government had not taken sufficient measures to curb respirable dust emissions of diesel vehicles:

> Bearing in mind its fundamentally subsidiary role with respect to issues of environmental policies, the Court finds that the applicants have not shown – and the documents submitted do not demonstrate – that the Contracting State, when it refused to take the specific measures requested by the applicants, exceeded its discretionary power by failing to strike a fair balance between the interests of the individual and of the community as a whole. Assessing all the material in its possession, the Court finds that the case does not disclose any appearance of a violation of Article 8.[20]

---

et seq.; N. Lavender, 'The Problem of the Margin of Appreciation', *European Human Rights Law Review*, 4 (1997), 380 at 387 et seq.

[18] *James and Others v. the United Kingdom*, ECtHR 21 February 1986, 8793/79, para. 51.

[19] *Ibid.*, para. 51. For some other examples, see *Rasmussen v. Denmark*, ECtHR 28 November 1984, 8777/79, para. 41; *Fretté v. France*, ECtHR 26 February 2002, 36515/97, para. 42; *Pla and Puncernau v. Andorra*, ECtHR 13 July 2004, 69498/01, para. 46; *Anheuser-Busch Inc. v. Portugal*, ECtHR 11 January 2007, 73049/01, para. 83; ECtHR (GC) 6 November 2017, 43494/09, para. 157.

[20] *Greenpeace e.V. and Others v. Germany*, ECtHR 12 May 2009 (dec.), 18215/06.

Lastly, in cases where the margin of appreciation is wide, the Court may apply a rather procedural test: if it finds that the national authorities have not assessed the case in an arbitrary or manifestly unreasonable manner, it will not find a violation.[21]

In other cases, the Court may leave the State only a narrow margin of appreciation. The Court will then closely consider the facts of the case, carefully identify and weigh the interests at stake and decide for itself where the appropriate balance between conflicting interests should have been struck. It is up to the national authorities in such cases to show that the limitation of rights was based on a careful and objective assessment of facts and interests and, more generally, that there were sufficiently weighty and important interests supporting it.[22] In many of these cases the Court applies a strict test of necessity, often mentioning the availability of less intrusive measures to underpin its judgment that the interference cannot be held to be justified, or criticising the lack of possibilities for individualised judgments on the national level.[23] Finally, in many such cases the Court requires additional procedural safeguards to be afforded by domestic law, such as access to judicial remedies and careful and individualised decision-making.[24]

Finally, there are many cases in which the Court leaves the respondent State 'a certain' margin of appreciation or just 'a' margin of appreciation.[25] This indicates an intermediate form of scrutiny on the scale ranging from very strict to very restrained review, and from a narrow to a wide margin of appreciation.[26] Usually, such an intermediate scope for the margin of appreciation means that the Court will apply a relatively neutral approach, allowing the State some leeway for making its own decisions, yet not limiting itself to a pure review of arbitrariness or manifest unreasonableness.

---

[21] E.g. *Fretté v. France*, ECtHR 26 February 2002, 36515/97, para. 42; *Maurice v. France*, ECtHR 6 October 2005, 11810/03, paras. 118 et seq.; *Dimitar Yordanov v. Bulgaria*, ECtHR 6 September 2018, 3401/09, para. 56. On procedural review, see further Section 10.4.4.

[22] E.g. *Connors v. the United Kingdom*, ECtHR 27 May 2004, 66746/01, para. 94; *Makhmudov v. Russia*, ECtHR 26 July 2007, 35082/04.

[23] E.g. *Informationsverein Lentia v. Austria*, ECtHR 24 November 1993, 13914/88, paras. 39 and 42; *Fuentes Bobo v. Spain*, ECtHR 29 February 2000, 39293/98, para. 49; *S. and Marper v. the United Kingdom*, ECtHR 4 December 2008, 30562/04 and 30566/04, paras. 119–20. On the least restrictive means test, see further Section 10.2.3.

[24] E.g. *S. and Marper v. the United Kingdom*, ECtHR 4 December 2008, 30562/04 and 30566/04, paras. 103–4. See further Section 10.4.5.

[25] For some examples, see *Kurić and Others v. Slovenia*, ECtHR (GC) 26 June 2012, 26828/06, para. 387; *Eweida and Others v. the United Kingdom*, ECtHR 15 January 2013, 48420/10, paras. 84 and 88; *K.S. and M.S. v. Germany*, ECtHR 6 October 2017, 33696/11, para. 42; *Lupeni Greek Catholic Parish and Others v. Romania*, ECtHR (GC) 29 November 2016, 76943/11, paras. 89 and 102.

[26] See further J.H. Gerards, 'Intensity of Judicial Review in Equal Treatment Cases', *Netherlands International Law Review*, 51 (2004), 135–83 at 140 et seq.

Even if these different 'margins' can be distinguished in the Court's case law and there is a certain relationship between the scope of the margin and the intensity of the Court's review, it is important to note that they cannot be regarded as indicating specific tests or levels of scrutiny, nor is there a clear relationship between the different margins and the Court's substantive standards of review.[27] Moreover, the Court is often rather inconsistent in the way it uses the different margins.[28] Nevertheless, the flexibility of the margin of appreciation doctrine makes it a very useful tool.[29] Most importantly, the doctrine enables the Court to deal with the tension described in Section 7.1, since it can help the Court to determine the degree to which it will heed specific national values, standards and circumstances.[30] When limitations are related to deeply held constitutional or divisive issues, the Court can use the doctrine to defer to the national authorities' decisions and thereby visibly respect the principle of subsidiarity.[31] If the Convention right at stake is really important, however, and the Court considers a uniform and high standard of protection to be more important than the need to respect diversity, it can narrow down the scope of the margin of appreciation and apply a stricter test.[32]

7.3   Applicability of the Margin of Appreciation Doctrine

As was discussed in Sections 7.1 and 7.2, the main function of the margin of appreciation is to allow the States some leeway in deciding on the regulation of the enjoyment of fundamental rights. The logical consequence of this is that the margin of appreciation does not play a role in relation to absolutely absolute, non-derogable provisions of the Convention, such as Articles 3, 4(1) and 7 ECHR.[33] The absolute nature of these provisions and the prime importance of the rights contained in them means that it would be inappropriate to allow the States any leeway as regards their level of protection. Indeed, the Court has stressed that '[w]here allegations are made under Article 3 of the Convention the

---

[27] See in particular J.H. Gerards, 'Pluralism, Deference and the Margin of Appreciation Doctrine', *European Law Journal*, 17 (2011), 80–120 at 106; Christoffersen, *supra* n. 17, at 267 et seq.; J. Kratochvíl, 'The Inflation of the Margin of Appreciation by the European Court of Human Rights', *Netherlands Quarterly of Human Rights*, 29 (2011), 324–57 at 335; J.H. Gerards, 'Margin of Appreciation and Incrementalism in the Case Law of the European Court of Human Rights', *Human Rights Law Review*, 18 (2018), section 2.B.iv.

[28] *Ibid.*   [29] *Ibid.*, section 2.A.; see also Greer, *supra* n. 4, at 29.

[30] Gerards, 'Incrementalism', *supra* n. 27, section 2.A.   [31] *Ibid.*, with further references.   [32] *Ibid.*

[33] On the categories of Convention rights, see Section 1.5.

Court must apply particularly thorough scrutiny'.[34] In relation to Article 2 ECHR also, the Court has emphasised that there is little room for national discretion:

> The Court recalls that Article 2 ranks as one of the most fundamental provisions of the Convention – indeed one which, in peace time, admits of no derogation under Article 15. Like Article 3 of the Convention it enshrines one of the basic values of the democratic societies making up the Council of Europe. As such its provisions must be strictly construed. This is particularly true of the exceptions delineated in paragraph 2 of that Article which apply not only to intentional deprivation of life but also to situations where it is permitted to use force which may result, as an unintended outcome, in the deprivation of life.[35]

Consequently, the Court also does not leave any express margin of appreciation in relation to the positive obligations arising from these provisions, not even in cases which relate to policy matters where the Court would usually allow the national authorities some discretion.[36] Nevertheless, as has been shown in Section 5.4, in some of these cases the Court applies a test that clearly allows some leeway to the States and implies some judicial restraint, such as the reasonable knowledge and means test.[37] In relation to certain aspects of these positive obligations, such as if sufficient compensation has been offered to the victim or if prosecution of possible perpetrators was appropriate, the Court has mentioned that the State has a certain discretion.[38] Moreover, on rare and very sensitive occasions, the Court has even afforded a margin of appreciation to the States on core Article 2 issues.[39] This margin then concerns decisions such as whether to permit the withdrawal of life-sustaining treatment, or the means of striking a balance between the protection of the patient's right to life and the respect for the same patient's autonomy and private life.[40] Similarly, for Article 3, the Court has applied the margin of

---

[34] *Gäfgen v. Germany*, ECtHR (GC) 1 June 2010, 22978/05, para. 93; see also e.g. *Saadi v. Italy*, ECtHR (GC) 28 February 2008, 37201/06, paras. 128 and 138.

[35] *Andronicou and Constantinou v. Cyprus*, ECtHR 9 October 1997, 25052/94, para. 171. For a more recent confirmation, see e.g. *Shchiborshch and Kuzmina v. Russia*, ECtHR 16 January 2014, 5269/08, para. 204.

[36] See e.g. *Watts v. the United Kingdom*, ECtHR 4 May 2010 (dec.), 53586/09.

[37] The Court sometimes even translates this discretion to an application of the margin of appreciation doctrine; see e.g. *Cevrioğlu v. Turkey*, ECtHR 4 October 2016, 69546/12, para. 67.

[38] E.g. *Firstov v. Russia*, ECtHR 20 February 2014, 42119/04, para. 36; *Marro and Others v. Italy*, ECtHR 8 April 2014 (dec.), 29100/07, para. 46; *Armani da Silva v. the United Kingdom*, ECtHR (GC) 30 March 2016, 5878/08, paras. 267–9.

[39] E.g. *Lambert v. France*, ECtHR (GC) 5 June 2015, 46043/14, para. 148.

[40] *Lambert*, paras. 146–7. See also *Gard and Others v. the United Kingdom*, ECtHR 27 June 2017 (dec.), 39793/17, para. 84; *Afiri and Bidarri v. France*, ECtHR 23 January 2018 (dec.), 1828/18, para. 29.

appreciation doctrine in relation to certain aspects of sentencing policies, such as defining the conditions and setting the procedures in relation to lifelong sentences.[41]

While application of the doctrine is uncommon or even ruled out in relation to absolute rights, it is applied almost standardly in relation to derogable provisions of the Convention.[42] In particular, the Court frequently refers to the doctrine in relation to the assessment of restrictions under the express and general limitation clauses of Articles 8–11, Article 1 Protocol No. 1 and Article 2 Protocol No. 4 ECHR and the generic emergency clause of Article 15 ECHR.[43] The Court may also leave the States a margin of appreciation in relation to restrictions of Convention rights for which the Court has accepted implied limitations, such as restrictions of the right to access to a Court protected by Article 6 ECHR[44] and the right to free elections.[45] The same goes for restrictions of rights for which the Convention refers to the national laws of the States Parties, such as the right to marry in Article 12.[46]

In addition to the assessment of the reasonableness of restrictions, the Court may leave a certain margin of appreciation to the States as regards the definition of certain relevant terms in the limitation clauses of the Convention. Examples are the terms 'public emergency threatening the life of the nation' contained in Article 15 ECHR,[47] 'morals' in the limitation clauses of Articles 8–11 ECHR[48] and 'persons of unsound mind' in Article 5(1)(f) ECHR.[49] Very rarely, the Court has even recognised a margin of appreciation in relation to Convention terms that define the scope of application of the Convention. In the case of *Vo*, for example, it left a margin of appreciation to the States in determining when the right to life (protected by Article 2 ECHR) begins.[50] As a result, depending on national law and opinions, the States are free to determine whether the protection of Article 2 is granted at an earlier or

---

[41] E.g. *Vinter and Others v. the United Kingdom*, ECtHR (GC) 9 July 2013, 66069/09, para. 120; *T.P. and A.T. v. Hungary*, ECtHR 4 October 2016, 37871/14 and 73986/14 para. 45.

[42] For this classification, see Section 1.5.

[43] See *Ireland v. the United Kingdom*, ECtHR 18 January 1978, 5310/71, para. 207 and *A. v. the United Kingdom*, ECtHR (GC) 19 February 2009, 3455/05, para. 173.

[44] E.g. *Osman v. the United Kingdom*, ECtHR 28 October 1998, 23452/94, para. 147; *Kart v. Turkey*, ECtHR (GC) 3 December 2009, 8917/05, para. 79; *Arlewin v. Sweden*, ECtHR 1 March 2016, 22302/10, para. 67; *Tsezar and Others v. Ukraine*, ECtHR 13 February 2018, 73590/14, para. 51. The States may also have a margin of appreciation as regards other Article 6 aspects; see e.g. *A.N. v. Lithuania*, ECtHR 31 May 2016, 17280/08, para. 89.

[45] E.g. *Tanase v. Moldova*, ECtHR (GC) 27 April 2010, 7/08, para. 161; *Yabloko Russian United Democratic Party and Others v. Russia*, ECtHR 8 November 2016, 18860/07, para. 67.

[46] E.g. *Parry v. the United Kingdom*, ECtHR 28 November 2006 (dec.), 42971/05.

[47] E.g. *A. v. the United Kingdom*, ECtHR (GC) 19 February 2009, 3455/05, paras. 173 and 180.

[48] E.g. *Handyside v. United Kingdom*, ECtHR 7 December 1976, 5493/72, para. 48.

[49] E.g. *Luberti v. Italy*, ECtHR 23 February 1984, 9019/80, para. 27; *Salontaji-Drobnjak v. Serbia*, ECtHR 13 October 2009, 36500/05, para. 125.

[50] *Vo v. France*, ECtHR (GC) 8 July 2004, 53924/00, para. 85.

later point in time (e.g. at conception or only at birth) and, consequently, the degree to which unborn life is protected.[51] This is exceptional, however, since the Court normally adopts an autonomous approach in defining the scope of the Convention.[52]

The margin of appreciation doctrine also plays a role in connection to the right to non-discrimination of Article 14 ECHR, but in this particular context it is given a somewhat different shape. In these cases, the Court may decide to apply a so-called 'very weighty reasons test', which is particularly used in relation to unequal treatment based on certain a priori suspicious grounds, such as ethnicity, gender and sexual origin.[53] This test has a similar result to leaving a narrow margin of appreciation, in that, in practice, the very weighty reasons test implies very strict review by the Court.[54] However, the overall rationale for applying a weighty reasons test is somewhat different from the rationales discussed in Section 7.2, since it is related to the inherently problematic nature of certain grounds of discrimination.[55] For that reason, in Article 14 cases the fact that a difference in treatment is based on 'suspect' grounds, such as ethnic origin or birth, may trump other factors that normally help the Court determine the scope of the margin of appreciation, such as the better placed argument.[56] Non-discrimination cases are, to that extent, different from cases concerning other Convention rights.[57] Because of this specificity, these cases and the 'very weighty reasons' test are not specifically discussed in this chapter.

Finally, the Court also applies the margin of appreciation doctrine when defining the scope of the States' positive obligations.[58] States are usually granted quite some leeway to organise their health care and social security systems in a way they think fit, just like the organisation of their judicial and electoral systems, and the Court will not interfere with this lightly. Although the margin of appreciation will often be a wide one in this kind of policy area because of the 'better placed' argument (to be discussed hereafter, Section 7.4.3), this is not an absolute rule. The actual scope of

---

[51] See e.g. the Chamber judgment in *Evans v. the United Kingdom*, ECtHR 7 March 2006, 6339/05, para. 47.

[52] See Section 3.5.

[53] There are many examples: see *Alajos Kiss v. Hungary*, ECtHR 20 May 2010, 38832/06, para. 42. For a full overview of the 'suspect' grounds of discrimination to which the very weighty reasons test is applied, see J.H. Gerards, 'The Margin of Appreciation Doctrine, the Very Weighty Reasons Test and Grounds of Discrimination' in M. Balboni (ed.), *The European Convention on Human Rights and the Principle of Non-Discrimination* (Naples: Editoriale Scientifica, 2018), pp. 27–62.

[54] Cf. O.M. Arnardóttir, 'The Differences that Make a Difference: Recent Developments on the Discrimination Grounds and the Margin of Appreciation under Article 14 of the European Convention on Human Rights', *Human Rights Law Review*, 14 (2014), 647–70 at 655.

[55] See extensively Gerards, *supra* n. 53.

[56] See e.g. *Biao v. Denmark*, ECtHR (GC) 24 May 2016, 38590/10, paras. 94 and 138.

[57] See further Gerards, *supra* n. 53.   [58] See further Chapter 5.

the margin of appreciation in a concrete case is determined by a number of other factors, including the nature and importance of the individual interests at stake and the existence of European consensus.

7.4 Determining the Scope of the Margin of Appreciation

7.4.1 Factors Relevant to Determining the Scope of the Margin of Appreciation

In Section 7.2, it was explained that the main value of the margin of appreciation doctrine is in its flexibility and variability. Sometimes the margin will be wide (and the Court's review will be lenient), sometimes it will be narrow (and the Court's review will be strict) and sometimes there will be an intermediate or unclear margin (and intensity of the Court's review will be more or less neutral). The amount of discretion left to the States thus has a significant bearing on the Court's review, and for that reason, it is important to understand how the Court decides to grant a narrow, intermediate or wide margin of appreciation for the States. The Court has often explained that it uses a variety of factors in this respect, as it did for example in *S. and Marper*:

> A margin of appreciation must be left to the competent national authorities ... The breadth of this margin varies and depends on a number of factors including the nature of the Convention right in issue, its importance for the individual, the nature of the interference and the object pursued by the interference. The margin will tend to be narrower where the right at stake is crucial to the individual's effective enjoyment of intimate or key rights ... Where a particularly important facet of an individual's existence or identity is at stake, the margin allowed to the State will be restricted ... Where, however, there is no consensus within the Member States of the Council of Europe, either as to the relative importance of the interest at stake or as to how best to protect it, the margin will be wider.[59]

Based on such a list, three main factors can be distinguished which have the most impact on the scope of the margin of appreciation: the 'common ground' factor (Section 7.4.2), the 'better placed' factor (Section 7.4.3) and the nature and importance of the Convention right at stake (Section 7.4.4). In the academic literature on the margin of appreciation doctrine, many more factors have been distinguished, such as the character and weight of the aims pursued, the nature of the State's obligations, the seriousness of the interference and the context of the interference.[60]

---

[59] *S. and Marper v. the United Kingdom*, ECtHR 4 December 2008, 30562/04 and 30566/04, para. 102. An even more detailed version of this paragraph can be found in *Connors v. the United Kingdom*, ECtHR 27 May 2004, 66746/01, para. 82.

[60] See in particular Arai-Takahashi, *supra* n. 16, at p. 206 et seq.

In the Court's case law, however, these additional factors appear to be closely related to the three main factors distinguished in this chapter. To avoid too much detail, they are therefore not discussed separately.

7.4.2   The Common Ground Factor

The first intensity-determining factor is the existence or lack of a 'common ground'.[61] This common ground factor is closely related to the consensus method of interpretation discussed in Section 4.5, but it plays a different role. In the stage of interpretation (stage 1, see Section 1.4.2), the common ground method implies that the Court may accept a new definition of a Convention right if this interpretation is supported by (at least) an emerging consensus in the European States. The common ground factor plays a different role if it is applied in stage 3 (Section 1.4.4).[62] It then helps the Court determine how much leeway the States should have in deciding how they want to regulate and restrict the exercise of the Convention rights. In this context, the common ground factor may influence the Court's review in two ways.

First, the common ground factor may play a role in relation to the definition of the general interests that may be invoked to justify a restriction of a Convention right, or the test of legitimate aim.[63] If there is (virtually) no common ground between the States on a certain matter, the Court will usually leave a wide margin of appreciation to the States in this respect. This can be illustrated by *Wingrove*, a case that concerned the refusal of a certificate for distribution of the film 'Visions of Ecstasy'.[64] According to the applicant, the idea for the film was derived from the life and writings of St Teresa of Ávila, a sixteenth-century Carmelite nun who experienced powerful ecstatic visions of Jesus Christ.[65] The government, however, regarded the resulting film as blasphemous, and as shocking and insulting the religious feelings of believers. The Court considered the amount of European consensus to be an important factor in determining the leeway to be given to the State on whether to protect these feelings:

> The Court observes that the refusal to grant Visions of Ecstasy a distribution certificate was intended to protect 'the rights of others', and more specifically to provide protection against seriously offensive attacks on matters regarded as sacred by Christians ... As the observations filed by the intervenors ... show, blasphemy legislation is still in force in

---

[61] Cf. Judge Malinverni, concurring opinion in the case of *Egeland and Hanseid v. Norway*, ECtHR 16 April 2009, 34438/04, para. 6.

[62] E.g. *Dickson v. the United Kingdom*, ECtHR (GC) 4 December 2007, 44362/04, para. 78; *S. and Marper v. the United Kingdom*, ECtHR 4 December 2008, 30562/04 and 30566/04, para. 102; *Konstantin Markin v. Russia*, ECtHR 22 March 2012, 30048/06; *X. and Others v. Austria*, ECtHR (GC) 19 February 2013, 19010/07.

[63] See further Chapter 9.   [64] *Wingrove v. the United Kingdom*, ECtHR 25 November 1996, 17419/90.

[65] *Ibid.*, para. 8.

various European countries. It is true that the application of these laws has become increasingly rare and that several States have recently repealed them altogether … Whereas there is little scope under Article 10 para. 2 of the Convention for restrictions on political speech or on debate of questions of public interest … a wider margin of appreciation is generally available to the Contracting States when regulating freedom of expression in relation to matters liable to offend intimate personal convictions within the sphere of morals or, especially, religion. Moreover, as in the field of morals, and perhaps to an even greater degree, there is no uniform European conception of the requirements of 'the protection of the rights of others' in relation to attacks on their religious convictions. What is likely to cause substantial offence to persons of a particular religious persuasion will vary significantly from time to time and from place to place, especially in an era characterised by an ever growing array of faiths and denominations. By reason of their direct and continuous contact with the vital forces of their countries, State authorities are in principle in a better position than the international judge to give an opinion on the exact content of these requirements with regard to the rights of others as well as on the 'necessity' of a 'restriction' intended to protect from such material those whose deepest feelings and convictions would be seriously offended.[66]

Thus, the Court held that respect for religious opinions and feelings is an aim on which opinions in Europe clearly diverge. For that reason, the State should be given more leeway to make its own estimation of what is needed in this respect and, accordingly, the margin of appreciation is rather wide.[67] This will be different if the case concerns a general interest on which the views in Europe do not diverge. An example of this is the *Sunday Times* case, which concerned a prohibition of expressions that, according to the State, amounted to contempt of court.[68] The respondent government argued that the injunction had been necessary to maintain the authority and impartiality of the judiciary. The Court decided that it did not need to leave a wide margin of appreciation to the State in relation to this particular aim, and it contrasted the case to the above-mentioned *Handyside* case, which concerned a booklet which allegedly contained obscenities:[69]

---

[66] *Ibid.*, paras. 57–8. The Court also mentioned that the resulting margin of appreciation might be restricted again because of the nature of the interference (prior restraint of the freedom of expression); that factor is addressed in Section 7.4.4. For another example, see *Gough v. the United Kingdom*, ECtHR 28 October 2014, 49327/11, para. 172.

[67] If there is a particular context in which the definition of 'morals' less strongly diverges, however, the Court will leave considerably less margin of appreciation to the State; see e.g. *Bayev and Others v. Russia*, ECtHR 20 June 2017, 67667/09, paras. 66 et seq.

[68] *Sunday Times v. the United Kingdom (No. 1)*, ECtHR 26 April 1979, 6538/74.

[69] *Handyside v. the United Kingdom*, ECtHR 7 December 1976, 5493/72, para. 47; see further Section 7.2.

[T]he scope of the domestic power of appreciation is not identical as regards each of the aims listed in Article 10 (2). The Handyside case concerned the 'protection of morals'. The view taken by the Contracting States of the 'requirements of morals', observed the Court, 'varies from time to time and from place to place, especially in our era', and 'State authorities are in principle in a better position than the international judge to give an opinion on the exact content of these requirements' (... [*Handyside*], para. 48). Precisely the same cannot be said of the far more objective notion of the 'authority' of the judiciary. The domestic law and practice of the Contracting States reveal a fairly substantial measure of common ground in this area. This is reflected in a number of provisions of the Convention, including Article 6, which have no equivalent as far as 'morals' are concerned. Accordingly, here a more extensive European supervision corresponds to a less discretionary power of appreciation.[70]

The second situation in which the common ground factor may play a role relates to the assessment of the reasonableness, suitability, necessity or proportionality of restrictions.[71] The Court tends to leave a wider margin of appreciation to the States if there is little consensus in Europe on which modalities are best suited or most appropriate to serve a general interest. This can be seen in the *TV Vest* case, concerning the regulation of political television advertisements.[72] Norway had decided on an absolute prohibition of political television advertising with the aim of protecting smaller political parties, which would find it difficult to purchase advertising time. It could thus guarantee a level playing field and fair competition between such smaller parties and the bigger and richer ones, which could otherwise buy an undue advantage in the form of broadcasting time.[73] One of the questions the case presented was whether a full ban on political television advertisements would be acceptable under Article 10 ECHR. In this regard, the Court decided that Norway had a wide margin of appreciation to decide on the appropriateness and necessity of such a far-reaching measure because of the lack of common ground in this field:

The Court has ... considered whether ... the differences between domestic systems with regard to television broadcasting of political advertising could warrant a wide margin of appreciation. According to the comparative law reports compiled by the EPRA, out of the 30 European countries examined, (1) in 13 a statutory ban on paid political advertising in broadcasting applied; (2) in 10 such advertising was permitted; (3) in 11 there were provisions for free airtime for political parties and candidates during election campaigns (five of these were among the 13 under item (1)); (4) in several countries there was no

---

[70] *Sunday Times*, para. 59.   [71] See further on this in Chapter 10.
[72] *TV Vest As and Rogaland Pensjonistparti v. Norway*, ECtHR 11 December 2008, 21132/05.
[73] *Ibid.*, para. 41.

system of allocation of free airtime ... In so far as this absence of European consensus could be viewed as emanating from different perceptions regarding what is 'necessary' for the proper functioning of the 'democratic' system in the respective States, the Court is prepared to accept that it speaks in favour of allowing a somewhat wider margin of appreciation than that normally accorded with respect to restrictions on political speech in relation to Article 10 of the Convention.[74]

Although, eventually, the Court concluded that the ban constituted an altogether too absolute restriction of the freedom of expression, this consideration illustrates that the Court will show stronger deference if European approaches clearly diverge. This has proven to be the case for a wide variety of issues on which there appears to be little consensus in Europe, varying from recognition and establishing paternity[75] to the organisation of electoral systems[76].[77] By contrast, if there appears to be an emerging consensus on a certain topic, this may be an important factor in narrowing down the margin of appreciation, especially if other relevant factors also point in that direction.[78]

The cited paragraph of the *TV Vest* judgment further shows that the Court based its consensus argument on a comparative review of the modalities of regulation of political advertising. Thus, the approach taken to determining the level of consensus was similar to the approach the Court uses in interpretation, which is also true for other cases.[79] As was explained in Section 4.5.2, the Court can use various sources for its consensus interpretation. Next to comparative reviews of national law, these can be international or EU legal instruments and soft law. The use of the consensus argument as a tool of interpretation and as a factor to determine the margin of

---

[74] *Ibid.*, para. 67. See similarly *Animal Defenders International v. the United Kingdom*, ECtHR (GC) 22 April 2013, 48876/08, para. 123.

[75] See e.g. *Ahrens v. Germany*, ECtHR 22 March 2012, 45071/09, para. 70; *Konstantinidis v. Greece*, ECtHR 3 April 2014, 58809/09, para. 47; *L.P. and P.K. v. Bulgaria*, ECtHR 8 December 2016, 7949/11 and 45522/13, paras. 59–60.

[76] See e.g. *Yumak and Sadak v. Turkey*, ECtHR (GC) 8 July 2008, 10226/03, paras. 110 et seq.

[77] For other examples, see e.g. *Harroudj v. France*, ECtHR 4 October 2012, 43631/09, para. 48; *S.A.S. v. France*, ECtHR (GC) 1 July 2014, 43835/11, para. 156–7; *Dubská and Krejzová v. the Czech Republic*, ECtHR (GC) 15 November 2016, 28859/11 and 28473/12, para. 184; *Ebrahimian v. France*, ECtHR 26 November 2015, 64846/11, para. 65; *Armani da Silva v. the United Kingdom*, ECtHR (GC) 30 March 2016, 5878/08, para. 269; *Cumhariyet Halk Partisi v. Turkey*, ECtHR 26 April 2016, 19920/13, para. 70; *Klein and Others v. Germany*, ECtHR 6 April 2017, 10138/11, para. 87.

[78] For an example, see *Oliari and Others v. Italy*, ECtHR 21 July 2015, 18766/11 and 36030/11, paras. 177–85.

[79] See e.g. *Brauer v. Germany*, ECtHR 28 May 2009, 3545/04, para. 40; *Harroudj v. France*, ECtHR 4 October 2012, 43631/09, para. 48; *X. and Others v. Austria*, ECtHR (GC) 19 February 2013, 19010/07, paras. 149–50; *Parrillo v. Italy*, ECtHR (GC) 27 August 2015, 46470/11, paras. 176–82.

appreciation is also similar in the criticism that is often given of the Court's use of the factor. In particular, it has been argued in legal scholarship and dissenting opinions that it is much more difficult to establish the presence of a European consensus than the Court makes it appear, and some degree of 'cherry-picking' is almost unavoidable.[80] Perhaps for that reason, even if the consensus factor may play an important role in determining the margin of appreciation for the State, it is never decisive for the outcome of the case as such and it is usually combined with other factors.

7.4.3   The Better Placed Argument

As explained in Sections 7.1 and 7.2, the Court may leave a wide margin of appreciation to the States because they are in a better position to assess the necessity, suitability or overall reasonableness of a limitation of fundamental rights. Some of the judges of the Court have even contended that the 'better placed argument' should be the main or even only factor to be considered in deciding about the margin of appreciation.[81] Hereafter, the most relevant applications of the better placed argument are briefly discussed.

a   Moral and Ethical Issues

First, the Court usually leaves a wide margin in cases pertaining to morally or ethically sensitive issues. Examples are cases on the withdrawal of permission to use fertilised ova for IVF treatment;[82] same-sex relationships;[83] gender transformations;[84] surrogacy;[85] abortion;[86] the withdrawal of life-sustaining treatment;[87]

---

[80] This can be seen, for example, in the difference in views reflected in the judgment of the Court (paras. 54–5) and the separate opinion of Judge Malinverni in *Egeland and Hanseid v. Norway*, ECtHR 16 April 2009, 34438/04. See also Ostrovsky, *supra* n. 16, at 58; P.G. Carozza, 'Propter Honoris Respectum: Uses and Misuses of Comparative Law in International Human Rights: Some Reflections on the Jurisprudence of the European Court of Human Rights', *Notre Dame Law Review*, 73 (1998), 1217–37 at 1233.

[81] Cf. Judge Rozakis, dissenting opinion to *Egeland and Hanseid v. Norway*, ECtHR 16 April 2009, 34438/04.

[82] *Evans v. the United Kingdom*, ECtHR (GC) 10 April 2007, 6339/05, para. 77.

[83] E.g. *Schalk and Kopf v. Austria*, ECtHR 24 June 2010, 30151/04.

[84] E.g. *Hämäläinen v. Finland*, ECtHR (GC) 16 July 2014, 37359/09, para. 75; *Y.Y. v. Turkey*, ECtHR 10 March 2015, 14793/08, paras. 106–7.

[85] E.g. *Labassee v. France*, ECtHR 26 June 2014, 65941/11, paras. 57–8; *Paradiso and Campanelli v. Italy*, ECtHR (GC) 24 January 2017, para. 194.

[86] E.g. *A., B. and C. v. Ireland*, ECtHR (GC) 16 December 2010, 25579/05, para. 233.

[87] E.g. *Lambert v. France*, ECtHR (GC) 5 June 2015, 46043/14, para. 148; *Gard and Others v. the United Kingdom*, ECtHR 27 June 2017 (dec.), 39793/17, para. 84; *Afiri and Bidarri v. France*, ECtHR 23 January 2018 (dec.), 1828/18, para. 29.

the relationship between state and religion;[88] and the protection of religious feelings.[89] As the cases of *Handyside* and *Wingrove* have already illustrated, in the sphere of morals the 'better placed argument' is closely related to the existence or lack of a European consensus. Indeed, the Court often mentions these factors in one breath. It did so, for example, in the case of *A., B. and C. v. Ireland*, which concerned the Irish prohibition of abortion for reasons of health and well-being:

> The Court points out that a number of factors must be taken into account when determining the breadth of the margin of appreciation to be enjoyed by the State when determining any case under Article 8 of the Convention. Where a particularly important facet of an individual's existence or identity is at stake, the margin allowed to the State will normally be restricted ... Where, however, there is no consensus within the member States of the Council of Europe, either as to the relative importance of the interest at stake or as to the best means of protecting it, particularly where the case raises sensitive moral or ethical issues, the margin will be wider ... As noted above, by reason of their direct and continuous contact with the vital forces of their countries, the State authorities are, in principle, in a better position than the international judge to give an opinion, not only on the 'exact content of the requirements of morals' in their country, but also on the necessity of a restriction intended to meet them.[90]

Indeed, in many cases, the Court may find that the national authorities are better equipped than itself to decide about the reasonableness or appropriateness of certain measures, *because* there is hardly any consensus on a certain issue.

b   Socio-economic Issues; Political and Operational Policy Choices

In Section 5.3.1 it was shown that it is not possible to draw a sharp line between civil and political rights and socio-economic rights in the Court's case law. In particular, as a result of the Court's acceptance of positive obligations under the Convention and its wide interpretation of Articles 14 ECHR and Article 1 of Protocol No. 1, many cases concern, for example, social security and social benefits, housing, access to health care or planning policy. Regulation of such matters often requires complex assessments to be made of potential consequences of regulation, and budgetary and political choices are required. Not surprisingly, therefore, the Court has often held that the national authorities are generally better placed to make such choices and develop social and economic policies and strategies.[91] This can be

---

[88] *İzzettin Doğan and Others v. Turkey*, ECtHR (GC) 26 April 2016, 62649/10, paras. 112 and 132; *Osmanoğlu and Kocabaş v. Switzerland*, ECtHR 10 January 2017, 29086/12, para. 95; *Hamidović v. Bosnia and Herzegovina*, ECtHR 5 December 2017, 57792/15, para. 38.
[89] *Ibragim Ibragimov and Others v. Russia*, ECtHR 28 August 2018, 1413/08 and 28621/11, para. 95.
[90] *A., B. and C. v. Ireland*, ECtHR (GC) 16 December 2010, 25579/05, para. 232.
[91] For some early examples, see *James and Others v. the United Kingdom*, ECtHR 21 February 1986, 8793/79, para. 46; *Mellacher and Others v. Austria*, ECtHR 19 December 1989, 10522/83, 11011/84

illustrated by a series of cases on austerity measures that were introduced in response to the 2008 economic crisis and the subsequent recession. In many European States, budget cuts were made and public expenditure was reduced, for example by changing the way pensions were indexed or by ending social benefits. In *Da Conceição Mateus and Santos Januário*, the applicants complained that the Portuguese government had decided to reduce their holiday and Christmas subsidies for the year 2012.[92] In assessing the reasonableness of these reductions, the Court took account of the better placed factor:

> [A] wide margin of appreciation is usually allowed to the State under the Convention when it comes to general measures of economic or social policy. Because of their direct knowledge of their society and its needs, the national authorities are in principle better placed than the international judge to appreciate what is in the public interest on social or economic grounds, and the Court will generally respect the legislature's policy choice unless it is manifestly without reasonable foundation ... This margin is even wider when the issues involve an assessment of the priorities as to the allocation of limited State resources.[93]

In addition to austerity measures and economic and financial policy, the Court generally allows the States a wide margin of appreciation in relation to health care policy: 'Matters of health care policy, in particular as regards general preventive measures, are in principle within the margin of appreciation of the domestic authorities who are best placed to assess priorities, use of resources and social needs.'[94]

The same is true for operational choices the States must make in relation to, for example, the selection of the site where an installation, factory or plant will be located that poses certain risks for the health and lives of the people living in the vicinity:

---

and 11070/84, para. 45. See more recently also e.g. *The Church of Jesus Christ of Latter-Day Saints v. the United Kingdom*, ECtHR 4 March 2014, 7552/09, para. 33; *McDonald v. the United Kingdom*, ECtHR 20 May 2014, 4241/12, para. 55.

[92] *Da Conceição Mateus and Santos Januário v. Portugal*, ECtHR 8 October 2013 (dec.), 62235/12 and 57725/12.

[93] See similarly e.g. *Dimitru and Others v. Romania*, ECtHR 4 September 2012 (dec.), 57265/08, para. 41; *N.K.M. v. Hungary*, ECtHR 14 May 2013, 66529/11, para. 37; *Da Silva Carvalho Rico v. Portugal*, ECtHR 1 September 2015 (dec.), 13341/14, para. 37; *Mamatas and Others v. Greece*, ECtHR 21 July 2016, 63066/14, para. 88; *Fábián v. Hungary*, ECtHR (GC) 5 September 2017, 78117/13, para. 67; *Aielli and Others v. Italy and Arboit and Others v. Italy*, ECtHR 10 July 2018 (dec.), 27166/18 and 27167/18, para. 26.

[94] *Shelley v. the United Kingdom*, ECtHR 4 January 2008 (dec.), 23800/06. See also e.g. *Hristozov and Others v. Bulgaria*, ECtHR 13 November 2012, 47039/11 and 358/12, para. 119. In relation to clinical safety policy, see *Eweida and Others v. the United Kingdom*, ECtHR 15 January 2013, 48420/10, para. 99.

The Court acknowledges that it is not its task to substitute for the views of the local authorities its own view of the best policy to adopt in dealing with the social, economic and urban problems in this part of Istanbul. It therefore accepts the Government's argument that in this respect an impossible or disproportionate burden must not be imposed on the authorities without consideration being given, in particular, to the operational choices which they must make in terms of priorities and resources ... this results from the wide margin of appreciation States enjoy ... in difficult social and technical spheres such as the one in issue in the instant case.[95]

Similarly, the Court has generally accorded a wide margin of appreciation in matters of housing, spatial policy and planning. An example can be found in *Depalle*, which concerned a refusal of permission to continue occupying a house that was built (illegally) on maritime public land.[96] Although the refusal interfered with the right to property, the State was left much leeway to provide this type of restriction:

The Court has ... often reiterated that regional planning and environmental conservation policies, where the community's general interest is pre-eminent, confer on the State a margin of appreciation that is greater than when exclusively civil rights are at stake ... [I]t is first and foremost for the national authorities to decide which type of measures should be imposed to protect coastal areas. These will depend on urban and regional planning policies, which are, by definition, evolutive, and are, par excellence, spheres in which the State intervenes, particularly through control of property in the general or public interest.[97]

Finally, the same is true for matters of taxation, as the Court emphasised in *Berkvens*:

The Court has often stated that the national authorities are in principle better placed than an international court to evaluate local needs and conditions. In matters of general social and economic policy, on which opinions within a democratic society may reasonably differ widely, the domestic policy-maker should be afforded a particularly broad margin of appreciation ... With particular regard to taxation, the Court has held, under Article 1 of Protocol No. 1 taken alone, that when framing and implementing policies in

---

[95] *Öneryildiz v. Turkey*, ECtHR (GC) 30 November 2004, 48939/99, para. 107.
[96] *Depalle v. France*, ECtHR (GC) 29 March 2010, 34044/02.
[97] *Ibid.*, paras. 84 and 87. See also e.g. *Lohuis and Others v. the Netherlands*, ECtHR 30 April 2013 (dec.), 37265/10, para. 56. In relation to housing and tenancy policies, see e.g. *Nobel and Others v. the Netherlands*, ECtHR 2 July 2013 (dec.), 27126/11, para. 40; *Bittó and Others v. Slovakia*, ECtHR 28 January 2014, 30255/09, para. 96; *Zammit and Attard Cassar v. Malta*, ECtHR 30 July 2015, 1046/12, para. 62; *Landvreugd v. the Netherlands*, ECtHR (GC) 6 November 2017, 43494/09, paras. 137–9.

the area of taxation a Contracting State enjoys a wide margin of appreciation and the Court will respect the legislature's assessment in such matters unless it is devoid of reasonable foundation.[98]

Clearly, many such cases concerning these socio-economic policy issues are about positive obligations rather than interferences with Convention rights. On the other hand, it has been shown that many positive obligations cases require operational and policy choices to be made.[99] Accordingly, it is generally true that the margin of appreciation in positive obligations cases is a wide one. Nevertheless, there is no one-to-one relationship between positive obligations and a wide margin of appreciation. The Court emphasised in *Ališić* that the nature of an obligation as such makes little difference to the scope of the margin of appreciation:

> Whether the case is analysed in terms of a positive duty of the State or in terms of an interference by a public authority which needs to be justified, the criteria to be applied do not differ in substance . . . In both contexts the State enjoys a certain margin of appreciation in determining the steps to be taken to ensure compliance with the Convention.[100]

It is thus the better placed factor (together with other factors discussed above and below) that will be decisive in determining the margin's scope, not the nature of the obligation for the State. Indeed, there are many positive obligation cases where the Court either does not mention the margin of appreciation or it exercises strict scrutiny. Examples of this can be found in the many cases where the Court applies procedural positive obligations.[101] Apparently, the Court finds itself just as well placed as the national authorities to determine the compatibility of national acts and omissions with such procedural positive obligations.

c Special Context of the Case

The Court has further indicated that the special context of a case may mean that the States should be given extra leeway in deciding on reasonable restrictions. Importantly, however, in none of the situations discussed below is the element of context decisive in determining the overall margin of appreciation. As will be explained in Section 7.4.5, it may be outweighed by other factors, such as the importance of the individual rights at stake.

---

[98] *Berkvens v. the Netherlands*, ECtHR 27 May 2014 (dec.), 18485/14, paras. 31–2. See earlier also *Gasus Dossier- und Fördertechnik GmbH v. the Netherlands*, ECtHR 23 February 1995, 15375/89, para. 60 and the *Building Societies* case, ECtHR 23 October 1997, 21319/93, para. 80. See similarly e.g. *Arnaud and Others v. France*, ECtHR 15 January 2015, 36918/11, para. 27.

[99] For further elaboration, see Chapter 5.

[100] *Ališić and Others v. Bosnia and Herzegovina, Croatia, Serbia, Slovenia and the former Yugoslav Republic of Macedonia*, ECtHR (GC) 16 July 2014, 60642/08, para. 101. See similarly e.g. *Y.Y. v. Turkey*, ECtHR 10 March 2015, 14793/08, para. 59.

[101] See the examples mentioned in Section 5.3.2.

First, if a case concerns military matters or national security, for example, this context may be a factor in the Court's determination of the scope of the margin of appreciation. The Court explained this in *Smith and Grady*, which concerned the dismissal of some officers from the army because of their homosexuality:

> When the core of the national security aim pursued is the operational effectiveness of the armed forces, it is accepted that each State is competent to organise its own system of military discipline and enjoys a certain margin of appreciation in this respect … The Court also considers that it is open to the State to impose restrictions on an individual's right to respect for his private life where there is a real threat to the armed forces' operational effectiveness, as the proper functioning of an army is hardly imaginable without legal rules designed to prevent service personnel from undermining it.[102]

Another example can be found in relation to the prison context, where the Court has equally held that this particular context may require more leeway for the States to set restrictions on the exercise of rights such as the freedom of correspondence:

> The Court accepts … that the 'necessity' for interference with the exercise of the right of a convicted prisoner to respect for his correspondence must be appreciated having regard to the ordinary and reasonable requirements of imprisonment. The 'prevention of disorder or crime', for example, may justify wider measures of interference in the case of such a prisoner than in that of a person at liberty.[103]

More recently, however, the Court has held that the special prison context is less important in relation to the protection of private and family life.[104] The margin of appreciation therefore has narrowed in cases concerning, for example, family visits and the placement of detainees in prisons at a very large distance from their families.[105]

Just as the special military or prison context may play a role in widening the margin of appreciation, historical context can also explain the restrictive measures introduced by a State. Historical context is particularly relevant in cases concerning States that have made the transition from a dictatorial or communist regime to a democratic system.[106] Sometimes, to facilitate this transition, special measures are introduced that interfere with Convention rights. The context may then make it more difficult for the Court to assess the necessity and appropriateness of such

---

[102] *Smith and Grady v. the United Kingdom*, ECtHR 27 September 1999, 33985/96 and 33986/96, para. 89; see also *Konstantin Markin v. Russia*, ECtHR (GC) 22 March 2012, 30078/06, para. 128. In relation to national security, see also e.g. *Centrum för Rättvista v. Sweden*, ECtHR 19 June 2018, 35252/08, para. 112.
[103] *Golder v. the United Kingdom*, ECtHR 21 February 1975, 4451/70, para. 45.
[104] See *Koroshenko v. Russia*, ECtHR (GC) 30 June 2015, 41418/04, paras. 134–6.
[105] *Ibid.*; see also e.g. *Polyakova and Others v. Russia*, ECtHR 7 March 2017, 35090/09, para. 89.
[106] But it is not limited to that context; for another type of relevant historical context, see e.g. *Magyar Keresztény Mennonita Egyház and Others v. Hungary*, ECtHR 8 April 2014, 70945/11, para. 108.

measures, which may be a relevant factor in according a respondent State a somewhat wider margin of appreciation. In *Cichopek*, the Court summarised its relevant case law in this regard:

> Relying on the fundamentally subsidiary role of the Convention, the Court has consistently recognised that the national authorities, having direct democratic legitimation, are in principle better placed than an international court to evaluate local needs and conditions. In matters of general policy, on which opinions within a democratic society may reasonably differ widely, the role of the domestic policy-maker should be given special weight … In its many judgments given in the context of the political changes that commenced in central and eastern Europe in 1989–1990, the Court has stressed that these principles apply equally, if not *a fortiori*, to the measures adopted in the course of the fundamental reform of the country's political, legal and economic system in the transition from a totalitarian regime to a democratic State, phenomena which inevitably involve the enactment of large-scale economic and social legislation. Balancing the rights at stake, as well as the interests of the different persons affected by the process of transforming the State, is an exceptionally difficult exercise. In such circumstances, in the nature of things, a wide margin of appreciation should be accorded to the State.[107]

Another context that may be relevant to the Court's margin of appreciation doctrine is that of interferences in horizontal relations, that is, relations between private parties. As was discussed in Chapter 6, the Convention cannot be invoked directly against, for example, an employer who has spied on his employees and has thereby restricted their privacy rights. Nonetheless, the Court has held that there may be positive obligations for the State to prevent such interferences from occurring, but in this particular context, the States' margin of appreciation may be somewhat wider:

> The Court reiterates that the choice of the means calculated to secure compliance with Article 8 of the Convention in the sphere of the relations of individuals between themselves is in principle a matter that falls within the Contracting States' margin of appreciation. There are different ways of ensuring respect for private life, and the nature of the State's obligation will depend on the particular aspect of private life that is at issue.[108]

It may also be important for the scope of the margin of appreciation if a case is examined in the context of a pilot judgment procedure. This procedure allows the Court to identify structural or systemic problems of Convention compliance which

---

[107] *Cichopek and Others v. Poland*, ECtHR 14 May 2013 (dec.), 15189/10, para. 134; see also para. 142. See also e.g. *Velikovi and Others v. Bulgaria*, ECtHR 15 March 2007, 43278/98, paras. 178–80.
[108] *Bărbulescu v. Romania*, ECtHR (GC) 5 September 2017, 61496/08, para. 113; see also para. 119. See similarly e.g. *Söderman v. Sweden*, ECtHR 12 November 2013, 5786/08, para. 79.

have led to a great amount of similar complaints to be lodged in Strasbourg.[109] Having identified such problems in a judgment in one particular case – the pilot judgment – it is then for the respondent State to provide a general solution to the problem. After a certain amount of time has passed (usually a deadline set by the Court in its pilot judgment), the Court will decide another case on the same topic to see whether the problem has been adequately addressed and whether it can refer all similar pending cases back to be decided by the national authorities. In this particular context, the Court leaves a wide margin of appreciation to the States to assess which remedial measures should be taken. For example, in *Cocchiarella*, the Court had to decide on the measures Italy had introduced to offer a remedy in cases on excessively long national court proceedings:

> [T]he Contracting States are afforded some discretion as to the manner in which they provide individuals with the relief required by Article 13 and conform to their Convention obligation under that provision. It has also stressed the importance of the rules relating to the subsidiarity principle so that individuals are not systematically forced to refer to the Court in Strasbourg complaints that could otherwise, and in the Court's opinion more appropriately, have been addressed in the first place within the national legal system. Accordingly, where the legislature or the domestic courts have agreed to play their proper role by introducing a domestic remedy, the Court will clearly have to draw certain conclusions from this. Where a State has taken a significant step by introducing a compensatory remedy, the Court must leave a wider margin of appreciation to the State to allow it to organise the remedy in a manner consistent with its own legal system and traditions and consonant with the standard of living in the country concerned. It will, in particular, be easier for the domestic courts to refer to the amounts awarded at domestic level for other types of damage – personal injury, damage relating to a relative's death or damage in defamation cases, for example – and rely on their innermost conviction, even if that results in awards of amounts that are lower than those fixed by the Court in similar cases.[110]

Generally, it may therefore be relatively easy for States to justify a remedy introduced in response to a pilot judgment.

---

[109] See further e.g. J.H. Gerards, 'The Pilot Judgment Procedure before the European Court of Human Rights as an Instrument for Dialogue' in M. Claes et al. (eds.), *Constitutional Conversations in Europe* (Antwerp: Intersentia, 2012) pp. 371–97; L.R. Glas, 'The Functioning of the Pilot-Judgment Procedure of the European Court of Human Rights in Practice', *Netherlands Quarterly of Human Rights*, 34 (2016), 41 et seq.

[110] *Cocchiarella v. Italy*, ECtHR (GC) 29 March 2006, 64886/01, paras. 79–80. See also e.g. *Techniki Olympiaki A.E. v. Greece*, ECtHR 1 October 2013 (dec.), 40547/10, para. 41; *Preda and Others v. Romania*, ECtHR 29 April 2014, 9584/02, para. 115; *Domján and Others v. Hungary*, ECtHR 14 November 2017 (dec.), 5433/17, para. 27.

One last category of cases for which the Court has held that the States' margin of appreciation should be wide because of the context concerns the assessment of whether there is a state of emergency (Article 15 ECHR), and the evaluation of the need to take certain restrictive measures in this respect. The Court confirmed this in *A. v. the United Kingdom*, which concerned a special detention regime for suspects of terrorism:

> The Court reiterates that it falls to each Contracting State, with its responsibility for 'the life of [its] nation', to determine whether that life is threatened by a 'public emergency' and, if so, how far it is necessary to go in attempting to overcome the emergency. By reason of their direct and continuous contact with the pressing needs of the moment, the national authorities are in principle better placed than the international judge to decide both on the presence of such an emergency and on the nature and scope of the derogations necessary to avert it. Accordingly, in this matter a wide margin of appreciation should be left to the national authorities.[111]

d   The 'Fourth Instance' Argument: Interpretation of National Law and Establishing Facts

The Court has often emphasised that the national authorities are competent to construe and apply domestic law. This means that the Court will show some deference if a case primarily relates to questions of interpretation and application of national law. Indeed, usually domestic courts are better placed to answer such questions than the Court is, as the Court held in its ruling in *Pla and Puncernau*:

> On many occasions, and in very different spheres, the Court has declared that it is in the first place for the national authorities, and in particular the courts of first instance and appeal, to construe and apply the domestic law ... That principle, which by definition applies to domestic legislation, is all the more applicable when interpreting an eminently private instrument such as a clause in a person's will. In a situation such as the one here, the domestic courts are evidently better placed than an international court to evaluate, in the light of local legal traditions, the particular context of the legal dispute submitted to them and the various competing rights and interests ... When ruling on disputes of this type, the national authorities and, in particular, the courts of first instance and appeal have a wide margin of appreciation.[112]

---

[111]   *A. and Others v. the United Kingdom*, ECtHR (GC) 19 February 2009, 3455/05, para. 173. See earlier e.g. *Ireland v. the United Kingdom*, ECtHR 18 January 1978, 5310/71, para. 207 and see more recently *Mehmet Hasan Altan v. Turkey*, ECtHR 20 March 2018, 13237/17, para. 91.

[112]   *Pla and Puncernau v. Andorra*, ECtHR 13 July 2004, 69498/01, para. 46. See also already *Winterwerp v. the Netherlands*, ECtHR 24 October 1979, 6301/73, para. 46.

This argument may also play a role in cases regarding non-derogable rights or Convention provisions permitting only limited exceptions. There, the Court may even expressly distinguish between the margin of appreciation left to the State in establishing the facts and the level of scrutiny needed in assessing the compliance with the Convention. An example can be found in the *Van Colle* case, where a complaint regarding an alleged violation of Article 2 had been examined on the national level by the House of Lords of the United Kingdom:

> The Court recalls that, while it is not its task to substitute its own assessment of the facts for that of the domestic courts, where allegations are made under Articles 2 and 3 of the Convention the Court must apply a particularly thorough scrutiny … The Court considers that a similar approach should be applied to the House of Lords' application of the *Osman* test of State responsibility. Accordingly, while the Court must accord a certain margin of appreciation to the legal assessment made by the House of Lords, it must nevertheless apply a particularly thorough scrutiny since the complaint concerns the pre-eminent right to life guaranteed by Article 2.[113]

The Court has also left a wider margin of appreciation to the States in relation to issues of evidence and establishment of facts, as it did in *Kononov*:

> The Court notes that, in principle, it should not substitute itself for the domestic jurisdictions. Its duty, in accordance with Article 19 of the Convention, is to ensure the observance of the engagements undertaken by the Contracting Parties to the Convention. Given the subsidiary nature of the Convention system, it is not the Court's function to deal with alleged errors of fact committed by a national court, unless and in so far as they may have infringed rights and freedoms protected by the Convention … and unless that domestic assessment is manifestly arbitrary.[114]

This factor is often summarised as the 'fourth instance' argument, which implies that the Court is not to act as yet another national highest court that has the same competences and duties as the national courts, but it has to behave as a supra-national Court that supervises the compatibility of a national interference with the Convention.[115] The institutional argument of subsidiarity is particularly important to explaining this position, but the examples show that the epistemic 'better placed argument' also plays a role.

---

[113] *Van Colle v. the United Kingdom*, ECtHR 13 November 2012, 7678/09, para. 93.

[114] *Kononov v. Latvia*, ECtHR (GC) 17 May 2010, 36376/04, para. 189.

[115] See e.g. *Kemmache v. France (No. 3)*, ECtHR 24 November 1994, 17621/91, para. 44; *Somorjai v. Hungary*, ECtHR 28 August 2018, 60934/13, para. 53. See further e.g. Fahner, *supra* n. 10, section 2.3.4.

e Procedural Quality and Fairness

The Court often leaves a somewhat wider margin of appreciation to the States if it has transpired that their national judicial or legislative procedures are fair and of high quality, and if they have enabled a thorough scrutiny of all the interests involved.[116] On the other hand, if the quality of the national decision-making process was doubtful, the Court may intervene more easily. The Court held this, for example, in *Salontaji-Drobnjak*:

> [W]hilst Article 8 of the Convention contains no explicit procedural requirements, the decision-making process involved in measures of interference must be fair and such as to ensure due respect of the interests safeguarded by Article 8 ... The extent of the State's margin of appreciation thus depends on the quality of the decision-making process. If the procedure was seriously deficient in some respect, the conclusions of the domestic authorities are more open to criticism.[117]

Indeed, if there are serious procedural shortcomings, there is less reason to expect that the Court is worse placed than the national authorities to evaluate the need for certain restrictions. Moreover, from a perspective of effective protection of Convention rights, if there are such shortcomings there may be more reason to review more carefully whether the State's interferences can be justified on substantive grounds.

f Competing Convention Rights

The last category of cases in which the Court has generally left a wider margin of appreciation because of the 'better placed' factor comprises cases concerning a conflict between individual Convention rights. In *Chassagnou*, the Court held that such cases are often particularly complex and that, for that reason, the State should be given more leeway to strike a fair balance between the conflicting interests:

> In the present case the only aim invoked by the Government to justify the interference complained of was 'protection of the rights and freedoms of others'. Where these 'rights and freedoms' are themselves among those guaranteed by the Convention or its Protocols, it must be accepted that the need to protect them may lead States to restrict other rights or freedoms likewise set forth in the Convention. It is precisely this constant search for a balance between the fundamental rights of each individual which constitutes the foundation of a 'democratic society'. The balancing of individual interests that may well be

---

[116] See e.g. *Krisztián Barnabás Tóth v. Hungary*, ECtHR 12 February 2013, 48494/06, para. 37.

[117] *Salontaji-Drobnjak v. Serbia*, ECtHR 13 October 2009, 36500/05, para. 143; see also *A.N. v. Lithuania*, ECtHR 31 May 2016, 17280/08, para. 118. In relation to legislative procedures, see e.g. *Animal Defenders International v. the United Kingdom*, ECtHR (GC) 22 April 2013, 48876/08, para. 108 ('The quality of the parliamentary and judicial review of the necessity of the measure is of particular importance in this respect, including to the operation of the relevant margin of appreciation'); see also *S.A.S. v. France*, ECtHR (GC) 1 July 2014, 43835/11, para. 154.

contradictory is a difficult matter, and Contracting States must have a broad margin of appreciation in this respect, since the national authorities are in principle better placed than the European Court to assess whether or not there is a 'pressing social need' capable of justifying interference with one of the rights guaranteed by the Convention.[118]

The Court does not always mention this factor, however, even in cases which clearly concern conflicting rights, and it does not always leave a wide margin of appreciation in such cases for this particular reason.[119]

7.4.4 Nature and Importance of the Convention Issue at Stake
a Core Rights and Peripheral Rights

The Court has often stated that the nature of the Convention right and its importance for the individual are of great importance to the scope of the margin of appreciation.[120] In principle, the margin of appreciation will be narrow if the essence or 'core' of one of the Convention rights is affected, whereas it will be wider if a less important aspect of the Convention is at stake.[121] The importance of this factor can be understood from the perspective of effective protection of the Convention in relation to the principle of subsidiarity. The more important a certain right, the more reason there is for European supervision on the respect for that particular right.

The Court has given much attention to the definition of the core of certain Convention rights, even though it has not provided clear and general criteria to determine which elements belong to the core of those rights. As was explained in Section 3.4, the Court has found that there are four main values underlying the Convention: democracy, pluralism, human dignity and autonomy.[122] Core rights reasoning generally implies that the closer a certain aspect of a right is related to these central concepts, the more important it is considered to be. It is precisely because restrictions of such rights might endanger the achievement of the Convention's objectives that the Court finds it justified to apply strict scrutiny.

---

[118] *Chassagnou and Others v. France*, ECtHR (GC) 29 April 1999, 25088/94, para. 113. See also e.g. *MGN Limited v. the United Kingdom*, ECtHR 18 January 2011, 39401/04, paras. 142 and 150; *Eweida and Others v. the United Kingdom*, ECtHR 15 January 2013, 48420/10, para. 106; *Sindicatul 'Păstorul cel Bun' v. Romania*, ECtHR (GC) 9 July 2013, 2330/09, para. 160; *Delfi AS v. Estonia*, ECtHR (GC) 16 June 2015, 64569/09, para. 139.

[119] See e.g. *Pfeifer v. Austria*, ECtHR 15 November 2007, 12556/03; *X. and Others v. Austria*, ECtHR (GC) 19 February 2013, 19010/07, para. 151.

[120] See the general formula quoted *supra*, Section 7.2.

[121] E.g. *Evans v. the United Kingdom*, ECtHR 10 April 2007, 6339/05, para. 77; *Dickson v. the United Kingdom*, ECtHR (GC) 4 December 2007, 44362/04, para. 78; *S. and Marper v. the United Kingdom*, ECtHR 4 December 2008, 30562/04 and 30566/04, para. 102.

[122] See further Section 3.4.

Many examples of the Court's 'core-periphery approach' can be found in the case law about freedom of expression and freedom of association and assembly. According to the Court there is a clear connection between effective political democracy and the realisation of certain human rights and fundamental freedoms.[123] Consequently, the freedom of expression, assembly and association (especially the freedom to form political parties) are of prime importance to any well-functioning democracy.[124] In this light it is not surprising that the Court strictly reviews limitations of political expression and publications relating to subjects of general interest. In *Animal Defenders International*, for example, the Court explained that it should leave a narrow margin of appreciation and exercise strict review in relation to a restriction of political expression by an NGO:

> As to the breadth of the margin of appreciation to be afforded, it is recalled that it depends on a number of factors. It is defined by the type of the expression at issue and, in this respect, it is recalled that there is little scope under Article 10 § 2 for restrictions on debates on questions of public interest ... The margin is also narrowed by the strong interest of a democratic society in the press exercising its vital role as a public watchdog ... freedom of the press and other news media affords the public one of the best means of discovering and forming an opinion of the ideas and attitudes of political leaders. It is incumbent on the press to impart information and ideas on subjects of public interest and the public also has a right to receive them ... Accordingly, the Court scrupulously examines the proportionality of a restriction of expression by the press in a television programme on a subject of general interest ... In the present context, it must be noted that, when an NGO draws attention to matters of public interest, it is exercising a public watchdog role of similar importance to that of the press ... For these reasons, the margin of appreciation to be accorded to the State in the present context is, in principle, a narrow one.[125]

Likewise, the Court only accepts the dissolution of political parties if the national government has provided compelling and inescapable reasons to do so,[126] and it

---

[123] E.g. *Sørensen and Rasmussen v. Denmark*, ECtHR 11 January 2006, 52562/99 and 52620/99, para. 58.
[124] E.g. *United Communist Party of Turkey v. Turkey*, ECtHR 30 January 1998, 19392/92, para. 57; *Refah Partisi and Others v. Turkey*, ECtHR (GC) 13 February 2003, 41340/98, para. 86.
[125] *Animal Defenders International v. the United Kingdom*, ECtHR (GC) 22 April 2013, 48876/08, paras. 102–4. See also e.g. *Sunday Times v. United Kingdom*, ECtHR 26 April 1979, 6538/74; *Vajnai v. Hungary*, ECtHR 8 July 2008, 33629/06, para. 51; *Schweizerische Radio- und Fernsehgesellschaft SRG v. Switzerland*, ECtHR 21 June 2012, 34124/06, para. 51; *Morice v. France*, ECtHR (GC) 23 April 2015, 29369/10, para. 125.
[126] E.g. *United Communist Party of Turkey v. Turkey*, ECtHR 30 January 1998, 19392/92, para. 57; *Refah Partisi and Others v. Turkey*, ECtHR (GC) 13 February 2003, 41340/98, para. 86.

requires convincing arguments to justify limitations on meetings of associations or demonstrations.[127] To give an example, the Court explained in *Jerusalem* why it should leave a narrow margin of appreciation to the State in a case where the freedom of expression of a parliamentarian had been infringed:

> In this respect the Court recalls that while freedom of expression is important for everybody, it is especially so for an elected representative of the people. He or she represents the electorate, draws attention to their preoccupations and defends their interests. Accordingly, interferences with the freedom of expression of an opposition member of parliament, like the applicant, call for the closest scrutiny on the part of the Court.[128]

The value of pluralism may play a similar role in narrowing the margin of appreciation for the State. As explained in Section 3.4.5, the Court considers this value of great importance for individuals, in particular in the sphere of freedom of religion. In that sphere, pluralism is closely related to State neutrality: the State should not show any preference or bias for one particular religion or religious group. If such neutrality seems not to have been shown and the value of pluralism is affected by an interference, the Court will strictly scrutinise the interference to see if it can be justified by sufficiently objective and good reasons. In *Jehovah's Witnesses of Moscow*, for example, the Court was asked to judge on the compatibility with Article 9 of the dissolution of the Moscow Branch of the Jehovah's Witnesses:

> The Court reiterates that the State's duty of neutrality and impartiality prohibits it from assessing the legitimacy of religious beliefs or the ways in which those beliefs are expressed or manifested ... Accordingly, the State has a narrow margin of appreciation and must advance serious and compelling reasons for an interference with the choices that people may make in pursuance of the religious standard of behaviour within the sphere of their personal autonomy.[129]

In the same vein, the Court has devised a 'core' for rights related to the concepts of personal autonomy and human dignity. In particular, within the wide scope given to Article 8 ECHR (family life, private life, correspondence and housing), the Court has distinguished a (rather fuzzy) core of rights that it considers essential to the

---

[127] E.g. *Ouranio Toxo and Others v. Greece*, ECtHR 20 October 2005, 74989/01, para. 36; *Makhmudov v. Russia*, ECtHR 26 July 2007, 35082/04, para. 63. By contrast, if the case only concerns a more peripheral aspect of the freedom of demonstration, such as restrictions on the location, time or manner of conduct of an assembly, the margin may be wider; see e.g. *Kudrevičius and Others v. Lithuania*, ECtHR (GC) 15 October 2015, 37553/05, para. 156; *Les Authentiks and Supras Auteuil 91 v. France*, ECtHR 27 October 2016, 4696/11 and 4703/11, para. 84; *Lashmankin and Others v. Russia*, ECtHR 7 February 2017, 57818/09, para. 417.
[128] *Jerusalem v. Austria*, ECtHR 27 February 2001, 26958/95, para. 36.
[129] *Jehovah's Witnesses of Moscow v. Russia*, ECtHR 10 June 2010, 302/02, para. 119.

individual, and it has adapted the margin of appreciation accordingly. In *Evans*, for example, the Court held: 'Where a particularly important facet of an individual's existence or identity is at stake, the margin allowed to the State will be restricted.'[130] In line with this, the Court has held that measures that affect 'the most intimate' or 'sensitive' aspects of someone's life, such as someone's sexuality[131] or identity,[132] should generally be carefully scrutinised for their reasonableness and objectivity. Likewise, the Court has recognised several other issues that are closely connected to one's personal autonomy, such as the confidentiality of medical information[133] or the right to live in one's own house.[134]

Conversely, the ECtHR often leaves a wider margin of appreciation if no core values have been affected.[135] In relation to the freedom of expression, it compares the type of expression that has been limited to the core of the freedom of expression (mostly political speech), and it adapts the margin of appreciation accordingly. For example, in a case where internet pirates had enabled copyright protected materials to be freely shared on the internet, the Court held that the State enjoyed a wider margin of appreciation:

> In this connection, the Court would also underline that the width of the margin of appreciation afforded to States varies depending on a number of factors, among which the type of information at issue is of particular importance. In the present case, although protected by Article 10, the safeguards afforded to the distributed material in respect of which the applicants were convicted cannot reach the same level as that afforded to political expression and debate. It follows that the nature of the information at hand ... [is] such as to afford the State a wide margin of appreciation.[136]

Similarly, it has held that no intensive scrutiny has to be applied to restrictions of commercial expressions (such as television or radio commercials), as it did in *Sekmadienis*: '[The Court] observes that the advertisements had a commercial purpose – to advertise a clothing line – and were not intended to contribute to any public debate concerning religion or any other matters of general interest ... Accordingly, the margin of appreciation accorded to the national authorities in the

---

[130] *Evans v. the United Kingdom*, ECtHR (GC) 10 April 2007, 6339/05, para. 77.

[131] E.g. *Dudgeon v. the United Kingdom*, ECtHR 22 October 1981, 7525/76, para. 52; *Schlumpf v. Switzerland*, ECtHR 8 January 2009, 29002/06, para. 104.

[132] E.g. *Jäggi v. Switzerland*, ECtHR 13 July 2006, 58757/00, para. 37; *Mennesson v. France*, ECtHR 26 June 2014, 65192/11, para. 80.

[133] E.g. *Z v. Finland*, ECtHR 25 February 1997, 22009/93, paras. 95–6.

[134] E.g. *Gillow v. UK*, ECtHR 24 November 1986, 9063/80, para. 55; *Berger-Krall and Others v. Slovenia*, ECtHR 12 June 2014, 14717/04, para. 268.

[135] In addition, it leaves a wider margin of appreciation if the expressions themselves appear to conflict with core democratic values, as may be the case for hate speech; see e.g. *Stomakhin v. Russia*, ECtHR 9 May 2018, 52273/07, para. 92.

[136] *Neij and Sunde Kolmisoppi v. Sweden*, ECtHR 19 February 2013 (dec.), 40397/12.

present case is broader.'[137] This is different, however, if the expressions are, in reality, political in character or contribute to a debate about a topic of general interest.[138] The core value of such expressions then prevails.

Similarly, if the Court has found that the right at stake is not closely related to the applicant's autonomy or human dignity and the case concerns a rather more peripheral issue, the margin may be wider. The *Parrillo* case, for example, related to the applicant's wish that her embryos, which had been created through IVF treatment but had not been used for implantation, could be donated to scientific research instead of being destroyed. The Court decided to leave a wide margin of appreciation to the State in deciding on the fate of human embryos, taking into account that the issue did not concern a core right:

> The Court observes at the outset that ... the instant case does not concern prospective parenthood. Accordingly, whilst it is of course important, the right invoked by the applicant to donate embryos to scientific research is not one of the core rights attracting the protection of Article 8 of the Convention as it does not concern a particularly important aspect of the applicant's existence and identity.[139]

In a similar vein, the Court did not find a reason to restrict the State's margin of appreciation in a case that concerned the disclosure of an applicant's bank data, since this was purely financial information that did not concern intimate details or data closely linked to his identity.[140]

Finally, it is useful to note that the Court sometimes applies core rights reasoning without connecting the argument to the central values protected by the Convention. It did so in general terms, for example, in a case against the United Kingdom on trade union freedom:

> If a legislative restriction strikes at the core of trade-union activity, a lesser margin of appreciation is to be recognised to the national legislature and more is required to justify the proportionality of the resultant interference, in the general interest, with the exercise of trade-union freedom. Conversely, if it is not the core but a secondary or accessory aspect of trade-union activity that is affected, the margin is wider and the interference is, by its

---

[137] *Sekmadienis Ltd. v. Lithuania*, ECtHR 30 January 2018, 69317/14, para. 76. See also *Markt Intern Verlag GmbH and Klaus Beermann v. Germany*, ECtHR 20 November 1989, 10572/83, para. 33; *Demuth v. Switzerland*, ECtHR 5 November 2002, 38743/97, para. 42; *Mouvement raëlien suisse v. Switzerland*, ECtHR (GC) 13 July 2012, 16354/06, para. 61; *Ashby Donald and Others v. France*, ECtHR 10 January 2013, 36769/08; *Remuszko v. Poland*, ECtHR 16 July 2013, 1562/10, para. 64; *Bohlen v. Germany*, ECtHR 19 February 2015, 53495/09, para. 47.
[138] See e.g. *Hertel v. Switzerland*, ECtHR 25 August 1998, 25181/94, para. 47; *VgT Verein gegen Tierfabriken v. Switzerland*, ECtHR 28 June 2001, 24699/94, paras. 69–72; *Animal Defenders International Ltd. v. the United Kingdom*, ECtHR (GC) 22 April 2013, 48876/08, paras. 102–5.
[139] *Parrillo v. Italy*, ECtHR (GC) 27 August 2015, 46470/11, para. 174.
[140] *G.S.B. v. Switzerland*, ECtHR 22 December 2015, 28601/11, para. 93.

nature, more likely to be proportionate as far as its consequences for the exercise of trade-union freedom are concerned.[141]

The point of reference thus does not necessarily need to be democracy, pluralism, dignity or autonomy, but it may also be the purpose or 'telos' of the right as such.

b   Seriousness and Nature of the Interference

Closely connected to the importance of the individual interest concerned is the seriousness and nature of the interference with the right. In practice, this factor mainly influences the scope of the margin of appreciation if the interference makes it impossible (*de jure* or *de facto*) to effectively enjoy the right. Examples of this can be seen in relation to prior restrictions of the freedom of expression, such as seizure of all copies of a newspaper or an injunction prohibiting the distribution of a book. In *Observer and Guardian*, the Court explained the reasons for limiting the margin of appreciation of the State in such cases:

> Article 10 of the Convention does not in terms prohibit the imposition of prior restraints on publication, as such ... On the other hand, the dangers inherent in prior restraints are such that they call for the most careful scrutiny on the part of the Court. This is especially so as far as the press is concerned, for news is a perishable commodity and to delay its publication, even for a short period, may well deprive it of all its value and interest.[142]

Likewise, if the right to access to court is restricted by an immunity, the scope of the margin may be related to the nature of the immunity, since, as the Court has held, from the point of view of its compatibility with the Convention, the broader an immunity, the more compelling must be its justification'.[143] In other cases, the nature of the interference may help to widen the margin of appreciation. For example, the Court has mentioned that the identity of the person affected by the interference might make a difference. In *Bernh Larsen Holding*, the local tax authorities had decided to make a copy of the applicant company's server in relation to a tax audit.[144] In deciding on the margin of appreciation, the Court took account of the fact that in this case, it was a company that was affected by the measure:

> One factor that militates in favour of strict scrutiny in the present case is that the backup copy comprised all existing documents on the server, regardless of their relevance for tax assessment purposes ... On the other hand, the fact that the measure was aimed at legal

---

[141] *The National Union of Rail, Maritime and Transport Workers v. the United Kingdom*, ECtHR 8 April 2014, 31045/10, para. 87.
[142] *Observer and Guardian v. the United Kingdom*, ECtHR 26 November 1991, 13585/88, para. 60.
[143] *Kart v. Turkey*, ECtHR (GC) 3 December 2009, 8917/05, para. 83.
[144] *Bernh Larsen Holding AS and Others v. Norway*, ECtHR 14 March 2013, 24117/08.

persons meant that a wider margin of appreciation could be applied than would have been the case had it concerned an individual.[145]

Finally, there may be a difference in the scope of the margin of appreciation depending on the decision to regulate a certain matter as such, and the way in which the regulation is designed. The Court explained this difference in relation to the decision to create a bulk interception regime to protect national security in *Centrum för Rättvista*:

> The Court has expressly recognised that the national authorities enjoy a wide margin of appreciation in choosing how best to achieve the legitimate aim of protecting national security . . . [T]he Court considers that the decision to operate a bulk interception regime in order to identify hitherto unknown threats to national security is one which continues to fall within States' margin of appreciation. Nevertheless, it is evident from the Court's case-law over several decades that all interception regimes (both bulk and targeted) have the potential to be abused, especially where the true breadth of the authorities' discretion to intercept cannot be discerned from the relevant legislation . . . Therefore, while States enjoy a wide margin of appreciation in deciding what type of interception regime is necessary to protect national security, the discretion afforded to them in operating an interception regime must necessarily be narrower.[146]

In many cases, however, the intrusiveness and nature of the interference are more important for the test of reasonableness as such, in particular the fair balance test, than they are for the determination of the scope of the margin of appreciation.[147]

7.4.5   Balancing the Factors Determining the Margin of Appreciation

The above sections have shown that the margin of appreciation case law of the Court is refined and detailed. The Court has distinguished a range of different factors that may influence the scope of the margin and, thereby, the intensity of its review. An important remaining question is how these factors interrelate.[148] If all factors clearly point in one direction, this question is easily answered. For example, if there is little European consensus on how a socio-economic issue should be regulated and the case concerns an aspect of a right that cannot be regarded as a 'core aspect', it is fairly obvious that the margin of appreciation should be wide and the Court's review should be restrained.[149] Conversely, it is equally clear that a narrow margin of

---

[145] *Ibid.*, para. 159.
[146] *Centrum för Rättvista v. Sweden*, ECtHR 19 June 2018, 35252/08, paras. 112–13.
[147] The fair balance test is discussed in more detail in Section 10.4.
[148] See also M.R. Hutchinson, 'The Margin of Appreciation Doctrine in the European Court of Human Rights', *International and Comparative Law Quarterly*, 48 (1999), 641; see further in particular Gerards, 'Pluralism, Deference and the Margin of Appreciation Doctrine', *supra* n. 27.
[149] For such an example, see *Da Conceição Mateus and Santos Januário v. Portugal*, ECtHR 8 October 2013 (dec.), 62235/12 and 57725/12.

appreciation should be left if a core right is affected and there is a clear consensus in Europe that, in principle, such an interference is not acceptable.[150]

There does not seem to be a single standard, however, that helps the Court decide if intensity-determining factors pull in different directions. If a measure severely impedes an important right in a context where there is no common ground, the intensity-determining factors do not indicate an inevitable answer to the question of what margin of appreciation should be granted. Problems may also arise if an important right is infringed in an area where the national authorities are clearly better placed than the Court to assess the necessity of restrictive measures.[151] In some cases, the Court solves this problem by weighing the different factors and deciding accordingly. In *Perinçek*, for example, the Court established that there was little consensus on the need to criminalise genocide denial, but it also held that the case concerned a core right – the freedom of expression – and the applicant's speech had had little impact on the community whose interests the State sought to protect.[152] It concluded that the common ground factor therefore bore little weight in this case:

> The Court acknowledges this diversity.[153] It is nevertheless clear that, with its criminalisation of the denial of any genocide, without the requirement that it be carried out in a manner likely to incite to violence or hatred, Switzerland stands at one end of the comparative spectrum. In these circumstances, and given that in the present case there are other factors which have a significant bearing on the breadth of the applicable margin of appreciation ... the comparative law position cannot play a weighty part in the Court's conclusion with regard to this issue.[154]

Removing the consensus factor from the balance allowed the Court to apply a narrow margin of appreciation, since all remaining factors pointed in that direction.

In other cases, the Court has allowed the importance of a right to trump the better placed argument, for instance leaving a wider margin of appreciation in housing cases on Article 1 of Protocol No. 1 than in cases where the actual right to respect for the home of Article 8 ECHR had been infringed.[155] In most cases, however, the

---

[150] See e.g. *Dudgeon v. the United Kingdom*, ECtHR 22 October 1981, 7525/76, para. 52.

[151] E.g. *Sørensen and Rasmussen v. Denmark*, ECtHR 11 January 2006, 52562/99 and 52620/99, para. 58 (strict scrutiny because of the importance of the right at stake, regardless of the lack of consensus and the better placed argument); *Weber and Seravia v. Germany*, ECtHR 29 June 2006, 54934/00, para. 106 ('fairly wide margin of appreciation' in a case on secret surveillance in the interest of national security); *Soulas and Others v. France*, ECtHR 10 July 2008, 15948/03, para. 38 (in which the ECtHR finally settled on an intermediate level of review ('une marge d'appréciation assez large')).

[152] *Perinçek v. Switzerland*, ECtHR (GC) 15 October 2015, 27510/08.

[153] In national opinions on criminalisation of genocide denial.   [154] *Ibid.*, para. 257.

[155] *Berger-Krall and Others v. Slovenia*, ECtHR 12 June 2014, 14717/04, para. 268.

Court solves this kind of conflict by leaving 'a certain' margin of appreciation,[156] or by simply stopping short of making a real choice. It may occur, for example, that the Court considers that a case is about an important right, which would justify a narrower margin of appreciation, but it also mentions some reasons to justify a wider margin of appreciation.[157] It then does not provide a definitive margin of appreciation, but directly proceeds to discuss the reasonableness of the restriction. In such cases, part of the value of the margin of appreciation is lost, since there is then no clarity about the amount of deference the Court will pay and the concomitant intensity of its reasonableness review.

7.5   Continued Relevance of the Margin of Appreciation Doctrine?

The main function of the margin of appreciation doctrine is that it allows the Court to determine, based on objective factors, how strictly it will scrutinise the national compliance with the negative and positive obligations following from the Convention.[158] Its rationale is that it allows the Court to take account of its special position as a supranational Court that has to supervise the States to see whether they have provided effective protection of the Convention rights.[159] Moreover, insofar as the scope of the margin is translated into relatively clear standards of review and the factors determining the scope of the margin are well expressed, the doctrine has the advantage of providing clarity and predictability.[160] This makes it easier for national authorities to anticipate the Court's approach, and makes the standards to be applied by the Court predictable and reliable.

In academic literature, however, it has been noted that there is a disparity between the theory of the margin of appreciation and the way in which the Court formally refers to it in its case law, and the actual practice of application.[161] It has been seen in Section 7.4.5 that the Court may find it difficult to apply the doctrine if it is confronted with conflicting intensity-determining factors, and it may then sometimes stop short of determining any definitive margin of appreciation. In addition, there is often no clear

---

[156] E.g. *Otto-Preminger-Institut v. Austria*, ECtHR 20 September 1994, 13470/87, para. 50; *TV Vest AS and Rogaland Pensjonistparti v. Norway*, ECtHR 11 December 2008, 21132/05; *Stoll v. Switzerland*, ECtHR (GC) 10 December 2007 (GC), 69698/01, paras. 106–7; *Enver Aydemir v. Turkey*, ECtHR 7 June 2016, 26012/11, para. 81.

[157] For some examples, see *Aldeguer Tomás v. Spain*, ECtHR 14 June 2016, 35214/09, paras. 81–2 and 90; *British Gurkha Welfare Society and Others v. the United Kingdom*, ECtHR 15 September 2016, 44818/11, para. 81; *Khamtokhu and Aksenchik v. Russia*, ECtHR 24 January 2017, 60367/08 and 961/11, paras. 78–9. See in more detail Gerards, 'Margin of Appreciation', *supra* n. 27, section B.iii.

[158] See above, Section 7.2.   [159] *Ibid.*

[160] See further Gerards, 'Incrementalism', *supra* n. 27, section 4.

[161] See in particular Kratochvíl, *supra* n. 27; Gerards, 'Incrementalism', *supra* n. 27; Fahner, *supra* n. 10.

relationship between the scope of the margin of appreciation and the intensity of review. This is caused by the Court's tendency not to consistently establish the actual scope of the margin that is left in the concrete case, as well as not making a clear connection between the margin of appreciation and standards of review.[162]

In many cases, therefore, the references to the margin of appreciation have come to be rhetorical rather than functional in nature. This does not mean that the Court shows less judicial restraint or that it has grown increasingly activist. What has changed, however, is that the Court now increasingly also uses other argumentative devices to show such restraint. In particular, as was explained in Chapter 2, for many different situations, the Court has developed sets of general principles and standards that it can apply to the individual circumstances of the case. These have gradually added more details and specifics to the open-ended test of justification, which originally lacked such clear and precise standards. Based on the Court's judgments in its substantial case law, these general principles and standards also often incorporate the margin of appreciation considerations the Court has developed over time for a particular type or category of case.[163] Thus, elements of deference or, by contrast, elements of heightened review are often built into such concrete tests. If a case concerns a conflict between political speech and reputation rights, the Court therefore may no longer want to, first, determine how intensively it will assess the balance struck by the national authorities and, second, turn to the actual review of the justification. Instead, it may directly assess whether the national authorities have carefully applied the relevant standards developed in the Court's case law (including standards that relate to the margin of appreciation), and, if need be, it will check whether they have done so in a correct and fair manner.[164] This approach has the additional advantage that the Court can use techniques of distinguishing or revising if it is clear that a precedent would result in an altogether too intrusive review, or if the standards could be refined or further developed.[165]

It should be emphasised, though, that these lists of general principles have come to supplement rather than replace the margin of appreciation doctrine. As the many examples in this chapter have shown, the Court still relies on the doctrine and the factors determining its scope. The margin of appreciation doctrine is therefore of continuing relevance for the Convention system, but it is important to be aware that its function has changed and may continue to change in the future.

---

[162] For further elaboration and references, see Gerards, 'Margin of Appreciation', *supra* n. 27, section B.

[163] See e.g. *Winterstein and Others v. France*, ECtHR 17 October 2013, 27013/07, para. 148.

[164] See e.g. *Morice v. France*, ECtHR (GC) 23 April 2015, 29369/10, paras. 124 et seq.; *Satakunnan Markkinapörssi Oy and Satamedia Oy v. Finland*, ECtHR (GC) 27 June 2017, 931/13, paras. 162 et seq.

[165] See further Section 2.5.

8 Justification of Restrictions I – Lawfulness

8.1 Introduction

Most of the rights and obligations following from the Convention do not have an absolute nature.[1] As explained in Section 1.4.4, the Court's review is therefore usually not complete if it has found that there has been an interference with a Convention right. In order to determine if the Convention is actually violated, in stage 3 of its review the Court has to examine if the contested interference can be held to be justified by objective and convincing reasons of general interest that meet the relevant conditions and standards set out in the Convention and the Court's case law. When the case concerns a complaint about non-compliance with a positive obligation, the Court will apply similar standards as those contained in the various limitation clauses contained in the Convention.[2]

For that reason, these last three chapters are dedicated to the various standards and conditions for restriction and justification. It is important to recall that these are different for each of the rights protected in the Convention and the Protocols.[3] Nevertheless, the Court's case law discloses some general requirements which are relevant to almost all the Convention rights and freedoms, with the exception of the non-derogable rights.[4] The overall set of requirements that can be derived from the Convention and the Court's case law can be schematically represented as follows:

1. The interference with the Convention right must be 'prescribed by law' or 'in accordance with the law' (requirement of lawfulness):
    a) requirement of a 'basis in domestic law'
    b) requirement of accessibility of the legal basis
    c) requirement of forseeability of the interference, restriction or limitation
    d) requirement of non-arbitrariness and procedural due care.
2. The interference with the Convention right must pursue a legitimate aim (requirement of a legitimate aim).

---

[1] See Section 1.5.   [2] See Sections 5.2.1 and 5.4.   [3] See further Sections 1.4.4 and 1.5.
[4] See Section 1.5.

3. The interference must be necessary ('in a democratic society') to achieve the legitimate aim pursued (requirement of necessity; also often framed as the requirement of 'proportionality' or the requirement of a 'fair balance').

The lawfulness requirement is discussed in the present chapter, in which attention is paid to the autonomous and substantive interpretation of this notion (Section 8.3); the requirements of a basis in domestic law (Section 8.3), accessibility (Section 8.4) and foreseeability (Section 8.5); the requirement of the absence of arbitrariness (Section 8.6); and conditions of procedural fairness and procedural due care (Section 8.7). The test of a legitimate aim is discussed in Chapter 9. Finally, Chapter 10 is devoted to the test of necessity and its different expressions and aspects, such as the test of a pressing social need, the 'relevant and sufficient' test and the fair balance test.

8.2   Autonomous and Substantive Interpretation

One of the requirements for restrictions that is expressly laid down in almost all Convention provisions is that the interference must be 'prescribed by law' or, more generally put, must be lawful. The Convention notion of 'law' (or in French, 'loi') has been given an autonomous and substantive interpretation by the Court. The interpretation is substantive or qualitative in the sense that the Court does not set any standards for the procedure that needs to be followed in order to be able to speak of a valid legal basis, nor does it require a basis in specific types of 'law', such as an Act of Parliament.[5] Had the Court opted for a more procedural definition, it would not have been easy to apply the notion in the forty-seven States Parties with their widely varying constitutional and legal systems, where the legal basis for restrictions of fundamental rights can be found in a myriad of different instruments, varying from Acts of Parliament to bylaws and policy measures and from case law to unwritten law.

The qualitative standards are founded in what the Court regards as the core values served by the requirement of lawfulness, which are legal certainty and foreseeability. The Court sees it as essential that individuals and private legal entities can estimate the consequences of their behaviour, and can know about the limitations and restrictions set on the exercise of their rights and freedoms. In its judgment in *Sunday Times*, the Court formulated two requirements in this regard:

Firstly, the law must be adequately accessible: the citizen must be able to have an indication that is adequate in the circumstances of the legal rules applicable to a given case.

---

[5] See e.g. *Leyla Şahin v. Turkey*, ECtHR (GC) 10 November 2005, 44774/98, para. 88 (with many further references); *Biržietis v. Lithuania*, ECtHR 14 June 2016, 49304/09, para. 50.

Secondly, a norm cannot be regarded as a 'law' unless it is formulated with sufficient precision to enable the citizen to regulate his conduct: he must be able – if need be with appropriate advice – to foresee, to a degree that is reasonable in the circumstances, the consequences which a given action may entail. Those consequences need not be foreseeable with absolute certainty: experience shows this to be unattainable. Again, whilst certainty is highly desirable, it may bring in its train excessive rigidity and the law must be able to keep pace with changing circumstances. Accordingly, many laws are inevitably couched in terms which, to a greater or lesser extent, are vague and whose interpretation and application are questions of practice.[6]

In more recent case law, the Court sometimes adds a third standard, which is the protection against arbitrariness.[7] This standard is frequently expressed in requirements related to procedural fairness and availability of judicial remedies, as will be discussed in Section 8.7, but it may also be part of the general requirements of reasonableness and proportionality discussed in Chapter 10. In the next sections, the three qualitative requirements of accessibility, foreseeability and absence of arbitrariness are discussed in more detail. First, however, the more general and fundamental requirement of a basis in domestic law is addressed.

8.3   A Basis in Domestic Law

Any interference with a Convention right must have a 'basis in domestic law'. A clear example of a case where such a basis was lacking is *Khmel*.[8] Khmel, a regional parliamentarian, had been stopped on suspicion of drink-driving. Having been taken to a police station, he become agitated and started to verbally abuse the police officers. In connection with his behaviour, the police chief decided to record his actions on video and he notified the local broadcasting company, who sent a presenter and cameraman to film the applicant. The footage was then broadcast on television. Because the filming and broadcasting had been in clear violation of the applicable national legislation, the Court held that the interference did not meet the requirement of a 'basis in domestic law':

The Russian courts in the civil proceedings and the Government in their observations before the Court cited section 11(15) of the Police Act as a justification for the police chief's decision to invite television cameras and to have the applicant recorded on video. Section 11(15) of the Police Act granted the police the right to take fingerprints or to film individuals if it was impossible to identify them ... The Court fails to see how that provision

---

[6] *Sunday Times v. the United Kingdom*, ECtHR 26 April 1979, 6538/74, para. 48.
[7] See further Section 8.6.   [8] *Khmel v. Russia*, ECtHR 12 December 2013, 20383/04.

could be applicable in the instant case, where the applicant's identity had been established shortly after he had arrived at the police station . . . It is nevertheless not inconceivable that the filming was performed in accordance with the Operational-Search Activities Act which allowed the police to carry out 'observation' of individuals who were suspected of being in the process of committing criminal offences, using audio and video equipment . . . In any event, the interference in this case was not limited to the recording of the applicant's image, but also included making the footage available to the media, without restricting its subsequent use. Assuming that the footage was obtained in the framework of the operational-search activities, the same Operational-Search Activities Act expressly prohibited police officers from disseminating such information without the consent of the individual concerned . . . It follows that, in the absence of the applicant's consent, the release of the video recording to the regional television was in flagrant breach of the domestic law.[9]

Obviously, the requirement also will be breached if there is not a single legal provision available that can serve as a fitting legal basis for an interference.[10] The Court has further found a violation of the requirement of a legal basis if there is a clear mismatch between the objectives of the applicable legal provisions and the purpose for which they have been used. In *Huseynli*, for example, it had been established that the applicants had been arrested and sentenced to administrative detention in order to prevent their participation in a demonstration and to punish them for having participated in opposition protests. According to the Court, there was no proper legal basis for this detention:

The legal basis for those measures was Articles 296 and 310.1 of the CAO,[11] which prescribes an administrative penalty for 'minor hooliganism' and for 'failure to comply with a lawful order of a police officer' respectively. Thus, the measures in question were imposed relying on legal provisions which had no connection with the intended purpose of those measures. The Court cannot but agree with the applicants that the interference with their freedom of peaceful assembly on such a legal basis could only be characterised as arbitrary and unlawful.[12]

---

[9] *Ibid.*, paras. 47–9. See also e.g. *Giorgi Nikolaishvili v. Georgia*, ECtHR 13 January 2009, 37048/04, para. 128; *Mustafa Sezgin Tanrıkulu v. Turkey*, ECtHR 18 July 2017, 27473/06, paras. 50 et seq.; *N. v. Romania*, ECtHR 28 November 2017, 59152/08, paras. 150–61; *Mockutė v. Lithuania*, ECtHR 27 February 2018, 66490/09, para. 103; *Dimitar Yordanov v. Bulgaria*, ECtHR 6 September 2018, 3401/09, para. 65.

[10] See e.g. *Olsson v. Sweden (No. 2)*, ECtHR 27 November 1992, 13441/87, paras. 81–2; *Z.A. and Others v. Russia*, ECtHR 28 March 2017, 61411/15, paras. 97–9.

[11] The Code of Administrative Offences.

[12] *Huseynli and Others v. Azerbaijan*, ECtHR 11 February 2016, 67360/11, para. 98. See also e.g. *Antović and Mirković v. Montenegro*, 70838/13, paras. 59–60.

In other cases, the Court has been more lenient. If a provision has been found to be unconstitutional by a national constitutional court, for example, it can still provide a sufficient legal basis for an interference with a Convention right if this is possible according to national law. The Court accepted this in *Strack and Richter*, a case which concerned a statutory provision on the threshold for elections.[13] At the time of the elections of 2009, the relevant provision had been found to be unconstitutional by the German Federal Constitutional Court, but this court had approved the continuation of the application of the provision until the next elections. The Court explained that this could not be considered problematic from the perspective of lawfulness:

> The Court has accepted that a national constitutional court may set a time-limit for the legislature to enact new legislation with the effect that an unconstitutional provision remains applicable for a transitional period ... Moreover, in the German legal system, a measure generally remains lawful when the Federal Constitutional Court decides that nullifying a provision will only take effect at a later stage, sometimes defining transitional regulations ... This applies respectively to cases of electoral complaints in which the Federal Constitutional Court is given the power to decide what consequences an electoral error may entail ... The Court is therefore satisfied that the decision not to invalidate the 2009 elections of the German members of the European Parliament for the duration of the whole legislative period was in accordance with domestic law.[14]

This also shows that, in many cases, the Court is not willing to deeply scrutinise the existence of a domestic legal basis and it is usually ready to follow the national courts' views on the validity and interpretation of national law. In 1985, in *Barthold*, the Court had already emphasised its limited competence in this regard.[15] Barthold was a veterinary surgeon who offered a round-the-clock emergency service, but after he had advocated this kind of service in an interview in a local newspaper, a number of his fellow practitioners had started unfair competition proceedings against him. The national courts honoured their complaint and issued an injunction against Barthold's further advertising of this type of service. Complaining about a violation of the freedom of expression before the Court, Barthold alleged, among others, that the civil courts had based their decisions partly on inapplicable legal rules or rules they had no jurisdiction to apply. In this respect, the Court held that

> [w]hilst it is true that no interference can be considered as 'prescribed by law', for the purposes of Article 10 para. 2 of the Convention, unless the decision occasioning it complied with the relevant domestic legislation, the logic of the system of safeguard

---

[13] *Strack and Richter v. Germany*, ECtHR 5 July 2016 (dec.), 28811/12 and 50303/12.
[14] *Ibid.*, para. 29.   [15] *Barthold v. Germany*, ECtHR 25 March 1985, 8734/79.

established by the Convention sets limits upon the scope of the power of review exercisable by the Court in this respect. It is in the first place for the national authorities, notably the courts, to interpret and apply the domestic law: the national authorities are, in the nature of things, particularly qualified to settle the issues arising in this connection.[16]

Generally, thus, the Court will follow the national courts' judgment on the lawfulness of the applicable legislation.[17] In *Sindicatul 'Pastorul Cel Bun'*, for example, the argument was made that the applicable domestic legislation was unconstitutional and disregarded the hierarchy of norms, but the Court held that:

> it is not for the Court to examine this argument, which concerns the validity of a form of 'secondary legislation'. The interpretation of the Contracting Parties' domestic law is primarily a matter for the national courts . . . [T]he Court considers that since the County Court relied on the [relevant Statute] in its judgment, it implicitly took the view that the provisions of the Statute were not unconstitutional. Accordingly, the Court is prepared to accept, as the national courts did, that the interference complained of had a legal basis . . . and that these provisions satisfied the 'lawfulness' requirements established in its case-law.[18]

The Court may hold differently only if it is obvious from the facts of the case that the legal basis is flawed or the national interpretation is manifestly unreasonable.[19] As a result, the requirement of a basis in domestic law does not have much teeth compared to the other, substantive or qualitative lawfulness requirements.[20]

8.4   Accessibility

Since its landmark judgment in *Sunday Times*, the Court has consistently required that restrictions must be sufficiently accessible. This means that 'the citizen must be able to have an indication that is adequate in the circumstances of the legal rules

---

[16] *Ibid.*, para. 48. See also e.g. *Håkansson and Sturesson v. Sweden*, ECtHR 21 February 1990, 11855/85, para. 47; *Beyeler v. Italy*, ECtHR (GC) 5 January 2000, 33202/96, para. 108; *Maksymenko and Gerasymenko v. Ukraine*, ECtHR 16 May 2013, 49317/07, para. 54.

[17] See also *Berger-Krall and Others v. Slovenia*, ECtHR 12 June 2014, 14717/04, para. 189.

[18] *Sindicatul 'Pastorul Cel Bun' v. Romania*, ECtHR (GC) 9 July 2013, 2330/09, paras. 156–7. See also e.g. *N.K.M. v. Hungary*, ECtHR 14 May 2013, 66529/11, paras. 52–4; *Biržietis v. Lithuania*, ECtHR 14 June 2016, 49304/09, para. 51 and cf. *Rekvényi v. Hungary*, ECtHR (GC) 20 May 1999, 25390/94, para. 35.

[19] See e.g. *Ilias and Ahmed v. Hungary*, ECtHR 14 March 2017, 47287/15, para. 63.

[20] See also e.g. *Chagnon and Fournier v. France*, ECtHR 15 July 2010, 44174/06 and 44190/06, paras. 44–7, where the Court accepted that the legal basis was flawed, but it regarded this as acceptable because of the emergency situation and the need for urgent action to be taken. Moreover, even if the Court hesitates about the lawfulness, it usually does not give decisive importance to this; see e.g. *Lindström and Mässeli v. Finland*, ECtHR 14 January 2014, 24630/10, paras. 63–4.

applicable to a given case'.[21] The Court has accepted that this requirement is met when legislation is duly published.[22] More generally, the standards set in this regard are not very strict. In the case of *Groppera Radio*, for example, the applicable rules and restrictions were laid down in the international Radio Regulations, which had not been published; the 'Official Collection' of legislation only contained information about how they could be obtained and consulted.[23] In the Court's view this was sufficient to meet the accessibility requirement:

> In the instant case the relevant provisions of international telecommunications law were highly technical and complex; furthermore, they were primarily intended for specialists, who knew, from the information given in the Official Collection, how they could be obtained. It could therefore be expected of a business company wishing to engage in broadcasting across a frontier – like Groppera Radio AG – that it would seek to inform itself fully about the rules applicable in Switzerland, if necessary with the help of advisers. As the 1983 Ordinance and the International Telecommunication Convention had been published in full, such a company had only to acquaint itself with the Radio Regulations, either by consulting them at the PTT's head office in Berne or by obtaining them from the International Telecommunication Union in Geneva.[24]

It further appears from the Court's case law that the fact that certain regulations (e.g. policy regulations) have not been published can be compensated for if the restriction of the Convention right is still sufficiently foreseeable, for example if its meaning can be derived from underlying and duly published legislation or case law. In *Silver*, for example, the applicants – who were all detainees – had complained about the stopping or delaying of their correspondence by the prison authorities.[25] They stated that there had not been an accessible legal basis for this, since the conditions for stopping their correspondence were only contained in a number of unpublished Orders that supplemented the Prison Rules. Although this clearly limited the accessibility of the conditions, the Court did not regard this as problematic:

> In determining whether the foreseeability criterion was satisfied in this instance, account cannot be taken of the Orders which supplemented Rule 34(8): they were not available to prisoners nor do their contents appear to have been explained in cell cards . . . However, the wording of Rule 34(8) . . . is itself quite explicit: a reader would see not that correspondence with persons other than friends or relatives is allowed subject to certain exceptions but

---

[21] *Sunday Times v. the United Kingdom*, ECtHR 26 April 1979, 6538/74, para. 49.
[22] See implicitly e.g. *VgT Verein gegen Tierfabriken v. Switzerland*, ECtHR 28 June 2001, 24699/94, para. 54.
[23] *Groppera Radio AG and Others v. Switzerland*, ECtHR 28 March 1990, 10890/84.
[24] *Ibid.*, para. 68. Cf. also (though not very conclusively) *Roman Zakharov v. Russia*, ECtHR (GC) 4 December 2015, 47143/06, paras. 239–42.
[25] E.g. *Silver and Others v. the United Kingdom*, ECtHR 25 March 1983, 5947/72.

rather that it is prohibited save where the Secretary of State gives leave. Moreover, the Court considers that account should also be taken of Rule 33(2) – which contains a prohibition similar to that found in Rule 34(8) – and of Rule 34(2), from which it would be apparent that there were limits on the quantity of the correspondence of convicted prisoners . . . For these reasons, the Court concludes that the interferences in question were 'in accordance with the law'.[26]

By contrast, if the rules and practical details for receiving visits or making telephone calls are not made accessible in any way at all and a government cannot explain how prisoners can be aware of the relevant practical details, the Court will find a violation of the requirement of accessibility and it will hold that the restrictions are not 'prescribed by law'.[27]

8.5   Foreseeability

The requirement of foreseeability is closely related to the principle of legal certainty. As the Court emphasised in *Sunday Times*, legislation must enable 'the citizen to regulate his conduct: he must be able – if need be with appropriate advice – to foresee, to a degree that is reasonable in the circumstances, the consequences which a given action may entail.'[28] The Court also accepted in *Sunday Times* that a certain degree of vagueness and generality of the formulation is unavoidable and even necessary to allow for general applicability of legislation and for keeping pace with changing circumstances.[29] Sometimes, however, legislation is simply too vague to give any proper indications of its meaning. This can be illustrated by the case of *Hashman and Harrup*, where the applicants had disturbed a hunting party by blowing a horn and by 'hallooing'.[30] The domestic court had held that this behaviour could be qualified as '*contra bonos mores*'. For that reason, it obliged the applicants, in a so-called 'binding over order', 'to keep the peace and be of good behaviour' during a period of twelve months. The applicants complained before the Court that this order was not sufficiently clear as to meet the requirement of foreseeability. The Court agreed:

> The Court first recalls that in [a previous] judgment, it noted that the expression 'to be of good behaviour' 'was particularly imprecise and offered little guidance to the person bound over as to the type of conduct which would amount to a breach of the order' . . . Those considerations apply equally in the present case, where the applicants were not charged with any criminal offence, and were found not to have breached the peace. The Court next notes that conduct *contra bonos mores* is defined as behaviour which is 'wrong rather than

---

[26] *Ibid.*, para. 92.   [27] See *Lebois v. Bulgaria*, ECtHR 19 October 2017, 67482/14, para. 67.
[28] *Sunday Times v. the United Kingdom*, ECtHR 26 April 1979, 6538/74, para. 49.   [29] *Ibid.*
[30] *Hashman and Harrup v. the United Kingdom*, ECtHR (GC) 25 November 1999, 25594/94.

right in the judgment of the majority of contemporary fellow citizens' . . . Conduct which is 'wrong rather than right in the judgment of the majority of contemporary fellow citizens' . . . is conduct which is not described at all, but merely expressed to be 'wrong' in the opinion of a majority of citizens . . . With specific reference to the facts of the present case, the Court does not accept that it must have been evident to the applicants what they were being ordered not do [*sic*] for the period of their binding over . . . The Court thus finds that the order by which the applicants were bound over to keep the peace and not to behave *contra bonos mores* did not comply with the requirement of Article 10 § 2 of the Convention that it be 'prescribed by law'.[31]

Generally, the level of precision required of domestic legislation depends to a considerable degree on the content of the law in question, the field it is designed to cover, and the number and status of those to whom it is addressed.[32] Moreover, a lack of precision can be repaired or compensated for if sufficient clarification is offered by consistent case law or an administrative practice of application. Indeed, the Court has accepted that it is unavoidable that the meaning of legislation is gradually clarified, and sometimes changed, as a result of judicial interpretation and application. It did so even in relation to Article 7 ECHR, which contains the non-derogable prohibition of retroactive application of criminal law:

> As regards foreseeability . . . the Court notes that, however clearly drafted a legal provision may be in any system of law including criminal law, there is an inevitable element of judicial interpretation. There will always be a need for elucidation of doubtful points and for adaptation to changing circumstances. Indeed, in certain Convention States, the progressive development of the criminal law through judicial law-making is a well-entrenched and necessary part of legal tradition.[33]

In this respect, the Court has also noted that

> a margin of doubt in relation to borderline facts does not by itself make a legal provision unforeseeable in its application. Nor does the mere fact that a provision is capable of more than one construction mean that it fails to meet the requirement of 'foreseeability' for the purposes of the Convention. The role of adjudication vested in the courts is precisely to dissipate such interpretational doubts as remain, taking into account the changes in everyday practice.[34]

---

[31] *Ibid.*, paras. 37–41. See also e.g. *Association Les Témoins de Jéhovah v. France*, ECtHR 30 June 2011, 8916/05, para. 70; *Lindström and Mässeli v. Finland*, ECtHR 14 January 2014, 24630/10, para. 64; *Semir Güzel v. Turkey*, ECtHR 13 September 2016, 29483/09, para. 39; *De Tommaso v. Italy*, ECtHR (GC) 23 February 2017, 43395/09, paras. 118–26.

[32] E.g. *Mateescu v. Romania*, ECtHR 14 January 2014, 1944/10, para. 29; *Delfi AS v. Estonia*, ECtHR (GC) 16 June 2015, 64569/09, para. 122.

[33] *Kononov v. Latvia*, ECtHR (GC) 17 May 2010, 36376/04, para. 185.

[34] *Dogru v. France*, ECtHR 4 December 2008, 27058/05, para. 57.

Hence, the Court's standards in such matters are deliberately relaxed so as to allow the States to develop their case law and adjust it to the changing conditions of modern society.[35] Even if the case in which a certain interpretation is provided is the first of its kind, or the national courts have referred preliminary questions to the Court of Justice of the EU to ask for clarification of the underlying provisions of EU law, this is not necessarily problematic from a perspective of foreseeability.[36] Nevertheless, the Court has held that the resultant interpretation must be consistent with the essence of the original rules and it must be reasonably possible to foresee it.[37] A rather sudden departure from previous case law, as opposed to a gradual development or the introduction of new legislation, cannot always be reasonably expected and therefore may be in violation of the foreseeability requirement.[38]

In judging on the overall foreseeability of a limitation, the Court may also take account of another factor it mentioned in the *Sunday Times* case, namely that the individual 'must be able – *if need be with appropriate advice* – to foresee … the consequences which a given action may entail'.[39] In its case law the Court has used this factor mainly in relation to professionals, such as journalists, publishers, parliamentarians or lawyers. Indeed, it has held that 'persons carrying on a professional activity, who are used to having to proceed with a high degree of caution when pursuing their occupation, can on this account be expected to take special care in assessing the risks that such activity entails'.[40]

An example of the consequences of this assumption can be found in *Amihalachioaie*, which concerned the severe criticism which the then Moldovan Chairman of the Bar had levelled at a judgment of the Moldovan Constitutional Court.[41] He was fined because his criticism showed a 'lack of regard' towards the Constitutional Court, a term contained in the applicable Code of Constitutional Procedure which the applicant found unclear. The Court, however, held that

> although the acts that give rise to liability are not defined or set out with absolute precision in the legislation … in view of his legal training and professional experience as Chairman

---

[35] *Khodorkovskiy and Lebedev v. Russia*, ECtHR 25 July 2013, 11082/06 and 13772/05, para. 781; *Del Rio Prada v. Spain*, ECtHR (GC) 21 October 2013, 42750/09, para. 92; *Delfi AS v. Estonia*, ECtHR (GC) 16 June 2015, 64569/09, para. 121.

[36] *Satakunnan Markkinapörssi Oy and Satamedia Oy v. Finland*, ECtHR (GC) 27 June 2017, 931/13, para. 150. See also *Dmitriyevskiy v. Russia*, ECtHR 3 October 2017, 42168/06, paras. 82–3; *Savva Terentyev v. Russia*, ECtHR 28 August 2018, 10692/09, para. 58.

[37] *Kononov v. Latvia*, ECtHR (GC) 17 May 2010, 36376/04, para. 185. See also e.g. *Korbely v. Hungary*, ECtHR 19 September 2008, 9174/02, para. 71; *Khodorkovskiy and Lebedev v. Russia*, ECtHR 25 July 2013, 11082/06 and 13772/05, para. 780.

[38] See e.g. *Del Rio Prada v. Spain*, ECtHR (GC) 21 October 2013, 42750/09, paras. 111–18.

[39] *Sunday Times v. the United Kingdom*, ECtHR 26 April 1979, 6538/74, para. 49, emphasis added.

[40] *Satakunnan Markkinapörssi Oy and Satamedia Oy v. Finland*, ECtHR (GC) 27 June 2017, 931/13, para. 145.

[41] *Amihalachioaie v. Moldova*, ECtHR 20 April 2004, 60115/00.

of the Bar, the applicant could reasonably have foreseen that his remarks were liable to fall within the scope of the aforementioned provision of the Code of Constitutional Procedure.[42]

Yet, the Court has accepted some limits to the extent to which professionals need to inform themselves about the potential consequences of their acts. In *Mateescu*, the applicant – a medical specialist who had just finished his legal studies – was refused to the Bar because his practising as a lawyer would be incompatible with his medical profession.[43] The relevant legislative provision was phrased in general terms and it appeared that the national courts had given contrasting applications to it. The Court therefore found that the wording of the legal provision regulating the practice of the profession of lawyer was not sufficiently foreseeable 'to enable the applicant – even though, being aspiring [*sic*] lawyer, he was informed and well-versed in the law – to realise that the concurrent practice of another profession, not enumerated among those excluded by the law, entailed the denial of his right to practise as lawyer'.[44] Thus, if legislation is so obscure and generally worded that even specialists cannot foresee certain interpretations to be given to it, the Court is likely to find a violation of the lawfulness requirement.

For laymen, too, the Court has found that they must make a reasonable effort to understand the possible legal consequences of their behaviour. In several cases, the Court has found that individuals can be required to seek appropriate advice if the applicable legislation is not very clear, even if they are not legal experts themselves.[45] Moreover, if laymen have been issued official instructions or warnings, this can be enough to clarify the meaning of otherwise indeterminate legislation in a concrete case. In *Landvreugd*, for example, the applicant had complained about the lack of foreseeability of an order prohibiting him from entering a certain area in Amsterdam.[46] The prohibition order was based on a generally worded competence for the Burgomaster of Amsterdam to intervene if that would be necessary to quell or prevent serious disturbances of public order in so-called emergency areas. Although the Court noticed that the underlying legal basis was indeed rather general in terms, it also found that, in the circumstances of the case, Landvreugd could have known the consequences of his behaviour:

---

[42] *Ibid.*, para. 33. See also e.g. *Tourancheau and July v. France*, ECtHR 24 November 2005, 53886/00, para. 61; *Flinkkilä and Others v. Finland*, ECtHR 6 April 2010, 25576/04, para. 67; *Leandro da Silva v. Luxembourg*, ECtHR 11 February 2010, 30273/07; *Delfi AS v. Estonia*, ECtHR (GC) 16 June 2015, 64569/09, para. 129; *Karácsony and Others v. Hungary*, ECtHR (GC) 17 May 2016, 42461/13 and 44357/13, para. 126.

[43] *Mateescu v. Romania*, ECtHR 14 January 2014, 1944/10.   [44] *Ibid.*, para. 32.

[45] E.g. *Vereinigung Demokratischer Soldaten Österreichs and Gubi v. Austria*, ECtHR 19 December 1994, 15153/89, para. 46; *Ahmed and Others v. the United Kingdom*, ECtHR 2 September 1998, 22954/93, para. 46; *Perinçek v. Switzerland*, ECtHR (GC) 15 October 2015, 27510/08, para. 138.

[46] *Landvreugd v. the Netherlands*, ECtHR 4 June 2002, 37331/97.

It is not in dispute that in the instant case the applicant, after having been ordered on six different occasions to leave the area for eight hours – prohibition orders which are not challenged by the applicant as unlawful –, was finally told that he would have either to desist from using hard drugs or having hard drugs in his possession in streets situated in the emergency area – such use or possession constituting a disturbance of public order –, or to stay away from the area. He was informed that if he committed such acts again in the near future the Burgomaster would be requested to impose a prohibition order for fourteen days on him. After the applicant had neglected this warning on yet a further occasion, and had again been ordered to leave the area for eight hours, the Burgomaster in fact issued a prohibition order for fourteen days. It follows from the above that the applicant was able to foresee the consequences of his acts and that he was enabled to regulate his conduct in the matter before a prohibition order for fourteen days was imposed on him.[47]

These examples suggest that the Court accepts relatively easily that the requirement of foreseeability is met and that it even regards rather generally phrased legislation as sufficiently clear, as long as the addressees can reasonably be expected to know how it will be applied to their individual situations.[48] Nevertheless, there are many cases in which the Court finds a violation of the Convention because the requirement of 'foreseeability' was not met. It has done so mainly if the application of legislation or the interpretation thereof can objectively be seen to be unexpected, too broad or bordering on the arbitrary.[49] An example can be found in *Lelas*, where the applicant had complained about the delay in payment of a special daily allowance he was entitled to. He had asked his commanding officer why the allowances had not been paid.[50] To answer this question, the commanding officer had made enquiries of his superior, who had then contacted the General Staff of the Croatian Armed Forces. Eventually, the commanding officer had informed Lelas that his claims were not being disputed and that they would be paid once the funds for that purpose had been allocated in the State budget. When the allowances continued to be unpaid, Lelas started judicial proceedings, but they were

---

[47] *Ibid.*, paras. 64–5. See also e.g. *Dallas v. the United Kingdom*, ECtHR 11 February 2016, 38395/12, paras. 74–5; *Hamidović v. Bosnia and Herzegovina*, ECtHR 5 December 2017, 57792/15, para. 33.

[48] See also e.g. *Leela Förderkreis e.V. and Others v. Germany*, ECtHR 6 November 2008, 58911/00; *Dubská and Krejzová v. the Czech Republic*, ECtHR (GC) 15 November 2016, 28859/11 and 28473/12, paras. 169–71.

[49] See e.g. *Herczegfalvy v. Austria*, ECtHR 24 September 1992, 10533/83, para. 91; *Association Ekin v. France*, ECtHR 17 July 2001, 39288/98, para. 60; *Gawęda v. Poland*, ECtHR 14 March 2002, 26229/95, paras. 43–8; *Sud Fondi Srl and Others v. Italy*, ECtHR 20 January 2009, 75909/01, paras. 36–7; *Oleksander Volkov v. Ukraine*, ECtHR 9 January 2013, 21722/11, paras. 173–85; *Biblical Centre of the Chuvash Republic v. Russia*, ECtHR 12 June 2014, 33203/08, para. 56; *Yabloko Russian United Democratic Party and Others v. Russia*, ECtHR 8 November 2016, 18860/07, para. 76; *Navalnyy v. Russia*, ECtHR 17 October 2017, 101/15, para. 68.

[50] *Lelas v. Croatia*, ECtHR 20 May 2010, 55555/08.

unsuccessful because the domestic courts held that he could not have relied on the statements made by his commanding officer as that officer had not been authorised to make any declarations binding the government. In the Court's view, this had been unforeseeable for Lelas:

> [T]he question is whether, in the absence of a clear legal provision or a publicly available document that would support [the findings of the domestic courts], it was equally plausible for the applicant – who, under the rules of the military hierarchy, could have addressed his request only to his immediate superior – to assume that the information repeatedly communicated to him by his commanding officer came from a person or persons within the Ministry who had the authority to acknowledge the debt … In the Court's view, in the absence of a clear legal provision or publicly accessible documents as to who was authorised to acknowledge the debt on behalf of the Ministry of Defence, it was quite natural for the applicant to believe that the General Staff of the Croatian Armed Forces was an authority of sufficient rank whose statements could be binding on the Ministry. Therefore … the Court finds the impugned interference was incompatible with the principle of lawfulness and therefore contravened Article 1 of Protocol No. 1 to the Convention … because the manner in which [the domestic] court interpreted and applied the relevant domestic law … was not foreseeable for the applicant.[51]

Similarly, unpredictability and legal uncertainty as a result of inconsistent application by the national courts or of disagreement between the national authorities may result in a lack of foreseeability of the interference.[52] A further violation of the foreseeability requirement can be caused by a combination of vaguely and generally worded legislation and the lack of a clear implementation plan, the delayed implementation of relevant legislation or the existence of a legal vacuum.[53] Judicial interpretations of legislation may also be unforeseeable if the legislation is applied to facts that clearly do not fall within the scope of the relevant provisions.[54] Such applications of the foreseeability requirement demonstrate that in many cases, there is a significant overlap between the requirements of a basis in domestic law, foreseeability and the absence of arbitrariness.[55]

Lastly, it should be mentioned that the Court has formulated some special requirements of foreseeability for specific situation types. Best-known are the

---

[51] *Ibid.*, paras. 77–8.
[52] See also e.g. *Maširević v. Serbia*, ECtHR 11 February 2014, 30671/08, para. 50; *Cumhuriyet Halk Partisi v. Turkey*, ECtHR 26 April 2014, 19920/13, paras. 95–7; *Elberte v. Latvia*, ECtHR 13 January 2015, 61243/08, para. 113.
[53] E.g. *Centro Europa 7 S.r.l. and Di Stefano v. Italy*, ECtHR (GC) 7 June 2012, 38433/09, paras. 144–55; *Kurić and Others v. Slovenia*, ECtHR (GC) 26 June 2012, 26828/06, paras. 343–9.
[54] E.g. *Ahmet Yıldırım v. Turkey*, ECtHR 18 December 2012, 3111/10, para. 61.
[55] For illustrations of this overlap, see e.g. *L.H. v. Latvia*, ECtHR 29 April 2014, 52019/07, paras. 47–60; *Polyakova and Others v. Russia*, ECtHR 7 March 2017, 35090/09, paras. 116–18.

standards related to secret surveillance and interception of communications, for example by means of interception of bulk data, telephone tapping, audio-visual surveillance (e.g., placing a camera or a microphone in a room), placing a GPS-device in a car to trace someone's activities, or covert surveillance of conversations.[56] The Court has acknowledged that surveillance is often exercised in secret and that this is necessary for it to be effective, but it has also accepted that the exercise of such powers may interfere with the right to respect for one's private life and correspondence as protected by Article 8 ECHR. In *Malone*, the Court emphasised that this created a need for a specific definition of the foreseeability requirement:

Undoubtedly … the requirements of the Convention, notably in regard to foreseeability, cannot be exactly the same in the special context of interception of communications for the purposes of police investigations as they are where the object of the relevant law is to place restrictions on the conduct of individuals. In particular, the requirement of foreseeability cannot mean that an individual should be enabled to foresee when the authorities are likely to intercept his communications so that he can adapt his conduct accordingly. Nevertheless, the law must be sufficiently clear in its terms to give citizens an adequate indication as to the circumstances in which and the conditions on which public authorities are empowered to resort to this secret and potentially dangerous interference with the right to respect for private life and correspondence … Since the implementation in practice of measures of secret surveillance of communications is not open to scrutiny by the individuals concerned or the public at large, it would be contrary to the rule of law for the legal discretion granted to the executive to be expressed in terms of an unfettered power. Consequently, the law must indicate the scope of any such discretion conferred on the competent authorities and the manner of its exercise with sufficient clarity, having regard to the legitimate aim of the measure in question, to give the individual adequate protection against arbitrary interference.[57]

The Court has summarised its case law on the foreseeability of secret measures of surveillance in relation to national security in *Roman Zakharov*.[58] In that case, it held that legislation should contain the following minimum safeguards:

the nature of offences which may give rise to an interception order; a definition of the categories of people liable to have their telephones tapped; a limit on the duration of

[56] Cf. *Bykov v. Russia*, ECtHR (GC) 10 March 2009, 4378/02, para. 78.

[57] *Malone v. the United Kingdom*, ECtHR 2 August 1984, 8691/79, paras. 67–8. See more recently *Uzun v. Germany*, ECtHR 2 September 2010, 35623/05, para. 61; *Goranova-Karanaeva v. Bulgaria*, ECtHR 8 March 2011, 12739/05, para. 48; *Roman Zakharov v. Russia*, ECtHR (GC) 4 December 2015, 47143/06, para. 229; *Big Brother Watch and Others v. the United Kingdom*, ECtHR 13 September 2018, 58170/13, para. 306.

[58] *Roman Zakharov v. Russia*, ECtHR (GC) 4 December 2015, 47143/06.

telephone tapping; the procedure to be followed for examining, using and storing the data obtained; the precautions to be taken when communicating the data to other parties; and the circumstances in which recordings may or must be erased or destroyed.[59]

The Court has defined comparable requirements in relation to surveillance by private parties, such as insurance companies or employers.[60] It has done so by formulating a positive obligation for the State to ensure that the necessary clarity and safeguards are offered in these horizontal situations, for example by means of regulation or court decisions.[61] Similarly, the Court has obliged the States to formulate the relevant statutory legislation with special precision in relation to stop and search powers and other intrusive measures, such as data collection.[62] In *Gillan and Quinton*, for example, the Court warned that there is a clear risk of arbitrariness in granting wide discretionary search powers to the police, as they may easily be used in a discriminatory manner or misused against demonstrators or protestors.[63] Such powers must therefore be narrowly circumscribed, for instance only allowing their use if there is a reasonable suspicion against a person to be searched.[64]

In addition to such requirements relating to the foreseeability of secret surveillance and comparable measures, the Court has held that sufficient procedural safeguards must be offered to avoid arbitrary application.[65] In this respect, for example, it is necessary that individuals are notified at some reasonable point that secret surveillance measures have been used against them so as to enable them to make use of a legal remedy.[66] These safeguards are addressed separately hereafter, in Section 8.7.

8.6   Absence of Arbitrariness

In some cases, the Court has formulated the requirement of absence of arbitrariness as a separate requirement related to the overall lawfulness of an interference. In *R.Sz. v. Hungary*, for example, it held that 'the existence of a legal basis in domestic

---

[59] *Ibid.*, para. 231. See also e.g. *Weber and Saravia v. Germany*, ECtHR 29 June 2006 (dec.), 54934/00, para. 95. Specifically for bulk interception of communications, see *Big Brother Watch and Others v. the United Kingdom*, ECtHR 13 September 2018, 58170/13, paras. 339 et seq.

[60] See e.g. *Vukota-Bojić v. Switzerland*, ECtHR 18 October 2016, 61838/10, paras. 67 et seq.; *Bărbulescu v. Romania*, ECtHR (GC) 5 September 2017, 61496/08, paras. 120–1.

[61] See further Section 6.3.1.

[62] See e.g. *M.M. v. the United Kingdom*, ECtHR 13 November 2012, 24029/07, para. 195.

[63] *Gillan and Quinton v. the United Kingdom*, ECtHR 12 January 2010, 4158/05, para. 85.

[64] Cf. *ibid.*, paras. 86–7; see also *Colon v. the Netherlands*, ECtHR 15 May 2012 (dec.), 49458/06.

[65] E.g. *Roman Zakharov v. Russia*, ECtHR (GC) 4 December 2015, 47143/06, paras. 233–4.

[66] See already *Klass v. Germany*, ECtHR 6 September 1978, 5029/71, para. 78 and see more recently *Roman Zakharov v. Russia*, ECtHR (GC) 4 December 2015, 47143/06, paras. 234 and 286 et seq.

law does not suffice, in itself, to satisfy the principle of lawfulness. In addition, the legal basis must have a certain quality, namely it must be compatible with the rule of law and must provide guarantees against arbitrariness'.[67]

The *East/West Alliance* case can serve to illustrate the effect of this separate requirement.[68] This case concerned the seizure of fourteen aircraft owned by the applicant company and the various procedures the company had attempted to try to retrieve them or obtain compensation. After an extensive assessment of the decisions made and procedures conducted in the case, the Court formulated its conclusions as regards the lawfulness of the seizure:

> In the light of the foregoing, the Court cannot but conclude that the applicant company has been deprived of its six An-28 and eight L-410 aircraft in an utterly arbitrary manner, contrary to the rule of law principle. Furthermore, the Court notes that this interference was not of an instantaneous nature, but that the applicant company was denied access to its property for more than ten years. While it was taking strenuous efforts before various administrative, tax, prosecution and judicial authorities to recover its property, which remained fruitless regardless of their legal outcome, the aircraft were getting damaged and vandalised, or sold to third parties, or simply disappeared without anybody held accountable. Even though for brief periods the retention of the aircraft by the authorities complied with some of the principles inherent in Article 1 of Protocol No. 1, the concomitant abusive and arbitrary actions of the authorities negated in practice the effectiveness of those safeguards.[69]

The prohibition of arbitrariness can thus be used as an independent element of the test of lawfulness.[70] Many applications of this element can be seen in relation to specific provisions, such as the prohibition of arbitrary detention of Article 5 ECHR,[71] and in relation to secret surveillance, interception of data, or searches and seizures.[72] Otherwise, the application of the prohibition of arbitrariness as an independent requirement is rather uncommon. In most cases, the Court connects the

---

[67] *R.Sz. v. Hungary*, ECtHR 2 July 2013, 41838/11, para. 36.

[68] *East/West Alliance Limited v. Ukraine*, ECtHR 23 January 2014, 19336/04.

[69] *Ibid.*, paras. 215–17.

[70] E.g. *R.Sz. v. Hungary*, para. 37. For related examples in a different context, see *Vučković and Others v. Serbia*, ECtHR 28 August 2012, 17153/11; *Anđelković v. Serbia*, ECtHR 9 April 2013, 1401/08; *Polyakova and Others v. Russia*, ECtHR 7 March 2017, 35090/09, paras. 91–2; *Işıkırık v. Turkey*, ECtHR 14 November 2017, 41226/09, para. 58; *Ivaschenko v. Russia*, ECtHR 13 February 2018, 61064/10, para. 73. On the interconnectedness of foreseeability and arbitrariness, see also e.g. *Rolim Comercial, S.A. v. Portugal*, ECtHR 16 April 2013, 16153/09.

[71] See *Winterwerp v. the Netherlands*, ECtHR 24 October 1979, 6301/73, para. 45; for a more recent example (from many), see *Červenka v. the Czech Republic*, ECtHR 13 October 2016, 62507/12, para. 105.

[72] For one example taken from many, see *Roman Zakharov v. Russia*, ECtHR (GC) 4 December 2015, 47143/06, paras. 229–30.

prohibition of arbitrariness to the requirement of procedural safeguards, which is further addressed in Section 8.7, or to that of foreseeability. The *Ternovszky* case, for example, concerned the regulation of the possibility for pregnant women to give birth at home.[73] Hungarian legislation did not formally prohibit home births and it specifically recognised patients' right to self-determination. At the same time, specific regulations dissuaded medical professionals from assisting women when giving birth at home and there had been examples of such professionals being sanctioned. In the Court's view, the various provisions were contradictory, leading it to conclude that the legal situation on home births entailed a risk of arbitrariness and was therefore unforeseeable:

> These considerations enable the Court to conclude that the matter of health professionals assisting home births is surrounded by legal uncertainty prone to arbitrariness. Prospective mothers cannot therefore be considered as freely benefiting from such assistance, since a permanent threat is being posed to health professionals inclined to assist home births . . . as well as the absence of specific, comprehensive legislation on the matter. The lack of legal certainty and the threat to health professionals has limited the choices of the applicant considering home delivery. For the Court, this situation is incompatible with the notion of 'foreseeability' and hence with that of 'lawfulness'.[74]

Thus, the requirements of foreseeability, procedural safeguards and an absence of arbitrariness are intertwined, and they are often used in combination to establish the overall lawfulness of an interference.

8.7   Procedural Safeguards

In addition to the requirements of an accessible and foreseeable legal basis, and closely related to the primary responsibility of the States to secure the rights contained in the Convention, the Court has sought to ascertain that there is a procedural infrastructure on the national level to protect individuals and other private parties against arbitrary application of domestic legislation. In particular, the Court has emphasised the importance of such procedural guarantees in relation to interferences made in secret, such as interception of communications. In 1978, the Court acknowledged in *Klass* that additional guarantees are necessary because of the nature of these interferences:

> [T]he Contracting States [do not] enjoy an unlimited discretion to subject persons within their jurisdiction to secret surveillance. The Court, being aware of the danger such a law poses of undermining or even destroying democracy on the ground of defending it, affirms

---

[73] *Ternovszky v. Hungary*, ECtHR 14 December 2010, 67545/09.   [74] *Ibid.*, para. 26.

that the Contracting States may not, in the name of the struggle against espionage and terrorism, adopt whatever measures they deem appropriate. The Court must be satisfied that, whatever system of surveillance is adopted, there exist adequate and effective guarantees against abuse. This assessment has only a relative character: it depends on all the circumstances of the case, such as the nature, scope and duration of the possible measures, the grounds required for ordering such measures, the authorities competent to permit, carry out and supervise such measures, and the kind of remedy provided by the national law.[75]

In many subsequent cases the Court has further detailed which national procedural safeguards have to be offered in relation to the ordering of surveillance, during the actual surveillance and after the surveillance has ended.[76] In *Roman Zakharov*, the Court brought together all of this case law and defined very precise standards in relation to all of the following aspects of secret surveillance in relation to national security:

the accessibility of the domestic law, the scope and duration of the secret surveillance measures, the procedures to be followed for storing, accessing, examining, using, communicating and destroying the intercepted data, the authorisation procedures, the arrangements for supervising the implementation of secret surveillance measures, any notification mechanisms and the remedies provided for by national law.[77]

Similar requirements have been set in relation to interception of communications in criminal investigations, although the requirements are slightly less strict there.[78] It is also irrelevant to the applicability of these standards whether the case concerns 'bulk interception' of a large volume of communications, or whether it concerns targeted interception, although the Court has explained that their exact content can vary depending on the nature of the interception.[79] For example, in relation to targeted interception it might be reasonable to require objective evidence of a reasonable suspicion in relation to the person for whom the data is sought, but this would be an impracticable criterion in relation to bulk interception, which is by definition untargeted.[80]

To give an impression of the level of detail of the Court's requirements, the standards can be mentioned that the Court defined in *Roman Zakharov* in

---

[75] *Klass and Others v. Germany*, ECtHR 6 September 1978, 5029/71, paras. 49–50.

[76] *Roman Zakharov v. Russia*, ECtHR (GC) 4 December 2015, 47143/06, para. 233; *Big Brother Watch and Others v. the United Kingdom*, ECtHR 13 September 2018, 58170/13, para. 309.

[77] *Roman Zakharov*, para. 238. See also e.g. *Dragojević v. Croatia*, ECtHR 15 January 2015, 68955/11, para. 83; *Szabó and Vissy v. Hungary*, ECtHR 12 January 2016, 37138/14, para. 56; *Centrum för Rättvisa v. Sweden*, ECtHR 19 June 2018, 35252/08; *Big Brother Watch and Others v. the United Kingdom*, ECtHR 13 September 2018, 58170/13, para. 307.

[78] *Ibid.*, para. 307.   [79] *Ibid.*, para. 316.   [80] *Ibid.*, para. 317.

relation to just one of these aspects, that is, the authorisation of interception of telecommunications:

> As regards the authority competent to authorise the surveillance, authorising of telephone tapping by a non-judicial authority may be compatible with the Convention ... provided that that authority is sufficiently independent from the executive ... [The authorisation authority] must be capable of verifying the existence of a reasonable suspicion against the person concerned, in particular, whether there are factual indications for suspecting that person of planning, committing or having committed criminal acts or other acts that may give rise to secret surveillance measures, such as, for example, acts endangering national security. It must also ascertain whether the requested interception meets the requirement of 'necessity in a democratic society', as provided by Article 8 § 2 of the Convention, including whether it is proportionate to the legitimate aims pursued, by verifying, for example whether it is possible to achieve the aims by less restrictive means ... Lastly, as regards the content of the interception authorisation, it must clearly identify a specific person to be placed under surveillance or a single set of premises as the premises in respect of which the authorisation is ordered. Such identification may be made by names, addresses, telephone numbers or other relevant information.[81]

In addition, the Court has regularly stressed that it cannot base its judgments on the quality of the legislation and the existence of a system of procedural safeguards alone. Instead, it must focus on the manner in which all these guarantees have been applied in the particular circumstances of the case and whether, in the end, the requirement of lawfulness can be seen to have been met.[82] For example, in *Savovi*, the Court recalled that it had held in a previous judgment that the Bulgarian legislation on telephone tapping statutory procedure for authorising covert surveillance, if strictly adhered to, offered sufficient protection against arbitrary or indiscriminate surveillance.[83] The Court also noted, however, that in that judgment, it had already expressed some concerns in relation to the safeguards provided. It then turned to examining the facts of the case before it, and it found

> that these concerns are relevant to the instant case, seeing that ... no independent body has reviewed the lawfulness of the surveillance or the manner in which that material had been disposed of ... Indeed, when the [competent inspection] Commission arrived, the surveillance equipment was functioning and apparently no steps had been taken for its dismantling although the court warrant had expired three days before ... As to the manner in which the intelligence obtained in respect of the first applicant was handled and

[81] *Roman Zakharov v. Russia*, ECtHR (GC) 4 December 2015, 47143/06, paras. 257–66.
[82] See e.g. *Goranova-Karanaeva v. Bulgaria*, ECtHR 8 March 2011, 12739/05, para. 48; *Dragojević v. Croatia*, ECtHR 15 January 2015, 68955/11, para. 86; *Big Brother Watch and Others v. the United Kingdom*, ECtHR 13 September 2018, 58170/13, para. 320.
[83] *Savovi v. Bulgaria*, ECtHR 27 November 2012, 7222/05.

destroyed, the Court notes that it was taken away by members of the Commission in a cardboard box ... The subsequent proceedings before the domestic authorities do not reveal if, when or how it was destroyed.[84]

The Court held that the shortcomings in this case tainted the application of the legislation to such an extent that it could no longer be regarded as 'prescribed by law' and it was therefore in violation of the Convention. On the other hand however, the Court has held that some minor irregularities in the procedure do not necessarily lead to the finding of a violation if, overall, it appears that the surveillance powers have been applied in the individual case with sufficient safeguards against abuse.[85]

The Court has further held that procedural requirements on surveillance must be set in the context of surveillance by insurance companies or employers.[86] Moreover, the Court has required similar procedural safeguards in contexts other than secret surveillance and interception. For example, the Court has defined such requirements in relation to the protection of journalistic sources, given the vital importance of the freedom of the press:

> First and foremost among these safeguards is the guarantee of review by a judge or other independent and impartial decision-making body ... The requisite review should be carried out by a body separate from the executive and other interested parties, invested with the power to determine whether a requirement in the public interest overriding the principle of protection of journalistic sources exists prior to the handing over of such material and to prevent unnecessary access to information capable of disclosing the sources' identity if it does not ... It is clear, in the Court's view, that the exercise of any independent review that only takes place subsequently to the handing over of material capable of revealing such sources would undermine the very essence of the right to confidentiality. Given the preventive nature of such review the judge or other independent and impartial body must thus be in a position to carry out this weighing of the potential risks and respective interests prior to any disclosure and with reference to the material that it is sought to have disclosed so that the arguments of the authorities seeking the disclosure can be properly assessed. The decision to be taken should be governed by clear criteria, including whether a less intrusive measure can suffice to serve the overriding public interests established. It should be open to the judge or other authority to refuse to make a disclosure order or to make a limited or qualified order so as to protect sources from being revealed, whether or not they are

---

[84] *Ibid.*, para. 58; see also *Dragojević v. Croatia*, ECtHR 15 January 2015, 68955/11, para. 101.

[85] E.g. *Goranova-Karanaeva v. Bulgaria*, ECtHR 8 March 2011, 12739/05, para. 46. More generally, the Court has defined in *Roman Zakharov* when it will only look into the individual application of surveillance measures or also into the general legislation underlying such measures; see *Roman Zakharov v. Russia*, ECtHR (GC) 4 December 2015, 47143/06, para. 171; see also *Centrum för Rättvisa v. Sweden*, ECtHR 19 June 2018, 35252/08, paras. 92–3.

[86] *Vukota-Bojić v. Switzerland*, ECtHR 18 October 2016, 61838/10, paras. 67 et seq.; *Bărbulescu v. Romania*, ECtHR (GC) 5 September 2017, 61496/08, paras. 120–1.

specifically named in the withheld material, on the grounds that the communication of such material creates a serious risk of compromising the identity of journalist's sources . . . In situations of urgency, a procedure should exist to identify and isolate, prior to the exploitation of the material by the authorities, information that could lead to the identification of sources from information that carries no such risk.[87]

Comparable conditions for procedural fairness can be found in relation to the requirement of lawfulness in many other situation types, such as the collection, processing, retention and disclosure of personal data[88] (including finger prints and DNA samples),[89] the interception of correspondence,[90] the blocking of websites or publication bans,[91] and searches of homes, business premises or electronic devices.[92] Notably, however, the Court has held that these requirements can be somewhat less strict if the interference with the Convention right concerned (usually Article 8) is less intrusive, for example because it concerns only someone's movements in public places and therefore affects one's private life less seriously. The Court has accepted this, for example, in relation to GPS-tracking[93] and physical observation of the house where a suspect is living[94].[95]

On rare occasions, the Court has also inserted elements of procedural due care in the lawfulness test in cases unrelated to surveillance, searches and seizures, such as cases in deportation measures.[96] To mention another example, in the case of *Solska and Rybicka*, the Court explained that in cases on the exhumation of bodies in relation to an investigation of the causes of death, the national legislation has to

---

[87] *Sanoma v. the Netherlands*, ECtHR (GC) 14 September 2010, 38224/03, paras. 90–2.

[88] E.g. *L.H. v. Latvia*, ECtHR 29 April 2014, 52019/07, paras. 51–9.

[89] *S. and Marper v. the United Kingdom*, ECtHR (GC) 4 December 2008, 30562/04 and 30566/04, para. 99; *M.K. v. France*, ECtHR 18 April 2013, 19522/09, para. 35.

[90] *Dragoș Ioan Rusu v. Romania*, ECtHR 31 October 2017, 22767/08, para. 35.

[91] *Ahmet Yıldırım v. Turkey*, ECtHR 18 December 2012, 3111/10, para. 66; *Cumhuriyet Vakfı and Others v. Turkey*, ECtHR 8 October 2013, 28255/07, para. 61.

[92] E.g. *Robathin v. Austria*, ECtHR 3 July 2012, 30457/06, para. 44; *Ivaschenko v. Russia*, ECtHR 13 February 2018, 61064/10, paras. 93–4. Usually, however, such requirements are formulated in relation to the necessity test in this context; see this example taken from many, *K.S. and M.S. v. Germany*, ECtHR 6 October 2016, 33696/11, paras. 42 et seq. In *Ivaschenko*, the Court explained that, indeed, in this context, 'quality of law' may overlap with similar issues analysed under the heading of 'necessary in a democratic society' (para. 75).

[93] *Uzun v. Germany*, ECtHR 2 September 2010, 35623/05, para. 66; confirmed in *R.E. v. the United Kingdom*, ECtHR 27 October 2015, 62498/11, para. 127; but see also *Ben Faiza v. France*, ECtHR 8 February 2018, 31446/12, where the Court did not refer to *Uzun* and simply applied the standards developed in relation to secret surveillance.

[94] Cf. *El-Haski v. Belgium*, ECtHR 25 September 2012, 649/08, para. 107.

[95] See more generally *Big Brother Watch and Others v. the United Kingdom*, ECtHR 13 September 2018, 58170/13, para. 350.

[96] E.g. *Lupsa v. Romania*, ECtHR 8 June 2006, 10337/04, para. 34; *Liu v. Russia*, ECtHR 6 December 2007, 42086/05, para. 62; *I.R. and G.T. v. the United Kingdom*, ECtHR 28 January 2014 (dec.), 14876/12 and 63339/12, para. 60.

allow for the national authorities to strike a balance between the procedural positive obligations they incur under the right to life (Article 2 ECHR) and the respect for the interests and objections of the next-of-kin of the deceased.[97] If such a balance cannot be struck and no sufficient procedural guarantees are offered, the legislation will not be 'in accordance with the law'.[98]

Finally, it can be noted that, in many cases, the compatibility with these requirements is not reviewed as part of the test of 'foreseeability', but (also) as part of the tests of necessity and proportionality,[99] or as part of the compliance with procedural positive obligations.[100] The various requirements for restriction are thus interconnected.

---

[97] *Solska and Rybicka v. Poland*, ECtHR 20 September 2018, 30491/17 and 31083/17, paras. 118 et seq.

[98] *Ibid.*, para. 126.

[99] E.g. *S. and Marper v. the United Kingdom*, ECtHR (GC) 4 December 2008, 30562/04 and 30566/04, paras. 99 and 105–26; *Wieser and Bicos Beteiligungen GmbH v. Germany*, ECtHR 16 October 2007, 74336/01, para. 57; *Nagla v. Latvia*, ECtHR 16 July 2013, 73469/10, para. 98; *Szabó and Vissy v. Hungary*, ECtHR 12 January 2016, 37138/14, paras. 73 et seq.; *Cumhuriyet Vakfı and Others v. Turkey*, ECtHR 8 October 2013, 28255/07, paras. 61 et seq.; *Delta Pekárny A.S. v. the Czech Republic*, ECtHR 2 October 2014, 97/11, paras. 82 et seq.; *Pruteanu v. Romania*, ECtHR 3 February 2015, 30181/05, paras. 48 et seq.; *Ivaschenko v. Russia*, ECtHR 13 February 2018, 61064/10, para. 75.

[100] On procedural positive obligations, see Section 5.3.2.

9 Justification of Restrictions II – Legitimate Aim

9.1 Exhaustive Lists of Legitimate Aims and Their Importance

The second main requirement for an interference with a Convention right to be justifiable is that it pursues a legitimate aim. This requirement is explicitly mentioned in the provisions with express limitation clauses, such as Articles 8–11 ECHR, Article 1 of Protocol No. 1 and Article 2 of Protocol No. 4. In addition, the Court has consistently set this requirement in relation to Convention provisions which allow for implied or inherent restrictions, such as Article 14 ECHR. Indeed, it is a logical requirement, as it is hardly thinkable that a restriction of a fundamental right can be acceptable if it does not serve any reasonable purpose.

Notably, the express limitation clauses do not only require the aims pursued to be legitimate, but they also provide exhaustive lists of the aims which can legitimately be served. Interferences must be, for example, in the general interest or in the interests of national security or public safety, or they must be necessary for the protection of public order, health or morals, for the protection of the rights of others or, more specifically, for preventing the disclosure of information received in confidence. Theoretically, such clear and exhaustive definition of legitimate aims is very useful, as it narrows down the possibility for restricting fundamental rights to those situations in which such restrictions really can be considered reasonable and justifiable, and it makes the limitation clauses less indeterminate. The practical usefulness of the lists of grounds in the Convention's limitation clauses is considerably reduced, however, by the broadness of their wording. In reality, it has appeared that almost any general interest that reasonably could be served by a public authority is covered by them. In this light, it may not come as a surprise that the test of legitimate aim does not play a large role in the Court's review of justification for restrictions, as the Court itself has acceded: 'The Court's practice is to be quite succinct when it verifies the existence of a legitimate aim within the meaning of the second paragraphs of Articles 8 to 11 of the Convention.'[1] The Court has further admitted that

---

[1] *S.A.S. v. France*, ECtHR (GC) 1 July 2014, 43835/11, para. 114.

[i]n cases under those provisions[2] – as well as under Articles 1, 2 and 3 of Protocol No. 1, or Article 2 §§ 3 and 4 of Protocol No. 4 – respondent Governments normally have a relatively easy task in persuading the Court that the interference pursued a legitimate aim, even when the applicants cogently argue that it actually pursued an unavowed ulterior purpose ... The cases in which the Court has voiced doubts about the cited aim without ruling on the issue ... left the issue open ... or has rejected one or more of the cited aims ... are few and far between. The cases in which it has found a breach of the respective Article purely owing to the lack of a legitimate aim are rarer still ... although in a recent case the Grand Chamber found an absence of legitimate aim and yet went on to examine whether the interference had been necessary.[3]

Indeed, in most cases, the Court simply accepts that a measure or decision serves one of the aims mentioned in the Convention text, sometimes without even specifying which one it considers to be applicable,[4] or reclassifying a rather vague asserted aim as one that is clearly mentioned in a limitation clause.[5] The Court also prefers to focus on necessity and proportionality review, rather than review of a legitimate aim, when the parties disagree on whether a legitimate aim has been pursued or when the Court itself appears to cherish some hesitations as to the reasonableness and genuine nature of the stated objectives underlying a restriction.[6] In many cases, the Court will then proceed on the assumption that there was a legitimate aim, simply 'for the sake of argument'.[7]

9.2   Application and Interpretation of the Legitimate Aim Requirement

Even if the Court generally pays little attention to the requirement of a legitimate aim, there are a few cases where the Court has found that an aim does not meet the requirements of the Convention because it does not fit in the list of stated aims.

---

[2] Articles 8 to 11 ECHR.

[3] *Merabishvili v. Georgia*, ECtHR (GC) 28 November 2017, 72508/13, paras. 295–6, with many references to relevant case law.

[4] E.g. *Wasmuth v. Germany*, ECtHR 17 February 2011, 12884/03, para. 55; *Vrzić v. Croatia*, ECtHR 12 July 2016, 43777/13, para. 62.

[5] E.g. *Labassee v. France*, ECtHR 26 June 2014, 65941/11, paras. 53–4.

[6] See e.g. *Alekseyev v. Russia*, ECtHR 21 October 2010, 4916/07, 25924/08 and 14599/09, para. 69; in this case there might have been some doubts as to the legitimacy of the aims pursued and the parties clearly disagreed on this, but the Court chose to dispense with ruling on this point because, irrespective of the aim, it could easily hold that the restriction fell short of the necessity requirement. See further e.g. *Megadat.com Srl v. Moldova*, ECtHR 8 April 2008, 21151/04; *Temel and Others v. Turkey*, ECtHR 3 March 2009, 36458/02, para. 42; *Tănase v. Moldova*, ECtHR (GC) 27 April 2010, 7/08, paras. 164–70; *Dink v. Turkey*, ECtHR 14 September 2010, 2668/07, para. 118; *Bayatyan v. Armenia*, ECtHR (GC) 7 November 2011, 23459/03, para. 112; *Stamose v. Bulgaria*, ECtHR 27 November 2012, 29713/05; *Avilkina and Others v. Russia*, ECtHR 6 June 2013, 1585/09, para. 40; *Biržietis v. Lithuania*, ECtHR 14 June 2016, 49304/09, para. 54; *Baka v. Hungary*, ECtHR (GC) 23 June 2016, 20261/12, paras. 156–7; *Çölgeçen and Others v. Turkey*, ECtHR 12 December 2017, 50124/07, para. 53.

[7] See literally *Novikova v. Russia*, ECtHR 26 April 2016, 25501/07, para. 143.

It did so, for example, in *Nolan and K.*[8] Nolan, a Georgian national, worked in Russia for a religious organisation, but at a certain point in time, the authorities refused to extend his visa. They had concluded, based on a secret report, that Nolan's presence in Russia would be contrary to the interests of national security. The Court considered that, given Nolan's religious activities in Russia, the refusal to extend his visa interfered with his freedom of religion as protected by Article 9 ECHR. The aim of protecting national security could not be justifiably invoked in this respect:

> [I]n so far as the Government relied on the protection of national security as the main legitimate aim of the impugned measure, the Court reiterates that the exceptions to freedom of religion listed in Article 9 § 2 must be narrowly interpreted, for their enumeration is strictly exhaustive and their definition is necessarily restrictive ... Legitimate aims mentioned in this provision include: the interests of public safety, the protection of public order, health or morals, and the protection of the rights and freedoms of others ...
> However, unlike the second paragraphs of Articles 8, 10, and 11, paragraph 2 of Article 9 of the Convention does not allow restrictions on the ground of national security. Far from being an accidental omission, the non-inclusion of that particular ground for limitations in Article 9 reflects the primordial importance of religious pluralism as 'one of the foundations of a "democratic society" within the meaning of the Convention' and the fact that a State cannot dictate what a person believes or take coercive steps to make him change his beliefs ... It follows that the interests of national security could not serve as a justification for the measures taken by the Russian authorities against the applicant.[9]

Accordingly, it must be clear that the State's objectives fit into one of the aims expressly mentioned in the Convention. In this regard, the Court's emphasis that it will provide a restrictive interpretation of the aims listed in the Convention is also important. The Court explained the reason for this in *Perinçek*, where it was confronted with the difference in formulation and meaning between the French and English language versions of the legitimate aim of 'the prevention of disorder' and 'la défense de l'ordre':

> Bearing in mind that the context in which the terms at issue were used is a treaty for the effective protection of individual human rights ... that clauses, such as Article 10 § 2, that

---

[8] *Nolan and K. v. Russia*, ECtHR 12 February 2009, 2512/04.
[9] *Ibid.*, para. 73. For other examples, see *Open Door and Dublin Well Woman v. Ireland*, ECtHR 29 October 1992, 14234/88 and 14235/88, para. 63; *Khuzhin and Others v. Russia*, ECtHR 23 October 2008, 13470/02, para. 117; *Toma v. Romania*, ECtHR 24 February 2009, 42716/02, para. 92; *Tkachevy v. Russia*, ECtHR 14 February 2012, 35430/05; *P. and S. v. Poland*, ECtHR 30 October 2012, 57375/08, para. 133; *Khodorkovskiy and Lebedev v. Russia*, ECtHR 25 July 2013, 11082/06 and 13772/05, para. 844; *Baka v. Hungary*, ECtHR (GC) 23 June 2016, 20261/12, paras. 156–7; *Erményi v. Hungary*, ECtHR 22 November 2016, 22254/14, paras. 35–8; *Karajanov v. the Former Yugoslav Republic of Macedonia*, ECtHR 6 April 2017, 2229/15, para. 75.

permit interference with Convention rights must be interpreted restrictively ... and that, more generally, exceptions to a general rule cannot be given a broad interpretation ... the Court finds that, since the words used in the English text appear to be only capable of a narrower meaning, the expressions 'the prevention of disorder' and 'la défense de l'ordre' in the English and French texts of Article 10 § 2 can best be reconciled by being read as having the less extensive meaning.[10]

The Court also considered that the notion of 'ordre public', as it is contained in the French language version, appeared to bear a rather broad meaning, as it can be taken to refer to the body of political, economic and moral principles essential to the maintenance of the social structure, and in some jurisdictions even encompasses human dignity. By contrast, the English language notion of 'disorder' conveys a narrower significance, understood in essence as referring to riots or other forms of public disturbance.[11] For that reason, the Court rejected the moral arguments advanced by the Swiss government as being covered by the aim of 'prevention of disorder'.[12]

In some other cases, the Court has also undertaken to provide a further definition of the legitimate aims stated in the Convention. It has done so in particular for those provisions where the list of legitimate aims is open-ended or no such list is provided, such as in Article 14 ECHR. In general terms, for example, it has held that the national objectives must be compatible with the values underlying the Convention.[13] Thus, in *L. and V.*, it held that objectives which reflect negative attitudes towards a certain group or minority, such as a sexual or ethnic minority, cannot be accepted as justification for a difference in treatment: 'To the extent that [the applicable legislation] ... embodied a predisposed bias on the part of a heterosexual majority against a homosexual minority, these negative attitudes cannot of themselves be considered by the Court to amount to sufficient justification for the differential treatment any more than similar negative attitudes towards those of a different race, origin or colour.'[14]

---

[10] *Perinçek v. Switzerland*, ECtHR (GC) 15 October 2015, 27510/08, para. 151.   [11] *Ibid.*, para. 146.

[12] *Ibid.*, paras. 153–4. In other cases, the Court's interpretation has been much more lenient; see e.g. *Ivanova and Cherkezov v. Bulgaria*, ECtHR 21 April 2016, 46577/15, para. 51: 'The Court is satisfied that the demolition [of the applicants' illegally built house] would pursue a legitimate aim. Even if its only purpose is to ensure the effective implementation of the regulatory requirement that no buildings can be constructed without permit, it may be regarded as seeking to re-establish the rule of law ... which, in the context under examination, may be regarded as falling under "prevention of disorder" and as promoting the "economic well-being of the country".'

[13] See e.g. *Ebrahimian v. France*, ECtHR 26 November 2015, 64846/11, para. 53.

[14] *L. and V. v. Austria*, ECtHR 9 January 2003, 39392/98 and 39829/98, para. 52. See also e.g. *Smith and Grady v. the United Kingdom*, ECtHR 27 September 1999, 33985/96 and 33986/96, para. 102; *Bayev and Others v. Russia*, ECtHR 20 June 2017, 67667/09, para. 68.

A concrete application of this standard can be found in *Bayev*.[15] This case concerned the prohibition of so-called 'homo propaganda', which was in fact a prohibition of all open manifestations or public defences of homosexuality. Under Article 10(2) ECHR, the Russian government had argued that this prohibition, among other interests, served the legitimate aim of the protection of 'morals'. The Court did not agree with the Russian interpretation of this ground, however:

> The Court has consistently declined to endorse policies and decisions which embodied a predisposed bias on the part of a heterosexual majority against a homosexual minority ... The legislation at hand is an example of such predisposed bias, unambiguously highlighted by its domestic interpretation and enforcement, and embodied in ... references to the potential dangers of 'creating a distorted impression of the social equivalence of traditional and non-traditional marital relations' ... Even more unacceptable are the attempts to draw parallels between homosexuality and paedophilia ... The Court takes note of the Government's assertion that the majority of Russians disapprove of homosexuality and resent any display of same-sex relations. It is true that popular sentiment may play an important role in the Court's assessment when it comes to the justification on the grounds of morals. However, there is an important difference between giving way to popular support in favour of extending the scope of the Convention guarantees and a situation where that support is relied on in order to narrow the scope of the substantive protection. The Court reiterates that it would be incompatible with the underlying values of the Convention if the exercise of Convention rights by a minority group were made conditional on its being accepted by the majority. Were this so, a minority group's rights to freedom of religion, expression and assembly would become merely theoretical rather than practical and effective as required by the Convention ... In view of the above considerations, the Court rejects the Government's claim that regulating public debate on LGBT issues may be justified on the grounds of the protection of morals.[16]

Similarly, the Court will not easily accept objectives purely derived from tradition (such as the objective to maintain the traditional role of male heirs) as a justification for a difference in treatment,[17] although it has accepted that the interest of protecting the family in the traditional sense, in principle, constitutes a weighty and legitimate aim.[18] The Court has further rejected aims that are directly or indirectly

---

[15] *Bayev and Others v. Russia*, ECtHR 20 June 2017, 67667/09.   [16] *Ibid.*, paras. 68–71.

[17] E.g. *Pla and Puncernau v. Andorra*, ECtHR 13 July 2004, 69498/01, para. 62; *Ünal Tekeli v. Turkey*, ECtHR 16 November 2004, 29865/96, paras. 62 et seq.; *Brauer v. Germany*, ECtHR 28 May 2009, 3545/04, para. 43.

[18] E.g. *Karner v. Austria*, ECtHR 24 July 2003, 40016/98, para. 40; *Kozak v. Poland*, ECtHR 2 March 2010, 13102/02, para. 98; *X. and Others v. Austria*, ECtHR (GC) 19 February 2013, 19010/07, para. 138; *Vallianatos and Others v. Greece*, ECtHR (GC) 7 November 2013, 29381/09 and 32684/09, para. 83; *Tadeucci and McCall v. Italy*, ECtHR 30 June 2016, 51362/09, para. 87.

expressive of discrimination or prejudice,[19] that clearly reflect gender stereotypes,[20] or that more generally reflect biased assumptions or prevailing social prejudice in a particular country.[21]

9.3   Discrepancy Between Stated and Real Aims

It is not always easy for the Court to establish the presence of discriminatory or otherwise illegitimate objectives. After all, respondent governments will hardly be eager to admit that they have pursued such aims. The Court therefore will have to look closely into the context of the interference if it wants to discover the existence of any covert, illegitimate aims that were, secretly, more important than the objective and neutral arguments that have been presented to the Court. Given that this requires an intrusive review by the Court, it will usually only undertake such an investigation into the 'real' objectives of the States if it applies strict scrutiny and there is a narrow margin of appreciation for the State.[22] An example of a case where the Court embarked on such a contextual assessment is *Genderdoc-M*.[23] Genderdoc-M was an NGO that had applied for authorisation to hold a peaceful demonstration to advocate legalisation of homosexual partnerships, but this had been refused. Before the Court, the respondent government had argued that the reason for refusal was the existence of a systemic problem as to the right of assembly in Moldova during the period 2004–2006. The Court applied a 'very weighty reasons' test in this case because it suspected that the refusal was related to the prima facie unacceptable ground of sexual orientation.[24] This intrusive test allowed it to find that, in reality, no legitimate aim had been pursued:

> First, the Court observes that the applicant adduced as evidence decisions of the Chişinău Mayor's Office allowing various assemblies and which had been adopted during the same period of time referred to by the Government … The Government failed to offer an explanation as to this difference in treatment between the applicant association and the above-mentioned associations.

---

[19] Cf. e.g. *Y.Y. v. Turkey*, ECtHR 10 March 2015, 14793/08, paras. 77–8.

[20] *Konstantin Markin v. Russia*, ECtHR (GC) 22 March 2012, 30078/06, para. 143; *Emel Boyraz*, ECtHR 2 December 2014, 61960/08, paras. 52–6.

[21] *Biao v. Denmark*, ECtHR (GC) 24 May 2016, 38590/10, para. 126.

[22] See further Chapter 7. Even in such cases, however, the Court will not easily accept that there are illegitimate aims; the Court did not find sufficient proof, for example, to establish that forced sterilisations of Roma women in Slovakia were part of an organised policy and/or were intentionally racially motivated; see *V.C. v. Slovakia*, ECtHR 8 November 2011, 18968/07, para. 177; *I.G. and Others v. Slovakia*, ECtHR 13 November 2012, 15966/04, para. 165.

[23] *Genderdoc-M v. Moldova*, ECtHR 12 June 2012, 9106/06.   [24] See Section 7.3.

Second, the Court considers that the reason for the ban imposed on the event proposed by the applicant was the authorities' disapproval of demonstrations which they considered to promote homosexuality. In particular, the Court highlights that the Chişinău Mayor's Office – a decision-making body in the applicant's case – has insisted two times before the Court of Appeal that the applicant's assembly should be banned due to the opposition of many Moldovan citizens to homosexuality . . . In view of the above, the Court holds the view that there has been a violation of Article 14 in conjunction with Article 11 of the Convention in the present case.[25]

The fact that a public authority had acceded elsewhere that, in reality, the authorisation was refused for purely discriminatory reasons enabled the Court to find that there was no legitimate aim. Likewise, the Court may find an indication of fabrication of a legitimate aim for the purposes of the procedure before the Court if the government advances an objective that has not been discussed in the domestic proceedings or if it cannot be found in the preparatory works of domestic legislation.[26] Mostly, however, the Court can only find out about hidden objectives by extensively assessing the facts of the case in light of the contents of national decisions and legislation, if necessary taking account of supplementary sources such as legislative history and statements of politicians in the news media.[27]

9.4   Plurality of Aims

Another difficult situation arises when the Court has established that the interference has been motivated by different aims, some of which can be considered as legitimate, but some are more problematic, for example because they do not fit into one of the aims expressly contained in a limitation clause. In most cases, the Court solves this by leaving the problematic aim out of consideration and focusing on the other, legitimate objectives, to see whether they are sufficiently weighty as to support the interference under the necessity test. As the Court stated in *Merabishvili*: 'Even when it excludes some of the cited aims, if it accepts that an interference pursues at least one, it does not delve further into the question and goes on to assess whether it was necessary in a democratic society to attain that aim.'[28]

---

[25] *Genderdoc-M*, paras. 53–4.

[26] E.g. *Khordokovskiy and Lebedev v. Russia*, ECtHR 25 July 2013, 11082/06 and 13772/05, paras. 843–4.

[27] See e.g. *Tkachevy v. Russia*, ECtHR 14 February 2012, 35430/05, paras. 38–50; *Baka v. Hungary*, ECtHR (GC) 23 June 2016, 20261/12, paras. 143–51 and 156–7; *Volchkova and Mironov v. Russia*, ECtHR 28 March 2017, 45668/05 and 2292/06, paras. 118–21.

[28] *Merabishvili v. Georgia*, ECtHR (GC) 28 November 2017, 72508/13, para. 197.

An example of how this works can be found in *Sidiropoulos*.[29] This case concerned the refusal by the Greek government to register a new association, which was meant to further 'the cultural, intellectual and artistic development of its members', 'cultural decentralisation', folk culture and the protection of the region's natural and cultural environment.[30] The competent domestic court held, however, that the association was really meant to promote the idea that there is a Macedonian minority in Greece, which it considered an unacceptable objective. For that reason, the registration was refused.[31] The applicants argued before the Court that this refusal was incompatible with Article 11(2) ECHR. Regarding the legitimacy of the aims advanced by the government, the Court held that

> [t]he Government submitted that the interference in question pursued several aims: the maintenance of national security, the prevention of disorder and the upholding of Greece's cultural traditions and historical and cultural symbols. The Court is not persuaded that the last of those aims may constitute one of the legitimate aims set out in Article 11 § 2. Exceptions to freedom of association must be narrowly interpreted, such that the enumeration of them is strictly exhaustive and the definition of them necessarily restrictive. The Court notes nevertheless that the Salonika Court of Appeal based its decision on the conviction that the applicants intended to dispute the Greek identity of Macedonia and its inhabitants and undermine Greece's territorial integrity. Having regard to the situation prevailing in the Balkans at the time and to the political friction between Greece and the FYROM ... the Court accepts that the interference in issue was intended to protect national security and prevent disorder.[32]

Thus, the unacceptable aim was not allowed to play a role in the review of necessity and proportionality, which then focused on the remaining two objectives.[33]

9.5 Interconnectedness of Legitimate Aim and Proportionality

Finally, a review of the legitimacy of the aims pursued and a proportionality review are closely connected. *S.H. v. Austria*, for example, related to the prohibition of IVF

---

[29] *Sidiropoulos and Others v. Greece*, ECtHR 10 July 1998, 26695/95.   [30] *Ibid.*, para. 8.
[31] *Ibid.*, para. 10.   [32] *Ibid.*, paras. 37–9.
[33] See similarly in e.g. *Vereinigung Bildender Künstler v. Austria*, ECtHR 25 January 2007, 68354/01, para. 31; *Stoll v. Switzerland*, ECtHR (GC) 10 December 2007, 69698/01, paras. 54–6; *Khordokovskiy and Lebedev v. Russia*, ECtHR 25 July 2013, 11082/06 and 13772/05, paras. 844–5; *Mennesson v. France*, ECtHR 26 June 2014, 65192/11, paras. 61–2; *S.A.S. v. France*, ECtHR (GC) 1 July 2014, 43835/11, paras. 116–22; *Vintman v. Ukraine*, ECtHR 23 October 2014, 28403/05, paras. 94–9; *Y.Y. v. Turkey*, ECtHR 10 March 2015, 14793/08, paras. 78–9; *Perinçek v. Switzerland*, ECtHR (GC) 15 October 2015, 27510/08, paras. 146–57; *Hamidović v. Bosnia and Herzegovina*, ECtHR 5 December 2017, 57792/15, para. 35.

treatment with donated egg cells because of the moral and ethical objections that existed in Austria against such treatment. The Court considered that 'concerns based on moral considerations or on social acceptability are not in themselves sufficient reasons for a complete ban on a specific artificial procreation technique such as ova donation'.[34] It is not entirely clear from this consideration whether the Court did not accept the respondent government's justification because it regarded its grounds as unacceptable, or because it did not consider this aim to be sufficiently weighty to justify the restriction at hand. Most likely it was the combination of these factors which led it to reject the justification.[35] Indeed, such an approach is often taken, which is logical in light of the strong focus of the Court's review of necessity, proportionality and fair balance. This last part of the Court's review of restrictions of a Convention right is therefore separately and further addressed in Chapter 10.

---

[34] *S.H. v. Austria*, ECtHR 1 April 2010, 57813/00, para. 74.

[35] For similar examples of a mixed review of the legitimacy of the aims pursued and their weight in the overall balance of interests, see e.g. *Konstantin Markin v. Russia*, ECtHR (GC) 22 March 2012, 30078/06, paras. 138–52.

10 Justification of Restrictions III – Necessity, Proportionality and Fair Balance

10.1 Formulas, Tests and Standards

For a restriction of a Convention right to be justified, it is not enough for it to have a sound legal basis and to pursue a legitimate aim. Restrictions of Convention rights also must be shown to be necessary or proportionate, and there must be a fair balance between the aim being served and the right being restricted. The Court regards these requirements as central to the review of the legitimacy and justifiability of restrictions of fundamental rights. This is true in particular for the fair balance requirement, which also plays an important role in positive obligations cases.[1] Indeed, the Court has indicated that 'inherent in the whole of the Convention is a search for a fair balance between the demands of the general interest of the community and the requirements of the protection of the individual's fundamental rights'.[2] Consequently, some form of balancing review can often be seen in the case law on all derogable Convention provisions, including those which only contain implied possibilities for limitation, such as Article 14 ECHR.[3] The fair balance requirement as such is not, however, expressed in any of the Convention provisions. Instead, the express limitation clauses of Articles 8–11, Article 1 of Protocol No. 1 and Article 2 of Protocol No. 4 mention the requirement of necessity. More specifically, in several provisions, the requirement is formulated as one of 'necessity in a democratic society'. When applying the necessity test, the Court may indeed pay attention to the closeness of the connection between the interests served by a certain limitation and underlying core principles such as that of democracy.[4] Nevertheless, in the Court's case law, the formula 'in a democratic society' has never obtained the status of an independent standard of review. The element of necessity 'in a

---

[1] See further Chapter 5.2.1.

[2] *Soering v. the United Kingdom*, ECtHR 7 July 1989, 14038/88, para. 89.

[3] For Article 14, see *Case 'relating to certain aspects of the laws on the use of languages in education in Belgium' (Belgian Linguistics* case), ECtHR 23 July 1968, 1474/62; for Article 1(a) Protocol No. 1 see e.g. *Sporrong and Lönnroth v. Sweden*, ECtHR 23 September 1982, 7151/75 and 7152/85, para. 69.

[4] For an example, see *Refah Partisi (Welfare Party) and Others v. Turkey*, ECtHR (GC) 13 February 2003, 41340/98, paras. 86–100. See further also Section 10.4.1.

democratic society' is therefore not addressed separately in this chapter, but only in relation to the test of fair balance and proportionality (Section 10.4.1).

Not only does the wording of the test of necessity, proportionality or reasonableness of restrictions differ for the various Convention provisions, over time the Court itself has also defined a variety of specific tests and formulas to give shape to the test of necessity. The Court originally mentioned the following about the requirement of necessity as follows in the *Handyside* case:

> The Court notes … that, whilst the adjective 'necessary', within the meaning of Article 10 para. 2, is not synonymous with 'indispensable' (cf., in Articles 2 para. 2 and 6 para. 1, the words 'absolutely necessary' and 'strictly necessary' and, in Article 15 para. 1, the phrase 'to the extent strictly required by the exigencies of the situation'), neither has it the flexibility of such expressions as 'admissible', 'ordinary' (cf. Article 4 para. 3), 'useful' (cf. the French text of the first paragraph of Article 1 of Protocol No. 1), 'reasonable' (cf. Articles 5 para. 3 and 6 para. 1) or 'desirable'.[5]

Subsequently, in the *Sunday Times* case the Court provided further clarification, breaking down the necessity requirement into different elements: 'It must … be decided whether the "interference" complained of corresponded to a "pressing social need", whether it was "proportionate to the legitimate aim pursued", [and] whether the reasons given by the national authorities to justify it are "relevant and sufficient".'[6]

According to the *Handyside* definition, thus, 'necessary' is a point in the middle of a scale which ranges from 'indispensable' to merely 'useful'. In the *Sunday Times* formula, the Court further clarified this aspect of the relative weight and need for certain restrictions by means of its notion of a 'pressing social need'. The meaning of this notion can be illustrated by the case of *Vajnai*, which concerned a prohibition of wearing a communist star during a demonstration.[7] The Court showed itself aware of the potential risks for public order of wearing such a star in public, but it also pointed out that the red star can have multiple meanings and the Government had not referred to any instance where an actual or even remote danger of disorder triggered by the public display of the red star had arisen in Hungary.[8] It concluded that '[t]he containment of a mere speculative danger, as a preventive measure for the protection of democracy, cannot be seen as a "pressing social need"'.[9] Thus, it made clear that the necessity test in its form of a 'pressing social need' requirement refers to the existence of a genuine, objective and sufficiently important need to introduce certain restrictions.

---

[5] *Handyside v. the United Kingdom*, ECtHR 7 December 1976, 5493/72, para. 48.
[6] *Sunday Times v. the United Kingdom*, ECtHR 26 April 1979, 6538/74, para. 62.
[7] *Vajnai v. Hungary*, ECtHR 8 July 2008, 33629/06.   [8] *Ibid.* paras. 54–5.
[9] *Ibid.*, para. 55; see similarly e.g. *Christian Democratic People's Party v. Moldova (No. 2)*, ECtHR 2 February 2010, 25196/04.

With regard to the 'pressing social need' test, the *Sunday Times* formula contains a number of other factors relevant to establishing the overall 'necessity' of a restriction. The requirement of 'relevance and sufficiency' can be read to mean that there must be a certain importance to the restrictions, as well as a certain adequacy and appropriateness of the restriction to serving objectives of general interest. And finally, the *Sunday Times* formula contains an express reference to the principle of proportionality, which can be understood to refer to the need for a fair balance to be struck between the aims pursued and the Convention rights being harmed by the restriction.

The various tests and factors are not clearly delineated, however, and the above shows that there may be significant overlap. In addition, it must be noted that the Court does not strictly and consistently adhere to the *Sunday Times* formula and its different elements. Sometimes it may apply a proportionality test to determine if there was a pressing social need for a restriction, while in other cases it may opt for tests that are not mentioned in the formula, such as the least restrictive means test or a test of suitability. Moreover, in many cases, the aspect of relevance and sufficiency is not explicitly mentioned, and often the Court does not pronounce itself on the importance or pressing nature of the general interests that are being served. Furthermore, for several Convention provisions, the Court has defined alternative formulas to test the reasonableness of restrictions. In relation to restrictions of the right to property under Article 1 of Protocol No. 1, for example, the Court tends to examine whether the national measures caused the applicant to bear an 'individual and excessive burden';[10] in relation to Article 6 ECHR, the Court assesses whether restrictions have not affected 'the very essence' of the right to access to a court and to a fair trial;[11] and in relation to Article 14 ECHR, the Court investigates whether there is an 'objective and reasonable justification', which means that there should be 'a reasonable relationship of proportionality between the means employed and the aim sought to be realised'.[12]

Generally, therefore, the choice of factors and standards to be applied depends on the applicable Convention provision, the circumstances of the case, the nature of the complaints and the positions of the parties. The Court may be more easily inclined to pay attention to the least restrictive means test, for example, if the applicant has clearly set out that less intrusive measures would have been available to the State or if it has defined a narrow margin of appreciation for the State. In addition, as has been discussed in Sections 2.4 and 2.5, the exact choice of standards depends on the way in which the Court's case law on a specific topic has developed and the general principles it has formulated in this respect.[13] For cases on whistle-blowers, for

---

[10] See *Sporrong and Lönnroth v. Sweden*, ECtHR 23 September 1982, 7151/75 and 7152/75, para. 73.
[11] See *Ashingdane v. the United Kingdom*, ECtHR 25 May 1985, 8225/78, para. 57.
[12] See the *Belgian Linguistics* case, ECtHR 23 July 1968, 1474/62, para. B.I.10.
[13] On the practice of developing general principles, see Chapter 2.5. On the use of 'catalogues' of relevant factors and standards, see specifically J.H. Gerards, 'Procedural Review by the ECtHR –

example, the Court has defined a list of relevant factors to assess the reasonableness of any sanctions imposed,[14] which are different from the equally specific standards it has developed in relation to infringements of one's privacy by a press publication[15] or those relating to the disclosure of information covered by the secrecy of criminal investigations.[16] Similarly, the Court has developed lists of factors to be considered in the assessment of cases of expulsion of immigrants[17] or for the question of whether hearsay evidence may reasonably be considered in a criminal procedure.[18] Such catalogues of standards and factors help the Court determine whether an interference with a fundamental right was acceptable, without it having to resort to a general and fully open test of necessity or balancing. The unavoidable consequence is that the number of cases in which the Court only applies the very open standards discussed in this section is slowly decreasing, as was also discussed in Section 2.5.

Finally, it is important to recall that the Court usually leaves a certain margin of appreciation to the States to assess the necessity and proportionality of certain restrictions, as has been discussed in more detail in Chapter 7. It was explained in Section 7.2 that, generally, the scope of the margin of appreciation corresponds with a certain intensity of the Court's proportionality review. If the Court leaves the State a wide margin of appreciation, its review will be lenient, and it may not set very strict requirements for the effectiveness or proportionality of a restriction. If the margin of appreciation is narrow, the Court will be more critical and it may assess, for example, whether less restrictive measures could have been considered.

The result is that the shape and nature of the necessity test may vary considerably between the Court's judgments. In fact, to appreciate the exact requirements the Court sets in relation to the review of restrictions, it is necessary to understand the specific requirements and general principles developed and applied by the Court for each individual Convention right and, more specifically, for each individual topic that can be distinguished within the scope of such a right. Providing such detailed reviews of the precise tests to be applied is beyond the scope of this book. Nevertheless, it is possible and useful to provide some insight into the general standards and criteria that can be derived from the case law on necessity, proportionality,

---

A Typology' in J.H. Gerards and E. Brems (eds.), *Procedural Review in European Fundamental Rights Cases* (Cambridge University Press, 2017), pp. 127–60; see further also Section 8.4.4(a).

[14] See in particular *Guja v. Moldova*, ECtHR (GC) 12 February 2008, 14277/04, paras. 72–9.

[15] See in particular *Von Hannover (No. 2) v. Germany*, ECtHR (GC) 7 February 2012, 40660/08 and 60641/08, paras. 108–13.

[16] See in particular *Bédat v. Switzerland*, ECtHR (GC) 29 March 2016, 56925/08, paras. 55–81.

[17] See *Üner v. the Netherlands*, ECtHR (GC) 18 October 2006, 46410/99, para. 57; *Maslov v. Austria*, ECtHR (GC) 23 June 2008, 1638/03, para. 71.

[18] See *Al-Khawaja and Tahery v. the United Kingdom*, ECtHR (GC) 15 December 2011, 26766/05 and 22228/06, paras. 119–51; *Schatschaschwili v. Germany*, ECtHR (GC) 15 December 2015, 9154/10, paras. 119–31.

reasonableness and related tests. To this end, the general test of necessity is explored in Section 10.2, in which the pressing social need test and the least intrusive means test are also explained. Section 10.3 illuminates the 'relevant and sufficient' test, and Section 10.4 discusses the fair balance test and some related tests, as well as the related question of whether balancing should always be conducted on an individual and concrete basis on the national level, or whether blanket rules may sometimes suffice. Lastly, Section 10.5 briefly explores how procedural review can complement the Court's substantive reasonableness review of restrictions.

10.2   Necessity, a Pressing Social Need and the Least Restrictive Means Test

10.2.1   Necessity

As the Court clarified in *Handyside*, necessity can be defined in different ways.[19] One way of doing so is to examine whether, were it not for the restriction, a certain objective could have been achieved less easily.[20] This is what the Court meant by stating that 'necessary' could mean anything between 'indispensable' and 'merely useful'. The use of this general test of necessity can be further illustrated by the case of *Daróczy*, which was also discussed in Section 2.2.[21] To recall, when the applicant married in 1950, her married name was incorrectly registered on her marriage certificate as Tiborné Daróczy. She had used the surname ever since and no one had noted the mistake until she lost her identity card in 2004. A new card was then issued which indicated her name as Tibor Ipolyné Daróczy. The applicant asked for permission to continue to use the name Tiborné Daróczy, but this was not allowed. According to the government, the correct registration of the name was needed to protect the authenticity of the State Registry and the rights of others, and no exceptions could be made. The Court did not agree, in particular because it considered, in the circumstances of the case, that the refusal had not been necessary to achieve the stated aims:

> The Court draws attention to the fact that the applicant used this version of her name in all aspects of her official life. State authorities issued her with several official documents, including her identity card, she was entered on the electoral register and she opened a bank account using that name. The Government did not put forward any convincing argument to

---

[19]   *Handyside v. the United Kingdom*, ECtHR 7 December 1976, 5493/72, para. 48.
[20]   Cf. J.H. Gerards, 'How to Improve the Necessity Test of the European Court of Human Rights', *International Journal of Constitutional Law*, 11 (2013), 466–90; this section is partly based on the findings of this article.
[21]   *Daróczy v. Hungary*, ECtHR 1 July 2008, 44378/05.

show that the allegedly incorrect use of the applicant's name had in any way prejudiced the Hungarian system of State registries in 54 years. It is also difficult for the Court to accept that the restriction was necessary for the protection of the rights of others, namely the applicant's husband. There is nothing in the case file to indicate that the late Mr Tibor Daróczy used his name in another form and, therefore, it is implausible that the applicant's intention to continue using her name could infringe his rights, still less after his death.[22]

Thus, the Court concluded that the interference did not make any significant difference to the realisation of the aims pursued by the government. For that reason, and also in light of the importance of the interests of the applicant, the Court found a violation of the Convention. Indeed, in most of the cases in which the Court applies the general test of necessity, it appears to do so in this fashion.[23] The strictness of its review may vary, however, depending on the context and the scope of the margin of appreciation. Moreover, even if the Court expressly held in *Handyside* that 'necessity' is generally different from being 'indispensable', this standard still can be found in the Court's case law. The Court may reason, for example, that 'the national authorities were reasonably entitled to consider, having regard to all the circumstances of the case, that it was indispensable [to take the contested measures] . . . in order to protect health and morals, protect the rights of others and to prevent crime'.[24] Although the Court expressly mentioned the word 'indispensable', however, the necessity test was still applied here in a rather lenient manner: the Court did not actually require the State to prove that the aims could not have been achieved without the relevant restriction of a Convention right, but it accepted that they were 'reasonably entitled' to think the restriction of great importance.

10.2.2   Pressing Social Need

As the Court has held in *Sunday Times*, 'necessity' in the Convention context can also mean that there is a 'pressing social need' for a restriction. In fact, the test of a 'pressing social need' is a test which combines a judgment on the weight and importance of the stated aims and the overall effectiveness and necessity of a

---

[22] *Ibid.*, paras. 30–1.

[23] See also e.g. *Chabauty v. France*, ECtHR (GC) 4 October 2012, 57412/08, para. 54; *Kasparov and Others v. Russia*, ECtHR 3 October 2013, 21613/07, paras. 92–4; *Helsinki Committee of Armenia v. Armenia*, ECtHR 31 March 2015, 59109/08, paras. 49–52; *Mytilinaios and Kostakis v. Greece*, ECtHR 3 December 2015, 29389/11, para. 63; *Frumkin v. Russia*, ECtHR 5 January 2016, 74568/12, paras. 137–40; *Novikova and Others v. Russia*, ECtHR 26 April 2016, 25501/07, paras. 171 and 181–3; *Selmani and Others v. the former Yugoslav Republic of Macedonia*, ECtHR 9 February 2017, 67259/14, paras. 76–85.

[24] *Mouvement raëlien suisse v. Switzerland*, ECtHR (GC) 13 July 2012, 16354/06, para. 72. Cf. also *S.A.S. v. France*, ECtHR (GC) 1 July 2014, 43835/11, para. 141.

particular measure or decision to serving those aims.[25] It is thus a highly case-specific test, since it can only be determined on the basis of the particular circumstances of the case whether the need to restrict a Convention right really existed and whether it was sufficiently weighty to justify the interference with the Convention.[26] Its application can be illustrated by the judgment in *Éditions Plon*.[27] This case related to a court injunction prohibiting the distribution of a book about the former French President Mitterrand, because the book disclosed confidential details about his health. According to the competent national court, the distribution would violate the duty of medical confidentiality and affect the interests of Mitterrand's relatives. The initial injunction was later followed by an unlimited ban on publication and an obligation for the publisher to offer redress to the heirs of Mitterrand. The Court was not persuaded of the need of this continuation of the ban:

> It notes that by 23 October 1996, when the Paris *tribunal de grande instance* gave judgment, François Mitterrand had been dead for nine and a half months. Clearly, the context was no longer the same as on 18 January 1996, when the urgent-applications judge issued the interim injunction prohibiting the distribution of *Le Grand Secret*. The judge issued the injunction the day after the book's publication, which itself had taken place barely ten days after President Mitterrand's death ... Distribution of the book so soon after the President's death could only have intensified the legitimate emotions of the deceased's relatives, who inherited the rights vested in him ... In the Court's opinion, as the President's death became more distant in time, this factor became less important. Likewise, the more time that elapsed, the more the public interest in discussion of the history of President Mitterrand's two terms of office prevailed over the requirements of protecting the President's rights with regard to medical confidentiality. This certainly does not mean that the Court considers that the requirements of historical debate may release medical practitioners from the duty of medical confidentiality ... However, once the duty of confidentiality has been breached, giving rise to criminal (and disciplinary) sanctions against the person responsible, the passage of time must be taken into account in assessing whether such a serious measure as banning a book – a measure which in the instant case was likewise general and absolute – was compatible with freedom of expression. Furthermore, by the time of the civil court's ruling on the merits, not only had some 40,000 copies of the book already been sold, but it had also been disseminated

---

[25] Among many examples, see *Trade Union of the Police in the Slovak Republic and Others v. Slovakia*, ECtHR 25 September 2012, 11828/08, paras. 67–70; *Michaud v. France*, ECtHR 6 December 2014, 12323/11, paras. 120–32; *Erdoğan Gökçe v. Turkey*, ECtHR 14 October 2014, 31736/04, paras. 45–53; *Császy v. Hungary*, ECtHR 21 October 2014, 14447/11, paras. 18–20; *Party for a Democratic Society (DTP) and Others v. Turkey*, ECtHR 12 January 2016, 3840/10, paras. 72–100; *M.P. v. Finland*, ECtHR 15 December 2016, 36487/12, paras. 50–60; *Bektashi Community and Others v. the Former Yugoslav Republic of Macedonia*, ECtHR 12 April 2018, 48044/10, paras. 65–6.

[26] E.g. *Płoski v. Poland*, ECtHR 12 November 2012, 26761/95, para. 35; *Császy v. Hungary*, ECtHR 21 October 2014, 14447/11, para. 18.

[27] *Éditions Plon v. France*, ECtHR 18 May 2004, 58148/00.

on the Internet and had been the subject of considerable media comment. Accordingly, by that stage the information in the book was to a large extent no longer confidential in practice. Consequently, the preservation of medical confidentiality could no longer constitute an overriding requirement ... In conclusion, on 23 October 1996, when the Paris *tribunal de grande instance* gave judgment on the merits, there was no longer a 'pressing social need' justifying the continued ban on distribution of *Le Grand Secret*. There has therefore been a violation of Article 10 of the Convention from that date onwards.[28]

This lengthy quotation shows that the Court's pressing social need test helped it to establish the decreased weight of the interest of confidentiality that was said to be served by the restriction of the freedom of expression. Moreover, even to the extent that this aim would still bear some weight, the test allowed the Court to find that it would have been difficult to achieve this aim as thousands of copies of the book had already been distributed. Thus, the Court inserted an element of effectiveness or appropriateness of the restriction in achieving its stated aims in its 'pressing social need' test.[29] This is logical: if a measure, in fact, cannot contribute to realising the aims pursued, it can hardly be considered necessary to uphold such a measure, let alone that there is a 'pressing' need for doing so. Especially in cases where the Court has allowed a wide margin of appreciation to the State, however, it will usually leave the matter of effectiveness to the national authorities. More generally, in such cases, it is not likely to apply the pressing social need test in the fashion of *Éditions Plon*.[30] Instead, the pressing social need test then usually comes very close to a lenient and general test of manifest unreasonableness.

10.2.3   Least Restrictive Means

The test of necessity can also be given the shape of a 'least restrictive means test'. It can generally be said that most government objectives can be achieved in different ways, that is, by means of different kinds of measures, decisions or acts. The least restrictive means test requires that the option chosen is the least harmful or intrusive from the perspective of the Convention, yet still is able to effectively contribute to realising the legitimate objectives pursued by the State. The Court applies a test of least restrictive means only in rare cases, and usually only when it has left the State a narrow margin of appreciation and is strictly scrutinising the arguments the government has advanced in its defence. In relation to freedom of expression cases, for example, where the margin of appreciation is often narrow, the Court has stated

---

[28] *Ibid.*, para. 55.

[29] See also e.g. *Michaud v. France*, ECtHR 6 December 2014, 12323/11, para. 125. The Court may also insert such elements in its general test of necessity; see e.g. *Bartik v. Russia*, ECtHR 21 December 2006, 55565/00, paras. 49–52; *Soltysyak v. Russia*, ECtHR 10 February 2011, 4663/05, paras. 48 and 53.

[30] See e.g. *Garib v. the Netherlands*, ECtHR (GC) 6 November 2017, 43494/09, paras. 145–57.

rather generally that 'the authorities are required, when they decide to restrict fundamental rights, to choose the means that cause the least possible prejudice to the rights in question'.[31]

An example of the application of this test can be seen in *Ürper*, which concerned a complete prohibition on newspapers in which articles had been published in support of the activities of the PKK, a Kurdish independence movement that has been declared illegal by the Turkish government.[32] The Court did not find such a ban acceptable from the perspective of protection of the freedom of expression, as it considered that 'less draconian measures could have been envisaged, such as the confiscation of particular issues of the newspapers or restrictions on the publication of specific articles'.[33] In this case, the Court's judgment was based on the conceivable, hypothetical existence of alternative and less onerous options. Indeed, it is rare for the Court to point more concretely to the actual existence of alternatives; if it does so, these usually are derived from practices in other States.[34] Moreover, the Court may rely on the applicant's submissions of possible restrictive means.

Although the Court has also applied the least restrictive means test in some other cases where a strict review is called for, such as cases regarding the removal of a child from its parents,[35] the test is seldom decisive for the outcome of the case. In many cases, the existence of alternatives or the lack of domestic attention to the presence of such alternatives is merely one factor in determining the overall reasonableness of the interference.[36] In addition, if it is apparent from the facts of the case that the applicant can still enjoy the relevant Convention right in an effective manner, regardless of the restriction, the Court will not easily find that the State should have searched more actively for a different solution.[37]

---

[31] E.g. *Mouvement raëlien suisse v. Switzerland*, ECtHR (GC) 13 July 2012, 16354/06, para. 75; *Animal Defenders International v. the United Kingdom*, ECtHR (GC) 22 April 2013, 48876/08, para. 124; *Biblical Centre of the Chuvash Republic v. Russia*, ECtHR 12 June 2014, 33203/08, para. 59.

[32] *Ürper and Others v. Turkey*, ECtHR 20 October 2009, 14526/07.

[33] *Ibid.*, para. 43. See similarly e.g. *K.H. and Others v. Slovakia*, ECtHR 28 April 2009, 32881/04, para. 56; *Porubova v. Russia*, ECtHR 8 October 2009, 8237/03, para. 49; *Salontaji-Drobnjak v. Serbia*, ECtHR 13 October 2009, 36500/05, para. 144; *S.A.S. v. France*, ECtHR (GC) 1 July 2014, 43835/11, para. 139; *Gülbahar Özer and Yusuf Özer v. Turkey*, ECtHR 29 May 2018, 64406/09, paras. 34–7.

[34] E.g. *Tebieti Mühafize Cemiyyeti and Israfilov v. Azerbaijan*, ECtHR 8 October 2009, 37083/03, para. 82; *Fazliyski v. Bulgaria*, ECtHR 16 April 2013, 40908/05, para. 69.

[35] See e.g. *K. and T. v. Finland*, ECtHR (GC) 12 July 2001, 25702/94, para. 166; *P., C. and S. v. the United Kingdom*, ECtHR 16 July 2002, 56547/00, para. 116; *Hanzelkovi v. the Czech Republic*, ECtHR 11 December 2014, 43643/10, paras. 72 and 74.

[36] See e.g. *Ahmet Yıldırım v. Turkey*, ECtHR 18 December 2012, 3111/10, para. 64; *Lashmankin and Others v. Russia*, ECtHR 7 February 2017, 57818/09, para. 422.

[37] E.g. *Mouvement raëlien suisse v. Switzerland*, ECtHR (GC) 13 July 2012, 16354/06, para. 75; *Tierbefreier e.V. v. Germany*, ECtHR 16 January 2014, 45192/09, para. 58; *Animal Defenders International v. the United Kingdom*, ECtHR (GC) 22 April 2013, 48876/08, para. 124.

One of the reasons why the Court is reluctant to use the least restrictive means test is that it is relatively difficult for it to assess whether possible alternative means would be just as effective as the chosen measures.[38] These difficulties can be illustrated by the case of *Animal Defenders International*, where the applicant company had complained about the prohibition of political advertisements on television.[39] The government had defended this prohibition by stressing the need to prevent the distortion of crucial public interest debates, which would risk under-mining the democratic process.[40] The applicant had argued that this aim could equally well have been achieved by providing a more specific and thus less intrusive prohibition, such as narrowing the scope of the prohibition to allow advertising by social advocacy groups outside of electoral periods.[41] The Court, however, agreed with the government that such a less intrusive measure might be less effective:

> [T]he Court considers it reasonable to fear that this option would give rise to a risk of wealthy bodies with agendas being fronted by social advocacy groups created for that precise purpose. Financial caps on advertising could be circumvented by those wealthy bodies creating a large number of similar interest groups, thereby accumulating advertising time. The Court also considers rational the concern that a prohibition requiring a case-by-case distinction between advertisers and advertisements might not be a feasible means of achieving the legitimate aim. In particular, having regard to the complex regulatory background, this form of control could lead to uncertainty, litigation, expense and delay as well as to allegations of discrimination and arbitrariness, these being reasons which can justify a general measure . . . It was reasonable therefore for the Government to fear that the proposed alternative option was not feasible and that it might compromise the principle of broadcasting impartiality, a cornerstone of the regulatory system at issue.[42]

This consideration then played a supportive role in the Court's conclusion that the general prohibition could be regarded as a reasonable restriction of the freedom of expression.

The Court's reluctance to apply the least restrictive means test is especially apparent in cases where the Court exercises judicial restraint. In *James*, it even held in general terms that an application of this test would not be warranted in cases where the States have a wide margin of appreciation to regulate certain matters:

> The availability of alternative solutions does not in itself render the [contested] . . . legislation unjustified; it constitutes one factor, along with others, relevant for determining whether the means chosen could be regarded as reasonable and suited to achieving the legitimate aim being pursued, having regard to the need to strike a 'fair balance'. Provided

---

[38] On these problems, see also in more detail e.g. Gerards, *supra* n. 20, section 4.
[39] *Animal Defenders International v. the United Kingdom*, ECtHR (GC) 22 April 2013, 48876/08.
[40] *Ibid.*, para. 116.   [41] *Ibid.*, para. 122.   [42] *Ibid.*

the legislature remained within these bounds, it is not for the Court to say whether the legislation represented the best solution for dealing with the problem or whether the legislative discretion should have been exercised in another way.[43]

These considerations are closely connected to the 'better placed' argument that has been discussed in Section 7.4.3. The Court explained this connection even more clearly in *Mouvement raëlien suisse*, which concerned the management of public billboards. Having decided that the States should be left a considerable margin of appreciation in this respect, it held 'that certain local authorities may have plausible reasons for choosing not to impose restrictions in such matters . . . The Court cannot interfere with the choices of the national and local authorities, which are closer to the realities of their country, for it would thereby lose sight of the subsidiary nature of the Convention system.'[44] It is also clear from the test as defined in *James*, however, that even if the Court does not consider the least intrusive means test a decisive factor, the obvious existence of feasible alternatives may still play a role in its overall 'fair balance' test.[45]

10.3 The Relevant and Sufficient Test

According to the *Sunday Times* definition of the test of necessity, the Court has to examine for each restriction whether the reasons given by the national authorities to justify it are 'relevant and sufficient'.[46] Although the Court often refers to this relevant and sufficient test, it is difficult to unambiguously state its meaning, as its application varies according to the circumstances of each individual case. The case of *Standard Verlags (No. 3)* may serve as clarification, however.[47] In 2006, the daily newspaper *Der Standard* published an article dealing with an investigation into the losses incurred by a bank. The article mentioned that Christian Rauscher had been in charge of the treasury

---

[43] *James and Others v. the United Kingdom*, ECtHR 21 February 1986, 8793/79, para. 51; see more recently also *Garib v. the Netherlands*, ECtHR (GC) 6 November 2017, 43494/09, para. 157. There are exceptions to this rule, however; see e.g. *Vaskrsić v. Slovenia*, ECtHR 25 April 2017, 31371/12, para. 83.

[44] *Mouvement raëlien suisse v. Switzerland*, ECtHR (GC) 13 July 2012, 16354/06, para. 64.

[45] This test is discussed in Section 10.4.1. See also e.g. *Zelenchuk and Tsytsyura v. Ukraine*, ECtHR 22 May 2018, 846/16 and 1075/16, paras. 128–30.

[46] *Sunday Times v. the United Kingdom*, ECtHR 26 April 1979, 6538/74, para. 62.

[47] *Standard Verlags GmbH v. Austria (No. 3)*, ECtHR 10 January 2012, 34702/07. For some other examples, see *Vörður Ólafsson v. Iceland*, ECtHR 27 April 2010, 20161/06, paras. 77–83; *Peta Deutschland v. Germany*, ECtHR 8 November 2012, 43481/09, paras. 47–9; *Österreichische Vereinigung zur Erhaltung, Stärkung and Schaffung v. Austria*, ECtHR 28 November 2013, 39534/07, paras. 45–7; *Delfi AS v. Estonia*, ECtHR (GC) 16 June 2015, 64569/09, para. 162; *Pentikäinen v. Finland*, ECtHR 20 October 2015, 11882/10, paras. 95–114; *Lashmankin and Others v. Russia*, ECtHR 7 February 2017, 57818/09, paras. 435–42; *Podeschi v. San Marino*, ECtHR 13 April 2017, paras. 146–53; *Sekmadiensis Ltd. v. Lithuania*, ECtHR 30 January 2018, 69317/14, para. 79.

department of the bank and it connected him to the losses that had been sustained. This led Rauscher to bring proceedings against the publisher, Standard Verlags, for the unlawful disclosure of his identity. The Vienna Regional Criminal Court dismissed Rauscher's action based on a weighing of his interest in the protection of his identity and the public interest in its disclosure. In turn, the Court of Appeal granted Rauscher's appeal, finding that the Regional Court had wrongly balanced the conflicting interests at issue. Before the Court, Standard Verlags claimed that the Court of Appeal's judgment had violated its freedom of expression. The Court first addressed the relevance of the Court of Appeal's reasons to hold against the publisher:

> The Vienna Court of Appeal ... considered that the claimant was not a public figure. While accepting that the public had an interest in being informed of the speculation losses, it considered that this interest could not justify the disclosure of the claimant's name at an early stage of the criminal investigation where the suspicion was still vague. In the Court's view the reasons given by the Vienna Court of Appeal were undoubtedly 'relevant' reasons for the purposes of the necessity test to be carried out under Article 10 § 2.[48]

The Court then continued to examine if these reasons were also 'sufficient':

> In the present case, both the Vienna Regional Criminal Court and the Vienna Court of Appeal found that the claimant, as a senior employee of the bank in issue, was not a 'public figure' ... The Court agrees with this assessment ... However, the Court observes that the question whether or not a person, whose interests have been violated by reporting in the media, is a public figure is only one element among others to be taken into account ... Another important factor which the court has frequently stressed when it comes to weighing conflicting interests under Article 10 on the one hand and Article 8 on the other hand, is the contribution made by articles or photos in the press to a debate of general interest ... It is not in dispute in the present case that the article reported on an issue of public interest. It concerned a banking scandal which led to enormous losses by a bank, 45% of which was owned by the Land of Carinthia ... Moreover, it is not in dispute that the facts reported in the article were correct ... The Vienna Court of Appeal relied heavily on the aspect that the article reported on the opening of criminal proceedings and, by indicating the claimant's name, presented him as a suspect in the embezzlement of a huge sum of money ... [The Court] accepts the Vienna Court of Appeal's finding that the disclosure of a suspect's identity may be particularly problematic at the early stage of criminal proceedings. However, when assessing the necessity of an interference, the Court must have regard to the article as a whole. It observes that the article at issue is not a typical example of court reporting but focuses mainly on the political dimension of the banking scandal at hand ... The article's focus is ... on the extent to which politics and banking are intertwined and on the political and economic responsibility for the bank's enormous

---

[48] *Standard Verlags GmbH v. Austria (No. 3)*, ECtHR 10 January 2012, 34702/07, paras. 34–5.

losses ... Names, persons and personal relationships are clearly of considerable importance in this sphere. It is difficult to see how the applicant company could have reported on these issues in a meaningful manner without mentioning the names of all those involved, including the claimant ... Furthermore, the Court observes that the Vienna Court of Appeal referred to the Regional Court's finding that the disclosure of Mr Rauscher's identity had been detrimental to him, namely to his professional advancement. However, it did not counter the Regional Court's argument that his name and position at Hypo Alpe-Adria [the bank] must have been well known in business circles before the publication of the article at issue. In sum, the Court finds that the reasons adduced by the Vienna Court of Appeal, though being 'relevant' were not 'sufficient'.[49]

These quotations make clear that in this type of case, the test of 'relevance' mainly serves to identify the arguments that have been advanced in support of a restriction and to assess whether they make sense *in abstracto*. The 'sufficient' test then helps the Court to see if these arguments bear enough weight in the concrete case to justify the interference. The 'sufficient' test thereby comes very close to a test of balancing, but it is rather more one-sided. Whereas balancing or weighing implies a comparison of the interests served by a restriction and the interests affected by it, the 'sufficient' test is more focused on the question of whether the restriction actually and reasonably served to achieve the aims pursued.

This also means that the relevant and sufficient test comes very close to the pressing social need test. Indeed, the Court sometimes concludes in one single sentence that an interference meets (or does not meet) a pressing social need and the reasons adduced by the authorities were (or were not) 'relevant and sufficient',[50] it has derived from the fact that the reasons adduced were not relevant and sufficient that there was no pressing social need,[51] or – from the other direction – it has concluded from the fact that there was no pressing social need that there was not a sufficient justification for the interference.[52] Such overlap can be illustrated by another example: *Sáska*.[53] The applicant in this case had been refused authorisation for organising a demonstration in front of the Hungarian Parliament. The stated reason for the prohibition of the demonstration was that it would 'gravely endanger' the functioning of Parliament. The speeches and music might disturb the MPs' work and the participants might impede the MPs driving in and out of the Parliament's car park. The Court was not convinced by these arguments:

The Court notes the applicant's unrefuted assertion that another demonstration planned on exactly the same location for 15 October 2008 had not been forbidden by the authorities.

---

[49] *Ibid.*, paras. 38–46.   [50] See *Stomakhin v. Russia*, ECtHR 9 May 2018, 52273/07, para. 109.
[51] See e.g. *Sáska v. Hungary*, ECtHR 27 November 2012, 58050/08, para. 23; *Stomakhin v. Russia*, ECtHR 9 May 2018, 52273/07, para. 118.
[52] E.g. *Mladina D.D. Ljubljana v. Slovenia*, ECtHR 17 April 2014, 20981/10, para. 47.
[53] *Sáska v. Hungary*, ECtHR 27 November 2012, 58050/08.

For the Court, this is a remarkable element, since on that date ... five parliamentary commissions were in session ... evidently entailing the presence and movement of numerous MPs. In the light of this fact, the Court finds unconvincing the Government's argument that the restriction on the applicant's rights was necessitated by the requirement to secure the unimpeded work and movement of the MPs. This consideration cannot be regarded as a relevant or sufficient reason, especially since on the date of the event planned by the applicant no parliamentary activity was underway.[54]

It thus seemed decisive that the prohibition of the demonstration simply could not serve its stated aims and, accordingly, there was no need to impose it. This merger of the two tests shows that the Court often does not make a clear conceptual or argumentative distinction between the different tests and their functions, but it just uses the wording it thinks most fitting in the concrete case.

Finally, it can be noted that in some cases, the Court does not use the test to shape its own reasoning regarding the reasonableness of a restriction but imposes an obligation on the national courts to state 'relevant and sufficient' reasons in their own review in fundamental rights cases. In *Cumhuriyet Vakfi*, the Court explained that 'this obligation enables individuals, amongst other things, to learn about and contest the reasons behind a court decision that limits their freedom of expression, and thus offers an important procedural safeguard against arbitrary interferences with the rights protected under Article 10 of the Convention'.[55] This application of the relevant and sufficient test fits in an overall tendency of the Court to set procedural obligations for national courts to apply certain standards in their case law and limit its own review to examining whether such procedural requirements have been met. This use of this so-called procedural review is further discussed in Section 10.5.

10.4   Fair Balance, Proportionality and Related Tests

10.4.1   Balancing or Proportionality 'In the Strict Sense'

In many of its judgments, the Court resorts to a balancing test. Taking account of the weight of the individual interest affected, the seriousness of the interference, the importance of certain governmental aims and the need for the interference to

---

[54] *Ibid.*, paras. 22–3. See also e.g. *Sürek v. Turkey (No. 2)*, ECtHR (GC) 8 July 1999, 24122/94, paras. 39–42; *Kocherov and Sergeyeva v. Russia*, ECtHR 29 March 2016, 16899/13, paras. 101–20; *Strack and Richter v. Germany*, ECtHR 5 July 2016 (dec.), 28811/12 and 50303/12, para. 32; *Ibragim Ibragimov and Others v. Russia*, ECtHR 28 August 2018, 1413/08 and 28621/11, paras. 103 and 110.

[55] *Cumhuriyet Vakfi and Others v. Turkey*, ECtHR 8 October 2013, 28255/07, para. 68; see also e.g. *Österreichische Vereinigung zur Erhaltung, Stärkung und Schaffung eines wirtschaftlich gesunden land- und forstwirtschaftlichen Grundbesitzes v. Austria*, ECtHR 28 November 2013, 39534/07, para. 42; *Savva Terentyev v. Russia*, ECtHR 28 August 2018, 10692/09, para. 82.

achieve such aims, it makes an overall assessment of the reasonableness of the national act, measure or decision.[56] In legal scholarship, different terms are used to describe this type of balancing review, and the Court is equally versatile and flexible in its choice of wording. In particular, in many cases, the Court (also) refers to 'proportionality'. This notion is then sometimes used to describe all or several elements of the Court's reasonableness review (including the elements of necessity and relevant and sufficient reasons, discussed in Sections 10.2 and 10.3), but it is more commonly used in its strict sense, which means that it refers only to a balancing review.[57] It is in this last sense that the notion of 'proportionality' is used in this section.

a   Influence of the Margin of Appreciation

To understand the Court's balancing review, it is important to recall that its reasonableness assessment is influenced by the intensity of its review and the margin of appreciation left to the States.[58] If the margin is wide, the Court will generally leave the balancing exercise to the national authorities and it will only superficially assess it to see whether the national decision-making did not disclose a manifestly disproportionate or clearly unreasonable outcome. This can often be seen in cases where the 'better placed' argument plays an important role, such as cases on economic or social planning policy.[59] An example is the *Hardy and Maile* case, which concerned the construction and operation of two liquefied natural gas (LNG) terminals at Milford Haven harbour.[60] The applicants lived in the vicinity of this harbour and feared that the terminals would constitute a serious hazard for their right to life (Article 2 ECHR) and their private lives (Article 8 ECHR). The Court first noted that in this type of case, the State should have a wide margin of appreciation:

> It is for the national authorities to make the initial assessment of the 'necessity' for an interference. They are in principle better placed than an international court to assess the requirements relating to the transport and processing of LNG in a particular local context

---

[56] Among other examples, see *Odièvre v. France*, ECtHR (GC) 13 February 2003, 42326/98; *Segerstedt-Wiberg and Others v. Sweden*, ECtHR 6 June 2006, 62332/00, para. 88; *Öllinger v. Austria*, ECtHR 29 June 2006, 76900/01, paras. 42–50; *Phinikaridou v. Cyprus*, ECtHR 20 December 2007, 23890/02; *Neulinger and Shuruk v. Switzerland*, ECtHR (GC) 6 July 2010, 41615/07, para. 134; *Ali v. United Kingdom*, ECtHR 11 January 2011, 40385/06, para. 59; *Lindheim and Others v. Norway*, ECtHR 12 June 2012, 13221/08 and 2139/10, paras. 120–34; *Berger-Krall and Others v. Slovenia*, ECtHR 12 June 2014, 14717/04, paras. 196 et seq.; *Wolfert and Sarfert v. Germany*, ECtHR 23 March 2017, 59752/13 and 66277/13, para. 77; *Sekmadienis Ltd. v. Lithuania*, ECtHR 30 January 2018, 69317/14, para. 83. See also J. Christoffersen, *Fair Balance: Proportionality, subsidiarity and primarity in the European Convention on Human Rights* (Leiden/Boston: Martinus Nijhoff Publishers, 2009).
[57] See further e.g. Christoffersen, *supra* n. 56, at 69–72 and 614.
[58] On the margin of appreciation doctrine, see Chapter 7.
[59] On the 'better placed' argument, see Section 7.4.3.
[60] *Hardy and Maile v. the United Kingdom*, ECtHR 14 February 2012, 31965/07.

and to determine the most appropriate environmental policies and individual measures while taking into account the needs of the local community. The Court has therefore repeatedly stated that in cases raising environmental issues the State must be allowed a wide margin of appreciation.[61]

Taking this into account in its review of the decision-making process, the national valuation of the facts and the national authorities' balancing of interests, the Court concluded:

> In the present case, there was a coherent and comprehensive legislative and regulatory framework governing the activities in question. It is clear that extensive reports and studies were carried out in respect of the proposed LNG terminals ... in cooperation with the developers. The planning and hazardous substances authorities as well as the domestic courts were satisfied with the advice provided by the relevant authorities. In the circumstances, it does not appear to the Court that there has been any manifest error of appreciation by the national authorities in striking a fair balance between the competing interests in the case.[62]

The 'manifest error of appreciation' standard shows that the Court's balancing review was restrained. Indeed, the Court did not 'rebalance' the interests involved or replace the national valuations by one of its own, but it merely assessed the case to see whether there were no obvious procedural shortcomings in the national decision-making and the decisions were not tainted by arbitrariness.[63]

By contrast, when the Court's review is strict, the Court will require the States' arguments to be very weighty, convincing or even compelling, and it will not easily accept that the general interest is strong enough to outweigh the individual Convention right. In addition, the Court will then be very keen on any sign of incoherence or inconsistency in the national argumentation.[64] Such strictness can be particularly seen in cases regarding unequal treatment based on such grounds as ethnic origin, sexual orientation, birth or gender. An illustration can be found in *Kiyutin*, a case about Russian migration legislation which stipulated that residence permits could only be issued to foreign nationals who could show their HIV-negative status.[65] The Court determined that very weighty reasons must be adduced to justify such a measure:

---

[61] *Ibid.*, para. 218.   [62] *Ibid.*, para. 231.

[63] For some other examples of judicial restraint in other contexts, see *Communist Party of Russia and Others v. Russia*, ECtHR 19 June 2012, 29400/05, para. 87; *Hristozov and Others v. Bulgaria*, ECtHR 13 November 2012, 47039/11 and 358/12, para. 125; *Eweida and Others v. the United Kingdom*, ECtHR 15 January 2013, 48420/10, paras. 106 and 109; *Zagrebačka banka d.d. v. Croatia*, ECtHR 12 December 2013, 39544/05, para. 250.

[64] See e.g. *X. and Others v. Austria*, ECtHR (GC) 19 February 2013, 19010/07, para. 144.

[65] *Kiyutin v. Russia*, ECtHR 10 March 2011, 2700/10.

The Court ... considers that people living with HIV are a vulnerable group with a history of prejudice and stigmatisation and that the State should be afforded only a narrow margin of appreciation in choosing measures that single out this group for differential treatment on the basis of their HIV status. .... It appears ... that the exclusion of HIV-positive applicants from residence does not reflect an established European consensus and has little support among the Council of Europe member States. Accordingly, the respondent State is under an obligation to provide a particularly compelling justification for the differential treatment of which the applicant complained to have been a victim.[66]

Having closely considered the Russian arguments for the difference in treatment, in particular its argument that the measure was necessary to protect public health, it concluded that these arguments could not be considered 'compelling and objective' and the legislation disclosed a discrimination in violation of Article 14 of the Convention.[67]

b   Weight of the Interests Involved

The determination of the weight of the individual Convention right and the general interests at stake can be an important element in the Court's balancing review. Although the Court does not always pay express attention to this element, if it does so it bases its weight-determination on criteria that are similar to those that help it determine the scope of the margin of appreciation.[68] If a case affects an aspect of the Convention right that comes very close to the main values and principles underlying the Convention, or if there is a strong European consensus on the importance of a right, the Court will hold that the concomitant interest is particularly weighty, and it will require an equally weighty general interest to justify a restriction of that right. An example can be seen in *Michaud*, a case about the confidentiality of the professional relation between a lawyer and his client.[69] According to domestic law, if a lawyer discovered that a client might be engaged in an activity such as money-laundering, the lawyer should report this to the authorities. The Court reasoned that such an obligation of disclosure for lawyers affected a very important individual right: 'legal professional privilege is of great importance for both the lawyer and his client and for the proper administration of justice. It is without a doubt one of the

---

[66] *Ibid.*, paras. 64–5.

[67] *Ibid.*, paras. 66–74. For other examples of this approach, see *Fabris v. France*, ECtHR (GC) 7 February 2013, 16574/08, paras. 67–73; *X. and Others v. Austria*, ECtHR (GC) 19 February 2013, 19010/07, para. 151; *Dhahbi v. Italy*, ECtHR 8 April 2014, 17120/09, para. 53; *Pajić v. Croatia*, ECtHR 23 February 2016, 68453/13, para. 83; *A.H. and Others v. Russia*, ECtHR 17 January 2017, 6033/13, para. 426. The Court also sometimes refers to the need to advance compelling or convincing reasons outside the context of Article 14; see e.g. *Association of Victims of Romanian Judges and Others v. Romania*, ECtHR 14 January 2014, 47732/06, para. 34.

[68] See Section 7.4.4.   [69] *Michaud v. France*, ECtHR 6 December 2012, 12323/11.

fundamental principles on which the administration of justice in a democratic society is based.'[70] In this particular case, however, and notwithstanding the importance of the legal professional privilege, the Court found that it was outweighed by the general interest of the prevention of crime. It could do so because, from the same core value of democracy, this interest could also be regarded as very important and weighty:

> [The interest of upholding legal professional privilege] should ... be weighed against that attached by the member States to combating the laundering of the proceeds of crime, which are likely to be used to finance criminal activities linked to drug trafficking, for example, or international terrorism ... The Court observes in this connection that the European Directives at the origin of the obligation to report suspicions of which the applicant complained form part of a series of international instruments intended to prevent activities which constitute a serious threat to democracy.[71]

The specific weight of an interest may also depend on the circumstances of the case. In Section 9.2 for example, it was mentioned that the Court has considered that 'protection of the traditional family' is, in principle, a legitimate and weighty interest that may be pursued by the State. Applied in a different context, however, this particular interest may bear less weight:

> Although protection of the traditional family may, in some circumstances, amount to a legitimate aim under Article 14, the Court considers that, regarding the matter in question here – granting a residence permit for family reasons to a homosexual foreign partner – it cannot amount to a 'particularly convincing and weighty' reason capable of justifying, in the circumstances of the present case, discrimination on grounds of sexual orientation.[72]

This also shows that the scope of the State's margin of appreciation clearly influences the weight which the Court is ready to accord to the interests involved in a case.

c Intrusiveness of the Interference

The Court has found that stronger and more weighty reasons are needed if an interference is very intrusive or onerous in nature. This can be seen in *Biblical*

---

[70] *Ibid.*, para. 123. For similar analyses of the weight of the individual interest see e.g. *Eweida and Others v. the United Kingdom*, ECtHR 15 January 2013, 48420/10, para. 94.

[71] *Michaud v. France*, ECtHR 6 December 2012, 12323/11, para. 123; see also the Court's conclusion in para. 131. For an example of a case where the interest invoked by the government was considered to be less weighty, see *Magyar Helsinki Bizottság v. Hungary*, ECtHR (GC) 8 November 2016, 18030/11, paras. 191–6.

[72] *Taddeuci and McCall v. Italy*, ECtHR 30 June 2016, 51362/09, para. 93.

Centre of the Chuvash Republic, where a religious community had been dissolved after a fire and quality inspection had shown that there were several violations of the relevant safety and consumer legislation in the school run by the Centre, such as a lack of fire-safety signs and the decoration of windows with flowers in pots.[73] The Court held that the dissolution of the Centre was a particularly intrusive measure and therefore it could only be justified by very convincing reasons:

> The Court would observe at the outset that the measure in question consisted in the dissolution of the applicant religious organisation with immediate effect, which was a harsh measure entailing significant consequences for the believers … Such a drastic measure requires very serious reasons by way of justification before it can be considered proportionate to the legitimate aim pursued; it would be warranted only in the most serious of cases.[74]

After having looked into the objectives of the government more deeply, the Court concluded that such a severe interference could not be regarded as proportionate 'to whatever legitimate aims were pursued'.[75]

d Reconciliation

A 'fair balance' does not always imply an actual choice to be made between conflicting rights and interests, in the sense that one interest or right has to prevail over another one. Instead, it may be important to look for reconciliation or for a middle ground. This standard of reconciliation is often applied in relation to positive obligations, where the Court strives to formulate an obligation in such a way that it serves the individual Convention right without imposing an unreasonable burden on the State.[76] The Court may also use this approach in cases on negative obligations, however, as can be seen in *Öllinger*.[77] Öllinger, who was an MP for the Green Party, planned to hold a commemorative meeting at the Salzburg municipal cemetery in front of the war memorial on All Saint's Day. The authorities decided not to give him authorisation for the meeting, because 'Comradeship IV', an association whose members were mainly former SS members, also announced it would be present at the cemetery to lay a wreath in front of the war memorial in memory of SS soldiers killed in World War II. The national authorities argued that the concurrence of the two meetings might disrupt the peace at the cemetery, which would be particularly problematic as All Saint's Day was a religious holiday on

---

[73] *Biblical Centre of the Chuvash Republic v. Russia*, ECtHR 12 June 2014, 33203/08, paras. 12–13 and 21.
[74] *Ibid.*, para. 54.
[75] *Ibid.*, para. 61. See similarly e.g. *Ivanovski v. the Former Yugoslav Republic of Macedonia*, ECtHR 21 January 2016, 29908/11, paras. 177 and 186; *Vaskrsić v. Slovenia*, ECtHR 25 April 2017, 31371/12, paras. 83 and 87.
[76] See further Chapter 5.　　[77] *Öllinger v. Austria*, ECtHR 29 June 2006, 76900/01.

which many people visited cemeteries to commemorate the dead. The Court found that the domestic authorities had been too quick to dismiss Öllinger's request for authorisation and they had not done enough to find a middle ground:

> [T]he Court is not convinced by the Government's argument that allowing both meetings while taking preventive measures, such as ensuring police presence in order to keep the two assemblies apart, was not a viable alternative which would have preserved the applicant's right to freedom of assembly while at the same time offering a sufficient degree of protection as regards the rights of the cemetery's visitors. Instead, the domestic authorities imposed an unconditional prohibition on the applicant's assembly. The Court therefore finds that they gave too little weight to the applicant's interest in holding the intended assembly and expressing his protest against the meeting of Comradeship IV, while giving too much weight to the interest of cemetery-goers in being protected against some rather limited disturbances. Having regard to these factors, and notwithstanding the margin of appreciation afforded to the State in this area, the Court considers that the Austrian authorities failed to strike a fair balance between the competing interests.[78]

e   Lists or Catalogues of Factors in a Balancing Review

Finally, although there are many cases in which the Court resorts to a balancing or proportionality review, it often structures and rationalises its assessment of the justification for a restriction by using lists or catalogues of relevant factors and standards.[79] An example of such a list of factors can be seen in *Üner*,[80] which concerned the intended expulsion of a Turkish national from the Netherlands after a serious offence. In such a case, the right to respect for one's private and family life, protected by Article 8 ECHR, has to be balanced against the general interest of the State to protect public order and prevent disorder or crime.[81] Recalling that it had already defined some relevant factors to facilitate this type of balancing in the earlier *Boultif* case,[82] the Court briefly summarised these factors and it specified the list by adding two further criteria:

> In *Boultif* the Court elaborated the relevant criteria which it would use in order to assess whether an expulsion measure was necessary in a democratic society and proportionate to the legitimate aim pursued. These criteria ... are the following:
>
> – the nature and seriousness of the offence committed by the applicant;
> – the length of the applicant's stay in the country from which he or she is to be expelled;

---

[78] *Ibid.*, paras. 48–50. See also e.g. *Moser v. Austria*, ECtHR 21 September 2006, 12643/02, paras. 68–73.

[79] For a brief review with examples, see Section 10.1; see also e.g. Gerards, *supra* n. 13, at 151.

[80] *Üner v. the Netherlands*, ECtHR (GC) 18 October 2006, 46410/99.

[81] See also *Boultif v. Switzerland*, ECtHR 2 August 2001, 54273/00, paras. 45–6.   [82] *Ibid.*, para. 48.

- the time elapsed since the offence was committed and the applicant's conduct during that period;
- the nationalities of the various persons concerned;
- the applicant's family situation, such as the length of the marriage, and other factors expressing the effectiveness of a couple's family life;
- whether the spouse knew about the offence at the time when he or she entered into a family relationship;
- whether there are children of the marriage, and if so, their age; and
- the seriousness of the difficulties which the spouse is likely to encounter in the country to which the applicant is to be expelled.

The Court would wish to make explicit two criteria which may already be implicit in those identified in *Boultif*:

- the best interests and well-being of the children, in particular the seriousness of the difficulties which any children of the applicant are likely to encounter in the country to which the applicant is to be expelled; and
- the solidity of social, cultural and family ties with the host country and with the country of destination.[83]

A list such as this one cannot serve as mathematical formula which can predict the Court's judgments, especially because the Court does not indicate what relative weight should be attached to each factor. The Court acknowledged this in a later case on the same topic, *Maslov*:

The Court would stress that while the criteria which emerge from its case law and are spelled out in the *Boultif* and *Üner* judgments are meant to facilitate the application of Article 8 in expulsion cases by domestic courts, the weight to be attached to the respective criteria will inevitably vary according to the specific circumstances of each case. Moreover, it has to be borne in mind that where, as in the present case, the interference with the applicant's rights under Article 8 pursues, as a legitimate aim, the 'prevention of disorder or crime' . . . the above criteria ultimately are designed to help evaluate the extent to which the applicant can be expected to cause disorder or to engage in criminal activities.[84]

Hence, the Court uses such lists mainly as interpretative aids which help it to structure its reasoning and make its balancing review more transparent. Usually, after having reiterated the relevant standards, the Court explains in considerable detail how each factor, criterion or step is to be applied to the facts of the case. Based on that explanation, it may arrive at a conclusion on the overall reasonableness of

---

[83] *Üner v. the Netherlands*, ECtHR (GC) 18 October 2006, 46410/99, paras. 57–8.
[84] *Maslov v. Austria*, ECtHR (GC) 23 June 2008, 1638/03, para. 70.

an interference. In *Maslov*, for example, it concluded as follows regarding the reasonableness of the exclusion order:

> Having regard to the foregoing considerations, in particular the – with one exception – non-violent nature of the offences committed when a minor and the State's duty to facilitate his reintegration into society, the length of the applicant's lawful residence in Austria, his family, social and linguistic ties with Austria and the lack of proven ties with his country of origin, the Court finds that the imposition of an exclusion order, even of a limited duration, was disproportionate to the legitimate aim pursued, 'the prevention of disorder or crime'. It was therefore not 'necessary in a democratic society'. Consequently, there has been a violation of Article 8 of the Convention.[85]

The Court thus conducted a balancing exercise by looking into all relevant facts and circumstances of the case to see whether the general interest could be held to outweigh the Convention right to respect for one's family and private life. In other cases, it may opt for a different approach, that is, it may mainly consider whether and how such factors have been taken into account by the national authorities. This then comes down to a type of procedural review, which is discussed separately in Section 10.5.

10.4.2   The Individual and Excessive Burden Test

As explained in Section 10.1, the fair balance test may manifest itself in different forms and formulations. Especially in relation to the right to property protected by Article 1 Protocol No. 1, the Court often applies an 'individual and excessive burden' test to find out if an interference has not been disproportionate to its stated objectives. This is apparent from the first case in which the Court defined this test, *Sporrong and Lönnroth*.[86] In ruling on a number of long-term expropriation permits and prohibitions of use, the Court held that

> the two series of measures created a situation which upset the fair balance which should be struck between the protection of the right of property and the requirements of the general interest: the Sporrong Estate and Mrs. Lönnroth bore an individual and excessive burden which could have been rendered legitimate only if they had had the possibility of seeking a reduction of the time-limits or of claiming compensation.[87]

In applying the individual and excessive burden test, the Court usually assesses whether a measure or decision affects individual property rights to a degree that is manifestly unreasonable or disproportionate. An example of this can be found in *Béláné Nagy*.[88] The applicant in the case had been granted a disability pension in

[85] *Ibid.*, paras. 100–1.
[86] *Sporrong and Lönnroth v. Sweden*, ECtHR 23 September 1982, 7151/75 and 7152/75, para. 73.
[87] *Ibid.*, para. 73.   [88] *Béláné Nagy v. Hungary*, ECtHR (GC) 13 December 2016, 53080/13.

2001, but after a change in the methodology to determine the degree of disability in 2010, her pension was withdrawn because she no longer met the statutory qualification criteria. After she had undergone further medical examinations, she was reassessed at the qualifying level, but in the meantime, new legislation had entered into force that introduced new eligibility criteria. In particular, the duration of the social security cover had now become relevant. Since the applicant's cover just fell short of this new requirement, she lost her disability pension and, consequently, her means of support. The Court applied the individual and excessive burden test to determine the reasonableness of this interference with her property rights:

> The Court notes that the applicant was subjected to a complete deprivation of any entitlements, rather than to a commensurate reduction in her benefits . . . in view of the fact that her social-security cover was only 148 days short of the required length. This element gains particular importance in view of the fact that the applicant did not have any other significant income on which to subsist . . . and that she evidently had difficulties in pursuing gainful employment and belonged to the vulnerable group of disabled persons . . . In the light of the above considerations, the Court is of the view that the disputed measure, albeit aimed at protecting the public purse by overhauling and rationalising the scheme of disability benefits, consisted in legislation which, in the circumstances, failed to strike a fair balance between the interests at stake . . . It should also be noted that the applicant was deprived of entitlement to any allowance, despite the fact that there is no indication that she failed to act in good faith at all times, to co-operate with the authorities or to make any relevant claims or representations . . . The Court thus considers that there was no reasonable relation of proportionality between the aim pursued and the means applied. It therefore finds that, notwithstanding the State's wide margin of appreciation in this field, the applicant had to bear an excessive individual burden . . . amounting to a violation of her rights under Article 1 of Protocol No. 1.[89]

This example shows that, in many cases, the individual and excessive burden test is a concrete balancing test. The Court looks into the impact of the application of a decision or of legislation in the particular circumstances of the case and if it turns out that it has very serious or 'excessive' consequences for the applicant, such as a total deprivation of property or income, the need of effective protection of the Convention may outweigh the general interest served by the measure or decision. By contrast, if there is a reduction that is limited in extent or temporary in nature, or

---

[89] *Ibid.*, paras. 123–6. For similar examples where the Court found an individual and excessive burden, see e.g. *Hutten-Czapska v. Poland*, ECtHR (GC) 19 June 2006, 35014/97, para. 223; *Hüseyin Kaplan v. Turkey*, ECtHR 1 October 2013, 24508/09, para. 47; *Pyrantienė v. Lithuania*, ECtHR 12 November 2013, 45092/07, para. 72.

if the essence of a right has not been affected, the Court will more easily find that the restriction was justified.[90]

In the Court's application of the individual and excessive burden test, the element of an 'individual' burden may play a role in that the Court may consider it unfair if a measure affected a particular person or a particular group much more severely compared to others. This can be seen, for example, in *N.K.M.*, where the severance pay of the applicant, who had been recently dismissed as a civil servant, was taxed on a rate of 52 per cent.[91] This tax rate was about three times the overall income tax rate of 16 per cent, which the applicant considered unfair. In assessing the reasonableness of the tax measure, the Court took account of the objectives of the severance pay and the personal burden the applicant had sustained as a result. In addition, it looked into the size of the group of persons affected by the measure:

> [T]he Court finds that the measure complained of entailed an excessive and individual burden on the applicant's side. This is all the more evident when considering the fact that the measure targeted only a certain group of individuals, who were apparently singled out by the public administration in its capacity as employer. Assuming that the impugned measure served the interest of the State budget at a time of economic hardship, the Court notes that the majority of citizens were not obliged to contribute, to a comparable extent, to the public burden.[92]

If a general burden is not distributed fairly and equally over the entire public, this may thereby provide an indication of unfairness and disproportionality. This is not to say, however, that the test of an 'individual' and excessive burden means that it must always be established that the individual applicant or a small group have been affected much more severely than the general public. Even if the group of persons affected by a measure is very large, the Court may still find a violation of Article 1 Protocol No. 1 if their property rights had been affected to an exceptionally strong degree.[93] Moreover, in many cases the actual 'excessiveness' of the disadvantage is decisive for the Court's findings and, indeed, the Court therefore often speaks of a

---

[90] E.g. *Arras and Others v. Italy*, ECtHR 14 February 2012, 17972/07, para. 83; *Cichopek and Others v. Poland*, ECtHR 14 May 2013, 15189/10, paras. 136 and 156; *Da Conceição Mateus and Santos Januário v. Portugal*, ECtHR 8 October 2013 (dec.), 62235/12 and 57725/12, para. 29; *Fábián v. Hungary*, ECtHR (GC) 5 September 2017, 78117/13, paras. 78–82 and 84; *P. Plaisier and Others v. the Netherlands*, ECtHR 14 November 2017 (dec.), 46184/16, para. 95.

[91] *N.K.M. v. Hungary*, ECtHR 14 May 2013, 66529/11.

[92] Cf. also e.g. *Kjartan Ásmundsson v. Iceland*, ECtHR 12 October 2004, 60669/00, paras. 43–5; *Khonakina v. Georgia*, ECtHR 19 June 2012, 17767/08, para. 78; *Krajnc v. Slovenia*, ECtHR 31 October 2017, 38775/14, paras. 50–1. See more implicitly also *Lindheim and Others v. Norway*, ECtHR 12 June 2012, 13221/08 and 2139/10, para. 134; *O'Sullivan McCarthy Mussel Development Ltd. v. Ireland*, ECtHR 6 June 2018, 44460/16, paras. 128 and 130.

[93] See in particular *Hutten-Czapska v. Poland*, ECtHR (GC) 19 June 2006, 35014/97, where the interests of around 100,000 landlords were involved.

'disproportionate and excessive burden' test, leaving out the 'individual burden' aspect.[94] Thus, although the fact that a measure only or mainly affects an individual or a small group can clearly help in deciding on the 'excessiveness' of the effects of the measure, it is not a strict requirement.[95]

10.4.3 The Essence of a Right

As was discussed in Section 2.5, many ECHR provisions do not contain dedicated limitation clauses, but the Court may still accept certain implied or inherent limitations. In relation to such implied limitations, the Court also applies balancing or proportionality review, but it then often uses a different formula: 'the limitations applied must not restrict or reduce the access left to the individual in such a way or to such an extent that the very essence of the right is impaired'.[96] In relation to Article 6 ECHR, which protects the right to a fair trial and access to a court, the Court has used this test, for example, to find a violation in relation to excessively formalistic limitations to the access to a court, unreasonable admissibility requirements or extremely high court fees.[97] Also, for the right to access to education (Article 2 of Protocol No. 1), the Court has mentioned that restrictions may be imposed, but they may not curtail the right to such an extent as to impair its very essence.[98] In addition, the same approach is taken in relation to the right to free elections of Article 3 of Protocol No. 1.[99] Similarly, the Court has required that limitations of the right to marry (Article 12 ECHR) leave the very core of this right unaffected.[100] In the case of *O'Donoghue*, the Court in this basis rejected a blanket

---

[94] See e.g. *Jahn and Others v. Germany*, ECtHR (GC) 30 June 2005, 46720/99, para. 95; *Hutten-Czapska v. Poland*, ECtHR (GC) 19 June 2006, 35014/97, para. 167; *Pietrzak v. Poland*, ECtHR 8 January 2008, 38185/02, para. 103; *Cichopek and Others v. Poland*, ECtHR 14 May 2013, 15189/10, paras. 136 and 156; *Da Conceição Mateus and Santos Januário v. Portugal*, ECtHR 8 October 2013 (dec.), 62235/12 and 57725/12, para. 23.
[95] See e.g. *Lindheim and Others v. Norway*, ECtHR 12 June 2012, 13221/08 and 2139/10, para. 134.
[96] *Ashingdane v. the United Kingdom*, ECtHR 25 May 1985, 8225/78, para. 57.
[97] E.g. *Platakou v. Greece*, ECtHR 11 January 2001, 38460/97, para. 49; *Kreuz v. Poland*, ECtHR 19 June 2001, 28249/95, para. 66; *Melikyan v. Armenia*, ECtHR 19 February 2013, 9737/06, para. 48; *Eşim v. Turkey*, ECtHR 17 September 2013, 59601/09, para. 26; *Al-Dulimi and Montana Management Inc. v. Switzerland*, ECtHR (GC) 31 July 2016, 5809/08, paras. 129 and 151; *Marc Brauer v. Germany*, ECtHR 1 September 2016, 24062/13, para. 34; *Tsezar and Others v. Ukraine*, ECtHR 13 February 2018, 73590/14, paras. 51 and 55; *Naït-Liman v. Switzerland*, ECtHR (GC) 15 March 2018, 51357/07, para. 114.
[98] E.g. *Folgerø and Others v. Norway*, ECtHR (GC) 29 June 2007, 15472/02, para. 98; *Hasan and Eylem Zengin v. Turkey*, ECtHR 9 October 2007, 1448/04, para. 73; *Catan and Others v. Moldova and Russia*, ECtHR (GC) 19 October 2012, 43370/04, para. 140; *Velyo Velev v. Bulgaria*, ECtHR 27 May 2014, 16032/07, para. 32; *Çölgeçen and Others v. Turkey*, ECtHR 12 December 2017, 50124/07, para. 49.
[99] E.g. *Mathieu-Mohin and Clerfayt v. Belgium*, ECtHR 2 March 1987, 9267/81, para. 52; *Podkolzina v. Latvia*, ECtHR 9 April 2002, 46726/99, para. 33.
[100] E.g. *Frasik v. Poland*, ECtHR 5 January 2010, 22933/02.

prohibition on the exercise of the right to marry for all applicants with no valid leave to enter or remain in the United Kingdom. In the Court's view,

> [e]ven if there was evidence to suggest that persons falling within these categories were more likely to enter into marriages of convenience for immigration purposes ... a blanket prohibition, without any attempt being made to investigate the genuineness of the proposed marriages, restricted the right to marry to such an extent that the very essence of the right was impaired.[101]

In some cases, the Court has also referred to this notion of the 'essence' of the right in relation to provisions containing a general and express limitation clause, such as Article 9,[102] Article 10,[103] Article 11[104] or Article 1 of Protocol No. 1.[105]

How the Court conceptualises this type of review is not clear from its case law. It sometimes seems as if the 'essence' of the right constitutes an inviolable and absolute core that no national measure or decision is allowed to affect and that cannot be 'balanced away' by any governmental interest, however weighty it might be. Such an absolute reading implies that the Court must define more or less clearly and in general terms what, then, constitutes the 'very essence' or the 'core' of a Convention right.[106] This requires an interpretative exercise which takes due account of the underlying principles of the Convention, the existence of a European consensus on what constitutes the core of the right, and the definitions provided in the case law of the Court. Indeed, in some cases the Court seems to undertake such an exercise.[107] In relation to trade union freedom, for example, it has held on the basis of its previous judgments that 'the following essential elements of the right of association can be established: the right to form and join a trade union ... the prohibition of closed-shop agreements ... and the right for a trade union to seek to persuade the employer to hear what it has to say on behalf of its members'.[108]

---

[101] *O'Donoghue and Others v. the United Kingdom*, ECtHR 14 December 2010, 34848/07, para. 89. See also e.g. *Chernetskiy v. Ukraine*, ECtHR 8 December 2016, 44316/07, paras. 28 and 33.
[102] E.g. *Süveges v. Hungary*, ECtHR 5 January 2016, 50255/12, para. 155.
[103] E.g. *Novikova and Others v. Russia*, ECtHR 26 April 2016, 25501/07, para. 196.
[104] E.g. *Demir and Baykara v. Turkey*, ECtHR (GC) 12 November 2088, 34503/97, paras. 97, 144; *Matelly v. France*, ECtHR 2 October 2014, 10609/10, para. 57.
[105] E.g. *Janković v. Croatia*, ECtHR 12 October 2000 (dec.), 43440/98; *Kjartan Ásmundsson v. Iceland*, ECtHR 12 October 2004, 60669/00, para. 39; *Da Silva Carvalho Rico v. Portugal*, ECtHR 1 September 2015 (dec.), 13341/14, para. 42; *Fábián v. Hungary*, ECtHR 5 September 2017, 78117/13, para. 74.
[106] For more elaboration on this point, see A.E.M. Leijten, *Core Rights and the Protection of Socio-Economic Interests by the European Court of Human Rights*, PhD thesis, Leiden University (2015), Chapter 4.
[107] See further Section 3.4. Indeed, the Court sometimes relies on such criteria to define the importance of certain aspects of rights. See e.g. *Folgerø and Others v. Norway*, ECtHR (GC) 29 June 2007, 15472/02, para. 98; *Hasan and Eylem Zengin v. Turkey*, ECtHR 9 October 2007, 1448/04, para. 73; *Demir and Baykara v. Turkey*, ECtHR (GC) 12 November 2088, 34503/97, paras. 140 et seq.
[108] *Ibid.*, para. 145.

In cases where the Court has concluded that the very essence of the right has been affected, moreover, it will not even look into the arguments the States may have for their restriction of a right.[109] In those cases, no real balancing exercise can be seen and the core is really seen as a 'limit of limits'.[110] By contrast, if the core of such a right does not appear to be affected, the Court will conduct a normal proportionality review.[111]

Nevertheless, even if it uses the absolute core approach, the Court does not always appear to regard the resulting core as completely inviolable, as can be derived from its judgment in *Demir and Baykara*:

> [T]he evolution of case-law as to the substance of the right of association enshrined in Article 11 is marked by two guiding principles: firstly, the Court takes into consideration the totality of the measures taken by the State concerned in order to secure trade-union freedom, subject to its margin of appreciation; secondly, the Court does not accept restrictions that affect the essential elements of trade-union freedom, without which that freedom would become devoid of substance. These two principles are not contradictory but are correlated. This correlation implies that the Contracting State in question, while in principle being free to decide what measures it wishes to take in order to ensure compliance with Article 11, is under an obligation to take account of the elements regarded as essential by the Court's case-law.[112]

This approach still seems to allow for a certain degree of restriction and balancing. More often, moreover, the Court uses the 'essence of the right' approach in a very similar way as its normal balancing approach or the individual and excessive burden test.[113] It then applies a general proportionality test, taking due account of the individual right concerned as well as the government's argument. The main difference with a balancing review is that if the Court finds that the national authorities have struck a manifestly unreasonable balance, it frames this in terms of the essence of the right having been affected.[114] The other way around, if it concludes that, in the end, the restriction could be held to be justified, it must be presumed that the essence of the right has not been affected.

---

[109] See e.g. *Matelly v. France*, ECtHR 2 October 2014, 10609/10, para. 75; *Chernetskiy v. Ukraine*, ECtHR 8 December 2016, 44316/07, para. 33.

[110] For this notion, see e.g. E. Örücü, 'The Core of Rights and Freedoms: the Limit of Limits' in T. Campbell et al. (eds.), *Human Rights. From Rhetoric to Reality* (Oxford: Basil Blackwell, 1986), pp. 37–59 at 37. See also G. Van der Schyff, 'Cutting to the Core of Conflicting Rights: The Question of Inalienable Cores in Comparative Perspective' in E. Brems (ed.), *Conflicts Between Fundamental Rights* (Antwerp/Oxford/Portland: Intersentia, 2008), pp. 131–47 at 140.

[111] See in relation to trade union freedom e.g. *Tek Gıda İş Sendikası v. Turkey*, ECtHR 4 April 2017, 35009/05.

[112] *Demir and Baykara v. Turkey*, ECtHR (GC) 12 November 2008, 34503/97, para. 144.

[113] See further also Christoffersen, *supra* n. 56.

[114] E.g. *Phinikaridou v. Cyprus*, ECtHR 20 December 2007, 23890/02, para. 65; *Süveges v. Hungary*, ECtHR 5 January 2016, 50255/12, paras. 152–5; *Marc Brauer v. Germany*, ECtHR 1 September 2016, 24062/13, paras. 35–44.

10.4.4   Individualised Decision-making on the National Level and Blanket Rules

It will be evident by now that the Court highly values the existence of a fair balance in the individual case before it. An important question in this regard is to what extent the Court requires that the national authorities, too, should always engage in such concrete balancing exercises.[115] Indeed, generally, the Court appears to object to restrictions on the possibilities for an individualised application or individualised balancing review.[116] Especially in the area of family law,[117] the Court has stressed time and again that generic legislative presumptions are problematic and should be replaced by particularised judicial decision-making. The *Schneider* case can be mentioned as an illustration, which related to a legal presumption that the mother's husband is the legal father of the child, even if another man claims to be the biological father and even if he has recognised the child.[118] According to the Court, such a general legal presumption is untenable:

> Having regard to the realities of family life in the 21st century ... the Court is not convinced that the best interest of children living with their legal father but having a different biological father can be truly determined by a general legal assumption. Consideration of what lies in the best interest of the child concerned is ... of paramount importance in every case of this kind ... Having regard to the great variety of family situations possibly concerned, the Court therefore considers that a fair balancing of the rights of all persons involved necessitates an examination of the particular circumstances of the case.[119]

Thus, the Court's own overall presumption is that individualised balancing exercises by national courts are to be favoured over legislative rules.[120] Exceptions can be seen, however, in cases where moral issues are at stake and where legal certainty can be held to prevail over individual justice,[121] and in cases concerning social

---

[115] See further J.H. Gerards, 'The European Court of Human Rights and the National Courts – Giving Shape to the Notion of "Shared Responsibility"' in J.H. Gerards and J.W.A. Fleuren (eds.), *Implementation of the European Convention on Human Rights and of the judgments of the ECtHR in national case law. A Comparative Analysis* (Antwerp: Intersentia, 2014), pp. 13–94, section 5.2.2; Gerards, *supra* n. 13, section 2.3.2.

[116] For a while, an example of this could be seen, in the Court's case law on voting rights for prisoners; see e.g. *Hirst (No. 2) v. the United Kingdom*, ECtHR (GC) 6 October 2005, 74025/01, para. 82; *Frodl v. Austria*, ECtHR 8 April 2010, 20201/04, para. 34. In later cases on the topic, the Court has nuanced its position; see e.g. *Scoppola (No. 3) v. Italy*, ECtHR (GC) 22 May 2012, 126/05, paras. 99 and 102.

[117] But certainly not limited to that – see e.g. *Bjedov v. Croatia*, ECtHR 29 May 2012, 42150/09, a case that related to the occupation of a social tenancy flat.

[118] *Schneider v. Germany*, ECtHR 15 September 2011, 17080/07.   [119] *Ibid.*, para. 100.

[120] See also *Ādamsons v. Latvia*, ECtHR 24 June 2008, 3669/03.

[121] See e.g. *Evans v. the United Kingdom*, ECtHR (GC) 10 April 2007, 6339/05; for a similar example, see *S.H. and Others v. Austria*, ECtHR (GC) 3 November 2011, 57813/00; on this, see also J. Bomhoff and L. Zucca, 'The Tragedy of Ms Evans: Conflicts and Incommensurability of Rights',

security and planning issues.[122] An example of such an exception can be seen in *Evans*, which presented the national authorities and the Court with a dilemma.[123] The applicant in the case was a woman who could only give birth to a child genetically related to her if fertilised ova would be placed *in uterus*. Her ova had been fertilised by her partner, but after their separation, he had withdrawn his consent with their use. Consequently, either the applicant could not become a biological mother against her own wishes, or her former partner would be compelled to become a biological father against his wishes. To solve such a dilemma, the Court held, it is not problematic to rely on general legislation:

> While the applicant criticised the national rules on consent for the fact that they could not be disapplied in any circumstances, the Court does not find that the absolute nature of the Act is, in itself, necessarily inconsistent with Article 8 ... Respect for human dignity and free will, as well as a desire to ensure a fair balance between the parties to IVF treatment, underlay the legislature's decision to enact provisions permitting of no exception to ensure that every person donating gametes for the purpose of IVF treatment would know in advance that no use could be made of his or her genetic material without his or her continuing consent. In addition to the principle at stake, the absolute nature of the rule served to promote legal certainty and to avoid the problems of arbitrariness and inconsistency inherent in weighing, on a case-by-case basis, what the Court of Appeal described as 'entirely incommensurable' interests ... In the Court's view, these general interests pursued by the legislation are legitimate and consistent with Article 8.[124]

Moreover, in its judgment in *Animal Defenders International*, the Court defined a number of criteria to determine when general measures are acceptable and when an individualised balancing exercise can be required:

> It emerges from [the Court's previous] case-law that, in order to determine the proportionality of a general measure, the Court must primarily assess the legislative choices underlying it ... The quality of the parliamentary and judicial review of the necessity of the measure is of particular importance in this respect, including to the operation of the relevant margin of appreciation ... It is also relevant to take into account the risk of abuse if a general measure were to be relaxed, that being a risk which is primarily for the State to assess ... A general measure has been found to be a more feasible means of achieving the

European Constitutional Law Review, 2 (2006), 424 at 429–30. However, the case law is not entirely consistent; see e.g. *Dickson v. the United Kingdom*, ECtHR (GC) 4 December 2007, 44362/04.

[122] See e.g. *Twizell v. the United Kingdom*, ECtHR 20 May 2008, 25379/02; *Maggio and Others v. Italy*, ECtHR 31 May 2011, 46286/09.

[123] *Evans v. the United Kingdom*, ECtHR (GC) 10 April 2007, 6339/05; see also Bomhoff and Zucca, *supra* n. 121, at 424.

[124] *Evans v. the United Kingdom*, ECtHR (GC) 10 April 2007, 6339/05, para. 89. See also Bomhoff and Zucca, *supra* n. 121, at 429–30.

legitimate aim than a provision allowing a case-by-case examination, when the latter would give rise to a risk of significant uncertainty . . . of litigation, expense and delay . . . as well as of discrimination and arbitrariness . . . The application of the general measure to the facts of the case remains, however, illustrative of its impact in practice and is thus material to its proportionality . . . It follows that the more convincing the general justifications for the general measure are, the less importance the Court will attach to its impact in the particular case . . . [T]he core issue is whether, in adopting the general measure and striking the balance it did, the legislature acted within the margin of appreciation afforded to it.[125]

Clearly, thus, the Court accepts that there may be good reason to adopt a blanket rule that does not allow for (much) individualisation, especially from a perspective of legal certainty.[126] It is equally clear, however, that in many cases the Court will still reject automatically and indiscriminately applied legislation if individual balancing would have been the better way to provide effective protection of the Convention rights on the national level.[127]

10.5   Procedural Review

The tests of necessity and fair balance usually focus on the substance of the arguments and interests involved in a certain case. In many cases, however, arguments related to the quality of the decision-making process also play a role in the Court's review.[128] Although such 'procedural' arguments usually do not replace substantive reasonableness review, they may supplement substantive balancing and the Court may draw inferences from the quality of the procedure that have a bearing on the outcome of the case. For that reason, they are separately discussed in this last section.

First, if it is clear that a decision or rule has been prepared with the greatest care and after extensive deliberation, in an open or transparent decision-making process, the Court may more readily accept the conformity of such a decision or rule with the

---

[125] *Animal Defenders International v. the United Kingdom*, ECtHR (GC) 22 April 2013, 48876/08, paras. 108–10.

[126] See also *The National Union of Rail, Maritime and Transport Workers v. the United Kingdom*, ECtHR 8 April 2014, 31045/10, paras. 101–4.

[127] E.g. *Ivanova and Cherkezov v. Bulgaria*, ECtHR 21 April 2016, 46577/15, para. 54 (but see also para. 73); *Lashmankin and Others v. Russia*, ECtHR 7 February 2017, 57818/09, para. 434.

[128] See further e.g. P. Popelier and C. Van De Heyning, 'Procedural Rationality: Giving teeth to the proportionality analysis', 9 *European Constitutional Law Review* (2013), 230; L.M. Huijbers, 'The European Court of Human Rights' Procedural Approach in the Age of Subsidiarity', *Cambridge International Law Journal*, 6 (2017), 177–201; Gerards, *supra* n. 13.

Convention. An example of this can be seen in *Maurice*, which related to the sensitive and complex issue of compensation in cases of wrongful birth.[129] The applicants argued that the relevant legislation, the 'Loi Perruche', violated their rights under Article 8 of the Convention because it offered a generally lower level of compensation than they could have obtained under the former case law of the French courts. In its judgment in the case, the Court paid close attention to the quality of the process that had led to the adoption of the 'Loi Perruche'. It noted that there had been a 'stormy nation-wide debate' on the issue, in which politicians, interest groups and individuals had participated, and that close attention had been paid to all relevant legal, ethical and social considerations. It concluded that 'there is no serious reason for the Court to declare contrary to Article 8 ... the way in which the French legislature dealt with the problem or the content of the specific measures taken to that end'.[130] The Court thus hardly addressed the substantive issue of necessity and proportionality of the legislation, implicitly accepting that a sound national decision-making procedure, in a sphere where the margin of appreciation is wide, can be supposed to deliver reasonable outcomes.

A second variety of the Court's procedural review can be seen mainly in relation to decision-making by national courts. Many Convention cases require difficult balancing exercises to be made by the national courts, or they require complex evaluations of fact. In such cases, the Court may check mainly whether sufficient procedural guarantees have been offered and the national courts have respected the requirements of a fair trial,[131] and, in particular, whether they have duly and fairly applied the Convention standards as developed in the Court's case law. If a case shows a lack of procedural due care or an inadequate proportionality review by the domestic courts, the Court may take this into account in deciding on the overall reasonableness of the interference. For example, in *Winterstein*, a case that related to the eviction of a number of Roma families from their houses, the Court noted important shortcomings in this respect:

> The Court reiterates that the loss of a dwelling is a most extreme form of interference with the right to respect for one's home and that any person at risk of being a victim thereof should in principle be able to have the proportionality of the measure determined by a court. In particular, where relevant arguments concerning the proportionality of the interference have been raised, the domestic courts should examine them in detail and provide adequate reasons ... In the present case, the domestic courts ordered the applicants'

---

[129] *Maurice v. France*, ECtHR (GC) 6 October 2005, 11810/03.   [130] *Ibid.*, para. 124.

[131] See e.g. *Haase and Others v. Germany*, ECtHR 12 February 2008 (dec.), 34499/04; *Koons v. Italy*, ECtHR 30 September 2008, 68183/01; *Kopf and Liberda v. Austria*, ECtHR 17 January 2012, 1598/06; *Ahrens v. Germany*, ECtHR 22 March 2012, 45071/09; *Nacic and others v. Sweden*, ECtHR 15 May 2012, 16567/10; *Krisztián Barnabás Tóth v. Hungary*, ECtHR 12 February 2013, 48494/06; *Ibragim Ibragimov and Others v. Russia*, ECtHR 28 August 2018, 1413/08 and 28621/11.

eviction without having analysed the proportionality of this measure ... Once they had found that the occupation did not comply with the land-use plan, they gave that aspect paramount importance, without weighing it up in any way against the applicants' arguments ... The Court thus finds that the applicants did not, in the eviction proceedings, have the benefit of an examination of the proportionality of the interference in compliance with the requirements of Article 8.[132]

These procedural considerations formed an important basis, next to a number of other arguments, for the Court's final conclusion that Article 8 of the Convention had been breached.

Conversely, if the national courts have duly taken the Court's standards into account and the procedure has been sufficiently open and transparent, the Court will not readily overturn the national court's findings. In *Palomo Sánchez*, the Court clearly emphasised its limited role in this respect:

> In the present case, the Spanish courts were required to balance the applicants' right to freedom of expression, as guaranteed by Article 10 of the Convention, against the right to honour and dignity of Mr G., Mr A. and Mr B. ... Article 10 of the Convention does not guarantee an unlimited freedom of expression and the protection of the reputation or rights of others – in the present case the reputation of the persons targeted in the drawings and texts at issue – constitutes a legitimate aim permitting a restriction of that freedom of expression. If the reasoning of the domestic courts' decisions concerning the limits of freedom of expression in cases involving a person's reputation is sufficient and consistent with the criteria established by the Court's case-law, the Court would require strong reasons to substitute its view for that of the domestic courts.[133]

Nevertheless, regardless of such considerations and in most similar cases, the Court still looks into the facts and interests at stake to see whether the balance struck was not unreasonable.[134] Thus, the reasoning of the Court is usually based on a combination of procedural-type review and a substantive assessment of arguments relating to the necessity and proportionality of a restriction.[135]

---

[132] *Winterstein v. France*, ECtHR 17 October 2013, 27013/07, paras. 155–7.

[133] *Palomo Sánchez and Others v. Spain*, ECtHR (GC) 12 September 2011, 28955/06, para. 57. See also e.g. *MGN Limited v. the United Kingdom*, ECtHR 11 January 2011, 39401/04, paras. 150 and 155; *Von Hannover (No. 2) v. Germany*, ECtHR (GC) 7 February 2012, 40660/08 and 60641/08, para. 107; *Satakunnan Markkinapörssi Oy and Satamedia Oy v. Finland*, ECtHR (GC) 27 June 2017, 931/13, para. 198; *A.-M.V. v. Finland*, ECtHR 23 March 2017, 53251/13, para. 87.

[134] See e.g. *Ojala and Etukeno Oy v. Finland*, ECtHR 14 January 2014, 69939/10; *Axel Springer SE and RTL Television GmbH v. Germany*, ECtHR 21 September 2017, 51405/12, paras. 53–8.

[135] See e.g. *Lindheim and Others v. Norway*, ECtHR 12 June 2012, 13221/08 and 2139/10, paras. 120–34.

Index

absence of arbitrariness in rights restrictions, 212

absolute (non-derogable) rights. *see* Convention rights

accessibility of rights restrictions, 203

assembly and association. *see* freedom of assembly and association

autonomous interpretation
dependency principle, 74
effectiveness principle as rationale for, 67
limits to, 68
public authority, definition of, 138

autonomous positive obligations, 130

autonomy as interpretative principle, 62

balance, obligation to provide for fair, 152

burden of proof, margin of appreciation as to assignment of, 166

case-based review of rights. *see* Convention rights, review

civil and political rights, positive obligations in relation, 122

collective enforcement of rights, 10

common ground (consensus) interpretation
European law as source, 97
European Union law as source, 102
international law as source, 97
and margin of appreciation, 97
national law as source, 95
rationale for, 93

sufficient common ground, 104

compliance
ECtHR's role. *see* European Court of Human Rights

conscience. *see* freedom of thought, conscience and religion

Convention. *see* European Convention on Human Rights

Convention rights
absolute (non-derogable) rights
absolutely absolute rights, 20
not notstandsfest, 19
application of
determination of applicability, 12
responsibility of national courts for, 155
assembly and association. *see* freedom of assembly and association
categories, 19
competing rights, 187
conscience. *see* freedom of thought, conscience and religion
definition of, uncertainties as to, 160–1
discrimination. *see* prohibition of discrimination
effect. *see* effect
essence of, 253
exercise of
determination of interference with, 14
interference with, seriousness and nature of, 193
justification or reasonableness review of interference, 18

restriction of. *see* restriction of rights
rights typology based on permissible restriction, 19

expression. *see* freedom of expression

fair trial. *see* right to a fair trial

family life. *see* right to respect for private and family life

freedom of thought. *see* freedom of thought, conscience and religion

interference with. *see* restriction of rights

interpretation. *see also* autonomous interpretation; common ground (consensus) interpretation; evolutive interpretation; meta-teleological interpretation
autonomous interpretation, 67
case-based refinement of general principles, 41
common ground (consensus) interpretation, 93
Convention as living instrument, 51
democracy, principle of, 64
dependency principle, 74
determination of, 12
effectiveness principle, 67, 119
European law as source, 97
European Union law as source, 102
evolutive interpretation principle, 51
general interpretative role of ECtHR, 11, 31, 36, 46

Convention rights (cont.)
　human dignity, principle
　　of, 61
　incremental formulation of
　　general principles, 41
　individual interpretative
　　role of ECtHR, 31, 36, 46
　internally consistent
　　(harmonious)
　　interpretation, 87
　international law as
　　source, 97
　legal effect of
　　interpretations (res
　　interpretata), 44
　limits to, 56
　meta-teleological
　　interpretation, 59
　methods, 78
　minimum level of
　　protection by rights,
　　clarification of, 10, 160
　national law as source, 95
　object of review, 32
　personal autonomy,
　　principle of, 62
　pluralism, principle of, 66
　precedent, use of, 37, 78,
　　120
　principles of, 46
　progressiveness of, 58
　reflective equilibrium as
　　aim of, 43, 46
　sufficient common ground,
　　104
　temporal effect of, 53
　textual interpretation, 79
　travaux préparatoires as
　　guide, 48, 83
　and underlying values of
　　Convention, 59
　and Vienna Convention on
　　the Law of Treaties, 47, 83
liberty. see right to liberty
life. see right to life
limitation. see restriction of
　rights
marriage. see right to marry
non-absolute (derogable)
　rights
　legitimate aim requirement
　　for restriction, 220
　necessity requirement for
　　restriction, 229

with express, general
　limitation clauses, 25
with express, specific
　limitation clauses, 24
without express limitation
　clauses, 26
other non-absolute rights,
　28
obligations. see obligations
private life. see right to
　respect for private and
　family life
protection
　collective enforcement of
　　rights, 10
　compliance obligations
　　(subsidiarity principle),
　　5, 46
　ECtHR's role, 9, see
　　Convention rights,
　　protection
　effective remedy and fair
　　balance, obligation to
　　provide for, 152
　effectiveness principle, 3,
　　10, 46, 50, 67, 119
　margin of appreciation.
　　see margin of
　　appreciation
　maximalist approach,
　　reasons against use of,
　　160
　minimum level of,
　　clarification of, 10, 160
　positive obligations for,
　　145
　primary responsibility
　　(primacy principle), 5, 9
　regulatory obligation for
　　enforcement, 150
　subsidiarity and, 160
　subsidiary protection by
　　Convention, 9
　reconciliation with State
　　interest, 247
religion. see freedom of
　thought, conscience and
　religion
restriction. see restriction of
　rights
review
　case-based review, 41
　incremental approach
　　(incrementalism), 41

of legislation and/or
　individual application of
　legislation, 32
process of, 11
rights typology based on
　permissible restriction, 19
stage 1, determination of
　applicability of
　Convention, 12
stage 2, determination of
　interference with
　exercise of Convention
　right or freedom, 14
stage 3, justification or
　reasonableness review of
　interference, 18
slavery. see prohibition of
　slavery
thought. see freedom of
　thought, conscience and
　religion
torture. see prohibition of
　torture
typology based on permissible
　restriction, 19
weight of, determination of,
　245
criminal law, horizontal effect,
　136

democracy as interpretative
　principle, 64
dependency as interpretative
　principle, 74
dependent positive obligations,
　130
derogable (non-absolute) rights.
　see Convention rights,
　non-absolute
　(derogable) rights
dignity as interpretative
　principle, 61
discrimination. see prohibition
　of discrimination
domestic law. see national law

ECHR. see European Convention
　on Human Rights
ECtHR. see European Court of
　Human Rights
effect
　direct responsibility of States
　　for interferences with
　　Convention rights, 138

governmental organisation, definition of, 138

horizontal effect
  of Convention, 137
  of criminal law, 136, 147
  effective remedy and fair balance, obligation to provide for, 152
  indirect, 144
  limits to positive obligations in horizontal relationships, 154
  positive obligations to protect Convention rights, 145
  power imbalances and, 137
  of private law, 136, 149
  regulatory obligation to enforce, 150
  responsibility of national courts to apply Convention, 155
  private law acts by public authorities, 142
  public authority, definition of, 138
  State, definition of, 138
  vertical effect
  of Convention, 136

effective remedy, obligation to provide for, 152

effectiveness principle, 3, 10, 46, 50, 67

effectiveness-based definition of positive obligations, 119

enforcement of rights. see Convention rights, protection

essence of a right, test for impairment of, 253

ethical factors as to margin of appreciation, 177

European Convention on Human Rights (Convention, ECHR)
  application of. see Convention rights, application of
  development of Convention system, 1
  effect. see effect
  effectiveness principle, 3, 10, 46, 50, 67, 119

entry into force, 1
impact, 1
interpretation. see autonomous interpretation; common ground (consensus) interpretation; Convention rights, interpretation; evolutive interpretation; meta-teleological interpretation
  law-making nature of, 50
  as living instrument, 51
  margin of appreciation. see margin of appreciation
  obligations. see obligations
  primacy principle, 5
  restraint of State power, 136
  rights. see Convention rights
  subsidiarity principle, 5, 46
  underlying values of, 59
  and Vienna Convention on the Law of Treaties, 46, 48, 83

European Court of Human Rights (ECtHR)
  authors' approach to study of, 3
  compliance supervision role, 1, 9
  effectiveness principle, 3, 10, 46, 50, 67, 119
  establishment, 1
  influence worldwide, 1
  interpretative role. see Convention rights, interpretation
  judgments
    diversity of challenging topics, 2
    influence and effect of, 1
    precedent, use of, 37, 78
  jurisdiction, 1
  procedural review function, 258
  protective role. see Convention rights, protection; margin of appreciation
  recognition of positive Convention obligations of States, 108
  review of Convention rights. see Convention rights, review

subsidiarity principle, 5, 46
  and Vienna Convention on the Law of Treaties, 46, 83
  workload, 1

European law as source for interpretation, 97

European Union law as source for interpretation, 102

evidence and establishment of facts, margin of appreciation in relation, 186

evolutive interpretation
  Convention as living instrument, 51
  limits to, 56
  progressiveness of, 58
  temporal effect of, 53

exercise of rights. see Convention rights, exercise of

express limitation clauses. see restriction of rights, non-absolute (derogable) rights

expression. see freedom of expression

fair balance
  restriction of rights. see restriction of rights, necessity requirement
  test for positive obligations, 111

fair balance, obligation to provide for, 152

fair trial. see right to a fair trial

fairness factors as to margin of appreciation, 187

family life. see right to respect for private and family life

foreseeability of rights restrictions, 199, 205

freedom of assembly and association, 65, 88–9, 248–56

freedom of expression
  interpretation, 64
  limitation of, 17, 26, 65, 154, 176, 193, 235, 242
  margin of appreciation, 174, 195

freedom of expression (cont.)
  other rights in relation, 88,
    157, 188–9, 242–60
  pluralism and, 66
  protection of, 6, 68, 164
  violation of, 202, 240
freedom of thought, conscience
  and religion, 66, 68
freedoms under Convention. see
  Convention rights
fundamental rights. see
  Convention rights

governmental organisation,
  definition of, 138

harmonious interpretation, 87
horizontal effect. see effect
horizontal positive obligations,
  129
human dignity as interpretative
  principle, 61

incremental review of rights
  (incrementalism). see
  Convention rights,
  review
indirect horizontal effect, 144
individual and excessive burden
  test for rights restriction,
  250
interference with rights. see
  Convention rights,
  exercise of
internally consistent
  (harmonious)
  interpretation, 87
international law as source for
  interpretation, 97
interpretation. see Convention
  rights; Vienna
  Convention on the Law
  of Treaties
intrinsic positive obligations,
  130

lawfulness of rights restrictions.
  see restriction of rights
least restrictive means test for
  rights restriction, 231,
  236
legitimate aim of rights
  restrictions. see
  restriction of rights

legitimate aim requirement,
  proportionality and, 227
life. see right to life

margin of appreciation
  applicability of, 168
  burden of proof, assignment
    of, 166
  certain (degree of) margin,
    165, 167
  continued relevance of, 196
  development of doctrine of,
    163
  ECtHR's use of, 167–8
  introduction of, 163
  maximalist approach to
    rights protection,
    reasons against use of,
    160
  minimum level of rights
    protection, clarification
    of, 160
  narrow margin, 165, 167
  as to necessity requirement
    for rights restriction,
    232, 243
  scope of margin
    balancing of factors,
      194
    better placed argument,
      177
    common ground
      (consensus) factor, 173
    competing Convention
      rights, 187
    as to core rights, 188
    evidence and
      establishment of facts,
      issues of, 186
    extra margin due to special
      context of case, 181
    factors for determining,
      172
    fairness factors, 187
    fourth instance argument,
      181
    interference with right,
      seriousness and nature
      of, 193
    interpretation of national
      law, 185
    moral and ethical factors,
      177
    as to peripheral rights, 188

political and operational
  policy factors, 178
procedural quality factors,
  187
socio-economic factors,
  178
subject of case, nature and
  importance of, 188
as to States' capability and
  freedom to regulate
  (better placed
  argument), 162, 165
subsidiarity and, 160
subsidiary protective role of
  ECtHR in relation, 165
wide margin, 165
marriage. see right to marry
meta-teleological interpretation
  democracy, principle of, 64
  human dignity, principle of, 61
  personal autonomy, principle
    of, 62
  pluralism, principle of, 66
  and underlying values of
    Convention, 59
moral factors as to margin of
  appreciation, 177

national courts, responsibility to
  apply Convention, 155
national human rights
  authorities
  compliance obligations
    (subsidiarity principle),
    5, 46
  primary responsibility for
    Convention rights
    protection (primarity
    principle), 5, 9
national law
  interpretation of, and margin
    of appreciation, 185
  lawfulness requirement in,
    200
  as source for interpretation,
    95
national obligations under
  Convention. see
  obligations
necessity of rights restrictions.
  see restriction of rights,
  necessity requirement
negative obligations. see
  obligations

non-absolute (derogable) rights.
    see Convention rights
non-derogable (absolute) rights.
    see Convention rights,
    absolute rights

obligations
    compliance obligations
        (subsidiarity principle),
        5, 46
    negative obligations
        definition of, 108
        positive obligations in
            relation, 132
    positive obligations
        autonomous, 130
        civil and political rights in
            relation to, 122
        definition of, 110
        dependent, 130
        effectiveness-based
            definition of, 119
        fair balance test for, 111
        horizontal, 129
        and horizontal effect.
            see effect
        intrinsic, 130
        negative obligations in
            relation, 132
        no general theory of, 109
        precedent-based definition
            of, 120
        procedural, 126
        to protect Convention
            rights, 145
        reasonable knowledge
            and means test for,
            116
        recognition of, 108
        socio-economic rights in
            relation to, 122
        substantive, 122
        supporting, 130
        types of, 121, 129
        vertical, 129
operational policy factors as to
    margin of appreciation,
    178

personal autonomy as
    interpretative principle,
    62
pluralism as interpretative
    principle, 66

political policy factors as to
    margin of appreciation,
    178
positive obligations. *see*
    obligations
precedent, interpretative use of,
    37, 78
precedent-based definition of
    positive obligations, 120
preparatory works of treaty
    (*travaux préparatoires*)
    as guide to
    interpretation, 48, 83
pressing social need test for
    rights restriction, 230,
    234
private entities, definition as
    governmental
    organisations, 138
private law
    acts by public authorities, 142
    horizontal effect, 136
private life. *see* right to respect
    for private and family
    life
procedural positive obligations,
    126
procedural quality factors as to
    margin of appreciation,
    187
procedural review, 258
procedural safeguards as to
    restriction of rights, 214
prohibition of discrimination,
    27, 49, 74, 87, 98–9, 137
prohibition of slavery, 20
prohibition of torture, 18, 20,
    126, 132, 161
proof, margin of appreciation as
    to assignment of burden,
    166
proportionality. *see* restriction
    of rights, necessity
    requirement
protection of rights. *see*
    Convention rights,
    protection
public authorities
    definition of, 138
    private law acts by, 142

reasonable knowledge and
    means test for positive
    obligations, 116

relevancy test for rights
    restriction, 233
religion. *see* freedom of
    thought, conscience and
    religion
res interpretata, 44
restraint of State power by
    Convention, 136
restriction of rights
    accessibility of restrictions,
        203
    discrepancy between stated
        and real objectives of
        restriction, 225
    intrusiveness of interference,
        246
    justification
        conditions for, 198
        determination of, 198
    lawfulness requirement
        absence of arbitrariness,
            200
        accessibility of restrictions,
            203
        autonomous and
            substantive
            interpretation of, 199
        basis national law, 200
        elements of, 198
        foreseeability element,
            199, 205
        legal certainty element,
            199
        procedural safeguards, 214
    legitimate aim requirement
        application of, 221
        discrepancy between stated
            and real objectives of
            restriction, 225
        element of, 198
        exhaustive lists of
            legitimate aims, 220
        in express limitation
            clauses, 220
        interpretation of, 221
        plurality of aims, 226
        proportionality and, 227
    necessity (proportionality or
        fair balance)
        requirement
        application of, 231
        element of, 199
        essence of a right, test for
            impairment of, 253

restriction of rights (cont.)
  in express limitation
    clauses, 229
  factors in balancing
    review, 248
  individual and excessive
    burden test for, 250
  intrusiveness of
    interference with rights,
    246
  least restrictive means test
    for, 231, 236
  legitimate aim requirement
    and, 227
  margin of appreciation as
    to, 232, 243
  national-level balancing of
    rights decisions, 256
  need for, 229
  pressing social need test
    for, 230, 234
  procedural review and, 258
  reconciliation of
    Convention right and
    State interest, 247
  relevant and sufficient test
    for, 231–60
  scale of necessity, 230, 233
  strict sense of balancing or
    proportionality, 242
  tests for, 230
  weight of interests
    involved, 245
non-absolute (derogable)
  rights
  legitimate aim requirement
    for restriction, 220
  necessity requirement for
    restriction, 229
  with express, general
    limitation clauses, 25
  with express, specific
    limitation clauses, 24
  without express limitation
    clauses, 26
  other non-absolute rights,
    28
  rights typology based on
    permissible restriction,
    19

review of rights. see Convention
  rights, review
right to a fair trial
  applicability of, 69, 73, 75
  dependency approach, 77
  limitation of, 24, 26
  protection of, 69, 108, 253
right to liberty, 23–4, 130
right to life
  duty to protect, 4, 116, 130
  interference with, 16, 131,
    153, 243
  interpretation of, 57
  limitation of, 24, 82
  margin of appreciation, 71,
    169, 186
  procedural positive
    obligations, 126, 218
right to marry
  interpretation of, 57, 103
  limitation of, 28, 170, 253
  protection of, 70
  provision for, 11–12
right to respect for private and
  family life, 12, 25, 29,
  130, 157, 182, 248
rights under Convention. see
  Convention rights

slavery. see prohibition of
  slavery; right to liberty
social need test for rights
  restriction, 230, 234
socio-economic factors as to
  margin of appreciation,
  178
socio-economic rights, positive
  obligations in relation,
  122
State. see also national human
  rights authorities;
  national law; public
  authorities
  courts, responsibility to apply
    Convention, 155
  definition of, 138
  law as source for
    interpretation, 95
  margin of appreciation as to
    capability and freedom

  to regulate (better placed
    argument), 162, 165
  national-level balancing of
    rights decisions, 256
  obligations under
    Convention. see
    obligations
  power, restraint by
    Convention, 136
  State interests, reconciliation
    with Convention rights,
    247
subsidiarity
  and margin of appreciation,
    160
  principle of, 5, 46, 160
substantive positive obligations,
  126
sufficiency test for rights
  restriction, 233
supporting positive obligations,
  130

temporal effect of
  interpretation, 53
textual interpretation, 79
thought. see freedom of
  thought, conscience and
  religion
torture. see prohibition of
  torture
travaux préparatoires as guide
  to interpretation, 48, 83

vertical effect. see effect
vertical positive obligations,
  129
Vienna Convention on the Law
  of Treaties
  authentic language versions,
    48
  ECtHR's explanation of
    interpretation rules of, 48
  importance, 47
  main principles for
    interpretation of
    international treaties, 47
  travaux préparatoires as
    guide to interpretation,
    48, 83